COURTING DISASTER

COURTING

DISASTER

THE SUPREME COURT AND
THE UNMAKING OF AMERICAN LAW

MARTIN GARBUS

TIMES BOOKS
Henry Holt and Company
New York

Times Books
Henry Holt and Company, LLC
Publishers since 1866
115 West 18th Street
New York, New York 10011

Henry Holt® is a registered trademark of
Henry Holt and Company, LLC.

Library of Congress Cataloging-in-Publication Data

Garbus, Martin, date.
  Courting disaster : the Supreme Court and the unmaking of American law /
Martin Garbus.
    p. cm.
  Includes bibliographical references and index.
  ISBN 0-8050-6918-6 (HB)
  1. United States. Supreme Court—History.   2. Political questions and judicial
power—United States—History.   3. Constitutional history—United States.   I. Title.
KF8742 .G37   2002
347.73'26'09—dc21   2002020314

First Edition 2002

Designed by Kelly S. Too

Printed in the United States of America

1   3   5   7   9   10   8   6   4   2

To Sarina

Whether such decrees are wise or unwise, whether their subjects are citizens or not, if they are usurpation of power, our rights are both infringed and endangered. They are infringed because the power to decide and act is taken from the people without their consent. They are endangered because in a constitutional government every usurpation of power dangerously disorders the whole framework of the State.

Justice Benjamin R. Curtis
Thirty-second Justice of the United States Supreme Court
One of the Dissenting Justices in the *Dred Scott* case

CONTENTS

1

THE UNMAKING OF AMERICAN LAW

As I write, this U.S. Supreme Court is seizing power, and in doing so it is radically changing the law and this country. The Rehnquist Court rejects much of the last sixty-five years of America's constitutional law; rejects the balance between Congress, the Court, and the President; and rejects the form of our democracy that these cases establish. It does so to protect entrenched interests at the expense of unpopular minorities. It attempts to justify its new position by discarding prior cases and by looking to resurrect and reinterpret the Constitution as no other court has ever done. Instead of a balance of power, we have an attempt at judicial exclusivity at the expense of the Congress and "We the People."

The story goes that, as Benjamin Franklin left the Constitutional Convention, he was approached by a Mrs. Powell, who asked him, "What have you given us, Dr. Franklin?"

"A republic," he replied, "if you can keep it." Ideally, the Court is the bulwark of the republic. Instead, it is taking the republic away from us.

The American legal system, like no other legal system in the world, has expanded into the political arena and into our everyday lives. The questions it deals with are far more overtly political than narrowly legal. The great political and human issues of our time—race, abortion, women's rights, voting rights, campaign finance, and even the presidential election—are all fought out in the American courts. The same issues that are the bare-knuckled partisan politics manifest themselves on the bench. In truth, very few cases on the Supreme Court's dockets today are not political.

Politics has always been a prime element in the shaping of constitutional law. But no court in this century has seized power the way the Rehnquist Court has, and no court may leave as long a legacy. From 1937 until 1972, when Nixon appointee William Rehnquist came on the bench, the Supreme Court was basically an inclusive liberal body. If you believe, as I do, it did what a court interpreting our Constitution should do to deal with issues of race, class, poverty, religion, and power in such a way as to protect the majority of Americans, including the aged, the disabled, women, and minorities. Today, that has been turned around. It renders the disadvantaged more vulnerable, closes the courthouse door to lawsuits against states that violate constitutional rights, and puts state government assets into religious schools. In addition, as the Court's composition changes with right-wing appointees, it more and more sees itself as the guardian of a free market by keeping business free from congressional regulation. By nullifying acts legitimately passed by the people's elected representatives, it forces the people out of power. The Rehnquist Court elevates the protection of property rights over personal rights to protect big business—the drug, tobacco, and oil companies—at the expense of the environment, the consumer, and the citizens.

This is the Court's twenty-first-century agenda. By cloaking its states' rights and separation of power revolution in high-sounding legal rhetoric, the Court has obscured the real battles taking place over race, class, money, religion, guns, and control that are at issue. The Court is giving the Right control deep into the next century.

A lawyer's adage is, "If you can't change the facts and the law, then change the judges." The wretched *Bush v. Gore* decision ending election 2000, effectively decided by five, played a valuable role in showing us the naked partisanship of this Court. The entire legal spectacle of those proceedings drew attention to that fact; it briefly seemed to surprise and, for the first time, anger many Americans. Politics has always gone on in the judiciary, and the shock people expressed reminded me of Claude Rains's quip in *Casablanca* when he says, "I am shocked, shocked" to see gambling going on in Rick's back room. But after the sensation of the event died down, the public quickly lost interest in what the Court does and how it affects us. Part of that is because its deliberations are held in secrecy, part is because legalese obscures the true nature of its decisions, and part is because there exists a sense of apathy and disinterest.

The Supreme Court's decision in *Bush v. Gore* did not occur in a vacuum. It occurred against the background of a legal revolution that is an unabashed grab for power. By a vote of 5–4, the majority decided not only who would occupy the White House but also who would make the judicial appointments across America for the next four years. It gave the partisans of the political and religious right an opportunity not only to add to their Supreme Court majority but also to envision controlling nearly every one of the thirteen circuit courts. In many ways, as we shall see, control of the judicial branch is more long lasting than control of the executive branch.

The Right has not yet made a wholesale assault on the various and many benefits of the New Deal and Warren Courts, but they are creating a strong foundation for doing so through a steady accumulation of self-reinforcing and self-perpetuating precedents. If the bloc consisting of Rehnquist, Clarence Thomas, and Antonin Scalia enlarges from three to five, it can then act quickly in changing the structure of government, more aggressively championing the corporations' powers while disregarding established rights for the individual.

The Rehnquist Court has moved its agenda forward by looking backward. It has chipped away at our personal prerogatives and freedoms, finding its legal authority in the precedents from the nineteenth and early twentieth centuries. It has already substantially eviscerated the work of the Warren and early Burger Courts in areas of abortion, school prayer, affirmative action, and school integration, while its opinions lay a groundwork to reverse the effects of many New Deal Court decisions.

Imagine the effect on our lives if workplace standards for health and safety were severely cut back; if abortions were totally banned, no exceptions; if minimum hour and wage laws were so reduced as to be meaningless; if child labor laws were abolished or weakened; if there could be no gun control at all. Imagine what our world would look like if the law abolished equal rights, by use and misuse of dubious terminology like "color blind" and "reverse discrimination"; if the state took money from public schools and gave it to parochial schools; if regulatory agencies like the Food and Drug

Administration, the Securities and Exchange Commission, the Federal Trade Commission, or the Environmental Protection Agency were so gutted or handcuffed as to be ineffectual; if Congress's ability effectively to pass needed social legislation ended. All this and more are the declared goals of the radical right who now dominate the Republican Party on matters related to the judiciary. The judicial revolution that began under Richard Nixon, accelerated during Ronald Reagan's second term, and peaked in the last five years has become a runaway train. Since 1995, the Court has declared unconstitutional thirty acts of Congress. No other court in American history has ever done that. Today the law in America is what five justices say it is. Five people can put their thumbs up or down and determine some of the most important conditions of our lives. These unelected justices serving life terms have become an imperial judiciary.

Today's unprecedented Court, where a 5–4 split is more the rule than the exception, gives chilling new meaning to the idea of one man, one vote. This one justice today determines the law in the 12 federal circuit courts of appeals, consisting of 253 appellate judges and 942 federal trial judges.* One justice today upholds or strikes down the wishes of fifty state legislatures and millions of people who vote in elections and in referendums. It is one justice whose opinion overrules and rejects the laws that are passed by the Senate and the House of Representatives, then approved by a president who signs them into law after his attorney general has told him such legislation is necessary and proper. And that one justice's vote may control long after he or she has left the Court. But this one justice, and today's majority, do not reflect the country's will. There are many in the Republican Party, some of whom consider themselves true conservatives, who oppose the Radical Right's agenda. Rehnquist, Scalia, and Thomas are different than prior justices described as conservatives. The conservative side of the bench, from 1937 onward, deferred to the New Deal, honored precedent, and deferred to other branches of government. Conservatives generally have respect for precedent, for the institution of the law and the law itself. While each justice is different, there are similarities in the analysis of the three; their decisions are more reactionary than conservative. O'Connor and Kennedy have joined the three of them in their refusal to defer to the

*There are in fact thirteen circuit courts. The thirteenth, the Federal Circuit Court of Appeals, sitting in Washington, does not decide most of the issues discussed in this book. Its jurisdiction is basically limited to patents and appeals from administrative agencies.

legislature, and more often than not, have expressed similar disdain for the executive branch and precedent. This Court's specific agenda is like no other "conservative" Court that preceded it.

We are witnessing a judicial revolution, potent and purposeful, that seeks to do no less than unravel long-settled law reaching back to the cases Justice John Marshall decided in the early 1800s that gave structure to the new republic; to the legislative and judicial law created after the Civil War that extended equality to the newly freed; and to the new body of law created by the New Deal jurists to deal with the economic chaos of the Great Depression. The divisions in this country today are every bit as political as those that divided the justices in the 1840s (when the issues were property rights and slavery) or the 1930s (when the issue was the creation of the administrative states) or the 1950s (when the issue was race). But few other courts have moved in so many different fronts and may have as long a legacy.

With no economic depression or world war to motivate it, as FDR's Court did, and no explosive domestic movements to inspire, guide, or legitimize its actions, as the Warren Court had, the Rehnquist Court feels free to assert its supremacy and to cut back on federal power at a time when it is particularly dangerous and inappropriate to do so. Justices Scalia, Thomas, and Rehnquist are ideologically motivated, much like the secessionists during the Civil War, who argued that the states are "independent and autonomous." The states rights and the antifederal government movement they embrace are so deep-seated that even the September 11, 2001, tragedy—which has led both to the war against terrorism and to economic instability and which requires a powerful central government—will not stop this Supreme Court from drastically reducing federal power.

Time is on the side of the forces on the right. George W. Bush, even if he serves only one term, will probably appoint two or three justices to the Supreme Court. If he serves two terms, he may appoint up to five, a Bush majority to go along with Scalia and Thomas. One more reactionary like Scalia or Thomas would assuredly end abortion and reverse even those few recent cases in which the minority bloc won. Two or three more justices like Scalia or Thomas would put the Court in a choke hold that would last until well into the middle of this century. Justice John Paul Stevens, who was appointed to the Court by Gerald Ford in 1975, will turn eighty-one this year. Chief Justice William Rehnquist, named to the Court by Nixon in

1971, is seventy-six. Justice Sandra Day O'Connor, appointed by Reagan in 1981, will turn seventy-one. And Justice Ruth Bader Ginsburg, appointed by Bill Clinton, is now sixty-eight. Any one or more of the four may be expected to step down in the near future.

Replacing them with ultraright ideologues, as George W. Bush has said he would like to do, would mark a 180-degree change in the Court's direction on many issues of fundamental rights and liberties. Already Thomas and Scalia stand to the right of Rehnquist; replacing even him with their ideological compatriots would be devastating to the Court's balance. Even Clinton's nominees, Justices Ruth Bader Ginsburg and Stephen Breyer, are essentially moderates; they are often described as liberals only because the Court has shifted so far to the right. In fact, thirty-five years have passed since Democratic president Lyndon Johnson appointed the last unabashed liberal justice to the Court, Thurgood Marshall.

The current situation is without historical precedent. Since 1937, one vacancy has occurred on the average of every two years, but this Supreme Court has not had a vacancy since 1994. Only once before, in 1824, have we been seven years without a vacancy. FDR made nine appointments in less than six years, Lincoln five in less than three years, Truman four in four years, Nixon four in thirty months, Clinton two in eight years. Given the age and health of the present members of the Court, George W. Bush, by appointing younger justices who will join Thomas and Scalia in serving into the second quarter of this century, may very well leave the changes in the law as his greatest legacy.

Justices Anthony Kennedy and Sandra Day O'Connor, famously thought of as swing votes, are now nearly always added to the reactionary three-justice bloc that rules the Court. Even so, right-wing leaders have expressed bitter dissatisfaction with four Republican-appointed justices, Stevens, Kennedy, and O'Connor but most especially with Justice David Souter. Televangelist and Christian Coalition founder Pat Robertson has called Justice Souter a "stealth candidate" who "pulled the wool over the eyes of the White House Chief of Staff" in order to be nominated by the elder George Bush. Both O'Connor and Kennedy have been called traitors because of their votes not to overrule *Roe v. Wade* (1973) and because of their failure thus far to take consistent, hard-line stands on church-state issues. Neither Bush nor future Republicans so deep in debt to the far right will make those mistakes again.

Ginsburg became the first Democratic appointee in a quarter of a century, after ten straight Republican appointees. Given past history, it is no surprise that seven of today's nine justices are Republican appointees. Over the past fifty years, Democratic presidents have appointed six Supreme Court justices, while Republican presidents have appointed fifteen, representing more than 70 percent of the total. By relentlessly and carefully concentrating on judicial appointments at federal trial and appellate court levels during these last twenty years, the right wing has been extremely successful in changing both the law and, perhaps more important, the faces of the lifetime-appointed jurists who make the law.

Most people pay little attention to Supreme Court appointments and no attention to federal circuit court appointments. A recent poll of Americans showed that two-thirds of them could not name a single Supreme Court justice. As Senator Patrick Leahy said, most people pay more attention to National Pickle Week than to who gets nominated to the judiciary. As a result, nine of the twelve federal circuit courts, after the Supreme Court the nine most powerful courts in the country, defining the way most Americans live under law, will, by the end of this year, become securely right-wing conservative courts—not Republican, but to the far right of the Republican center. Most of the nominations made to those courts were never challenged; most of the judges who sit there are unknown; most of their decisions are obscure.

So successful was the Republican-driven judicial avalanche that not even Bill Clinton could stop it. Scandals, and the limits imposed upon him by a Republican Congress after 1994 (the first time in forty years that one party controlled both houses), forced him to pick his battles, and the judiciary was not a priority. Determined not to get into court fights, Clinton sought to paper over his ideological giveaways by claiming that he helped diversify the Court by appointing more women and more blacks, with the result that most of his appointments were moderates and some even conservatives.

Bush is moving aggressively forward to consolidate these gains. Even now, with our country focused on other matters and with little attention being paid to battles over the courts, his administration is pushing hard on circuit court judgeships. Although the 1,195 federal district and appeals court judges enjoy far less visibility than the Supreme Court justices, their significance to the nation's legal process is acutely understood by the current Bush White House, for it is there where the political battles that most divide us—abortion, voting rights, religion, economic controls—are first joined, and even ultimately decided. Most of these appointments are far below the radar screen; they will go unnoticed and unchallenged.

The lower courts are critical because the Supreme Court hears less than 1 percent of the cases presented to it. As a result of this and of changes in the law, the Rehnquist Court shapes its own docket. As in *Bush v. Gore*, it can reach out and take cases it wants even though there may be no clear legal qualifications. Merely agreeing to take a case often signals which way the Court wants to go. And for the 99 percent of cases it does not hear, the decisions reached by the very same federal judges that conservative Republicans worked with such care and calculation to appoint are the ones that stand.

I acknowledge my bias as to what the law is, and what our Constitution stands for. I agree with Justice William Brennan's reaction to the conservative view of the Constitution. "It is not," says he, "the living charter I have taken to be the Constitution, it is instead [in the eyes of conservatives] a stagnant, hidebound, archaic document steeped in the prejudices and superstitions of a long time past. This Constitution does not recognize that times change, does not see that sometimes a practice or rule outlives its foundations."

As a trial lawyer, I felt the law change beneath my feet. Trying and arguing appeals in constitutional, civil, and criminal cases in courts throughout the country—Mississippi, Alabama, New York, California—I have witnessed how the law's most radical changes greatly influence most people's lives. Practicing under the Warren Court, the Burger Court, and now the Rehnquist, have been very different experiences. Until recently, trial and appellate justices knew they had to adhere to Warren or early Burger Court principles or they would be reversed. It was a dominant Court that reached out to correct what it saw as injustice. When voters were disenfranchised, when poor people were denied access to the courts because they could not pay filing fees, when women were sexually harassed and had no rights, the lower courts often went further left than the liberal Warren Court dictated, believing their decisions would be upheld. This led to a new creativity in the law. Today there is still a new creativity, but it goes the other way. Today, lower federal courts go further to the right than the Supreme Court because they can anticipate the high court's judgments and know that few of the circuit courts' rulings will be reviewed.

In 1990 I wanted to write a book showing where the Rehnquist Court was going. The primary struggle had moved, it seemed to me, from fighting in the courts to changing the composition of the courts. But I felt it was premature; the lines of the future were not yet clearly defined. They now are. Twelve years later, the path of law and the path of the judiciary allow us to look back at the last twenty years and forward thirty or forty years, nearly to the middle of this century, to see the effects of Reagan's legal revolution. All that I then imagined now is true; more is not only possible but highly probable.

The public, informed, should be involved in shaping constitutional law through political debates, social movements, and elections. But tracing the Rehnquist Court's path has been, for most of us, hard to do. The decisions that are unalterably and disturbingly reshaping our lives are obscured by several factors. Today building a constituency focusing on the Court is harder than it was in the past. First, because the Court hears half the number of cases that it heard ten years ago, it is in the news less often. And the cases it does pick to decide are often harder for the public to see clearly— the cases seem to announce few new dramatic changes in society, while the language and the decisions themselves are more technical. The Court's docket therefore appears to be largely concerned with debates over legal matters that seem purely procedural. Federalism and the Eleventh Amendment arguments are not as compelling as images of Governor George C. Wallace and National Guardsmen standing in classroom doorways at the University of Alabama in 1963 opposing the enrollment of black college students. The collective media, particularly television, covers the Court less rigorously than they did years ago. There is less hard news of every sort. And lastly, of course, the country's interest and politics have changed.

As if all this were not enough, the stream of 5–4 decisions are today more nuanced and complex than they were before. Recently there were eight separate opinions rendered in one case, a result that discourages even the most dedicated of Court followers. It is nearly impossible to see long-term patterns, most especially during the last months of the term, called the June "crunch," when most of the Court's decisions come down, some of which may run hundreds of pages. Although these decisions are available to anyone, and journalists and onlookers may watch oral arguments in the Supreme Court, television coverage is minuscule and Internet coverage is limited. Given all the other noise, the Court operates nearly invisibly.

Many of today's Supreme Court justices and circuit court judges see the overriding principle of the law as the maximization of wealth, not social justice, as they aggressively champion corporate interests. Today, the Court is giving away rights desperately fought for over the last century so that in the future the "benevolent employer," not the state, is the one we will have to look toward for minimum wages and safety in the workplace. These and other hot-button issues that mobilize voters and make people and groups pay attention to the Court are the conservatives' issues. When Jerry Falwell and Pat Robertson blame feminists, abortionists, and liberals for creating an atmosphere that spawns terrorists, they articulate the feelings of a significant part of the country's voters. Issues of obscenity, limits on free speech and dissent, gun control, voting rights, and race infuriate committed right-wingers. Only in the abortion area is there a powerful committed group that fights the right over Supreme Court issues. It is not surprising. The Democratic Party, heavily committed to labor, traditionally pays much of its attention to, and spends much of its political capital on, labor-related issues. Until very recently it was left primarily to private groups like the Alliance for Justice in Washington, D.C., which are underfunded and underequipped to fight the evangelists and Bible Belt conservatives on social issues. The judicial selection process for much of the last twenty years has been virtually ceded away.

Constitutional interpretation is often just politics under a different name. While it may be true that there are as many different interpretations of the Constitution as there are of *Hamlet*, there are, in fact, limits. Yet, its malleability and susceptibility to different interpretations are broad enough to enhance nearly all the extreme left- and right-wing justices—to allow justices to interpret the Constitution in whatever way suits their needs in any particular case. Furthermore, what Scalia and Rehnquist can clearly see in the Constitution, Stevens and Souter cannot. In truth, law is underdetermined by precedent. As Chief Justice Charles Evans Hughes said, 90 percent of "judicial decisions are based on bias, prejudices and personal and political motivations, and the other 10% is based on the law."

Judges do not live as our peers. They occupy a different world than most of us and even most of our public figures. They are largely unknown, and unaccountable, tacking between applause-filled rooms at universities or grand ballrooms and the isolation of their chambers. Their black robes, unique among politicians, recall our glorious history of two hundred years ago—with echoes of George Washington, Thomas Jefferson, and Abraham Lincoln, visions of noble men drafting a Constitution in Philadelphia. The justices' secrecy, their professional seclusion, only add to their aura; nine people regarded with reverence and awe, thought to be far smarter and more judicious than the rest of us, distinguished in a way that none of us are, and engaged in a lofty legal dialogue, with politics and self-interest rarely intruding. It is, of course, not true. Like nine scorpions in a bottle, they disagree sharply, fight one another with bare-knuckled determination, and get angry with one another as they argue over the political issues in the law.

Increasingly, those who come to the Court have as their prime credential political activity and a track record working the political judicial ladder. Politics has always been a selection criteria, but it has now moved to a new level. It wasn't scholarship, or greatness, or long years of excellence in judging that brought these justices to the court. Rehnquist, Kennedy, and O'Connor worked hard on the political campaigns of Barry Goldwater and Richard Nixon, while powerful mentors in the Senate advanced the judicial careers of Thomas, Souter, and Breyer. Aggressive partisanship is the necessary credential.

It's only natural that today's Supreme Court reflects right-wing voting patterns. The Roosevelt Court reflected New Deal politics. The fact that the Court is political does not mean we disregard it, or that we should not respect its authority. Politics can lead a court to choose many different values: political stability, moderate policy choices, social satisfaction, social justice, or economic efficiency. In order for the "nine scorpions in a bottle" to live together, there will be, and always has been, horse trading and compromise, an essential element of both politics and judging. The justices will allow a case to be lost on the narrowest grounds in order to save larger principles. The image of the law being an anchor in the political waters is still somewhat true because there are limitations on it that do not exist on other branches of government. But it also has certain freedoms the other branches do not have.

The law generally moves incrementally. Today's decisions built on foundations of the last twenty years do not seem radical. But momentum is turning these incremental decisions into a landslide. Prior to the New Deal, and during the early years of the Great Depression, the courts refused to allow the federal government to try to end the brutal economic conditions most Americans experienced, striking down child labor and minimum wage laws that in effect prohibited the New Deal from regulating business. Fought by conservative jurists, FDR openly acknowledged the political nature of the Court by threatening to pack it with his own appointees, ultimately crushing his legal and economic opponents.

The pro–free market Rehnquist Court has found its own tactical weapons through its fresh and idiosyncratic reading of "newly" discovered parts of the Constitution to protect business and economic rights at the expense of individual rights. Rehnquist, Scalia, and Thomas want to reinstitute the free market to the extent they can. "Let's do away with the SEC" was the headline on a recent Federalist newsletter. That America's biggest private financial disaster, Enron, occurred in a deregulated market will not stop the rush to deregulation.

The evangelical right wing wants to change sixty years of law by taking down the constitutionally created wall of church and state, by getting direct funding to religious schools, by putting prayer back in the classroom, and by implementing faith-based initiatives. The political Right wants to end affirmative action in education, at the workplace, and in the awarding of government contracts. They want to get the courts out of the school integration business and give back to the states the power they believe the Roosevelt and Warren Courts took away. And, through their black-robed allies, they do this in the way they read the Constitution. They can find it in the original intent of those who drafted the Constitution, or they find it in natural law, in a Constitution created under God.

I have chosen not to write about certain areas—such as free speech—in chapters of their own. Instead, I have discussed the First Amendment in the abortion area—in which, for example, the Supreme Court precluded doctors from giving family counseling advice—and in the church-state area—in which the Supreme Court required the state to fund a religious magazine at a university. Also I have not treated separately gender discrimination and racial discrimination because the facts and law surrounding these issues parallel each other. Nor will I write exhaustively about each particular battlefield. In this, as in much else, the raindrop mirrors the universe.

I will begin by examining Ronald Reagan's attempt to politicize every part of the federal judiciary, and then I'll turn to the different areas in which the present law has already dramatically changed and will continue to so change in the future. As we explore the direction in which our nation is heading, we will see that we must do more not to fail Benjamin Franklin's challenge.

2

THE RIGHT'S TWENTY-YEAR ATTACK ON THE FEDERAL JUDICIARY

As a rule, only presidents with powerful mandates can transform the judiciary. Franklin D. Roosevelt and Ronald Reagan had those mandates. Roosevelt, in his first election in 1932, received 472 electoral votes to Herbert C. Hoover's 59. Ronald Reagan, during his first election in 1980, received 489 to Jimmy Carter's 49. During his second election, Roosevelt won the electoral vote 523 to Alfred M. Landon's 8, while Reagan won 525 to Walter F. Mondale's 13. They each received approximately 60 percent of the popular vote in their reelection bids, and each succeeded in changing the course of the law. But today, with Reagan supporters solidly entrenched in Washington, the momentum of Reagan's legal revolution lives, in the administrations of the elder Bush and now the younger Bush; indeed it thrives.

Prior to both FDR and Reagan, the courts were already beginning to reflect the changing political circumstances. But each president wanted more dramatic change, and although the judiciary originally was not a top priority for FDR, it was for Reagan. Reagan, like Roosevelt, understood the political nature of the courts: that judges make new laws and reject old ones, and that court decisions can change society in profound and often unforeseeable ways. Both helped expand the courts to become a powerful influence on a wide range of issues that are far more political than legal, and while Roosevelt had an advantage that Reagan did not have—a Congress of his own party—both made judicial appointments to further their political agendas. Each achieved their objective. Roosevelt's justices created a judicial revolution against nineteenth-century conservatism; Reagan and his supporters, the Federalist Society and the Religious Right, created a judicial counterrevolution to twentieth-century liberal law. As Reagan declared, "It is doubtful that the net contribution of the Constitution to our national well-being has been positive and it is certain that the net contribution of judicial review has been negative." In other words, constitutional law ought to complement the results sought, not interfere with them. These views have been mirrored by the Republican presidents and their judiciaries ever since.

Reagan, like Barry Goldwater in 1964, made the courts a major campaign issue. He married money interests, conservatives, and right-wing populism, attacking long-established laws governing the rights of property owners, race issues, state-federal relations, affirmative action, the separation of powers, the wall of separation between church and state, big government, and individual entitlement programs. Specific issues that would gain mass support were publicly targeted, *Roe v. Wade* more than any other. But with a solid .Democratic House making legislative gains in these areas nearly impossible, Reagan began to look closely at court appointments. The Supreme Court, of course, was the ultimate political prize, but Reagan's people now focused, as never before, on the circuit court as a high-stakes political incubator, turning to it (especially the circuit court in Washington, D.C.) when the time came to search for Supreme Court nominees.

Beginning in 1981, Reagan nominated four federal appeals judges to fill High Court vacancies. While only a third of the fifteen judges nominated to the Supreme Court between 1945 and 1968 were federal appeals judges, sixteen of nineteen nominees since then have emerged from this elite pool. This means that a different type of person now becomes a justice. Formerly they were prominent elected political figures, such as an Earl Warren or Hugo Black, figures who had their hand on the pulse of the people, figures who knew the problems of government and knew how to make society work. Many justices of the past had larger views of the world than courts composed of longtime federal appeals judges who had never been leading players in the world of political currents and their changes.

Reagan's first term was a time for consolidation and planning. His first attorney general, California corporate lawyer William French Smith, was not, in style or substance, what the right wing wanted. Smith's selection of his friend Sandra Day O'Connor angered conservatives who never believed, as Smith and Reagan had promised, that she would vote to ban abortions. Once Edwin Meese replaced Smith as the attorney general in charge of the Justice Department in 1985, and Charles Fried became solicitor general in charge of lawyers who represent the United States before the Supreme Court, the Right was in a position to start the rewriting of American law. As in most other areas, Reagan maintained a hands-off approach, simply outlining goals and delegating responsibilities.

Meese wanted justices and judges to stop busing; to stop the Court's involvement in schools, prisons, and abortions; and to assert states rights: "One of the things, of course, that we're doing is to be sure that the Justice Department is not a party to any actions that would encourage additional forced busing of school children. At the same time, we are working with many school districts that have successfully eliminated segregation to be relieved of the requirements of forced busing that might have been included in a previous decree." In 1986, Meese told the American Bar Association (ABA) that he believed if a judge agrees with *Roe*, he is unsuitable to be a judge: "I think that a potential judge's views on *Roe v. Wade*, which I view as a usurpation of the legislative authority, might be indicative of the way in which that judge would generally approach the whole subject of judicial activism." For this reason, he and many of Reagan's nominees, including William Rehnquist, believed *Brown v. Board of Education* to be wrongly decided.

Meese sought confrontation; he was the most vocal and ideological attorney general of the previous forty years. He and Reagan were perfect for each other. As a driving force and architect of the revolution done in Reagan's name, he spoke wherever and whenever he could, vigorously laying out his political agenda. A look at some of his speeches shows us where the legal revolution has yet to go.

In a speech prepared for a July 1984 ABA meeting, Meese argued that the "doctrine of incorporation," a body of decisions over the last sixty years holding that the Fourteenth Amendment gave citizens the protection of the Bill of Rights against the states, was wrong, thereby attacking concepts that most jurists then and today accept as being set in stone. Meese criticized the Supreme Court's criminal law decisions—the right to competent counsel; the right not to be precluded from the Courts because you are indigent;

and the right not to be brutally, wantonly, and sadistically beaten in the state system. He forwarded his view of state-supported religion, and he offered his opinion that originalism—interpreting the Constitution by looking only at the intent of framers, resulting (its critics say) in a document that is static, unchanging, and "dead"—was the proper model of constitutional orientation. On another occasion, he attacked the existence of independent regulatory agencies, and he called black civil rights groups a "pernicious lobby" and the American Civil Liberties Union (ACLU) a "criminals' lobby."

Meese made changing the entire federal bench's membership a priority. Under his tutelage, the justices Reagan sent up for nominations—Robert Bork, Antonin Scalia, Anthony Kennedy, Sandra Day O'Connor, and William Rehnquist for chief justice—were as right wing a group of justices as had ever been nominated. Indeed, a thorough search of Scalia's circuit court opinions uncovered not a single opinion that disagreed with Meese's politics.

When Harvard law professor Charles Fried became solicitor general in 1985, the political war disguised as a constitutional war began in earnest. The solicitor general has often been referred to as the "Tenth Justice," being seen as a kind of permanent, dispassionate friend to the Court, interpreting and protecting the Constitution. But that was not Fried's or Meese's view of the position. Fried became far more politically aggressive than any previous solicitor, advocating the Court to depart from its own precedents and adopt the administration's political view through its decisions.

Although they had their disagreements, Fried and Meese were a perfect fit. Fried, European born, thin, elegant, well educated, gave Meese's programs intellectual cover. While Meese laid out a fifty-year plan to limit access to the federal courts and railed against the New Deal and the administrative state, Fried and the bright conservative lawyers he attracted to government created legal rationales to support the strategy.

Fried drew little distinction between political and judicial ideology as jurisprudence as he argued against decades of Court decisions. During the 1960s and early 1970s, I and other liberal lawyers learned to go to federal court as often as we could to try to get quickly to the Supreme Court. Once Fried's effect was felt, it was clear that the federal courts should be avoided. The conservatives learned to use the courts in the '80s and '90s as the liberals had in the '50s, '60s, and early '70s. Now it is the Far Right that goes to the Court; the Center or Left seeks to avoid it. Under Charles Fried, the solicitor general's office turned into a political lobbyist, not only arguing the cases before the Court but advising the Court which cases it should pick out to hear or reject, a practice continued by the present officeholder, Theodore Olson.

Reagan and Meese—like Scalia, Thomas, and Rehnquist—believed Congress's role in governance begins and ends with the passage of statutes. Once a statute becomes law, the executive and judiciary take over and congressional control ends. The people are thus driven out of the process. The executive enforces the law while the judiciary determines its constitutionality. Under this system, should a law, in fact, be challenged, today's majority argues that Congress's fact-finding and the law's legislative history should be given little if any weight—a view and construct that have helped the Court to strike down thirty congressional statutes in the last five years alone.

Lani Guinier, in her book *The Tyranny of the Majority*, summarizes these events.

> With the loss in 1986 of the Republican advantage in the United States Senate, the Supreme Court replaced the legislature as the war zone. The strategy was to enlist conservative lawyers as jurists to soldier on, to tame past precedents that attempted "rough justice," and instead to "stand up" for a conservative agenda in which government is color blind and minimalistic, and in which the power of the President is "clear and unitary." The objective was to reinterpret and reclaim a "liberal, individualistic" conception of justice, personified in the heightened power of the Presidency.

Reagan's openly political stance on the law, accompanied by a more ideologically compatible judiciary, revolutionized the entire judicial process. The courts today look even more like what Reagan wanted than when he left office: Republican strongholds presided over by Republican appointees. Sandra Day O'Connor aside, Reagan appointed few women, and fewer blacks, than any president since Eisenhower. And although he entered office as our oldest president, his appointees were younger than those made by the four preceding presidents, thereby ensuring his longer legacy. Whereas during Reagan's first years few of the justices were ready to enlist in the Right's project, that is no longer true.

The framers writing Article III of the Constitution wanted justices, men of law, to sit on courts—for men above politics, just as the law would be. But they were not naive; they knew that government is politics. They saw early on, in the original fighting between Justice John Marshall and Thomas Jefferson, the inevitable entangling of politics and law. The framers understood that when the appointments process becomes an extension of politics, independent judicial review is seriously questioned, and they tried, as best they could, to take politics out of the judiciary. But life tenure is not a sufficient measure of independence when politics demands the appointment of one set of judges rather than another.

Party politics were inevitable. Alexander Hamilton's Federalists, passing measures for the benefit of the Northeast, for the benefit of the wealthy, for "gentlemen of principle and property," offended "the people of no particular importance." He showed little respect for other interests, for the South, and for those rough pioneers expanding the country. When the Federalists lost control of Congress with Jefferson's election in 1800, John Adams used the lame-duck congressional session of 1801 to adopt a Judiciary Act creating new judgeships, to which Federalists were immediately appointed and confirmed. John Marshall's appointment as chief justice was politically manipulated, to prevent Jefferson from making that nomination.

Adams was the last Federalist president, but during more than thirty years of Republican control, Justice Marshall continued to hand down a Federalist interpretation of law. Prior to his appointment, each Supreme Court justice wrote a separate opinion on each case. The decision was then based on the majority vote, regardless of the different and often contradicting reasoning of each judge. The Court had little meaning in our government's structure. But Marshall changed all that. For the next thirty-three years, he wrote almost all the important decisions, the other justices simply concurring or dissenting. America was lucky. The Court resembled an autocracy under the control of a benevolent autocrat. Marshall, the Federalist, established judicial review when he first struck down a Republican statute. Jefferson, like Roosevelt and Reagan after him, railed against the Court, and he sought by impeachment to get at Federalist justices who disagreed with his politics. Later presidents mostly waited for retirements.

Roosevelt did not want to wait and exerted presidential power with his threat of court packing. Between 1930 and 1967, presidents nominated twenty-four justices to the Supreme Court without a single rejection. Five of the next fifteen nominees were rejected. While controversial nominations (Abe Fortas, Homer Thornberry, and Harold Carswell), and anti-Semitism (Louis Brandeis and Felix Frankfurter), racism (Thurgood Marshall), and politics (Earl Warren and William Brennan) were always part of the mix, the nomination process became most explosive with Reagan's appointments of Robert Bork and the elder Bush's nomination of Clarence Thomas.

Since Reagan, with prosperity and the absence of the cold war, and with the rise and permanence of the Far Right, internecine, ongoing judicial politics seemed to have reached new highs of viciousness. The Supreme Court nomination process has, in fact, become so political that justices forewarn the executive branch of their leaving to give the president as much time as possible to begin in secret the replacement process. Associate Justice Potter Stewart in 1981 and Chief Justice Warren Burger in 1986 each gave the Reagan administration a private warning about their plans, enabling the administration quietly to get to work to unveil fully vetted nominees as soon as the justices announced their retirements publicly. By the time Congress learned the names of the nominees, the candidates had months of preparation and politicking done on their behalf. Reagan introduced the tactic of surprise.

Chief Justice Burger indeed helped the Republicans recruit judges who would carry out the conservative mission—he helpfully supplied a list of proposed replacements for himself, which included William Rehnquist, then an associate justice, and Antonin Scalia, who eventually was named to fill the vacancy created when Reagan elevated Rehnquist to take Burger's position. Justice Lewis F. Powell Jr., on the other hand, who prided himself on remaining aloof from party politics, gave the Reagan administration four days' notice before announcing his June 1987 retirement. That lack of turnaround time may have contributed to the infamous Bork debacle, because the Reagan team basically plucked Bork from the list of nominees it had prepared the previous year without allowing itself sufficient time to reflect on the Senate's changed politics and on Bork's recent writings.

Reagan's appointment process was unusual because it was so totally driven by age and politics and because it has been so successfully institutionalized since 1980. But if Bork was the most conspicuous misstep, there were other nominations that just barely stayed alive.

The Reagan appellate appointee Daniel Manion, whom the Senate Judiciary Committee considered on May 8, 1986, was one of the first judges to become the object of a national campaign to defeat a lower court nomination. Prior to his appointment, Manion praised the John Birch Society for "being on the front line of the fight for constitutional freedom"; as a lawyer, Manion had handled almost no litigation of any complexity, had shown no intellectual distinction, and had written no scholarly or any other articles. The ensuing vote promised to be close until Republican senator Arlen Specter of Pennsylvania and Democrat Dennis DeConcini of Arizona, both of whom had voted against the nomination in committee, changed their votes. Manion then received his appointment, clearly unqualified to serve on a court that ranks just below the Supreme Court in the judicial structure.

Sid Fitzwater, another nominee, had drawn a letter of complaint from the Justice Department for posting intimidating and misleading signs in minority districts to discourage minority votes. Yet when the Senate voted 64–33 to confirm, he became, at thirty-two years of age, the youngest federal district court judge in the nation.

J. Harvie Wilkinson was a former editorial-page writer and University of Virginia law professor. When he was nominated to the U.S. Court of Appeals for the Fourth Circuit, at the age of thirty-nine, he had never had a private client and had never tried a case in court. Nonetheless, the nomination succeeded. Now on the fourth circuit, Wilkinson is one of the most conservative judges on the nation's most conservative circuit. His name had been floated by George Bush and now by White House Federalists as a possible Supreme Court nominee.

Alex Kozinski was appointed to the ninth circuit when he was only thirty-four. He received a split ABA rating, a majority voting him "qualified" and a minority voting him "not qualified." A bitter debate resulted in a vote of 52–43 in his favor. A brilliant eclectic arch conservative, his name, too, had been floated by both Bush administrations as a potential nominee for the Supreme Court. Only the fear of a Senate fight will stop the nominations of Wilkinson and Kozinski.

Some of the Reagan nominations were so far beyond minimum limits of dignity and fairness, they were defeated. Jefferson B. Sessions, who called

the National Association for the Advancement of Colored People
(NAACP) and the National Council of Churches (NCC) "un-American"
and "Communist-inspired" organizations that were "trying to force civil
rights down the throats of people," was one such nonstarter. Sessions said
the Ku Klux Klan was "OK until I learned they smoke pot." He referred to
a white civil rights lawyer "as a disgrace to his race." Years later, he has
come back to haunt the Democrats as a senator who sits, of all places, on
the Senate Judiciary Committee, the committee responsible for judicial
appointments.

Another Reagan appointee, Lino A. Graglia, a law professor, told a Texas
community it was "under no obligation" to obey federal court busing
orders. He published scholarly articles saying that white parents should be
allowed to evade federal court orders by sham custody arrangements,
referred to black children as "pickaninnies," and condemned judicially created constitutional safeguards for individual rights as "just bad ideas." When
the ABA found him "not qualified" to sit on the U.S. Court of Appeals for
the Fifth Circuit, Reagan withdrew the nomination. Yet when the ABA also
issued nominee Sherman Unger a poor rating in 1982, the Reagan administration dug in its heels. Only Unger's death during the confirmation process
saved the administration from a loss.

Bernard Siegan, a San Diego law professor nominated to the U.S. Court
of Appeals for the Ninth Circuit, had written two books advocating vigorous
judicial protection of property rights while at the same time arguing for the
limitation of personal rights and limited government. Natural law, he wrote,
was the basis of the Constitution. Siegan, who at his hearing underwent
confirmation conversion, dismissed his previous written views as irrelevant,
and promised he would follow Supreme Court decisions. The Senate Judiciary Committee first rejected him and then decided not to send the nomination to the floor; while his nomination was withdrawn, his name
resurfaced on the elder Bush's early nominee lists. His writing today is as
intemperate as his writings in the past—he has influenced a group of young
scholars, with eyes on the Court, who have learned to avoid paper trails
such as that which defeated Siegan.

By contrast, many highly qualified conservative nominees were attacked
by the extreme right wing of the Reagan administration. Judith Whittaker,
an outstanding conservative jurist on the U.S. Court of Appeals for the
Eighth Circuit, survived the attack; former U.S. deputy solicitor general

Andrew Frey, selected for the District of Columbia appeals court by Reagan, did not: Whittaker had made a small contribution to Planned Parenthood, and Frey had made a contribution to a gun-control group.

Supreme Court confirmation hearings have a long history and are now considered commonplace. The first justice to be called before the Senate Judiciary Committee for a hearing was Harlan Fiske Stone in 1925. Despite hostile questioning, he "came through with flying colors in a performance marked by strength, dignity, and articulateness." Recent Supreme Court nominees have shown little of these qualities in their own Judiciary Committee appearances. We can expect each future hearing to be a war—a war that can, one hopes, educate the voters on what is at stake.

The same issues will be raised in this century as in the past but with everyone realizing that so much more is at stake, one question may, and should become, a hundred. Decades ago, during Judge Roger J. Miner's confirmation hearing for the circuit court, Senator Strom Thurmond asked him whether he understood that it was a judge's duty to interpret, not make the law. Miner said he did. Senator Paul Simon, on behalf of the Democrats, asked if Miner understood that it might not always be the case that a judge should interpret the law and not make the law. Miner said he understood that, too. That was it. He was unanimously confirmed. Those days are gone.

When on May 27, 1986, Chief Justice Burger told Reagan he was stepping down, Rehnquist was nominated for the chief justice's seat and Antonin Scalia for Rehnquist's associate justice spot. Prior to Bork, the Republican Right had had a nearly free ride. While Rehnquist's controversial nomination saw him get the largest negative vote of any Supreme Court justice (the vote was 65–33), after a nasty acrimonious debate, Scalia, the first Italian American to be designated, sailed in with a 98–0 vote. Scalia and Bork both enjoyed parallel records as brilliant, successful, ideological conservatives who had been academics and then judges on the prestigious Washington federal appeals court. Both were originally considered for the same seat. In fact, the White House concluded that Scalia was the more radical of the two, that Bork would be more inclined "to give broader effect to a 'core' constitutional value." Ultimately Scalia's younger age (Bork was fifty-nine, Scalia fifty) was determinative.

Scalia, appointed by Reagan, is the justice that George Bush, George W. Bush, the Federalists, and the Religious Right use as a model for future justices. Born on March 12, 1936, in New Jersey, Antonin Scalia later moved to Queens, New York, and grew up in a strict Roman Catholic family. Characterized as an arch conservative by friends in high school, he was class valedictorian at Georgetown University, and law review editor and magna cum laude at Harvard Law School. After a brief stint at practice and teaching, he joined the Nixon administration in 1972, ultimately becoming head of the Justice Department's Office of Legal Counsel. After Nixon left, while working for the Ford administration Scalia argued that Nixon, not the government, had title to the tapes and documents of Watergate and that the executive was superior to the courts or to Congress, a position soundly rejected by the Supreme Court.

During Carter's presidency he went to the conservative American Enterprise Institute (AEI), where he coedited a journal promoting the free market and deregulation. Nominated by Reagan in 1986 for the vacant seat left by Rehnquist, he benefited by the fight over the chief justice nomination by quietly slipping through at his hearing. He took a hard-line radical revisionist view, was against abortion, and defended an article he wrote attacking Powell's opinion in *Regents of the University of California v. Bakke* (1978), the affirmative action case as "thoroughly unconvincing as an honest" decision. Those liberals who did pay attention to Scalia's record and statements were numbed. Although Alabama Democrat Howell Heflin said Scalia "had been elusive, evasive and perhaps overly hidden behind some concept of separation of powers," he passed the Senate unanimously and became the Court's youngest judge.

Some Democrats may have voted for Scalia believing his extreme views would result in his being an isolated voice, but the Court is turning his way, and he is a powerful member of the new majority. He is much sought after politically and gives more public appearances in support of his agenda than any other justice.

A devout Catholic, he is married and has nine children. His wife regularly attends meetings of the ultra-orthodox Opus Dei. Scalia recently criticized the Catholic Church for its anti–capital punishment position, pointing out that for two thousand years the Church had not been against it. Catholic judges who were against the death penalty and had any hesitancy in applying it should resign, he said, because it was the law of the land.

Then at the end of the Reagan period came Robert Bork; with his nomination, politics came to the front of the nomination process as never before. From a liberal point of view, the fight over Rehnquist the year before had far greater urgency, and, had the liberal community been more organized, that nomination might have been defeated. But the residual anger over the Democrats' failure to stop Rehnquist, along with a host of other factors, led to the Bork war.

Some of it was Bork's fault; some of it was not. Powell, suffering from old age and ill health, wanted a Republican president to appoint his successor. Bork, nominated four days after Powell announced his retirement on June 26, 1987, was already a controversial figure. As Nixon's acting attorney general, he agreed to fire Watergate special prosecutor Archibald Cox during the infamous "Saturday Night Massacre." When Elliot Richardson, Cox's nominal successor, resigned rather than do Nixon's bidding, it made Bork's actions seem unsavory.

But the Right could not imagine that Bork's distinguished academic and judicial background would not lead to a nomination. Only a year earlier Scalia had waltzed through. Senator Kennedy, leading the attack on Bork, argued that since Bork was getting Powell's swing seat, the fight was not only over Bork, but also over a concern about unbalancing the Court. Kennedy—describing a Robert Bork America as a land of repression, regression, and fear—declared that the future and present political path of the Court's decision-making process was at stake; the combination of Bork and Scalia on the same Court would, because of their intellect and deep ideological commitments, drive present and future appointments further right. Unlike Rehnquist, Bork had not previously been on the Court, and while it would have been unheard of to turn down a sitting justice for the chief justice position, defeating Bork's nomination was another matter.

Senator Kennedy's remarks, unleashing the anger and frustration of the last seven years, helped seal Bork's doom. The nomination went down that October, 58–42. But the years have been kind to the Reagan judicial vision. If Powell's ultimate replacement, Anthony Kennedy, would turn out to be not quite all things to all Reaganites, the agenda had nonetheless affixed itself to the national consciousness. With Scalia now on the Court, and with Rehnquist leading it, the American judiciary had dramatically changed.

The Bork defeat was only one battle lost in the right wing's successful attempt to dominate the judiciary. Reagan's change in the criteria for appointment was extraordinary. In only eight years he had changed the nature of the judiciary and the law itself and had left a legacy that would last for generations. We live today with those grim results. Ronald Reagan's mechanism for selecting justices would be refined by his successors. Both Bush administrations would embrace the tactic of surprise to get a jump on their critics by moving quickly to announce Court nominations, and both would be open in their quest for youth and unabashed in their ferocious politicization of the judiciary.

Even the Bork disappointment, the elder Bush thought, could be reframed to the Republicans' political advantage. David Souter, Bush's test nominee, was seen as "a home run," a Bork clone without political baggage or a writing trail. Clarence Thomas, nominated for the "black seat" vacated by Marshall, split some of the opposition to his conservatism because of his race. While his nomination might have been contentious, until Anita Hill surfaced he was assured of easy success. The only real loser was the confirmation process itself, which might never fully recover its integrity.

The questions themselves in subsequent hearings have become overloaded with rhetoric absent of follow-up, and provide argument rather than information. Ranking Democratic Committee member Joseph Biden's questioning continues to be nearly always uniform; Arlen Specter's every question tries to permit only the partisan answer he wants. We are now treated to what is in effect a staged, inept performance from both sides. It is aimed at public relations; it is senatorial posturing beamed toward national television. The nominee—aided by public relations experts, Justice Department briefers, and supporters of the confirmation—tries to say as little as possible.

After his hearing, Bork accurately predicted that direct answers would never again be the norm, because nominees would be selected from those who have not written or spoken about important issues. Those who followed him have studiously avoided any controversial responses to questions put to them, in Thomas's case even ignoring what he himself had said and written previously. The hearings have been allowed to become an exercise in near futility. If the senators were to come better prepared and were to acknowledge that the hearings are about politics and partisanship and that highly qualified judges, depending on their politics, can answer the same question ten different ways, then we could deal with the reality and choose the justices that further the political and legal agenda the people want.

The potent partnership forged by the Reagan team and the Religious Right carried over to the first Bush administration. Bush's 187 lifetime appointments—a very large number—were bookended by the Bork defeat at the end of the Reagan presidency and by the success of the Thomas nomination. But to talk about the Bush Sr. years is to talk about the addition of some of the most powerful forces in creating and structuring the new legal system— the private organizations created by the Right. The most powerful is the Federalist Society, whose emblem is a silhouette of James Madison, advocate of a strong federal government. It is an appalling, outrageous reversal of Madison's dream and intent. Although in reality they are against a strong national government, they took the Federalist name in part to tweak it, and also because it is their view of federalism they claim to be correct.

Although the Federalists were formed during the Reagan administration, they came out of the closet during George Bush's first years, becoming more effective and visible, with little opposition, as the years went on. Much of the society's past and present leadership consists of formidable, active politicians (Orrin Hatch is cochair), important right-wing organizations (American Enterprise Institute), and judicial voices (Robert Bork and Antonin Scalia). Former Iran-Contra special prosecutor Lawrence Walsh wrote during George Bush's administration he was especially troubled that one of White House Counsel Boyden Gray's assistants had openly declared that no one who was not a member of the Federalist Society had received a judicial appointment from President George Bush Sr.

Edwin Meese helped form the Federalists, originally a right-wing lawyers group with a radical agenda. Calling themselves the "natural allies" of the administration, they had played no role in judicial selection previously and had lacked access to key officials at the Justice Department or the Supreme Court before. Meese changed all that.

Today, the Federalists have more authority than the ABA ever had in judicial selection. The significance of this cannot be underestimated. It rejected decades of established practices under both Republican and Democratic presidents. The Federalist Society for Law and Public Policy Studies was first begun, right after Reagan was elected in 1982, by a small group of radical conservative law students at the University of Chicago who had been undergraduates together at Yale—Steven Calabresi, David McIntosh, and Lee Lieberman Otis—and is backed by the prominent names in the right-wing legal establishment. Soon after, they were joined by Harvard law student Spencer Abraham, who started a Harvard chapter.

Calabresi went on to clerk for Robert Bork and Antonin Scalia on the U.S. Court of Appeals for the District of Columbia Circuit, and then worked in both the White House and in the Reagan and Bush Justice Departments. McIntosh became a special assistant to Attorney General Edwin Meese and to President Reagan and, later, a three-term congressman from Indiana who then lost a race for governor. Otis became an assistant attorney general under Meese, then clerked for Scalia at the Supreme Court. And Spencer Abraham became U.S. senator from Michigan and is now Secretary of Energy. Otis served as Abraham's chief counsel on the Senate Judiciary Committee before joining him at the Energy Department.

With seed money provided by the Institute for Educational Affairs (headed at the time by neo-conservatives Irving Kristol and the late William E. Simon) and millions of dollars over the years from the Lynde and Harry Bradley, John M. Olin, Sarah Scaife, Charles Koch, and Castle Rock Foundations, the Federalist Society grew quickly throughout the 1980s and '90s.

The Federalists—by targeting the courts, law schools, and the ABA, and now through coordinating litigation (with other right-wing groups) and advocacy—are radically transforming the entire American legal system. Indeed, senior appeals court judge Roger J. Miner warned in 1992 of a seismic power shift, that the power of appointment of federal trial, appellate, and Supreme Court judges "has shifted away from Presidents and Senators to staff." He went on: "The force of history and attachment to the coattails of political winners have catapulted them [the right-wing lawyers clustered around the Federalist Society] to positions of power, first as law clerks, then as movers and shakers in the office of the Attorney General, and now in the office of the President."

Reagan, as Miner acknowledged, successfully moved the nomination process out of the Department of Justice and into the White House; George Bush consolidated those gains. During the elder Bush's presidency, all activity relating to judicial appointments was centered in the office of the counsel to the president and controlled by its staff, and it has stayed there ever since. This staff, composed nearly entirely of Federalists and their allies in other private groups, many of whom consider Rehnquist not far enough to the right, have virtually hijacked the process. As Miner said, "The President has abdicated his duty to nominate, the Senate provides no advice whatsoever, and senatorial consent is a mere formality in most instances." Since 1982 most nominees to the circuit courts, and nearly all of the hundreds of district court judges, have been filtered and filled this way. "That this should be so," said Miner, "at a time when the appointment process is in the hands of those who profess a blind adherence to the doctrine of original intent, is strange indeed." So long as the nomination process continues wrongfully and tragically to reside in the White House, we shall continue to see both the partisanship and the spectacle.

Once the elder Bush installed the Federalists in power in the White House, they never left. They became prominent as clerks to Supreme Court and circuit court judges and in the law schools. Many continued, organizing against Clinton's judicial nominations at the state and federal political levels, from the base of the right-wing foundation world. The Federalist Society's members today include the most influential figures on the right in the current administration. Among them are two other members of George W. Bush's cabinet, Interior Secretary Gale A. Norton and Attorney General John D. Ashcroft. Other members or participants are sprinkled throughout high levels of the current Bush's administration. They include Solicitor General Theodore Olson, White House counsel Alberto Gonzalez (in charge of passing on all judicial nominations before they are submitted to Congress), and five of eleven lawyers on his staff. Donald Paul Hodel, Secretary of the Interior and Energy Department in the Reagan administration and later the president of the Christian Coalition, is a board member. Several sitting Supreme Court justices have spoken under the auspices of the society, and several leading judges on the federal bench serve in an advisory capacity to the society's local chapters.

The society membership includes more than forty thousand lawyers, policy experts, and business leaders who are involved in sixty Lawyers Division chapters nationwide. It offers continuing legal education (CLE) programs and promotes rightist views through publications and a number of sophisticated Web sites. There is a Faculty Division, as well as a Student Division containing five thousand members nationwide. Edward Lazarus, a former law clerk for Justice Harry Blackmun, wrote in 1990 that during the administration of the first Bush, membership had already "become a prerequisite for law students seeking clerkships with many Reagan judicial appointees as well as for employment in the upper ranks of the Justice Department and the White House." Theirs is an impressive effort. They are disciplined, helpful, effective, enormously polite, and gracious. I went to a number of their meetings and felt the same passions I found at Evangelical meetings.

With an annual budget in excess of $6 million, the society holds high-profile annual national student symposia and numerous local conferences targeting lawyers, law students, and faculty to argue conservative and right-wing views on key legal and political issues. The society claims the academic high ground by staging "balanced" debates through which it can introduce its agenda into the law school environment. Many leading liberal figures, including liberal senators, who totally disagree with them, feel it worth their while to participate in those seminars, thereby adding to the society's stature.

Federalist Society publications, think tank meetings, strategy sessions, and panel discussions target those cases that would place individual rights above economic rights; those agencies that place limitations on business; those judges who seek to expand the federal civil rights laws, the voting rights laws, and gender equality protections and desegregation orders. They are very specific and have an extensive enemies and friends list. And yet the Federalists do not litigate. Other right-wing legal groups do that on their behalf, like the Institute for Justice, the Washington Legal Foundation, the Center for Individual Rights, and the Pacific Legal Foundation. A proliferation of Religious Right litigation organizations coming out of the Evangelical movement has gained in resources, vastly increased the Right's power base, and successfully built a strategic litigation capacity. The Federalists get a great deal of credit for keeping disparate groups, often with conflicting agendas, under the same roof.

Because of the importance of keeping with them the organizations associated with Pat Robertson, the Federalists spend a great deal of energy on the Radical Right's issues. They argue for "school choice" and "charitable choice" (church involvement in state efforts to reform welfare), as well as creationist teachings and the distribution of religious materials in public schools, while sponsoring fifteen practice groups in separate areas, including religious liberty, national security, cyberspace, corporations law, and environmental law to help shape Federalist policy and promote the right-wing revisionist agenda throughout the country.

And it has made the ABA a constant target. In a keynote address on "judicial independence" at the 1999 Federalist Society Convention, Justice Clarence Thomas openly denounced the ABA, which he labeled "an interest group" probably incapable of reforming itself. More recently, the ABA's rating system role in the judicial confirmation process—those pesky ratings that had drubbed many Reagan/Bush nominees—has been, under George W. Bush, eliminated. The Federalist Society, not satisfied with taking the ABA out of the process, launched an ambitious attempt to take over the ABA itself by developing "voter guides" for ABA elections.

Thomas's successful nomination galvanized the Federalists. The judicial landscape at the end of the elder Bush's era was even better than at the end of the Reagan era. George Bush, with the Federalists and the Religious Right playing major roles, expanded and deepened the control over the circuit and trial courts. Thomas became the living triumph of that alliance, the Federalists and the Religious Right's most sought after speaker. His projection as a victim who refused to quit, and who then, because of his goodness, courage, and individuality, triumphed, blends biblical myth and free market thought. In 1991, at the time of his nomination, he was a fundamentalist who spoke in tongues (he became a Catholic four years ago, under the tutelage of Father Paul Scalia, the justice's son). Thomas is reputed to be a member of Opus Dei, the ultra-orthodox Catholic society that is often critical of what they see as the pope's liberalization of the faith. Thomas blends his own very reactionary instincts with Scalia-style legal conclusions, making him a poster boy for exactly what the Religious Right wants.

The Federalists, the administration of the elder Bush, and the future of the Republican Party are intertwined. Bush learned from Reagan to "appoint judges in the Reagan manner," meaning a far-right bench, and right-wing commentators lauded his appointments record. Clint Bolick, vice president of the Institute for Justice, called it "a tour de force. . . . He has been even better than Reagan. Bush has made the judiciary more solidly conservative without spending a lot of political capital on the issue." In fact, of the first seventy candidates interviewed for judgeships by George Bush's White House, twenty were directly recommended by the Federalist Society's

Washington headquarters. His appointees were even younger than Reagan's, and he did it all effectively and quietly, even after the Thomas storm broke.

As a result, during the election campaigns since, the Republicans placed less public emphasis on judicial selection than they did during the Reagan years. They didn't have to focus on establishing control of judicial machinery; it was already theirs.

The irony is that with Clinton's defeat of George Bush, the Right had to rethink their game plan—or at least figure out how to use their control of the Senate Judiciary Committee to frustrate the new president. They also turned their attention to the state courts, where they now play a formidable role. They succeeded during the Reagan-Bush years in giving new meaning to the phrase "packing the courts"—with or without a Republican White House, they "owned" the judiciary, as Bill Clinton was about to learn.

When Bill Clinton was first elected president in 1992, Republican appointees constituted 68.3 percent of all the active judges on the court of appeals. When he left office eight years later, although more than half of the appointees were nominally Democratic appointees, the circuit courts were more firmly in the hands of the right-wingers than ever before.

The Clinton presidency was, in fact, a disaster in trying to balance the federal courts. Part of the fault was his, part was the result of the midterm 1994 election that left the House Republican for the first time in forty years and Clinton powerless on this issue. Nonetheless, the judges Clinton appointed do not represent his politics or even the politics of most of his party. The profile for his appointees was to the right of Gerald Ford and even further to the right of his fellow Democrats Lyndon Johnson and Jimmy Carter. Of eighty-four nominees to the federal appellate courts, just forty-six were confirmed between 1995 and 2000. Some federal appellate judges waited up to four years for their nominations to go forward. And while Reagan and Clinton appointed similar numbers of appellate judges, 87 percent of Reagan's were confirmed, compared to only 61 percent of Clinton's.

What happened to Clinton's nominees was extraordinary and unique. Richard A. Paz, Clinton's nominee for the federal bench, waited a record 1,506 days until he was confirmed in 2000. Reached in his Los Angeles law office, Paz haltingly remembers his brush with the bench. He describes attending two judicial training sessions, dismissing his twelve law-firm employees, and selling all of his office furniture in 1995—only to be left hanging by a president who would not fight for his nomination when the political landscape changed. "There was no visible effort by the president to support the nominees," says Paz. "I think that's the most hurtful thing." Two other nominees to the ninth circuit court, which covers nine western states, also had long waits: William A. Fletcher spent more than three years waiting to be confirmed, while Marcia L. Berzon waited for more than two years. They are the lucky ones: among the many Clinton judicial appointments left still unconfirmed by the Senate at the end of his presidency were ten for positions the U.S. Judicial Conference and Chief Justice Rehnquist consider "judicial emergencies"—long-time vacancies on courts that are overworked.

Two of the ten were for the U.S. Circuit Court of Appeals for the Fourth Circuit. It is the most conservative court in the country, and the Senate members on the right are determined to keep it that way. By law, three of the court's fifteen judges are supposed to be from North Carolina. For some time now, there have been none. The fourth circuit court has always been the private domain of Jesse Helms. It is the only circuit court that, prior to 2001, never had a black member, although it covered an area that represents the largest African American area of any court. When, in fact, Clinton sent up the nomination of James Wynn, a black moderate with ten years of experience on the North Carolina court of appeals, Helms blocked the nomination. Helms's only excuse was to cite the dubious opinion of the Reagan appointee J. Harvie Wilkinson, now chief judge of the fourth circuit, who asserted that his court functioned better with fewer judges—the terseness of that circuit's opinions notwithstanding. In fact, the fourth circuit issued more one-sentence opinions than any other, suggesting that Wilkinson's resources were indeed severely taxed. When Clinton left office, Wynn was still waiting for his judgeship.

Roger Gregory, a respected black lawyer, was one of four Clinton nominees to the fourth circuit, all moderate lawyers or judges. All were savaged and stonewalled. None got so much as a hearing in the Senate. Finally, in January 1999, taking advantage of a congressional recess, Clinton named Gregory through a recess appointment to one of the circuit's five vacancies. The Senate at first did not confirm him to the permanent seat to which Clinton had renominated him. Finally, in 2001, George W. Bush made a deal: he got two of his judges on the bench in exchange for permitting Gregory to go on the circuit.

Bill Clinton's legacy was both that he made the federal judiciary "look more like America" and that he did not truly engage in the battle for ideological control of the courts. After 1992, judicial nominations went from a low priority to no priority, a practice he began while serving as Arkansas's governor. His presidential scandals kept him on the defensive, and after 1994, he refused to exhaust political capital on judicial fights. While diversification at the total expense of ideology was face-saving, Clinton helped to appease the Center and the Left by appointing women and blacks rather than strong opponents of the new tide. He appointed sixty-two black judges to the judiciary, only two fewer than his five predecessors had appointed in a twenty-four-year span. In all, 16.4 percent of his 378 appointees were black.

But while Clinton also outpaced all his predecessors in naming Hispanics and women to judgeships, many minority leaders expressed their disappointment at his sacrificing ideology for diversity. As Theodore Shaw, associate director of counsel to the NAACP Legal Defense and Educational Fund, suggested, "If there's anything we know, it's that to add more judges to the bench based on their race or ethnicity and regardless of their judicial philosophy, is a useless game." And, despite Clinton's claim, on leaving office, of racially integrating the judiciary, there was only one more African American judge confirmed to a federal court of appeals than at the end of Carter's term. Many of the circuit courts of appeals have no African American or Hispanic judges at all.

Not content to hold up the appointment pipeline, the Republicans in those years used attacks on sitting judges to advance their position and to unabashedly intimidate the current judiciary. In a speech before the American Society of Newspaper Editors on April 19, 1996, Senator Robert Dole made his opponent's judicial appointees a campaign issue. Describing Americans' confidence in their courts and trust in the rule of law as perhaps the most important issue of the presidential campaign, Dole identified a number of Clinton's appointees as allegedly being soft on crime. New York judge Harold Baer, Virginia judge Leonie Brinkema, third circuit judge H. Lee Sarokin, and eleventh circuit judge Rosemary Barkett were said to form a judicial "Hall of Shame" characterized by a willingness "to use technicalities to overturn death sentences for brutal murderers" and by an "outright hostility to law enforcement." Senator Dole's assault was followed by similar accusations made by other conservative political figures, including three separate floor speeches by Orrin Hatch, chairman of the Senate Judiciary Committee.

Circuit court judges then, and now, are helpless and powerless when they constitute a small minority. Several have resigned and made public their frustration. Lee Sarokin, a Carter appointee, resigned his seat on June 5, 1996, claiming that his political vilification had hampered his ability to render independent decisions. He said, "I see my life's work and reputation being disparaged on an almost daily basis and I find myself unable to ignore it." Dole's and Hatch's bullying tactics were insulting and demeaning, but they were also dead wrong. It was ludicrous of Dole to blame Sarokin and other Clinton appointees for the increase in crime. Sarokin argued pointedly, "To hold judges responsible for crime is like blaming doctors for disease. It is apparent that there are those who have decided to 'Willie Hortonize' the federal judiciary and I am to be part of that."

While some of Sarokin's right-wing critics claimed he used his resignation as an excuse to make a political statement, it was one of the few times anyone—in or out of the administration—did. Clinton's indifference to judgeships affected his entire organization. The shameful treatment received by his nominees in hearing—the most notorious being the humiliating and false charges Missouri judge Ronnie White was subjected to by John Ashcroft in 1999—point up the inadequacies of Clinton's judicial machinery versus the disciplined, organized effort of the Reagan-Bush team. In addition, the White House counsel's office suffered from significant turnover, beginning at the top. Lawyers ranging from Bernard Nussbaum to Lloyd Cutler to Charles Ruff moved in—and moved on—after a year or two in the job. The key players attended judicial nominee meetings each Thursday morning, but few of the people seated around that table remained after the Republicans took control of the Senate in 1994. The Republican Congress, in turn, refused to create the new judgeships necessary to handle an expanding population and caseload. Under Presidents Reagan and Bush, eighty-five additional federal judgeships were created; Clinton got just nine.

As soon as one of Clinton's appointments was threatened, he withdrew that name. Peter Edelman, once an aide to Robert Kennedy and a Georgetown University law professor, was the first appointee put forward by Clinton following the Democrats' 1994 loss of the Senate and House. Edelman and his wife, Children's Defense Fund founder Marian Wright Edelman, had a long-standing friendship with the Clintons. But his nomination to the high-profile U.S. Court of Appeals for the District of Columbia Circuit was quickly put into jeopardy when the right wing in the Republican Party objected to an old law review article of Edelman's that made the constitutional argument that poor Americans had a constitutional right to a guaranteed income. The candidate was pulled back and "spun," by Clinton advisor Eleanor Acheson, as an example of the administration's exemplary attempt to excise disputes from the nominations process.

Instead of an agenda for appointing liberal judges, Acheson stressed the administration's focus on the qualities of candidacy: "judicial temperament," "productivity," "energy," "integrity," "mental agility," and the nominee's understanding of the "court as an institution." Her remarks infuriated Judge Steven Reinhardt, a respected senior judge on the U.S. Court of Appeals for the Ninth Circuit. Furious, he wrote a stinging three-page letter attacking the administration's nominations process. It is a précis for all that went wrong during the Clinton years:

> Who in the world is not for judges with "judicial temperament"? Who is not for "productivity"? Who is opposed to judges with "energy," "integrity," or mental "agility"? Is there anyone—in Arkansas, Massachusetts or any other state—who doesn't believe that judges should have an understanding of the "court as an institution"?
>
> You must be aware by now that those most deeply committed to the judicial philosophy expounded by your predecessors laugh triumphantly at your protestations of philosophical objectivity. You must surely be aware how gleeful your predecessors are that this Administration has caved so quickly at almost every sign of opposition, even when it possessed a majority in both Houses. Certainly, you know how astonished they are that you have made life so easy for them. They never expected it to be that way. To say, as you do, that the Clinton Administration willingly accepts the Reagan-Bush administrations' successes in changing the philosophy of the federal courts so radically, and that it has no desire to redress the current judicial imbalance or to try to restore any glimmer of liberal representation to the courts is to abdicate, or more accurately repudiate, your historic responsibilities.
>
> Are you really seriously saying that you have no interest in which philoso-

phy your appointees have as long as they are otherwise qualified? Do you choose at random among those individuals who are "productive," "agile" and have "energy"? Would Charles Cooper, [a prominent Federalist] or Clint Bolick [legal director of the conservative Institute for Justice] be as acceptable to you and the President as Peter Edelman? Is there no limit to the panic and spinelessness these days? I'm beginning to think so.

Your comment has the same ring of verisimilitude as President Bush's, when he said that he was nominating Clarence Thomas because he was the most qualified lawyer in America. No one believed that either. Hypocritical declarations such as the one attributed to you cause people to lose confidence in government officials.

The Right's strategy—what Senate majority leader Trent Lott described as using "the process of moving nominees as a price for moving legislation"— worked with chilling efficiency. In 1996, an election year with a Democratic president in control, just seventeen trial court judges and no appeals judges made their way out of the Senate, barely a quarter the number confirmed by a Democratic Senate during 1992 when the elder Bush was in office.

The political bias of both the Judiciary Committee and the Congress was troubling, especially in light of the solid credentials of Clinton's nominees. One, Allen Snyder, appointed to the federal appeals court, clerked for Justice William Brennan and served as the chair of the lawyer disciplinary committee for the circuit and the D.C. court of appeals. He had bipartisan support, including that of the former D.C. circuit judge Robert Bork. It took him nine months to get a hearing. After the hearing, nothing happened. There was no committee vote. The nomination just died.

A report from Ohio University notes that, in contrast with George Bush, who also faced a Senate controlled by the opposition party, Clinton was greatly hampered in his ability to get circuit court nominees through the hearing and confirmation process. It took his appointees three times as long as Bush's to get nominated. The report said:

At the circuit level, Bush's nominees were confirmed in an average of 14.4 days after being reported out of committee in the Democratic 102nd Congress. . . . Clinton has not fared as well in divided government, with an average of 39.5 days until floor action in the 104th Congress and an average of 42.4 days in the 105th. It is impossible to escape the conclusion that the

Republican leadership in the Senate was engaged in a protracted effort to delay decision making on judicial appointments whether or not the appointee was, ultimately, confirmed.

Consequently, the courts were undermanned and overworked, several appeals courts averaged over a year from taking a case to rendering a decision, and the judiciary stayed as Reagan and Bush had created it.

No American president has been more vigorously attacked than Bill Clinton for appointing judges who were alleged to be extreme and uncompromising liberals. It was part of the pattern of attack that he faced during his entire administration. But this, at least, was totally untrue. Clinton saw both his Supreme Court nominees get in easily, not because they were exemplary but because Ginsburg and Breyer were anything but liberals.

Clinton was the first Democratic president since Lyndon Johnson to have the opportunity to appoint a justice to the Supreme Court. Ironically, the nomination of Abe Fortas to chief justice by lame-duck president Lyndon Johnson signaled the end of an era when most justices were easily confirmed by the Senate. By the time Clinton had the opportunity to make an appointment, the Radical Right was well poised to challenge any of his nominations; they were still smarting from the defeats of Robert Bork and the controversy surrounding Clarence Thomas's appointment. Moreover, Clinton was still reeling from the nomination debacles of Zoe Baird, Kimba Wood, and Lani Guinier. The prime criteria for Clinton henceforth was confirmability.

From a shortlist of candidates that posed few political risks to the administration, Stephen Breyer's ties with key Senate Judiciary Committee members seemed to make him the most confirmable of all. Although Clinton saw Breyer as economically too conservative, he could not afford to ignore Breyer's strengths as a nominee. Both Senators Ted Kennedy and Orrin Hatch were Breyer supporters, ensuring the nominee would receive crucial support from both sides of the aisle. Hatch, the Judiciary Committee's ranking Republican, in particular knew and liked Breyer. Clinton, battling scandal after scandal, could not afford a stormy confirmation process. Breyer was a lock, but because of Clinton's wariness of him, he became the second justice rather than the first.

Clinton's second nominee, Ruth Bader Ginsburg, was then advanced by

Bernard Nussbaum. Her candidacy was promoted through a fairly unprecedented letter-writing campaign, which was, if unorthodox, successful
enough to get her an interview with Clinton. Her nomination was
announced the next day in the White House Rose Garden after the president said he "fell in love" with her story. As Professor Karen O'Connor and
Professor Barbara Palmer, writing in the independent *Judicature*, said, "But
it was more than just infatuation. Both Ginsburg and Breyer are strikingly
like the other federal judges appointed by Clinton—non-controversial individuals with considerable judicial experience who behave as moderates."
They, as well as other political science and law professors, analyze each justice's decisions on a liberal-conservative continuum. President Clinton
often said he would go down in history as the most conservative Democrat
to occupy the White House in the twentieth century. The voting patterns of
his judicial appointees support that self-evaluation. In all analyses, Justices
Breyer and Ginsburg most often vote less liberally and with more restraint
than the other two members of the so-called moderate bloc—the two
Republican appointees, John Paul Stevens and David Souter.

Professor Sheldon Goldman and his colleagues, in their annual survey,
summed up the Clinton years:

> When the Clinton presidency came to a close on January 20, 2001, an
> extraordinary chapter in American political history ended. Clinton's first two
> years of unified government were followed by a tumultuous six years of
> divided government, bitter partisan and ideological acrimony, a sensational
> sex scandal involving the President, and a vindictive and relentless Indepen-
> dent Counsel whose referral to the House of Representatives of alleged
> offenses led to the attempted impeachment of the President and a trial by
> the Senate that ended in his acquittal. As if the American polity had not
> endured enough turmoil, a virtual tie in the presidential election of Novem-
> ber 7, 2000, resulted in five weeks of confusion, uncertainty, legal maneuver-
> ing, partisan wrangling, and finally a 5–4 Supreme Court ruling that handed
> the election to George W. Bush—a bitter coda to the Clinton years.

It is a gift that Bush is exploiting. His batch of nominees thus far sent up are
more conservative and ideological than those of either Reagan or his father.

At the outset, the younger Bush has made his power felt, dispensing with the ABA and letting it be publicly known that the Federalist Society was the employment center for judges and justices. "There is no question that Federalist Society lawyers are in control," said Ralph Neas, president of the liberal People for the American Way (PFAW), an organization that focuses on judicial selection. "These new lawyers in very key policy-making positions are even more conservative than those who served in the first Bush or even Reagan administrations. So what we see is the legal philosophy of Clarence Thomas and Antonin Scalia firmly ensconced in the White House, in the Department of Justice and throughout the executive branch."

Indeed, during the first one hundred days of the Bush administration, the influence of Federalist ideology was apparent in the rapid dismantling of workplace safety standards—the decision not to impose carbon dioxide emission standards and the decision not to ban water with high levels of arsenic—and the plans to open up the Alaskan National Wildlife Refuge to oil drilling. But these are only opening salvos; they want to gut agencies created by the New Deal, and destroy the entire architecture of regulations created by federal and state governments, both Democratic and Republican presidents and governors, and Democratic and Republican legislatures. This would include the Securities and Exchange Commission, state and federal Environmental Protection Agencies, and state and federal Equal Employment Opportunity Commissions. These agencies were designed to protect consumers and workers against a totally unregulated free-market system.

To achieve the breathtaking radical nature of their agenda, they are packing the government at every level of the state and federal bureaucracies. Many of these positions endure even though administrations change. People now being appointed as the new heads of those agencies that are severely cutting back personnel, enforcement, and regulation. Those who remain, or take their places—moderate Republicans among them—have no choice but to go along. They know where the control is.

But the Bush-Federalist coalition also knows acutely that without the courts, the right-wing populists and special interests cannot go forward. To that end, the control of the judiciary is its top priority. Moving with extraordinary swiftness, the incoming administration had many of its circuit and trial court nominees ready to roll even before Bush took the oath of office and announced that his administration would not allow Clinton's still-pending nominees to get a hearing. Nor did the defection of Vermont senator Jim Jeffords, or the bipartisanship that occurred after September 11, deter their pushing their agenda. If anything, these events have accelerated the administration's movement. They hoped Bush's high ratings would translate into an even more accommodating Congress.

The September 11 attack afforded the right wing an unwanted golden opportunity to push through its legal agenda. At both the state and federal levels, expansion of police powers and restrictions on individual liberties are being urged before legislatures and in cases totally unrelated to terrorism.

As this Court goes about its usual business, and because of the ages and politics of justices and judges who will be with us long into this century, we will see a torrent of precedent that fundamentally changes this democracy. Time is of the essence in the U.S. Supreme Court. The historical median age at which justices retire is seventy, following an average of fifteen years of service. But the ages of the present members belie that trend: John Paul Stevens is eighty-one; William H. Rehnquist is seventy-six; Ruth Bader Ginsburg is sixty-eight; Sandra Day O'Connor is seventy-one; Antonin Scalia is sixty-five; Anthony Kennedy is sixty-four; Stephen G. Breyer is sixty-two; David H. Souter is sixty-one; and Clarence Thomas is fifty-two. By the end of George W.'s first term, Rehnquist will have served thirty-two years, Stevens thirty years, and O'Connor twenty-three years. Bush's Supreme Court strategy, appoint more Scalias and Thomases, is clear. So, too, is his circuit court strategy.

To some, it would appear that George W.'s appointments would be more business as usual, particularly when his first nomination for the fifth circuit—which covers Mississippi, Texas, and Louisiana—turned out to be a judge appointed to the Mississippi federal trial court in 1990 by his father. The fifth circuit court serves a larger constituency of poor and African Americans than any other circuit. Charles J. Pickering, Bush's nominee, voted against the ERA and abortion, and wrote an article urging criminal penalties for miscegenation. He quit the Democratic Party in 1964 when it insisted on not having all-white delegations. Pickering lied about his very active involvement in the Mississippi Sovereignty Commission, a pro–Ku Klux Klan group dedicated to retaining separatism and opposing civil rights organizations. In a 1994 trial, he presided over a man who was convicted of burning a cross on the lawn of an interracial couple. Acting unethically, he contacted directly a member of the Justice Department to persuade the government not to seek a five-year sentence, which was required by the law. Senator John Edwards,

Democrat of North Carolina, read the canon of judicial ethics prohibiting a judge from making contact with one side. Neil Lewis reported in the *New York Times*, on February 8, 2002, that Pickering seemed taken aback by the line of questioning. He didn't "consider it to be a violation of judicial ethics" because he was not looking to achieve anything by his call. Asked *why* he had called, he said he was looking to express his frustration. He is a remarkable judge. In his eleven years on the bench, he published only 95 opinions, versus the federal average for that period of time of 1,235. He has seen twenty-one of twenty-three of his decisions reversed. Trent Lott, the Senate majority leader, is the judge's principal patron. Yet taking advantage of the spirit of congressional bipartisanship after September 11, 2001, Bush kept trying to push the nomination through. After Pickering was defeated in the Senate Judiciary Committee, the Republicans tried but failed to get a floor vote. Had there been a floor vote, Pickering might have won because three Democrats were prepared to vote for him. On the day after Pickering was defeated, Virginia Thomas, Clarence Thomas's wife, wrote an op-ed piece in the form of an open letter to the *Wall Street Journal* saying Pickering was opposed "because you will not rule in favor of the hard left's political agenda." Mrs. Thomas, an officer at the right-wing Heritage Foundation, said, "The Democrats on the committee and the outside groups that egg them on don't think of you as a human now."

As of this writing, the nomination of a jurist totally committed to the Far Right agenda is certain. Judge D. Brooks Smith, a federal trial judge nominated to the Third Circuit Court of Appeals by Bush, would join the rush to invalidate New Deal legislation. Appointed to the trial bench when he was 36, he gives an expansive reading of part of the Fifth Amendment, the Takings Clause (described in chapter 6) that renders nearly all regulation of business unconstitutional. His view of the Commerce Clause (described in chapter 5) would prohibit Congress from passing social legislation to protect women and minorities and would defeat any attempt at gun control. Reversed fifty times by the circuit court he seeks to join, he has consistently rendered decisions in favor of special interests, especially in environmental cases. A member of an all-male club, he rendered decisions in a case in which he and his wife had more than $100,000 in stock. Required by law to recuse himself, he refused to do so. Nonetheless, his nomination went to the Senate floor after an 12–7 vote in his favor by the Democratic-controlled Judiciary Committee. Democratic Senators Herb Kohn (from Wisconsin), John Edwards (from North Carolina), and Joe Biden (from Delaware) voted for him.

Hispanics are now the majority minority in the country, and this is being reflected in the judiciary wars. The Right has claimed that the Democrats are racist for not confirming Miguel Estrada because he is Hispanic, deliberately ignoring their refusal to even accord hearings to Jorge Rangel and Enrique Moreno, two Clinton nominees to the fifth circuit. Iowa Republicans admitted that Republicans had made a pact not to allow Clinton nominations, reserving the seats for a Republican president.

The circuit court was the big prize in the 2000 election. "As went the presidency, so goes the judiciary," observed right-wing activist Clint Bolick, vice president of the Institute for Justice. But Bush's strategy is more sophisticated as he contends with a Democratic-controlled Senate. In this post-Jeffords world, George W. Bush's plan is to solidify the judiciary's right-wing tilt by placing moderate Republicans on overwhelmingly liberal or conservative circuits where they will have little influence—and putting right-wing nominees on "battleground" circuits. It is being done in the incubator U.S. Court of Appeals for the District of Columbia, and the last of the remaining Democratic strongholds, the second, sixth, and ninth circuits.

Alberto Gonzales, Bush's White House counsel on the short list for Bush's anticipated Supreme Court nomination, worked for years with Vinson and Elkins, the law firm presently under attack for its Enron representation. As the chief judge of the Texas Appeals Court, the most conservative and pro-business court in the country, he received contributions from Enron. Gonzalez has staffed his office with former Scalia and Thomas clerks.

As of this writing, nine of the Bush circuit court and fifty-one of his federal trial appointments have been confirmed. It is only with the most visible appointments that he has been defeated.

Effective control of the circuits can negate Supreme Court losses and expand Supreme Court wins by radical or conservative interpretations of the High Court's decisions. Since every case is to some lesser or greater degree factually different than the one before it, the circuit courts can reframe the case to bypass both legal precedent, legislation, and agency regulations. So long as the circuit court doesn't patently ignore Supreme Court precedent, it is free to overreach, broaden, and distinguish. When the circuit courts sharply differ in their decisions, as they frequently do in abortion rights cases, the Supreme Court can step in. Yet Supreme Court precedent can be so easily distinguished, particularly given some Supreme Court justices' penchant for narrow, fact-driven rulings, as in reality to be put aside without the Supreme Court ever stepping into the case. The public never even sees it. What this means for the vast majority of Americans is that the de facto court of last resort is a circuit court of appeals.

In this way, George W. Bush can play a waiting game with the Supreme Court justices who may or may not be ready to step down. The sixth circuit has in recent years become a magnet for hot-button issues like school vouchers, campaign-finance reform, and affirmative action. With five vacancies already on that sixteen-judge circuit and two more expected, if the Democrats do not contest the nominees for it, it will become a right-wing bastion forever. A similar fight is likely over the composition of the U.S. Court of Appeals for the Tenth Circuit in Denver, where George W. has an opportunity to eliminate a 5–4 Democratic appointee advantage. Two seats are open, and another is expected to be vacant soon. And while there are two appeals courts where Democratic-appointed judges are least likely to soon be outnumbered, the ninth and the second circuits, many of the ninth circuit judges appointed by Clinton will easily follow the Right. There is also a great deal of pressure to break the ninth circuit into two separate circuits and add judges; with more appointments, both could become conservative.

But the Bush blitzkrieg is vulnerable to a well-prepared counterattack. Justice Priscilla Owen, a Texas Supreme Court justice, nominated to the fifth circuit court of appeals, was not only the most pro-business judge on the most right-wing state court in the country, she also wrote an opinion saving the Enron corporation $15 million after accepting an Enron campaign contribution. Enron, since 1993, had contributed $134,058 to Texas Supreme Court judges. In this, and elsewhere, the arrogance of the Republican Right, with their Federalist Society ties to Shell, Exxon, and Philip Morris, may come back to bite the hand that fed them.

The stakes are high, but we are not powerless before the juggernaut that is today's court system. The Reagan-Bush Supreme Court, when it ended its 2000–01 term, had a record of being both the most solidly, consistently divided Court in history and one of the most ideologically successful in achieving their stated, and unstated, goals. Tensions between the justices were many and frequent, often moving from the privacy of their chambers to the public courtroom. More and more opinions were written in dissent, but what had been rare before was now less rare—dissenting judges of both sides angrily reading their opinions in open court after the majority had its say. It is a fractious group, with some justices knowing that our liberties, our way of life, our democracy is on the line, and is in their hands.

Presidents have the power to put the justices and judges in place. But it is up to the nine to act, and the public plays a role in influencing this Court. Just as in Roosevelt's days, when some members of the Court, realizing the public would deeply disapprove of their rulings, did its "switch in time that saved nine." Some present members of the Court, in their decisions, have referred to the inappropriateness of reversing cases they disagree with because of the need for the public to perceive the Court as fair and nonpolitical. Other Court justices, not trusting elected officials, look at polls to determine exactly what the people want or feel.

For this reason, and because we have the vote, we can help shape judicial outcomes. The November 4, 2003, senatorial elections may well determine if the Right has a sufficient majority to push through Bush's nominees for the next two years.

We now turn to what the Rehnquist Court has achieved, and what it intends to have happen over the next many decades.

3

CRIME AND PUNISHMENT

In January 1972, the Burger Court was going through its transition from the Warren Court. Richard Nixon had the extraordinary opportunity to make four new appointments in three years after Chief Justice Earl Warren stepped down in 1969. First Warren E. Burger replaced Earl Warren; then, in rapid order, Harry Blackmun, appointed in 1970, and Lewis F. Powell Jr. and William Rehnquist both appointed in 1971, joined the Court as Justices Hugo Black, John Marshall Harlan II, and Abe Fortas stepped down. The liberal bloc lost three justices; the conservative bloc gained four. It was a seismic shift, a dramatic political change as great as any the country had seen in so short a time.

The Nixon appointees formed a new solid bloc of four when, in January 1972, in *Furman v. Georgia*, they heard the appeals of three African American men from death sentences handed down by juries in Georgia and Texas. Commentators, ignoring the fact that three of the liberal bloc still remained, described the counterrevolution against the Warren Court that would immediately take place. But it was not until the end of the second half of the Nixon-Burger Court's tenure that the conservative shift started.

Anthony Amsterdam, thin, intense, articulate, then a University of Pennsylvania law professor who had spent much of his professional life arguing that the death penalty was cruel and unusual, presented Furman's case. In considering his legal strategy, Amsterdam knew he could not persuade the Nixon four. He also knew that he had the liberal bloc of three, William Brennan, Thurgood Marshall, and William O. Douglas; therefore, the two swing votes of Byron R. White and Potter Stewart would be crucial.

Byron White, a Kennedy appointee, was liberal on race issues but conservative on criminal cases. Potter Stewart was conservative on both. Amsterdam would be arguing that the death penalty in Georgia and Texas was applied in a racially discriminatory manner. But he understood the brutality of the defendants' actions in committing rape and murder, and the incontrovertible facts proving guilt made it an unsympathetic case. The newest justice, William Rehnquist, was already on record concerning the way the judicial system handled capital appeals by allowing defendants to nitpick relentlessly and to use the federal courts to delay endlessly their executions. Rehnquist already knew what he wanted to say and do; Amsterdam had to hope he wouldn't take White or the like-minded Stewart with him.

In the January 17, 1972, argument, Amsterdam traced the history of how the law operated in Georgia and how juries there and in Texas imposed the death penalty without any guidelines or limits on their discretion. The juries were not given any criteria to help them decide if a defendant should be sentenced to death or given a life sentence, he argued. For centuries, Georgia has operated openly and formally a type of dual-justice system—one for whites and one for blacks—that is, in fact, still in place today. But as late as 1972, the criminal law expressly differentiated between crimes committed by and against blacks and whites, distinctions whose lineage traced back to the time of slavery. During the colonial period, black slaves who killed whites in Georgia, regardless of whether in self-defense or in defense of another, were automatically executed. Whites who killed or raped blacks were not.

By the time of the Civil War, the Georgia criminal code provided for a system of justice that applied only to black defendants. It contained separate sections for "Slaves and Free Persons of Color," and for all other persons. The code provided for an automatic death sentence for murder committed by blacks, but it declared that anyone else convicted of murder might receive life imprisonment if the conviction were founded solely on circumstantial testimony, or simply if the jury so recommended. This statute was never applied to a case of a white killing a black.

The history and laws of Georgia were not that different from the history and laws of the other southern states. The Tennessee handbook for criminal lawyers, the *Statement of the Law of Homicide in Tennessee*, predicted in colloquial language exactly what the empirical studies later found. "If a black man kill a white man, that be first-degree murder; if a white man kill a white man, that be second-degree murder; if a black man kill a black man, that be mere manslaughter; whereas if a white man kill a black man, that be excusable homicide (unless a woman be involved, in which case the black man died of natural causes)."

Although the NAACP Legal Defense Fund had been mounting a nation-wide attack on the death penalty, it did not seem that the new Burger Court, heavy with Nixon appointees, would accept the argument. The Court's decision, released that June, stunned everybody who overlooked the strength of the remaining liberal bloc.

In a 5–4 decision, the Supreme Court struck down the death penalty for the first time. Amsterdam had reached the two swing justices, White and Stewart, leaving the four Nixon appointees as dissenters. The *Furman v. Georgia* (1972) case stopped executions in the thirty-nine states that had the death penalty; the lives of more than six hundred people had been saved. Two events from the 1960s and '70s particularly stick in my mind: I remember where I was on November 22, 1963, when John F. Kennedy was shot, and I remember where I was on June 29, 1972, when the Furman decision came down. In 1963, I was at work in my twenty-first-floor office on Forty-fourth Street in New York City; in 1972, I was in the stacks of the Bar Association library, again at Forty-fourth Street, reading law review articles. I was astonished and jubilant when I heard the Court's decision.

In *Furman*, William Brennan spoke out eloquently against the death penalty, but as if to foreshadow those new right jurists who say our Constitution is frozen permanently in time two hundred years ago, he cautioned:

When this country was founded, memories of hanging horrors were fresh and corporal punishments were common. Death was not then a unique punishment. The practice of punishing criminals by death, moreover, was widespread and by and large acceptable to society. Indeed, without a developed prison system, there was frequently no workable alternative. Since that time, successive restrictions, imposed against the background of a continuing moral controversy, have drastically curtailed the use of this punishment. Today death is a uniquely severe punishment.

That language would frame the Court's subsequent capital punishment debate. He continued, "The genius of the Constitution rests not on any static meaning it might have had in a world that is dead and gone, but in the adaptability of its principles to cope with current problems and current needs."

If some hoped that with this battle won, the abolition of the death penalty would last forever, they were wrong. The Court's majority opinion was fractured and, therefore, left the door open. Douglas concluded that death was disproportionately applied to the poor and socially disadvantaged. Stewart and White found that the states' random use of the death penalty violated the Constitution. White said the statute could not be considered a deterrent when, even if there was a murder conviction, it could take ten years for the execution. Brennan and Marshall said even if it could be applied with precision, a penalty of death was, per se, cruel and unusual and violative of the Eighth Amendment. Under no conditions would they permit it, they concluded. In this they differed with White and Stewart: the term "random use" made clear that the votes of the two swing justices were conditional.

There was a strong negative reaction to *Furman*, with public opinion against it and many states passing new death penalty laws. Indeed, *Furman* probably did more to increase public support for the death penalty than anything else. Unlike the aftermath of *Roe v. Wade*, there was no real battle with regard to public opinion, because those who opposed the death penalty—having relied so heavily for so long on winning their battle through the courts—had no grassroots movement and did not engage in any real public education to try to stop new laws from being enacted. Instead, they continued to rely almost exclusively on legal battles, hoping that the Supreme Court really meant what its majority members said in their various opinions in *Furman*.

Not surprisingly, then, Georgia immediately redrafted and enacted a new and improved death penalty statute—and found itself the very next year, in the *Gregg v. Georgia* (1976) case, again before the Supreme Court defending an attack on their new law. But Justice William Douglas stepped down in 1975 and was replaced by Gerald Ford's nominee, Justice John Paul Stevens. There were now five straight Republican appointments, leaving instead of a liberal bloc only Marshall and Brennan.

There was, predictably, a new majority. Four years after *Furman*, seven justices, including White and Stewart, voted to uphold the death law; Marshall and Brennan did not. This time, the Georgia standard was upheld because it allegedly gave the jurors specific instruction as to when the death sentence could be applied. Jurors, the statute said, must consider aggravating circumstances, such as did the defendant, Troy Gregg, kill more than one person. Gregg had (two men were murdered during the armed robbery in which he participated). Did he have a previous conviction for murder or rape; did he kill a police officer; and did he try to escape. But the jurors, by statute, were also required to consider mitigating circumstances; for example, was the sentence motivated by passion or prejudice or any factor that might make the sentence too severe.

White and Stewart, following the logic of their *Furman* decision, said in separate opinions that no one in the Georgia case had proved that the state randomly sought to kill African Americans. The death sentence for the murder convictions was affirmed (although the sentence on the robbery convictions was reversed on the grounds that it was extremely rare in Georgia to impose murder sentences for armed robbery).

Marshall and Brennan, in their dissent, said the Eighth Amendment rule prohibiting cruel and unusual punishment has in it the concept of human dignity and that retribution or vengeance by state murder is inconsistent with human dignity. Moreover, penalogical evidence, they said, shows clearly that the death penalty does not deter. Retribution, they argued, has no place in the criminal law. They also argued that the people did not want it: opinion polls showed conclusively the public preferred life imprisonment without parole over the death penalty. Present public opinion polls are the same.

After *Gregg*, defense lawyers, hoping to get White and Stewart back in the next cases, would try to show that prosecutors in Georgia routinely sought the death penalty for blacks but not for whites; that the death sentence was random; and that the determinate factor was not the crime committed but the race of the defendant.

Then in 1989 the Rehnquist Court, in *McCleskey v. Kemp*, firmly ended the argument that the death penalty in Georgia discriminated against individual black defendants, even though the Court accepted as true the condemned man's proof that there was discrimination against blacks in murder cases. This time, there was more to the case than "just" the death penalty. The result raises serious questions about the Court's commitment to justice.

The facts of the case were these: Warren McCleskey was sentenced to death in Fulton County, Georgia, in 1978 for the killing of a police officer who had responded to a silent alarm set off when four armed men, including the defendant, attempted to rob a furniture store. McCleskey was black, the dead officer white. A jury consisting of eleven white jurors and one African American juror convicted McCleskey of murder and sentenced him to death. Since *Furman,* death penalty opponents had been amassing statistical evidence proving that in both the North and South, the penalty was applied in a racially discriminating manner. Now, the Legal Defense Fund, after years of trying to get the right case to the Court, was surprised when the McClesky case was accepted by the Court. Their pleasure at having the Court take the case was tempered by their concern that it had picked the case to reaffirm *Gregg.* McCleskey's guilt was not in doubt, and the fact that he killed a police officer made his case an especially unsympathetic one for the Court.

Nevertheless, McCleskey's lawyer argued that the death penalty was infected with racial applications. Appropriately, the McCleskey case came from Georgia, one of the big four states in executions. While thirty-six states authorized the death penalty and shipped convicts to death row, executions remained a phenomenon primarily of the South. By 1990, 120 persons had been put to death since the *Gregg* ruling restored capital punishment; 86 of them, or nearly three-fourths of the total, had been executed in four southern states: Texas, Florida, Louisiana, and Georgia.

In the *McCleskey* case, the Legal Defense Fund put in a great deal of evidence at trial in the event the Supreme Court should review the case. The proof at the *McCleskey* trial showed that the defendant's death sentence was the only one imposed in Georgia's Fulton County for the killing of a police officer between 1973 (when Georgia's post-*Furman* statute was enacted) and 1980 (when the appeal started). Elsewhere in the nation during those years, sixteen other killers of police officers had been sentenced to life imprisonment—there were no executions. In only one police-killing case other than McCleskey's did the state of Georgia seek the death penalty, and in that case a black defendant convicted of killing a black officer had been given a life sentence.

McCleskey's lawyer claimed his client's sentence was the product of a statewide pattern of racially biased death sentences in Georgia, and thus violated both the Eighth Amendment prohibiting arbitrary and discriminatory capital sentencing and the Equal Protection Clause of the Fourteenth Amendment. In support of these claims, McCleskey's lawyers presented an extensive study of how Georgia prosecuted and punished murderers between 1974 and 1979.

The study, directed by Professor David C. Baldus of the University of Iowa, and based on documents obtained from official state records kept by the Georgia Supreme Court and the Georgia Board of Pardons and Paroles, showed that 2,484 homicides took place in Georgia between 1974 and 1979 in which a suspect was arrested. About two-thirds of those murders involved blacks—as victims and/or as defendants. However, the murder cases that resulted in death sentences revealed quite clearly that race factors made for the differences. For instance, the study showed that fewer than 40 percent of Georgia's homicide cases involved white victims, but that in 87 percent of the cases in which a death sentence was imposed, the victim was white. Most compelling was the fact that defendants charged with killing whites were 4.3 times as likely to receive the death penalty as defendants charged with killing blacks. Baldus showed the taking of a black life was far less onerous than the taking of a white life. Blacks who kill whites are sentenced to death far more often than whites who kill blacks.

Baldus's findings were based on information collected from more than five hundred factors in each case. These included demographic and individual characteristics of the defendant and victim; the circumstances of the crime; the strength of the evidence of guilt; and the aggravating and mitigating factors in each case—both the factors specified by Georgia law for consideration in capital sentencing, and every other factor recognized in the legal and criminological literature as theoretically or actually likely to affect the choice of life or death. While presenting the results on the witness stand, Professor Baldus re-analyzed the data several more times to take in account every additional factor, combination of factors, or alternate models for analysis of factors suggested by the state of Georgia's expert witnesses, its lawyers, and the state trial judge. Other experts supported his findings.

But the trial judge said the study was not accurate; that the disparity may have occurred because prosecutors have discretion in deciding which penalty to seek in murder cases, and the courts do not interfere with that discretion. In this particular case, there was no proof, the judge said, that showed the prosecutor singled out McCleskey for the death penalty because he was black. This reasoning places a preposterous "proof" requirement on a defendant. The only way for the defendant to make his case—because facts in each case are different—is for the defense to get the prosecutor to say, "I chose the death penalty in this case solely because the defendant was black," an unlikely event.

Months later, the court of appeals, sitting in New Orleans, said the trial judge was wrong about the study—it was accurate—but, nonetheless, legally insufficient to prove a constitutional violation and thus affirmed the death sentence. It was then up to the Supreme Court, which heard the argument in October 1986.

The *McCleskey* majority did not want to write its opinion with a broad brush. So far as they were concerned, the case involved only the procedures used in a single trial. Justice Powell, a southerner, feared that if the Court ruled in favor of McCleskey because of the studies, similar statistics would be used to attack the fairness of the entire criminal justice system in other southern, and perhaps northern, states—not just death row cases but all criminal cases. Powell's supporters claim he was naive and an innocent about the realities of southern justice; others, less kind, accused him and the Court of cowardice. The Court's refusal to tackle the issue head-on is incomprehensible. The Court said it would not look, because if it did, it was afraid of what it would see. It calls to mind those who hear no evil, see no evil, and speak no evil.

The opinions, for the majority and the dissenters, went back and forth among the chambers. On April 22, 1987, six months after argument, the decision was finally released. Powell was the swing justice for a 5–4 majority against McCleskey. "At most, the Baldus study indicates a discrepancy that appears to correlate with race," Powell said, writing for the majority. "Apparent discrepancies in sentencing are an inevitable part of our criminal justice system." He candidly admitted that "if we accept McCleskey's claim that racial bias has impermissibly tainted the capital sentencing decision, we could soon be faced with similar claims as to other types of penalty."

McCleskey was a deplorable decision for other reasons. It may be the single most important decision the Court ever issued on the subject of race and crime. Because the racial challenge was so "fundamental to our multi-racial society," said Powell, the issue should be addressed by the legislature. Powell said McCleskey's claim, taken to its legal conclusion, throws into serious question the principles that underlie our criminal justice system. He then effectively cut off the right to examine whether the entire system of justice is pervaded by racial inequality. As a practical matter, the *McCleskey* decision made it impossible to attack state or federal convictions and practices on the grounds of discrimination. *McCleskey* would henceforth require the Court to consider only the particular defendant before it. Prior to that, constitutional challenges to the death penalty had a class action effect; a defendant's win could change a local, state, or federal practice. But no more: the time and cost involved for each individual defendant made it nearly impossible to mount any effective attack based on race, class, or gender illegality in the criminal system. The Court, in Powell's opinion, was setting limitations on the judiciary's ability to solve racial discrimination in the system.

Justice Blackmun, in dissent, said the Reconstruction Congress that wrote the Fourteenth Amendment was most concerned about unequal criminal punishments for blacks and whites. An original intent argument, Blackmun said, favored by conservatives on the Court, as well as by then Attorney General Edwin Meese, in fact compelled a victory for McCleskey. Rhetorically, Blackmun went on to ask why was discrimination in capital punishment being treated differently than in other bias cases. When presented with statistical evidence of discrimination in hiring, housing, and jury selection, the Court had said that the party accused (often the government) bore the burden of proving that no discrimination had taken place. But in this case, the Court was placing the burden on the victim, who rarely, if ever, would have the resources to bear that burden.

Here, Blackmun referred to a Santa Clara County affirmative action case in which Justice O'Connor (who voted in the *McCleskey* majority) focused on one statistic—not one woman in 237 skilled jobs—and opined that it offered a "firm basis" for believing discrimination had occurred there. In the *McCleskey* case, however, O'Connor silently signed on to Powell's majority opinion, discounting the numbers. Blackmun found the Court's opinion in *McCleskey* inconsistent. Brennan, in his searing dissent, stated precisely the conversation that McCleskey's lawyer would have to have with him if McCleskey wanted to know why he was going to be executed:

At some point in this case, Warren McCleskey doubtless asked his lawyer whether a jury was likely to sentence him to die. A candid reply to this question would have been disturbing. First, counsel would have to tell McCleskey that few of the details of the crime or of McCleskey's past criminal conduct were more important than the fact that his victim was white. . . . In addition, frankness would compel the disclosure that . . . every eleven [black] defendants convicted of killing a white person would not have received the death penalty if their victims had been black, while . . . 20 of every 34 would not have been sentenced to die if their victims had been black. Finally, the assessment would not be complete without the information that cases involving black defendants and white victims are more likely to result in the death sentence than cases involving any other racial combination of defendant and victim. The story could be told in a variety of ways, but McCleskey could not fail to grasp its essential narrative line: There was a chance that race would play a prominent role in determining whether he was to live or die.

Brennan's words, grounded in reality, unlike the majority justices who refused to see how the legal system actually operated, are a haunting and stirring reminder: "It is tempting to pretend that the minorities on death row share a fate in no way connected to our own, that our treatment of them sounds no echoes beyond the chambers in which they die. Such an illusion is ultimately corrosive, for the errors of injustice are not so easily confirmed."

What Blackmun could not know was that the Rehnquist Court's future rulings would shift the burden in all cases onto the victims and away from the government—an immense change in the law that, because it is procedural, goes largely unnoticed. Indeed, the Court, from this point on, would focus more on the *appearance* of criminal justice than on its realities.

The 5–4 ruling in the *McCleskey* case sent out a clear message that the Rehnquist Court was not going to overturn the death penalty irrespective of the evidence presented to it, and would, given the chance, look away from any claims of racial inequality. In fact, just the day before, on April 12, 1987, in *Stanford v. Kentucky*, another 5–4 decision, the Court had actually expanded the grounds for a sentence of death. Before, the Court had reserved the ultimate punishment for the actual killer, not the accomplices who did not pull the trigger—and most certainly not when the offenders were still juveniles. But, faced with the gruesome murder of an Arizona family by a convict whose two sons helped him escape from prison, the Court set down a new rule. The sons, sixteen-year-old Heath Wilkins and seventeen-year-old Kevin Stanford, could be executed because they were "major participants" in the murder, even though they did not have guns and pleaded with their father not to harm the family. The majority was the same as in *McCleskey v. Kemp*: Rehnquist, White, Powell, O'Connor, and Scalia.

After long deliberation, O'Connor would not go along with the minority in the Arizona case even though it involved death sentences for unarmed minors, who pleaded for the victims' lives. Presumably, most juries would not vote to execute a juvenile under such circumstances, but O'Connor did not believe the Constitution absolutely prohibited such a sentence in all instances.

Her colleague, Justice Scalia, on the other hand, writing for the majority, could barely contain his zeal: "The punishment is either 'cruel AND unusual' or it is not," he said, and since children of fourteen could be executed when the Constitution was ratified, similar executions should be allowed today. The death sentence, he said, would not have been considered cruel and unusual in the eighteenth century; at that time it was perfectly appropriate to kill a teenage murderer. Indeed, many hundreds of children under the age of seventeen have been killed since the founding of the republic. Since it was not barbarous to do so in the eighteenth century, it is not barbarous today, Scalia said, as he argued that it was wrong for justices to use today's moral standards in their evaluations. Such punishment, he concluded, is not unusual, even though some may consider it cruel.

He also dismissed what he labeled the "socioscientific and ethicoscientific evidence" that had been furnished by human rights groups concerning "an evolving standard of decency." So what if learned societies find the death penalty abominable or if European governments oppose it, as the defense had shown. State lawmakers, reflecting the popular will, wrote the death penalty into law. "The audience for these arguments [against the death penalty] is not this Court, but the citizenry of the United States. It is they, not we, who must be persuaded," he said. It is entirely irrelevant, as Scalia's colleagues had argued, that since 1979 there had been only eight executions of offenders under the age of eighteen and that three of those were in the United States while the others were in Rwanda, Bangladesh, and Pakistan. This is America, and it is only American law and values we are looking at.

After *McCleskey*, Rehnquist accelerated his lobbying for new legislation to cut back murder defendants' access to the courts. He has long been frustrated by the amount of time it takes criminal cases to go through the federal system, by the endless appeals as lawyers and sometimes prisoners travel up and down the appellate ladder with frivolous claims, and he sees it as his job to reduce the number of appeals. Murder cases, particularly, bother him. The heinousness of the allegations, often true but sometimes not, and the death sentence that he feels causes courts to review cases they otherwise would not, irritate and anger him, his conservative colleagues, and some liberals, as well.

The chief justice's lobbying efforts have been extraordinarily successful. He is primarily responsible for the 1996 Anti-Terrorism and Effective Death Penalty Act, which expanded restrictions on the right to file habeas corpus proceedings that require the government to come before a court and give its reasons for detaining or jailing an individual. Called the Great Writ, habeas corpus has always been seen as a cornerstone of this democracy. Now, in a large number of instances, the government was no longer required to do so. Orrin Hatch, aided and abetted by Bill Clinton, succeeded in having legislation passed that, in the wake of the Oklahoma City bombing, was never able to be passed when there were Republican presidents. Under the 1996 law, a state inmate must show that a state court conviction is "contrary to or involved in an unreasonable application of federal law," as interpreted by the Supreme Court. But states' murders are rarely tried in federal court, and the way Rehnquist defines "unreasonable" makes it very difficult for a murder defendant to get into federal court. The Rehnquist Court, in a series of prior cases, said the Warren Court was wrong in allowing the defendants to challenge state convictions in a federal court. This law, consistent then with his Court's decisions, effectively makes federal courts off limits for convicted defendants looking at a state death sentence. O'Connor and Kennedy felt that the Court had already done such a fine job of curtailing habeas corpus, and could further eviscerate it if it chose to do so, that Congress should at that point have left a good thing alone.

In habeas corpus cases, Rehnquist reversed Warren Court concepts when he wrote the majority in *Wainwright v. Sykes* (1977), which held that federal courts were barred from considering an issue that was not raised at the appropriate time of the state criminal proceedings. And he authored *Brecht v. Abrahamson* (1993), which held that for a conviction to be reversed by a federal court on a writ of habeas corpus, the prisoner has the burden of showing not only that there were constitutional errors, but that those errors had a "substantial and injurious effect or influence in determining the jury's verdict"—a nearly impossible standard to meet.

Years ago, the federal court was the venue toward which every innocent or guilty defendant looked hopefully. No longer. Winning in the federal courts has been made exceedingly difficult at a time when it becomes clearer that a substantial number of innocent people have been wrongfully convicted. In truth, Supreme Court decisions, and Rehnquist's lobbying with Congress, have set a high bar for state inmates seeking judicial review of murder cases as well as all other criminal cases in the federal courts. Since nearly all murder cases that come before the Court began with state convictions, by nearly totally cutting that pipeline, the Supreme Court ensures that its previous rulings will go unchallenged, and the circle is completed.

While the reach of Rehnquist's arm is long, it is the legacy of *McCleskey* that affects all capital cases involving juvenile killers, the mentally disabled, and the poor (i.e., those who can't afford to hire private attorneys or pay for DNA testing). The Court—now that it has rid itself of having to fight off death penalty challenges based on hard statistical numbers, and now that race discrimination is no longer a viable defense—is today free to close whatever loopholes still exist. These would include juveniles and the mentally disabled—society's most vulnerable members—messy exceptions for whom the same laws must nonetheless apply. O'Connor would seem to be the justice most likely to be persuaded otherwise, but thus far she has not been.

Justice Sandra Day O'Connor has sought to pass herself off as more of a humanist than the other justices. And certainly even the most hard-core pro-death advocates must agonize over killing a child. But O'Connor's indifference was shown again in August 2001, when Napoleon Beazley, a seventeen-year-old black honors student with no criminal record, caught in a carjacking went bad, asked the High Court for a stay of his Texas execution on the grounds that he had additional evidence that the jury should have considered and that his lawyer admitted he wrongly did not raise the issue of his client's age at the time of his offense. Papers filed in both the U.S. Supreme Court and the Texas Court of Appeals (that state's highest court) also set forth one juror's statement after Beazley's sentence, "The nigger got what he deserves," and the fact that another juror flies a confederate flag on her front lawn. Yet the Supreme Court justices split 3–3 on whether to execute the student. (Three of the justices—Souter, Thomas, and Scalia—recused themselves because of their relationship to the victim's son, a fourth circuit judge.)

In *Beazley v. Texas*, the opposing justices saw different worlds with different values. With a claim of incompetent counsel, a potentially tainted jury, a juvenile offender, and as many justices against execution as for it, the Supreme Court preferred to let the boy die. The decision set off a torrent of national and international attention. The *Weekend Australian*, in an article entitled "The Land Where a Tied Vote Means Death," expressed the outrage of many most eloquently: "In sports, the solution to a tied championship game is to play extra time until one team prevails. Nowhere is this truer than in the U.S. where baseball, football and hockey games have been known to go all night. Yet, if you are a black man who killed a white man whose son was a federal judge, a tie means death."

When Beazley's request for a stay was denied by the Court, they had every reason to believe that Texas, the state that leads the nation in executions, would kill him. They also knew the Texas high court rarely stays executions when the Supreme Court has denied the "last" story. So Beazley's lawyer was "amazed" when the Texas court did grant a stay. "They knew no one should be executed on a 3–3 vote," he said. The Texas court then changed its mind and allowed Beasley to be killed.

The *Beazley* case brought the tie-vote death sentence practice to public attention. Too often these isolated cases get swept under the rug. A take-no-prisoners attitude is this Court's capital punishment history. On January 9, 1985, Roosevelt Green was electrocuted after his stay application was denied in a bitter 4–4 vote. The Green defense argued, as did the McCleskey defense, that the Georgia system of capital punishment was racially discriminatory, and they asked that the execution be delayed until *McCleskey* was decided. Studies similar to the Baldus study were part of his record; the issue of cruel and unusual punishment was raised; and all executions other than Green's from Georgia had been stayed. But because Green slipped between the cracks, he was executed. The *New York Times*'s scathing editorial was titled "Kill Him."

Two years later, in 1987, Alpha Otis O'Daniel Stephens, an indigent black man sentenced in Georgia to death for killing a white man, was before the Supreme Court seeking a stay of execution and filing a petition for review. While five justices approved his stay application—the issues it raised were the same as those in the *McCleskey* case, which was then before the Supreme Court—only three justices voted to have the Court hear the argument. This meant that Stevens would die, for if the

Court did not take the case, the stay application would become moot as the defendant could no longer challenge his conviction. Brennan was infuriated. Writing to members of the Court, he said that if review were denied, he was going to go public and write a formidable dissent and say the Court's action "is at best an example of result-orientation carried to its most cynical extreme. At worst, it is outright lawlessness." Ultimately, although Justices White and Blackmun offered to be the "gentlemanly" votes necessary to stay the execution, the other justices—in part enraged at Brennan's description of the Court's process—refused to have any part of the agreement. Review was denied. The execution was marked by the *New York Times*, which accused the Court of "a new brazen insensitivity to the need for special care in death cases."

Another 5–4 decision in January 2002 saw O'Connor switch to the moderate side when the Court overturned a South Carolina death sentence because the judge refused the defendant's request to inform the jurors that a convicted murderer would serve a life sentence and never be released. Polls showed that juries would, if told of that option, in the majority of cases choose it over the death penalty.

The four dissenters said the prosecution's statement suggesting future potential danger, and the trial judge's refusal to tell the jury of the possible sentencing option, did not require reversal. But Justice Souter, writing for the majority, said the "clear inference" of the prosecutor's argument was that the defendant would be dangerous if not executed.

In September 2001, shortly after Anthony Beazley's execution, Justice Sandra Day O'Connor gave a speech to Minnesota women in which she indicated she was rethinking her views on aspects of capital punishment. She said that as a result of capital punishment "some innocent defendants may be executed" and that "perhaps it's time to look at minimum standards for appointed counsel in death cases and adequate compensation for appointed counsel when they are used." People with more money, she was saying, get better defenses.

And yet her Court has dramatically lowered the bar on what constitutes minimum standards; it has refused to overturn or review decisions in which lawyers fell asleep at trial while defending murder cases yet were found competent; in which lawyers failed not only to speak to their own clients, but did not speak to any witnesses against their clients; in which lawyers saw the defendant for the first time in court. The Court has not reversed cases in which capital defendants spend weeks or months before they meet their lawyer; in which the amount the state pays is insufficient to represent any person, let alone a man charged with murder; in which no funds exist at all for investigations; in which lawyers are paid $65 per hour to represent defendants facing murder charges.

O'Connor, in her Minnesota speech, noted that DNA testing can help prove innocence. It has, thus far, in more than two hundred cases. Eleven were death cases in which volunteer lawyers represented men on death row. But she knows that, in nearly every state where no fees, or such tiny fees, are permitted for DNA expert witnesses to counter the state's experts, defendants rarely use DNA experts. Few murder or rape defendants have any access to DNA experts, and those who do cannot get the caliber of experts that the state can get. But O'Connor, on the Court for more than twenty years, helped eviscerate the great 1963 case *Gideon v. Wainwright,* decided 9–0, that said defendants accused of serious crimes in state courts must be represented by adequate appointed counsel, and she was also in the majority in a Rehnquist Court case that overruled the Warren Court's decision that had expanded the power of the federal courts to release innocent men convicted in the state courts.

O'Connor was also in the majority when the Court made the execution of innocent defendants far more likely by denying them the chance to raise nearly all competence-of-counsel issues, by cutting off access to the federal courts in nearly all murder cases, and by so diminishing the constitutionally guaranteed writ of habeas corpus as to make it nearly meaningless for all murder defendants. She has joined in Rehnquist-driven opinions expressing hostility and anger that it takes so long for the legal system to kill defendants, and she has urged the shortcutting of many procedures that could have allowed defendants to prove their innocence. She has consistently voted against the claim that the death penalty is racially discriminatory, for she believes the Constitution ought to be "color blind." And she has consistently voted for the execution of children and, until this year, the mentally disabled.

And yet she knows, as a former Arizona state judge, how bad the capital defendant's representation is, and how Arizona, as well as other states, are always in budget crunches, and do not have the defense of murder one defendants high on their list of priorities. While private law firms will sometimes help defend capital cases (at a cost, they estimate, of not less than $1 million to adequately do so), they are in large part withdrawing from the field, leaving these defenses nearly entirely to state public defenders. Law school professors, private law firms, and private lawyers such as Ronald Tabak have a far greater success rate than government officers in upsetting convictions. Local legal aid offices have never had less funding in the last thirty years than they have today, while the federal public defender's office has gone out of business because of lack of funds. States today are not looking, and they cannot put in the substantial funds, to protect defendants, many of whom are black, poor, and accused of having committed atrocious crimes.

While it is unlikely that Justice O'Connor will alter her basic death penalty opinions any time soon (she may relent in the *Atkins v. Virginia* case, see page 64, when she is faced with the execution of a mentally disabled youth)—she made it clear at the Minnesota talk that the life of the defendant should be decided in state courts not in federal courts. If she changes her mind, she would not be the first Supreme Court justice to go through an execution conversion. Four years after writing the Court's 5–4 decision upholding the death penalty in *McCleskey*, Justice Lewis Powell, now retired, was asked by his biographer whether he would have changed his vote in any case. "Yes," he replied, "*McCleskey v. Kemp.*" Capital punishment should be abolished, he said, because it could not be regularly and fairly administered.

Justice Harry Blackmun, too, the conservative law-and-order Nixon appointee, who was on the pro-death-penalty side in both *Furman v. Georgia* and *Gregg v. Georgia*, switched sides, as we saw in *McCleskey*, to join the defeated liberals. Eighty-five years old and near the end of his tenure on the Court, Blackmun decided he could no longer support the death penalty. In a solitary dissent from the Court's refusal to stop a Texas execution, he wrote in 1994, "The problem is that the inevitability of factual, legal and moral error gives us a system that we know must wrongly kill some defendants, a system that fails to deliver the fair, consistent and reliable sentence of death required by the Constitution. The path the Court has chosen, lessens us all." Believing that the Court had tried to make capital punishment fair, he admitted that "the death penalty experiment has failed." But he continued to hope the Supreme Court would ultimately agree with him. "I may not live to see that day but I have faith it will arrive."

At the time the Constitution was passed, capital punishment was permitted in the United States. Then, as now, it was driven by racism and Christian fundamentalism. Like slavery, the great stain on the Constitution, capital punishment is inconsistent with its basic values. A document then, and still now, unique in the Western world, it evinces a respect for human dignity, two words that Justices Brennan, Marshall, and Blackmun continually evoked in their death penalty opposition. If we look at other countries, we see none that attempted to govern a system where so many individuals' rights were protected, including the right not to be subject to cruel and unusual punishment. When the Constitution was written in 1789, the values it expressed, and the limited government it sought to create, made this country a leader in seeking justice.

Today, we seem, under the same Constitution, to be the Western country consumed with punitive sentences and excessive periods of incarceration—a condition that would have appalled Franklin, Jefferson, Madison, Adams, and Hamilton. The decisions of Justices Thomas, Scalia, and Rehnquist pay no homage to the concept that underlies the Constitution and makes it such a luminous document and, considering the time when it was written, a document remarkable for being the most advanced human rights declaration of its time.

The U.S. Supreme Court had refused to hold that the use of the electric chair violates the federal Constitution. But in October 2001, Georgia's highest court held that the electric chair violated the state's constitution because it "inflicts purposeless physical violence and needless mutilation that makes no measurable contribution to accepted goals of punishment." The Georgia Supreme Court was specifically referring to the executions of Warren McCleskey and Alpha Otis O'Daniel Stephens, which, according to tape recordings and eyewitness accounts, were grotesquely botched. Perhaps the Supreme Court's tolerance for "searing flesh" and "excruciating pain" (as reported in the Georgia case) remains high, but, it now appears, the tolerance of the American public does not.

As I write this, we are at the twenty-sixth anniversary of *Gregg v. Georgia*, when the Supreme Court reinstated the death penalty. Scalia, in a number of unrelated cases, has icily advised to look at what the people want, not what the Courts want. But he will not do this with the death penalty. Americans' support for the death penalty can be directly correlated with the number of state executions in any given year. In the early 1950s, the Gallup Poll showed support was quite high, 68 percent, but then as executions slowed down, people favored it less. In 1966, a low execution year at the end of a long, steady downward cycle, public support dropped to only 42 percent. After *Furman v. Georgia*, and after some states changed their laws to conform to the *Gregg* standard, however, the number of Americans supporting it climbed again, to a 1994 high of 80 percent. The most recent polls show 60 percent of the population favoring the death penalty, with 38 percent opposed, but when offered the alternative of life imprisonment without parole, that number drops precipitously. Due to education efforts, media outreach, and grassroots organizing—including activity by bar associations— public opinion on the death penalty has begun to shift in recent years, and the moratorium movement has built up steam. Americans are having second thoughts. Seventy-two percent favored the immediate suspension of the penalty until studies can determine if it's fair; 91 percent favored DNA usage in every capital case; over 82 percent favored requiring experienced counsel in death penalty cases and making funds necessary to provide such counsel available. These are the very issues the Court is on record as opposing.

The Supreme Court notwithstanding, the declining use of capital punishment reflects the decade-long reduction in the crime rate as well as a public less enthusiastic about punishment by execution. As discussion has grown about the fairness and reliability of capital convictions, judges and governors also have become more willing to stop them and to take a second look at questionable cases. In 1994, for example, Virginia governor L. Douglas Wilder at the last moment stayed the execution of Earl Washington, a mentally disabled defendant, and DNA tests later proved he was innocent. Wilder did so because in a previous case two years before he had refused a defendant's request for a stay to get DNA evidence, and an innocent man may have been put to death. And in 2000, Governor George Ryan, the first governor to do so, banned all executions in Illinois after it was shown that more than a dozen men sentenced to death in his state were later found to be innocent. The number exonerated exceeded by one the number who had been executed. On May 9, 2002, Maryland became the second state to suspend the death penalty. Governor Parris N. Glendening said he was troubled by concerns in Maryland and across the country "about the fairness of a death procedure that may racially discriminate." This year the Senate will vote on the Innocence Protection Act. The House version that had 218 sponsors—half the House—requires preservation of biological evidence and gives federal and state death row inmates access to DNA testing.

One of the more important cases this year before the Supreme Court will be whether the Court will continue to sanction the execution of a mentally disabled person. States over the years have executed many such people. Wanda Jean Allen, who in January 2000 became the first woman ever executed in Oklahoma, had an IQ of below 70. Her application to the Supreme Court failed, even after it was shown that the state lied at a clemency hearing when it said she had graduated from high school and attended college. John Paul Penry, first before the Court in 1989, will this year petition the Court for the third time this year, claiming that his mental disability prohibits his execution.

What makes Penry's case especially worth watching is that it not only has already become a rallying cry for capital punishment opponents worldwide, it also challenges what O'Connor and others on the Court have implied that we must wait for the majority of Americans to be against the death penalty before it is appropriate for the Court to consider stopping it. When the Court first considered Penry's case twelve years ago, only two of the thirty-eight death penalty states barred execution of the mentally disabled. In that 1989 case, *Penry v. Lynaugh,* members of the Supreme Court implied they would consider banning the killings if there was a national consensus against it, but that consensus did not then exist. It does today. Eighteen states ban the death sentence in such instances, and there is legislation pending in other state houses. In addition, twelve states ban the death penalty; thus, a majority of the states prohibit the execution of the mentally disabled. In North Carolina, after the Court accepted the appeal of Ernest P. McCarver, a mentally disabled defendant sentenced to death, the state legislature changed the law, prohibiting that execution, and the case was mooted out. The federal death penalty law excludes execution of the mentally disabled.

By the Court's own logic, the time is now. The Court, by deciding in

2001 to review the case of Daryl Renard Atkins, an eighteen-year-old with an IQ of 59, who is facing death for a Virginia kidnapping and murder, tipped its hand. Virginia had never before executed a defendant with such a low IQ score. Atkins, wanting money to buy beer, shot his victim eight times. The jury that decided on the death penalty heard that Atkins previously had eighteen felony convictions, including one in which he hit a victim over the head with a bottle and another in which he shot a woman in the stomach without provocation. A defense psychiatrist said Atkins was retarded; a prosecution expert witness sharply disagreed, testifying that Atkins could use sophisticated words such as "orchestra," "decimal," and "parable," and that although his school record was poor, he had passed the Literacy Passport Test and also understood what he was doing when he committed the murder and understood the consequences of his act.

The Court's taking of the *Atkins v. Virginia* case may be driven by O'Connor. She has previously said that executions of fifteen-year-olds were unconstitutional. Today, affirming the death penalty of Atkins, who has a mental age of ten, would give the Court a black eye. The case was argued on February 22, 2002. As a result of the positions taken at the argument, it is most likely she will be the fifth for a majority that will prohibit such killings. Breyer, at the hearing, said it appears "settled" that the American people do not want mentally retarded people to be executed. A Columbia University team in 1999 found that 68 percent of all death sentences reviewed by appellate Courts between 1973 and 1995 had been reversed because of serious error. The study found the errors were not technical—they ranged from improper jury instructions from judges, evidence wrongfully withheld by prosecutors, and incompetent counsel. A follow-up study by some teams found that the death penalty was applied at random, rather than for the "worst of the worst." Pamela Rumpz, a Virginia assistant attorney general arguing for the execution of Atkins, disagreed, saying that laws exempting the mentally disabled have existed on average for five years, not long enough to create a national consensus. She shocked and stunned the courtroom as well as the justices when she said "public opinion would change" if Osama bin Laden were captured and found to be mentally retarded. Desperately stretching to make a point, she lost her audience. If Atkins wins, the celebrated *Penry* case, in which the defendant's mental age is seven, will be mooted.

Now, and certainly since September 11, 2001, when America recognizes it must work with other countries of the world, our death penalty is an obstacle. Spain has refused to extradite suspected terrorists because of its use here. France is refusing to turn over evidence that can be used in a terrorist death penalty case. In fact, the Supreme Court's enthusiasm for capital punishment is shocking to much of the world. It surfaces at economic or political summit discussions that are totally unrelated. Often at diplomatic conferences, before the U.S. officials are able to get to topics on the agenda—like Kosovo or other security issues—they must answer for the practice to their European counterparts. As a result, American diplomats filed an unprecedented brief in the *Atkins* death case. They noted that even the International Court of Justice, which will try Slobodan Milosevic, refuses to use the death penalty, and that the practice subjects the United States to "daily and growing criticism from the international community."

"For practically the full four years I was in Paris," recalled former U.S. Ambassador to France Felix G. Rohatyn, a signer of the brief, "there was not a single speech I made where the first or second question was not: 'How can you people do this? Why do you execute the mentally retarded? Why do you execute minors? Why are there so many minorities on death row? . . . When you think of what we've done for human rights in the world, that's an enormous treasure we have. And we're allowing it to be wasted, giving something to people who can attack us with relative impunity."

Since the Supreme Court revived the death penalty twenty-six years ago, 725 people have been executed. Today's death row population is 3,726, 54 percent of whom are people of color. This U.S. death row inmate population also includes 57 women and 72 juveniles; Texas presently holds 465 people on death row, California 591. These are numbers that exceed the total number of people—510 men and women—who were executed from 1893 to 2000. These are staggering figures, and they cost us not only in our prestige abroad, but in the chain of monies that could be used for schools, hospitals, and social service programs aimed at cutting back crime. A California study says the state would save $90 million a year if death penalty cases were abolished. The average cost to try such a case is $2.8 million, twice what it costs to house a prisoner for life. It is also four times as costly to house a prisoner on death row as in the general population. Yet, defense lawyers seeking to get DNA evidence that might acquit some of those men have found themselves in legal battles with the state, which has refused to open old death cases. The capital punishment debate heated up in early 2001 as the new pro-death administration assumed office.

Bush's choice for attorney general, John W. Ashcroft, is famously remembered as a senator who denied a judicial nomination to a respected black law-and-order judge, Ronnie White, for being soft on criminals because the judge reversed one of five death sentences. Following his appointment, Ashcroft hit the ground running. He said that a study by his predecessor, Janet Reno, which proved that the death penalty was unfair and discriminatory, was incomplete. In fact, Ashcroft, in a whitewash report, claimed he completed Reno's study and was led to a different conclusion. The Bush Department of Justice, under pressure, then agreed to carry out the comprehensive study Ashcroft promised. That study has yet to be completed. Reno's study, which made far more persuasive arguments for abolishing the death penalty than did any previous study, even those created by anti–death penalty advocates, examined every execution under federal law since 1988. In reviewing each state, there could be no doubt as to the racial application of the law. In Virginia, for example, fifty-five members of minorities and five whites were sentenced to death. The five whites were convicted of espionage. That meant in Virginia the balance was effectively 55–0.

Soon after the release of Reno's Justice Department study, judicial and prosecutorial circles were rocked again. Oklahoma City's police scientist, and the chief witness in a number of death cases, Joyce Gilchrist, was found to have testified falsely in a number of cases, including twelve in which defendants were put to death because her oral testimony, under oath, helped persuade the jury of their guilt. In at least two cases, both involving rape and murder, she produced evidence of the men's semen that "conclusively" tied them to the victim. But DNA findings and the examination of her slides (which had no semen) proved otherwise. Ms. Gilchrist worked on twelve hundred cases; they are all under review.

The majority justices form a solid wall of support for the death penalty. O'Connor and Kennedy are likely to continue to join the reactionary three, whenever they can, leaving capital punishment, as meted out by the Rehnquist Court, as firmly entrenched as ever. The same must be said about race discrimination, wherever the justice system finds it.

Most recently, the Rehnquist Court attacked previous Supreme Court decisions that tried to racially integrate juries by changing the law on the use of peremptory jury challenges. These are challenges that allow either side to strike a potential juror for any reason whatsoever—no cause need be shown. Each side has an equal and limited number. The sole arbiter of what is or is not an appropriate challenge is the trial judge, and his decision can rarely be successfully appealed. The Rehnquist Court put racial bias back into jury selection by allowing prosecutors again to have all-white juries—a practice people complained about throughout the first half of this century. Refusing to look at the composition of jury pools and the real effect of his decision, Rehnquist declared there was nothing wrong with all-white juries, and because the criminal justice system should be color blind, race ought not be a factor in its decision making.

> In my view there is simply nothing "unequal" about the state's using its peremptory challenges to strike blacks from the jury in cases involving black defendants, so long as such challenges are also used to exclude whites in cases involving white defendants. . . . This case-specific use of peremptory challenges by the state does not single out blacks, or members of any other race for that matter, for discriminatory treatment. Juries are the first and most important original triers of fact. If they are biased, the entire American legal process is biased. It is no answer to say it is as biased against whites as against blacks.

Scalia, agreeing, concluded that bias is part of life, directed not only at blacks, and that it can, therefore, be part of nearly every criminal trial in the country.

If the *Gregg v. Georgia* decision, overturning the opinion on *Furman v. Virginia*, is, arguably, a decision conservatives most enthusiastically champion, then *Miranda v. Arizona* (1966) joins *Roe v. Wade* and *Brown v. Board of Education* (1954) as those cases they most strenuously criticize. *Miranda* attempted to strike a balance between the need for the police to solve crimes and the need to have constitutional protections in the station house. It held that the privilege against self-incrimination applies to police interrogations as well as to proceedings in a courtroom or a Congress. The Warren Court, recognizing that pressure to speak can be compulsory under the

Fifth Amendment, said there is always some element of coercion merely by holding a suspect in custody. The *Miranda* rule—that the suspect being questioned be told he has a right to remain silent, a right not to incriminate himself, a right to counsel, and a right to make a knowing waiver of that right—was aimed at stopping the egregious practice of the coerced confession, often extracted when police told their suspects that if they did not confess, the criminal justice system would penalize them.

The attack on *Miranda* began most seriously when Rehnquist joined the Court. He claimed *Miranda* was not constitutionally required. The Court, in a series of cases, decided after he became chief justice, in effect today encourages law enforcement to violate the *Miranda* standard by rewarding them when a confession is legally coerced. The Court held that a coerced confession may be used against the defendant if he takes the stand—a surefire procedure for stopping him from testifying on his own behalf. If the defendant's family hires a lawyer and the police refuse to let the lawyer see his client, or do not tell the defendant a lawyer has been hired and is waiting to see him, statements made during that period are admissible as well. If a coerced confession produces the names of witnesses to testify against a defendant, then those witnesses could be called. A police officer need not give the warning if he is "reasonably prompted by a concern for public safety"; and if a defendant claims he was arrested and placed in the station house, and the officer demurs, insisting he was "invited" to the station house to discuss the crime, the defendant's statements are admissible because the "warnings" need not be given. In sum, because prosecutors and police know that the Supreme Court will nearly always back them up, the *Miranda* protection is nearly totally ineffective.

Any criminal law case may contain elements in its fact pattern and issues that make it unique and render interpretation subjective. What constitutes a "knowing" waiver? When does an interrogation become too long? How long can you question a subject even after you have read his rights and he says he wants a lawyer or remains silent? How can the Court decide all the tiny facts, decide if the police or the suspect is telling the truth? It all depends on whether the Court is committed to the Warren Court's attempt to stop coercion in the interrogation room.

There are many ways the Court could have built on *Miranda*. It could have said a ten-hour interrogation is too long, that anyone subjected to such questioning can be worn down and will ultimately confess. It could have more clearly defined what a knowing waiver is. Instead, the intent of the Warren Court to stop coercion in the interrogation room has been determinedly undermined: as a practical matter, police practice today in the coerced confession area is the same as before *Miranda*. With sixty *Miranda*-related cases decided since that time, in only two have the rulings favored the defendant.

The most important of these cases upheld *Miranda*'s constitutionality. In *Dickerson v. United States* (2000) Congress passed a law attempting to render *Miranda* ineffectual—a goal originally championed by Chief Justice Rehnquist—and so his opinion in June 2000 for a 7–2 majority was seen by many in the media as evidence that perhaps the Rehnquist Court was not as revisionist as we thought. But upon careful reading, we see that Justice Rehnquist upheld, at best, a severely damaged *Miranda*. His opinion reaffirmed earlier decisions of his Court that had "reduced the [adverse] impact of the Miranda rule on legitimate law enforcement." All the *Dickerson* decision did was to institutionalize that new balance articulated in those previous cases. In effect, Rehnquist put *Miranda* on legal life support.

But why then would Rehnquist, long interested in tearing *Miranda* down, write the majority *Dickerson* opinion seeming to uphold it? There are two reasons. First, he wanted to show that in upholding *Miranda*, he could point out how little there was to uphold. Second, had he not been in the majority, then John Paul Stevens, as the senior judge for the majority, could have written a majority opinion that would reaffirm *Miranda*'s broad sweep. Rehnquist's opinion was, in fact, a compromise opinion—he would have preferred to write a majority opinion directly overruling it, but he did not have those five votes. Clearly, Rehnquist wanted the *Dickerson* majority to speak with one voice. Then why did the moderate justices go along? Why didn't they say that the weakened *Miranda* is not the law; that the law is as the Warren Court wrote it and that the subsequent cases that weakened it are wrong? Because if they had, they would have been in the minority; O'Connor and Kennedy would have joined Scalia, Thomas, and Rehnquist to make the five-judge majority to override it. The liberal justices instead joined a majority, opinion that contradicted their own words, when, in the minority, they had voted against those very cases that cut *Miranda* back. By joining the majority, Stevens, the most ardent critic of the Rehnquist Court's treatment of *Miranda*, was effectively silenced. Only Thomas and Scalia, the two dissenters, were consistent; they were opposed to *Miranda* in any form. And because of this, Rehnquist's failure to join Thomas and Scalia was attacked by the right wing, which was not sympathetic to the needs of the Court's internal politics, or understanding of the public relations coup it had scored by a liberal press that soundly missed the significance of what had just happened.

In truth, *Miranda* is now an empty symbol, still respected as the icon of an ideal, but one the courts are free to disregard after performing appropriate rituals of rationalization and reversal. When the Rehnquist Court affirmed *Miranda,* in the *Dickerson* decision, they knew studies had conclusively shown that, once weakened, it had no significant effect on law enforcement. Indeed, many of these cases were merely a blueprint of how law enforcement could avoid convictions being invalidated. No doubt, if the same exact case as *Miranda* came up again, the Supreme Court would uphold it in spirit. But every case has different facts, and cases with facts very close to those of *Miranda* have come up, and the Court has distinguished them. Its trajectory totally altered, Rehnquist's Court has allowed lower courts to endlessly cut *Miranda* back, knowing the Supreme Court will not reverse them. What happened to *Miranda* happened to a long string of Warren and early Burger Court cases that protected individual rights. Most, like *Miranda*, are "good law" but effectively meaningless.

As I review all these cases, we see a cradle-to-grave approach to criminal defendants being systematically and deliberately taken by the Court: their rights are set back in search and seizure and evidence collection (cradle), to arrest (*Miranda*), to defense and appeals, and finally to incarceration and death (grave), where the application of the Bill of Rights ends.

William Rehnquist has also authored opinions or joined the Court when it comes to making it more difficult for criminal defendants to challenge a search and seizure, in expanding the scope of police searches, and in establishing a "good faith" exception to the exclusionary rule that says that evidence illegally seized by the state in violation of the Fourth Amendment must be excluded. Prior to Rehnquist, the government was severely penalized if it did not follow the law. But the Supreme Court has now created a set of rules that allows the evidence in. In addition, it has held that evidence obtained by police relying, in good faith, on a defective search warrant may be used, even if the search was illegal.

As a practical matter, this permitted police to request, and judges to issue, potentially illegal warrants, knowing that even if the search was no good, the evidence was useful and admissible. Now, as Justice Brennan pointed out, there is nothing to prevent the police from stopping any car or person, or entering any home they wanted to, without a warrant, and then using the evidence. Justice John Paul Stevens said these decisions, taken together, "provide government agents with an affirmative action to engage in unconstitutional violations of the privacy of the home." All it need come down to is the word of one or two officers against a defendant probably thought guilty for the courts to resolve warrantless search issues in the government's favor.

America's punitive prison sentences, shaped in part by a frontier culture and an emphasis on individual accountability, are routinely upheld by the Court. Our criminal system has far longer sentences and a higher percent of its people in jail than any European nation (except Russia), most of which stress rehabilitation not punishment. America's overwhelming commitment to prisons and long sentences has been greatly aided by Stephen Breyer who, years before his nomination to the Court, had a major role in creating sentencing guidelines in criminal cases that make racial disparities in sentencing harsher. For this, he was severely criticized by liberals at his confirmation hearings.

Nonetheless, sentencing guidelines have as many supporters as critics. They were adopted because of concerns that convicted criminals were being punished in a random manner as judges misused their broad discretion to allow criminals to either avoid severe punishment or be punished in excess of what was considered reasonable.

As such, the guidelines sharply cut down the number of cases that went to trial, thereby achieving Rehnquist's goal of streamlining the federal courts. But defendants, presumably innocent, who elect to go to trial are punished for doing so. By going to trial and rejecting a plea agreement, these defendants are denied the sentence reduction for acceptance of responsibility that routinely accompanies plea bargains. It means the addition of several years to a sentence. Statutes for a fairer way to accomplish the goals of evenhanded sentencing are now before Congress, but they are unlikely to be passed. This Supreme Court has rejected any attempt to strike down the sentencing guidelines.

The issue of cruel and unusual punishment, generally considered to be the defining one in capital offenses, was raised in a different form in a 1992 case. This time, the moderates seemed to win, but like *Dickerson v. United States*, it was a hollow victory. The case, *Hudson v. McMillian,* decided in 1992, was one of Clarence Thomas's earliest cases, and in this decision we saw the anger and fury he exhibited during the nomination process focused on the plaintiff.

Keith Hudson, black, charged with burglary and held in segregation, was taken in shackles from his cell at Louisiana's notorious Angola prison by Jack McMillian, a white sergeant with whom he had previously had a run-in. He was then handed over to two white guards, who severely beat him. Hudson filed a complaint in federal court against the officers for assault. He argued his own case before the federal magistrate, claiming that the guards had used excessive force that violated the cruel and unusual punishment prohibition, winning damages in the sum of $800. The magistrate found the guards had acted maliciously, unnecessarily, and wantonly. The police guards appealed and lost, then appealed again to the U.S. Supreme Court.

Hudson won a 7–2 decision, the majority opinion written by O'Connor, with only Scalia and Thomas in dissent. Whether Rehnquist believed in Hudson's position, or joined the majority, as he did in *Dickerson,* in order still to have influence with O'Connor and Kennedy, is hard to say.

Even so, it's a cautious decision. Afraid of opening the floodgates to prisoner litigation, O'Connor distinguished the *Hudson* case from those cases where deliberate indifference to a prisoner's health is not a violation unless there is serious injury. She said the use of excessive physical force against Hudson could constitute a violation of the Eighth Amendment even if his injuries were not serious. The test, she said, was "whether force was applied in a good faith effort to maintain or restore discipline, or maliciously and sadistically to cause harm." She and six other judges found the beating to be wanton and sadistic.

Thomas, speaking for himself and Scalia, reading the same factual records as the other seven judges, declared that "a use of force that causes only insignificant harm to a prisoner may be immoral, it may be tortious, it may be criminal, and it may even be remarkable under other provisions of the Constitution, but it is not cruel and unusual punishment." He agreed that the prison guards' conduct was unacceptable but said, "The Eighth Amendment is not, and should not be turned into a National Code of Prison Regulation."

Hudson, written early in Thomas's career, shows us his methodology and

the legal theory he applies to most constitutional issues. In reaching his conclusions, he first examined the culture and values existing at the end of the
eighteenth century. Then he examined the history of the cruel and unusual
punishment clause, the Constitutional Convention and state ratifying con-
ventions debates, and then the text itself. His decision also examines early
prison jurisprudence, and he notes that the Courts had all rejected "conditions of complaint" claims by prisoners until well into the twentieth century.
For the first 185 years of this country, Thomas wrote, "this Court did not so
much as intimate that the Cruel and Unusual Punishment Clause" was relevant to prison conditions. He made his point clear: "Today's expansion of
the Cruel and Unusual Punishment Clause beyond all bounds of history
and precedent is, I suspect, yet another manifestation of the pervasive view
that the Federal Constitution must address all the deplorable ills of our
society . . . [including] any hardship that might befall a prisoner during
incarceration." Reaching that conclusion, and looking at the law since, he
argued that not only should Hudson's claim be denied, but that many previous cases also affirming prisoners claims of unlawful beating and torture
were wrong and should be overturned.

  While both the *Hudson* and *Dickerson* cases saw Rehnquist in the
majority, in the final analysis, the two dissenters, Clarence Thomas and
Antonin Scalia, finally won far more than they lost. It was also evident that
Rehnquist, while not voting with Thomas in the *Hudson* case, agreed with
him more than disagreed. In 1996, after Rehnquist's extensive lobbying, the
Prison Litigation Reform Act was passed by Congress, stating that a prisoner such as Hudson cannot recover damages under the Cruel and Unusual
Punishment Clause of the Eighth Amendment if there is no permanent
damage. He cannot recover merely for pain and suffering, even if the beating is long, brutal, malicious, and wanton. The congressional bill is a manual
for the police on how to conduct beatings and not be sued.

Many veteran Court observers were surprised to see the chief justice aban-
don Scalia and Thomas in these last two key decisions, but explainable shifts
have also gone the other way.

  Fourth Amendment law is one such area where justices surprise Court
watchers and switch sides. In *Kyllo v. United States* (2001), Justice Scalia
joined the liberals for a 5–4 majority, that "thermal imaging," the use of a

heat-seeking device outside a house in order to determine if criminal acts were being committed inside, was violative of that amendment. But another Fourth Amendment decision saw Justice David Souter swing over to the Right's side; *Atwater v. City of Lago Vista* (2001) is a case worth looking at if for no other reason than to dispel the commonly accepted view that Souter is a consistent part of the moderate bloc. He had joined the Right early in his career, then veered toward a liberal position. Then, recently, he came up with an unusual decision sharply narrowing the Fourth Amendment. And as we shall see, in the *Vernonia School District 47J v. Wayne Acton* (1995) case, Justice Ginsburg joined the Right in a case that infringes not upon the rights of America's criminal class, but on the rights of its middle class to be free of inappropriate police conduct and wrongful invasions of privacy.

In March 1997, Gail Atwater was driving her pickup truck in Lago Vista, Texas, with her three-year-old son and five-year-old daughter; all were in the front seat and none was using a seat belt. A sixteen-year resident of Lago Vista, she was driving fifteen miles an hour on a residential street. In Texas, front-seat passengers must wear seat belts if they are installed, and any small child riding in the front must be secured. Violation of either provision is a misdemeanor punishable by a modest fine.

Bart Turek, a Lago Vista police officer, pulled Atwater over, then handcuffed her with her hands behind her back, placed her and her children in the police car, and drove to the police station. The police refused to help her make arrangements for the children—fortunately, she found a friend to take them. At the station, she was forced to remove her shoes, relinquish her possessions, and wait in a holding cell until she posted a $310 bond—all this for a $50 seat belt offense, which she ultimately paid after pleading no contest.

Atwater filed suit in Texas state court for damages against Turek, claiming he and the city had violated her Fourth Amendment rights. A three-judge panel of the fifth circuit concluded that "an arrest for a first-time seat belt offense" was an unreasonable seizure under the Fourth Amendment, but when an appeal was made to the entire fifth circuit, the court reversed.

Atwater's lawyer went to the Supreme Court and argued that the common law forbade peace officers from making warrantless misdemeanor arrests except in cases of "breach of peace." Breach of the peace, according to Atwater, meant only offenses "involving or tending towards violence."

Justice Sandra Day O'Connor, one of the Court's traditional swing votes, remarked during oral argument that the defendant's counsel had "the perfect case," thus leading most to believe it was a safe bet that the Fourth Amendment was due for another win.

Writing for the majority, Justice Souter conceded that "[i]n cases of misdemeanor, a peace officer . . . has at common law no power of arresting without a warrant except when a breach of the peace has been committed in his presence or there is reasonable ground for supposing that a breach of peace is about to be committed or renewed in his presence." Souter wrote, "If we were to derive a rule exclusively to address the uncontested facts of this case, Atwater might well prevail." She was a known and established resident of Lago Vista with no place to hide and no incentive to flee, and common sense says she would almost certainly have buckled up as a condition of driving off with a citation. But this was not enough to protect Ms. Atwater against the police. The five-judge majority rejected the legal issue at the heart of her argument concerning Officer Turek's warrantless arrest, pointing out that, gratuitous humiliations aside, the police cannot, on the spot, tell whether the offender is jailable or not, and if the officer makes a mistake, the suit for damages must be dismissed.

Given the Court's claim of extraordinary pressures on its time, this case should have been treated perfunctorily. Instead, Justice Souter, evoking the language of originalism usually associated with his colleagues Scalia, Rehnquist, and Thomas, wrote that if a practice was accepted when the Fourth Amendment was adopted, the party advocating change "bears a heavy burden of justifying a departure from the historical understanding."

In another unusual lineup of justices, Justice Ginsburg switched to the conservative side to join Justice Scalia in a Fourth Amendment case, this time going after child athletes in *Vernonia School District 47J v. Wayne Acton*, the 1995 majority opinion that upheld random drug testing for a twelve-year-old boy who had sought to try out for the Vernonia High School football team. Here, as in *Atwater*, what is surprising is who the Court is targeting. "Original intent" and "original meaning" theory, the majority admitted, did not justify forcing young James Acton to take the test. There was no suspicion of any kind by anyone that the boy had ever taken a drug. Acton's parents objected, saying their child was their responsibility and that the drug testing was an unreasonable search of his body, prohibited by the Fourth Amendment. While the ninth circuit said the school was unjustified in requiring random drug tests where students never before had a problem, a 6–3 Supreme Court majority disagreed and said Acton could be forced to take the test. President Clinton, sensitive to the temper of the times and his own political problems, was caught between a rock and a hard place. He lauded Ginsburg's ruling in the *Vernonia* decision as another way of combating drug use.

Sandra Day O'Connor tried to make a factual distinction between random drug testing if it were limited to students with disciplinary problems, which she would uphold, and the school's mass, suspicionless search, which she could not. Justice Ginsburg tried to limit the holding to athletes and not all high school students. The three dissenters, claiming a constitutional violation, referred to Justice Robert Jackson's description of the significance of the Fourth Amendment as belonging ". . . in the catalogue of indispensable freedoms. Among deprivations of rights, none is so effective in cowing a population . . . and putting terror in every heart. Uncontrolled search and seizure is one of the first and most effective weapons in the arsenal of every arbitrary government." In 2002, based on the *Vernonia* case, the Supreme Court extended drug testing to all students, not just athletes and not just those with drug problems. Justice Ginsburg's view that she could control *Vernonia*'s path was wrong.

Another area of controversy in the criminal arena is whether the Bill of Rights, originally enacted to protect citizens from federal infringement, protected them as well from state infringement. Without the incorporation doctrine, the Fifth Amendment right to avoid self-incrimination, the Fourth Amendment's protection against wrongful search, the Sixth Amendment's right to counsel, the Eighth Amendment's right to be free of cruel and unusual punishment, and other of the first ten amendments, would not apply to citizens in state courts; the "states rights" argument being that each state should be free to set its own standards. But in the 1947 *Adamson v. California* case the Court said that while the Fourteenth Amendment "does not draw all of the rights of the federal Bill of Rights under its protection," it does incorporate those rights that are so fundamental that they are implicit "in the concept of ordered liberty." Felix Frankfurter, writing for the majority, in a 5–4 decision, adopted a fundamental fairness test to decide which amendments should be incorporated. Justice Hugo Black's "total incorporation" concept, that the entire Bill of Rights protected state citizens, was rejected.

This so-called doctrine of "incorporation" has drawn acrimonious criticism. Meese told the bar association in 1984 that the sixty years of law supporting incorporation was wrong and correcting it was high on his agenda. Thomas, Scalia, and Rehnquist are dead set against the application of many of the Bill of Rights amendments against the states. They want to take the federal judiciary (where these rights are now protected) off central stage in deciding the major social and political conflicts in our society. They achieve this result by saying some of the most important portions of the federal Bill of Rights do not apply to states and by denying citizens' rights to sue over these rights in the federal courts. Conservatives saw, correctly, that the process of incorporation is part of a process of nationalization—like the Commerce Clause, it channels power into central government at the expense of the states. But incorporation has been the settled law for half a century, and until the last few years it was inconceivable the Court would try to strip the American people of these cherished Bill of Rights protections. Nevertheless, as Daniel Troy, a former clerk to Bork and one of the Federalist founders presently in the Bush administration, says, "Incorporation is in play." And the Federalists have held meetings to formulate a legal strategy on how to attack this solidly decided law of the last sixty years.

Jeffrey S. Sutton, a Bush nominee to the circuit court, has also openly called for the end to the incorporation doctrine. He has already briefed and argued the wrongness of it before, in an unrelated 1993 Supreme Court case. Justice Breyer found his attack hard to believe. "Are you really now saying incorporation was totally wrong?" "Yes," answered Sutton. There are, for the Right, few sacred principles in American constitutional jurisprudence.

As we see in the next chapter, the relentless assault on *Roe v. Wade* shows the reactionary determination to keep on attacking, in as many ways as possible, a principle that is accepted by an overwhelming number of Americans.

4

MORALITY AND VALUES:
Sex, Abortion, and Women's Rights

No other nation permits its legal system to resolve so broad a range of judicial disputes as does the United States. No judicial issue of our time has been as intertwined with politics for as long a time as the Supreme Court's decision in *Roe v. Wade*. It was, and still is, one of the most momentous political and social issue dividing our country. Every national political campaign since 1973 has had abortion as one of its most significant elements. A substantial part of the American vote turns on it. And every justice nomination since 1973 has pivoted on whether he (or she) would vote to overrule it or support it.

For the past thirty years, demonstrations and public outrage have attended each abortion case the Supreme Court faced. Thirty years after *Roe*, on June 28, 2000, in *Stenberg v. Carhart*, a 5–4 decision, the Court rejected a ban on so-called partial birth abortion, a term created by the anti-abortion movement. Justice Scalia, dissenting, said combatively, "We can now look to at least another term with boxes full of mail from the public and streets full of demonstration." Justice Breyer recognized the still "controversial nature of the problem" and "the deep and seemingly absolute convictions that the subject inspires."

Three justices are firmly against abortion—Rehnquist, Scalia, and Thomas—while Anthony Kennedy became a fourth minority vote in the

Stenberg decision to uphold the ban. What Justice Blackmun, *Roe's* author, observed sadly in the 1989 *Webster v. Reproductive Health Services* case, that *Roe's* life is fragile, is as true today. "In one sense, the Court's approach is worlds apart from that of the Chief Justice and Justice Scalia. And yet, in another sense, the distance between the two worlds is short—the distance is but a simple vote. I am 83 years old, I cannot remain on this Court forever, and when I do step down, the confirmation process for my successor may well focus on the issue before us today. That, I regret, may be exactly where the choice between the two worlds will be made."

Roe v. Wade was decided in 1973. Since then there have been more than 40 million abortions in the United States. The women's movement, the Supreme Court's privacy cases, as well as cultural and social forces all contributed to the decision. One hundred fifty years ago a married woman could not normally own or control her property or enter contractual agreements. If she worked outside her home, her husband legally owned her wages. Myra Bradwell was denied admission to the bar in 1873. Her petition to the Supreme Court was denied. Justice Bradley's concurring opinion explained why: "The Constitution of the family organization which is founded on the divine ordinance, as well as in the nature of things, indicates the domestic sphere as that which properly belongs to the domain and functions of womanhood."

During the nineteenth century and most of the twentieth, women were seen primarily as serving as housewives, helpless to guide their own lives or even to make moral choices. In 1937, a Georgia poll tax excusing women from payment was upheld when the Supreme Court said, "The tax being on persons, women may be exempted on the basis of special considerations to which they are naturally entitled. . . . The laws of Georgia declare the husband to be the head of the family and the wife to be subject to him. To subject her to the levy would be to add to his burden." The law is fair, said the Court, "in view of the burdens necessarily borne by them for the preservation of the race." State laws in jury service, job eligibility, voting, and taxes that did not include women in the definition of persons were upheld by the courts, and so women could be treated differently than men.

Eleven years later, in 1948, Justice Felix Frankfurter, writing an opinion for the Court, said that a law prohibiting the employment of women bartenders unless they were related to a male bar owner was appropriate so that men could look after the morals of their wives or daughters. And the

Court, in 1961, refused to let Gwendolyn Hoyt challenge her murder conviction that was a result, she claimed, of a jury selection process that led to her all-male jury, because, said the Courts, "woman is still regarded as the center of home and family life. . . . We cannot say that it is constitutionally impermissible for a state, acting in pursuit of the general welfare, to conclude that women should be relieved from the civic duty of jury service unless she herself determines that such service is consistent with her own special responsibilities." And so it went.

The law dramatically began to shift when Ruth Ginsburg, the present justice, argued before the Supreme Court in 1971, in *Reed v. Reed*, that the Fourteenth Amendment was violated by statutory gender discrimination. It was the first such decision in a century, and *Reed* became a most important building block toward the establishment of women's rights.

Then, on January 22, 1973, in *Roe v. Wade*, the Supreme Court decided 7–2 that state laws from Georgia and Texas proscribing most abortions violated the right of privacy. Justice Harry Blackmun's opinion divided pregnancy into trimesters—during the first trimester the woman had a nearly unrestricted right to abortion after speaking to her physician; in the second trimester states could regulate abortion to protect a women's health; and in the third trimester the states' interest in protecting the fetus was great enough to warrant severe restrictions on abortion, but even then the states must permit abortions to save a woman's life. The anti-abortion forces' attempts to overrule that decision by lawsuit, constitutional amendments, and bills submitted to Congress have composed one of the more enduring battles of the last thirty years.

Brown v. Board of Education in 1954 and *Roe* in 1973 are bookends for the liberal decisions of the Warren and Burger Courts. *Roe v. Wade*, decided early in Chief Justice Burger's tenure, with a majority that included three Nixon-appointed justices, has been the Right's greatest disappointment. It is seen as such not only because it legalizes abortion, for later cases severely cut back that right, but because of the method of constitutional interpretation that was used in the case and that barely keeps it alive today.

To understand the political, legal, and social dispute over *Roe*, we first look at a case that forms the foundation for the abortion case. *Griswold v. Connecticut*, decided in 1965, was a high-water mark for the Court—without a right of privacy, there would not be a right to abortion today or the line of cases dramatically expanding the privacy rights over the last three decades. Had *Griswold* or *Roe* been presented to this Supreme Court any-time after 1990, the cases would have had a different outcome. If *Roe* and *Griswold* did not exist, our country would be different in many ways besides abortion, ranging from privacy protections in the bedroom to protections against privacy invasion by the new technologies. The *Griswold* case, decided eight years before *Roe*, drew a heavy storm of criticism. Like *Roe*, the justices who decided it were accused of creating new law, acting with their hearts rather than their heads, and finding constitutional rights that do not exist in the Constitution.

In *Roe*, as in *Griswold*, the majority justices who "discovered" these new rights often found different sources for them. The *Griswold* case began four years before the Supreme Court heard it. Dr. Estelle T. Gris-wold, the executive director of Planned Parenthood of Connecticut, and Dr. C. Lee Buxton, a physician and professor at the Yale Medical School, created a test case to challenge a state law banning them from making con-traceptives publicly available. The 7–2 decision that followed (the same vote as in *Roe*), written by Justice William Douglas, found that the right of privacy, although not mentioned in the Constitution, is the privilege of every American.

The key sentence that supports the *Griswold* opinion is also the sen-tence that most infuriates the Right, as well as many conservatives. Justice Douglas said, "The specific guarantees in the Bill of Rights [as, for example, privacy], have penumbras formed by emanations from those guarantees that help give them life and substance." This phrasing has been relentlessly attacked as idiosyncratic and beyond the Constitution, reflecting totally subjective lawmaking. Justices Arthur Goldberg, Brennan, and Warren, agreeing that there is a right to privacy, found it in different places in the Constitution, in the Ninth Amendment, and in the word "liberty"—a word that contains rights beyond those described by the Bill of Rights. Justice Brennan wrote that "liberty" protects rights so rooted in the tradition and conscience of our people as to be ranked fundamental. In a letter to Doug-las sent during the Court's later internal debate on *Roe*, Justice Brennan observed that privacy is a species of liberty:

. . . I would identify three groups of fundamental freedoms that "liberty" encompasses . . . first, freedom from bodily restraints or inspection, freedom to do with one's body as one likes and freedom to care for one's health and person; second, freedom of choice in basic decisions of life, such as marriage, divorce, procreation, contraception, and the education and upbringing of children; and, third, autonomous control over the development and expression of one's intellect and personality.

The Constitution, the *Griswold* majority agreed, is not exclusionary; it does not list all the rights we have. But the Ninth Amendment, on which some of the majority justices relied, talks of unenumerated rights that the people have, and that is a constitutional reservoir from which a right of privacy can be drawn. The majority argued that although the Constitution does not say a child has a right to an education, or that we have a right to associate with anyone we wish, the Courts have found those rights by their interpretation of the Constitution, and that logic, the majority said, supports and establishes a right of privacy.

Potter Stewart, dissenting, said that while the anticontraception law was "an uncommonly silly law," the Constitution does not protect a right to privacy. Hugo Black went further: If you can derive the right of privacy and abortion from the Constitution, why can't you also find a right to "freedom of contract"? He asked what the difference was between the well-discredited *Lochner v. People of State of New York* (1905) denying the employer the right to freely contract with his employee, and *Griswold*, finding a right to privacy. Consistency and adherence to the text, Black believed, required the Court to reject both. Otherwise, Black claimed (and to some extent Scalia and Robert Bork—strange bedfellows, indeed), a new Constitution would be created each time a Court finds a new right. "I think it approaches the fantastic," he wrote

for judges to create from these general, all embracing constitutional provisions guaranteeing a general right to privacy. And I think it fantastic for judges to use these specific constitutional guaranties as an excuse to arrogate to themselves authority to create new and different alleged constitutional rights where judges believe modern conditions call for new constitutional rights. For judges to have such power would amount to authority on their part to override the people's Constitution. I prefer to have the people's liberty measured by the constitutional language the Founders wrote rather than by new views of new judges as to what liberty it is safe for the people to have.

Douglas's response in *Griswold* to Black was that it all comes down to which kind of rights are most worth protecting. In language hauntingly like the *Roe* opinion to come, he wrote, rejecting the *Lochner* analogy, "We do not sit as a super legislature to determine the wisdom, need and propriety of laws that touch economic problems, business affairs, or social conditions. The contraception law operates directly on the intimate relationship of husband and wife and that makes all the difference. The right of a woman to control her body, to decide whether to terminate or not to terminate her pregnancy, flows directly from that right to privacy which is based on our traditions and history."

Another response to Black's argument is that for the last sixty years we have quite properly decided that personal rights are entitled to a higher degree of protection than economic rights, and that this double standard is required by the Constitution. The conservative rejoinder to that formulation is that what the Court was doing during those sixty years was wrong; that the writers of the Constitution made clear the very high value they placed on property rights; and that some of the framers even believed those rights were entitled to more protection than individual rights. Why, ask the conservatives, is it less dangerous for unelected justices to impose their preferences on legislators and society in economic relations than personal rights? Overrule *Roe*, they say; previous cases do not require us to reaffirm years of wrong decisions. *Brown v. Board of Education* overruled *Plessy v. Ferguson* (1896), thus overturning school segregation; FDR's Court overruled the cases that prohibited minimum wage laws or child labor.

The vitality of these debates before and since the *Roe* decision is suggestive. The ability to derive or not derive privacy and abortion rights from the Constitution illuminates the discretionary nature of legal interpretation and the basic truth that textual constraints on judges are often far less important than cultural and political forces. The *Roe* opinion, following *Griswold*, to which it owed so much, was itself stirring, elegant, and deserving of its status as a constitutional landmark. Blackmun, building on *Griswold*, found the women's right to privacy in the Due Process Clause of the Fourteenth Amendment. Formerly counsel to the Mayo Clinic, Blackmun spent the summer of 1972 in an extensive study of medical materials on abortion. He hoped to discover when a fetus could be considered viable. Blackmun, writing *Roe*, said, "It perhaps is not generally appreciated that criminal abortion laws are in effect today and of relatively recent vintage." After examining

Persian, Greek, and Roman times, and English and American law, he pointed out that in the United States, it was not until 1980 that the majority of the states banned abortion. He concludes that women can be harmed if they cannot abort. Specific and direct harm medically diagnosable even in early pregnancy may be involved. Maternity or additional offspring may force upon a woman a distressful life and future. Psychological harm may be imminent. Blackmun pointed out that, through the ages, the concept of "liberty" had been expanded to cover many freedoms not already found in the Constitution.

Rehnquist, representing the minority, looked at the same American traditions and history and saw reason for rejecting the abortion right. The fact that a majority of the states, reflecting, after all, the majority sentiment in those states, have had restrictions on abortion for at least a century is a strong indication, it seemed to Rehnquist, that the asserted right to an abortion is not "so rooted in the traditions and conscience of our people as to be marked as fundamental." His position drives the conservative argument.

Sixteen years later, in 1989, after Justice Rehnquist became Chief Justice Rehnquist, anti-abortionists throughout the country thought they had the perfect vehicle to overrule *Roe* in a case called *Webster v. Reproductive Health Services*. The Court's composition had dramatically changed since *Roe*'s days, with four new appointees—Stevens, O'Connor, Scalia, and Kennedy—Republicans all. Missouri, the state in which the case originated, had long been a leading anti-abortion state, regularly passing tougher and tougher laws, getting as close to the heart of *Roe* as it could. It was supported in its legal battles by the administration of George Bush. That state's newest law declared in a preamble that life begins at conception and that "unborn children have protectable interests in life health and well-being." Another provision precluded state hospitals from providing abortions, even if the women could pay for it; another required a physician to determine the viability of the fetus, when the doctor believed the fetus was twenty or more weeks. This gave the states the ability to stop abortions earlier. Rehnquist seized on that preamble and sought to make it the law of the land—that a fetus at any time in the pregnancy has a right not to be killed—but he ultimately failed. Up until the end, he thought he had forged a majority, with five justices ready to uphold Missouri's statute and write a decision that had the practical effect of reversing *Roe* without specifically overruling it. On May 25, Rehnquist circulated what he understood was to be the majority opinion. His draft said that although precedent was "a cornerstone of our legal system," it should give way where the previous case is "unsound in principle and workable in practice."

Depending on the constitutional test used, a statute either lives or dies. Chief Justice Rehnquist wanted the same constitutional test for abortion and personal rights as previous courts had used to test economic rights statutes—what is called a rational scrutiny test. Nearly all laws survive a rational scrutiny test, just as nearly all laws fail a strict scrutiny test. Strict scrutiny requires that the statement be closely related to government interest. Rational scrutiny requires only that the statute be "reasonable" in relation to a statute that the government has less of an interest in. The rational scrutiny test is the least vigorous test to be used in determining constitutionality. Much of the abortion fight wages over these fine, subjective tests of constitutional interpretation.

Justice Stevens, who was actually undecided at the *Webster* conference, was pushed into joining what became the minority bloc after he saw a draft of Rehnquist's opinion. Rehnquist's test, said Stevens in a letter to the chief justice, would uphold all and nearly any abortion restrictions and override *Roe* without saying it was doing so. After implying that this was dishonest, Stevens said the following restrictions would be appropriate under Rehnquist's new test: a tax on abortions, a requirement that the pregnant woman must be able to stand on her head for fifteen minutes, or that she must first pass a test on Shakespeare or American history before she could have an abortion. If *Roe* is to be killed, he said, "I would rather see the Court give the case a decent burial instead of tossing it out the window of a fast moving caboose."

Blackmun's draft, in response to Rehnquist's, adopted the caustic, mocking tone of Stevens's letter. Whatever opinion the majority would write would damage *Roe* severely, Blackmun said. Under Rehnquist's standards, he continued, a woman could be denied an abortion if she could not "memorize and recite" Rehnquist's opinion before seeking one. Scalia's draft opinion agreed with a portion of both Blackmun's and Rehnquist's views. "Yes," he said, "Rehnquist's opinion overrules *Roe*, and yes, that is what we're all doing and it's about time." Yet if the chief justice thought he finally had the majority to overrule *Roe*, he was premature. Not only did Stevens join the pro-abortion forces, O'Connor, too, refused to sign Rehnquist's *Webster* opinion.

The *Webster* holding dramatically shifted the standard of review in abortion cases, moving from the much more demanding requirement that the legislature establish a "compelling state interest" to a far less difficult requirement that any regulation not place an "undue burden" on the person seeking the abortion. The Rehnquist plurality opinion, announcing the judgment of the Court but not the Court's majority, was vintage Rehnquist. It reargued *Griswold* and *Roe*, said privacy and abortion were not in the Constitution, and held that *Roe*'s "web of rules" were fallacious.

In framing his *Webster* opinion, Rehnquist had tried to sway O'Connor with an opinion that quoted from her earlier writings. Rehnquist rejected the *Roe* test, which said that the states' interest in protecting the fetus increased as the potential life increased. His plurality said that the states' interest in protecting the fetus was the same throughout the pregnancy. Had O'Connor joined him, Rehnquist could have cleared the way for broad state regulation of abortion, even though the basic right to choose abortion would have survived. But, to his surprise, O'Connor instead wrote a separate, narrow opinion that permitted Missouri to halt abortions in its public hospitals—but no more. She refused to tamper with the *Roe* decision at all, asserting that a "fundamental rule of judicial restraint" requires us to avoid reconsidering it. Abortion cases such as this, as well as affirmative action cases, show O'Connor's important role in the formation and division of majorities. Rehnquist was left with a majority to rule for Missouri but no majority to cut back on *Roe*.

Pro-choice groups nonetheless saw in *Webster* the beginning of the end of *Roe*. Blackmun advised Rehnquist he would read part of his dissent in open court after the chief justice read the majority opinion. Tormented and angry, soft but firm, Blackmun told those attending the Court that "today a bare majority of the Court disserves the people of this nation and especially the millions of women who have lived and come of age in the sixteen years since *Roe*. I rue this day. I rue the violence that has been done to our legal fabric and to the integrity of this Court. . . . For today, the women of this nation still retain the right to control their destinies. But the signs are evident and ominous and a chill wind blows."

Webster can be seen as the Supreme Court's invitation to states to pass restrictive laws that would end abortion without saying so. It would set the stage. All sides waited for the next big case, several of which were already in the lower courts. As they did, Justice William Brennan stepped down and was replaced by David Souter. His arrival coincided with a case that would give everybody their first look at the new justice, in the abortion area the one who John Sununu had promised the elder Bush would be "a home run." The case was *Rust v. Sullivan* (1991).

The background to the *Rust* case was as follows. Congress had originally passed a 1970 law providing federal funds to support family planning services for low-income women, a population that faced disproportionately high rates of teenage pregnancy, infant mortality, and impaired health. But the law also said that funds would not go where abortion was part of family planning, and later regulations banned federal funds to clinics that provided abortions. Then came a directive by George Bush's Secretary of Health and Human Services, Dr. Lewis W. Sullivan, that went further. It had a gag rule that said that clinics receiving federal funds could not even counsel pregnant women about the availability of abortions; that if they referred their patients elsewhere, they could not mention it; and that if a patient asked about abortion specifically, they were to say words to the effect of, "We do not consider abortion an appropriate method of family planning." Notwithstanding *Roe*, Dr. Sullivan said the new restrictions reflected changed attitudes toward the "elimination of unborn children by abortion." The monies at stake were substantial. In New York alone, $6 million was distributed to thirty-seven agencies and hospitals. Dr. Irving Rust, the director of a Bronx Planned Parenthood clinic that received from the government $439,391, half of its family planning budget, saw the issue as one of free speech. He became the plaintiff in a federal suit to declare that directive violative of the physicians' free speech right fully to advise his patient, and thus unconstitutional.

The case was heard in the Supreme Court on October 30, 1990. A large part of the argument was whether or not the gag rule violated the First Amendment rights of doctors to talk, and patients to hear full medical advice. During oral arguments, it became clear that a decision could be rendered that would leave *Roe* untouched. Souter was the swing vote, and the lawyers now made him the focus of attention. Dr. Rust's lawyers, in addition to arguing that the First Amendment was violated and that the physician-patient privilege was invaded by dictating what a doctor must or must not tell his patient, also claimed that the patient's rights, as enumerated in *Roe*, were interfered with. After the argument, Dr. Rust and his lawyers believed Souter was on their side and, given the free speech argument, believed they might also carry another justice. They were mistaken.

In yet another bitterly contested 5–4 decision, the Court held for Dr. Sullivan and against Dr. Rust. But *Roe* still stood. Souter was indeed the swing vote, and he cast it with the Right. Finding there had been speech violations, the majority said the government could impose the Bush restrictions to make sure that the planning clinics did what they wanted. Chief Justice Rehnquist said that the clinics were not required to take federal monies and that had they operated only out of private funds, they could do what they wanted. But if they wanted federal monies, they must also take it with whatever strings were attached.

Rehnquist again wrote the majority opinion, asserting that speech was not stopped merely because of what was excluded in the counseling advice. He said the government has a right to fund one activity (family planning excluding abortion considerations and seeking alterations) and not another (family planning with pro-abortion counseling), and he suggested that the women denied advice were no worse off than if Congress had never set up the grant system. The woman's poverty blocked her ability to get an abortion, not the gag rules.

His argument was disingenuous. The speech being stopped was clearly aimed at limiting speech about abortion. In a dissent better grounded in legal principles and the reality of women's lives, *Roe*'s author, Harry Blackmun, countered that because many poor pregnant women receive their only information about their pregnancies from federally funded clinics, restricting those clinics from providing information was tantamount to ending their ability to have abortions. He concluded that, while technically leaving intact the fundamental right protected by *Roe*, the Court "through a relentlessly formalistic catechism once again has [in fact destroyed the right to abortion] . . . for if a right is found to be unenforceable, even against a flagrant attempt by government to circumvent it, then it ceases to be a right at all." Women today still die of illegal abortions, and *Rust* is in part responsible. O'Connor voted with the moderates, infuriating Scalia. Souter's joining in the majority created fear in the pro-choice movement. Was it a predictor of his future abortion voting?

Now, with *Webster* and *Rust* decided, and with the newly installed Clarence Thomas filling the seat vacated by Thurgood Marshall, abortion opponents saw the case they were awaiting appear in the form of *Planned Parenthood of Southeastern Pennsylvania v. Robert P. Casey* (1992), a Pennsylvania official. The Pennsylvania law was supposedly "justified" by *Webster*—it aimed to eliminate abortion by imposing time-consuming and potentially embarrassing regulations that would force women to take their pregnancies to term. Under *Casey*, a woman had to wait twenty-four hours after a doctor provided her with information about the abortion procedure and gave her alternatives; minors had to obtain the consent of one parent; and married women had to tell their husbands if they intended to abort. Failure to do so could result in jail time. At this point, there was no longer any way to avoid confronting *Roe* head-on. The Pennsylvania restrictions were too harsh and too clear; it would be pure hypocrisy to say both *Roe* and the guts of the Pennsylvania statute survived.

Kathryn Kolbert, arguing for Planned Parenthood against the Pennsylvania law, believed that at best she could salvage a 5–4 decision upholding *Roe*. Rehnquist, Thomas, Scalia, and White seemed totally predictable. Only Blackmun of the original *Roe* majority was still on the Court, and although Stevens would no doubt now join him, Souter's swing vote in the *Rust* decision made him problematic. All the anti-abortion forces had to do was to get one vote out of Kennedy, O'Connor, and Souter. Kolbert had to get all three Republican appointees.

She began by trying to answer the argument previously expressed by Rehnquist and Scalia, that "traditional concerns" surrounding the sanctity of family and marriage require the practice of abortion to be ended, by forcefully arguing the Court must look generally to whether a right is reflected in our nation's history and traditions, rather than at whether the activity was illegal at the time of the adoption of the Fourteenth Amendment. She argued that our nation has "respected interests of bodily integrity and autonomy," and there is a "tradition of respect for equality of women." Kolbert further asserted that "those are the central and core values" of the abortion issue.

Justice Scalia would not let her get off that easily. He said the nation's history and tradition were to reject abortion. Kolbert responded that you could not rely exclusively on what fifty states have legislated to determine the scope of liberty, for that approach, she argued, would imperil numerous freedoms. "If we were only to look at whether State legislatures prohibited activity in determining whether or not an activity is fundamental, many of the most precious rights that we now have: rights to travel, rights to vote, rights to be free from racial segregation would not be accorded status because in fact, State legislators have acted to inhibit those rights at the time of the adoption of the Fourteenth Amendment."

Scalia asked her what was the status of abortion when the Constitution was signed. Looking for votes elsewhere, she tried to quickly answer Scalia so she could address the swing justice's concerns, "If the Court was only to look at whether abortion was illegal in 1868, at the time of the adoption of the Fourteenth Amendment, it would be placed in a very difficult situation, because at the time . . . the Constitution was adopted, abortion was legal."

But Justice Scalia would not let her go: "Pick 1968, I gather you wouldn't accept 1968 either though."

Knowing Scalia's factual point was correct, that abortion was illegal in the majority of states in both 1868 and 1968, Kolbert tried to make a larger argument, that more important was the path America wanted to follow today. This country historically and today, she said, accepts "that private autonomous decisions made by women in the privacy of their families ought to be respected and accorded fundamental status."

Now the attorney general for Pennsylvania, Robert Preate, rose to begin his argument. His first words were careless. He said *Roe* permitted abortion on demand. Justice Blackmun jumped to the front of his seat and cut him right off. *Roe* "does not provide for abortion on demand. Have you read *Roe*?" Preate admitted he had. Blackmun said, "Thank you," and then sat back.

Stevens then asked Preate about *Webster*'s "undue burden" test: "Do you think it refers to the number of persons burdened by the law on the one hand or the severity of the burden on a particular individual affected by the law on the other hand? Which is the right analysis?" Preate said it was the number of women affected, not the effect on individual women.

O'Connor asked whether the provision compelling the women to tell her husband of the intended abortion posed First Amendment problems. Preate replied it did not.

Kenneth Starr, then solicitor general, rose and argued that *Roe* should be overruled, that the *Webster* plurality opinion written by Rehnquist ought to become the law of the land. O'Connor rejoined by pointing out that *Roe* said the fetus is not a person under the Fourteenth Amendment. Starr responded that the state had an interest in protecting the fetus.

"But given that *Roe* said otherwise," Stevens asked, "what is the textual basis in the Constitution? What is the textual basis for your position that there's a compelling interest in something that is not a person within the meaning of the Fourteenth Amendment?"

Starr avoided the question, but Stevens repeated himself, "What is the textual basis for it?"

Starr finally answered: "The State has an interest in its potential citizen, it does not have the basis in the Constitution. Justice Stevens, it is my view that the State can look out and say we, historically, regulate and legislate in the interest of those who will come into being, who will be born."

"That's not responsive to my question. My question is what is the textual basis in the Constitution. If you're going to say there is none, fine, that's perfectly all right," Stevens said.

Starr responded: "I think it's in the nature of our system. And if nothing else, the Tenth Amendment, Justice Stevens, suggests that the State can order its relationships in ways that reflect the morality of the people, within limits."

Scalia then jumped in to make his own rhetorical point and to help Starr out: "General Starr, why does there have to be something in the Constitution? There's nothing in the Constitution that requires the State to protect the environment, is there?"

"Of course not," said Starr, giving the answer Scalia wanted.

"And yet that can be a compelling State interest, may it not?" Scalia finished.

Finally, in *Casey*, four justices voted against *Roe*, two justices, Blackmun and Stevens, thought *Roe* rightly decided, and three justices, O'Connor, Kennedy, and Souter, felt *Roe* should be reaffirmed because of precedent—because a failure to do so "would seriously weaken the Court's capacity to exercise the judicial power and to function as the Supreme Court of a Nation dedicated to the rule of law." A troubled Anthony Kennedy told a reporter before the Court announced its *Casey* decision that it was hard for the justices to know "if you're Caesar about to cross the Rubicon or Captain Queeg cutting your tow line."

In an unusual step, the three Republicans appointed to help overrule

Roe, but who had reaffirmed it here, jointly wrote the opinion for the Court. Different sections of the opinion were assigned to each. Reading the opinion, one can see individual paragraphs that are more reflective of one judge rather than another. They were joined, in part, by Justices Blackmun and Stevens.

The *Casey* decision demonstrates the three justices' attempts to make clear that any efforts to overturn *Roe* would divide the nation, pose profound questions about the Court's legitimacy, and make it appear that the justices were merely giving in to political pressures. They wanted to assure the country that they did not vote against abortion merely because they were Republicans, and merely because Republican presidents had appointed them. Kennedy, who frequently writes about the substantial role ideology plays in legal decisions, set forth the standard by which the Court acquires legitimacy. It "depends on making legally principled decisions under circumstances in which their principled character is sufficiently plausible to be accepted by the nation."

Scalia, Thomas, White, and Rehnquist dissented. Rehnquist, attacking his fellow Republicans Souter, O'Connor, and Kennedy who voted to uphold *Roe*, observed they could not bring themselves "to say that *Roe* was correct as an original matter, but the authors are of the view that the immediate question is not the soundness of *Roe*'s resolution of the issue, but the precedential force that must be accorded to its holding." But Rehnquist argued that the Court's own historical logic renders this argument specious: After all, *Plessy* and *Lochner* were overruled—-why not *Roe*? Rehnquist argued that the mere fact that there are political pressures, demonstrations, and conflicts over abortion does not mean we must give in to a wrong decision. He noted that the political pressure that exists in capital punishment cases had not deterred the majority of the Court from resisting it.

Justice Scalia furiously attacked O'Connor, saying that Justice O'Connor's assertion that a "fundamental rule of judicial restraint requires us to avoid reconsidering *Roe*" cannot "be taken seriously." Her *Casey* opinion, relying on precedent to uphold *Roe*, Scalia continued caustically, was "a sort of Judicial Potemkin village." Scalia was still angry that O'Connor had not voted with Kennedy in *Webster*. It was also likely that Scalia's scathing attack on the icy, proud O'Connor's position in *Webster*, and his lecturing of her as if she were a first-year law student, had now pushed her, in *Casey*, more firmly against Scalia's position.

Perhaps Scalia's ire should bave been directed instead toward his colleague Anthony Kennedy. Kennedy had taken the seat Bork did not get. Had Bork been on the Court instead of Kennedy, the decision could easily have gone the other way and might even have been 6–3. O'Connor would most likely have felt the combined power of a Bork, Rehnquist, White, Scalia, and Thomas coalition irresistible, and *Roe* would be a dead letter.

The 1993 *Casey* decision reaffirmed the undue burden test of *Webster*. Because *Roe* was left standing, *Casey* persuaded many that abortion had at least a small window of viability; that there are certain precedents that now are foundations of the law. Overlooked then was the truth that the important restrictions *Casey* kept in place would permit other legislatures to go fishing to find additional restrictions. Perpetuating the right to abortion with so many restrictions, including the lack of funding for low-income women, makes this option far more difficult, if not wholly out of reach, for a large part of the population.

Indeed, *Casey* gave Rehnquist much of what he wanted on *Webster* but could not get: a test for abortion laws that made it harder for courts to overturn state laws. As she began her *Casey* argument, Kathryn Kolbert noted presciently, "The central question in the case is what is the standard that this Court uses to evaluate the restrictions that are at issue." It is, in fact, on that issue—the acceptance of a rational scrutiny test—that abortion and other personal rights will end if the younger Bush gets the Supreme Court justices he wants.

The Supreme Court today has declined to overrule *Roe*, has declined to make abortion a crime, but by continuing not to review circuit court decisions that come very close, and sometimes exceed, the very worst restrictions of *Casey* and *Webster*, it has for many women, primarily young, low-income women living in rural areas, rendered the essence of *Roe* nearly meaningless. There was little need for O'Connor, Kennedy, and Souter to publicly hammer the last nail in the coffin. As Stevens said, these laws abolished *Roe* without saying so, by protecting restrictions that are not vulnerable to legal challenge under *Casey* and *Webster*.

Following the *Casey* "victory," it took seven years before the Supreme Court looked at any lower courts' interpretation of that decision. Countless women were bound by laws upheld by circuit courts, putting more of a burden on them than *Casey* permitted. As the Supreme Court becomes more conservative on abortion issues, and, as the appellate courts become more conservative (the majority of the circuit courts today are hostile to abortion rights), there will be fewer conflicts between circuits that trigger Supreme Court review. If *Roe* is not totally dead, the circuit court appointees of our sitting or future conservative president will do the job for it.

After *Casey*, the Evangelicals focused their attack on so-called partial-birth abortions, a term that had a high emotional impact. In fact, they were attacking the safest medical procedures available, used in first and occasionally second trimester abortions. Grisly pictures and stories of such abortions were sent to members of Congress, which in turn twice tried to pass laws making it a serious crime. President Clinton vetoed those bills, driving the Right to Lifers to lobby the states, many of which adopted these criminal bans. Then, in 1999, Dr. Leroy Carhart sought, in *Stenberg v. Carhart*, to challenge a Nebraska law that made performing partial-birth abortions— defined as "a procedure in which the doctor delivers vaginally, a living unborn child, before intentionally killing the child"—a felony punishable by up to twenty years in prison, a fine of $25,000, and revocation of the doctor's license. In fact, the statute was intentionally vague and could be used to apply to the safest first and second trimester procedures. It put physicians at constant risk of criminal prosecution, thus making abortions less accessible. The lower court and appeals court held the Nebraska law unconstitutional, and Justice Breyer, writing for a five-justice majority, agreed, for the Nebraska law permitted the misnamed partial-birth abortion if the mother's life was at stake.

Donald Stenberg, the named defendant and the attorney general of Nebraska, rose to present his case on April 20, 2000. His first sentence stopped his argument when he loudly declared that partial-birth abortion "borders on infanticide." The moderate members of the Court jumped on that rhetoric, pointing out there are criminal laws for killing infants, and there can be no infanticide until there is an infant. "Have you read *Roe v. Wade?*" Blackmun asked. Stenberg said he had. Justice Scalia jumped in to help Stenberg; permitting the killing of a fetus, he observed, "can coerce public perception to other forms of killing fetuses or children outside the womb, right?" Yes, agreed Mr. Stenberg, that is what he meant.

Stenberg was the first case since *Casey* in the Supreme Court that might define the outer limits of what constitutes an undue burden. Simon Heller, who argued the case for Dr. Carhart, focused his argument on Justices Kennedy and O'Connor. He felt that O'Connor might be disturbed by the details of the abortion procedures while Kennedy might not be; and that O'Connor might be bothered that there was no health exception for the women.

Heller said, "The Nebraska statute seeks to eliminate the central principle of *Roe* and *Casey*. It seeks to reverse the supremacy of women's health over fetal interests throughout pregnancy." He said that if the doctor decides to use a particular procedure that is the safest for the mother, then he should be permitted to do it.

And, indeed, it was on these points that Breyer's opinion focused. He said that *Casey* held that laws "designed to further the state's interest in fetal life" are unconstitutional if they place an undue burden on the woman's decision prior to "fetal viability." *Casey* prohibits laws having the "purpose or effect of placing a substantial obstacle in the path of a woman seeking an abortion of a nonviable fetus," and Breyer concluded that the Nebraska statute is such an obstacle because of its vagueness. He rejected Nebraska's argument that the legislature intended to ban only D & C procedures. In reviewing the medical evidence, Breyer cited the rulings of other federal courts that had reached a similar conclusion.

Stenberg could have been lost and yet *Roe* saved. But it would have been another deep wound. Kennedy, voting in the minority, said that if the procedure was offensive to one's conscience (as this was to his), then it could not be used, even if it were the safest procedure. From there to a state statute that prohibits, on moral grounds, the safest procedure, effectively stopping abortions, is but a short step.

On the same day as *Stenberg*, the Court vacated the seventh circuit court of appeals' ruling in *Hope Clinic v. Ryan*, upholding the Illinois and Wisconsin partial-birth abortion bans, sending the case back to the seventh circuit to be reconsidered in light of the Court's decision in *Stenberg*. Federal courts since have struck down all of the nineteen remaining bans that have been challenged. Bans enacted in eleven states—Georgia, Indiana, Kansas, Mississippi, North Dakota, Ohio, Oklahoma, South Carolina, South Dakota, Tennessee, and Utah—are currently enforceable, but only three

(Utah, Ohio, and Kansas) would likely survive the Court's *Stenberg* ruling since they include a health exception.

But those who thought that *Stenberg* resolved the issue underestimated the relentlessness of the Right. On February 3, 2002, the Justice Department asked a federal appeals court to review an Ohio ban on the procedure. The Ohio law passed the month before the *Stenberg* decision could satisfy O'Connor; she said in *Stenberg* that a narrowly written ban, which allowed the procedure to be done only if it was necessary to preserve the life and health of the woman, could be acceptable. When the federal judge struck down the Ohio procedure, he said the health exception did not ensure that physicians would provide the best procedure. Ohio appealed, and the government jumped in.

It is rare for the Justice Department to intervene in a state abortion dispute in a lower U.S. court rather than wait for a showdown at the Supreme Court. Not since 1992, when the first President Bush was in office, has the White House backed an abortion restriction in court.

President Clinton twice vetoed bills calling for a federal ban on "partial-birth" abortions. The White House's support of Ohio's law could lead other states to write laws matching Ohio's. In the brief it filed with the U.S. Court of Appeals for the Sixth Circuit, the Justice Department justified its intervention because President Bush supports a federal ban. The same week, the Bush administration announced to the twenty-ninth annual Conservative Political Action Conference that it would broaden the definition of a child eligible for coverage under the Children's Health Insurance Program to begin with conception. The crowd erupted in cheers.

Representative Henry A. Waxman, a California Democrat, argued that the administration could have broadened coverage to pregnant women by many other means and that the new rule was not a serious policy effort but "an ideological statement" aimed at pleasing the administration's conservative base. But, it's even more dangerous. There will be new legislation and regulations in different social services areas, passed by the federal and state governments, which establish that the unborn fetus at conception has rights that are different and perhaps superior to the rights of the mother.

Abortion for all hangs on by a slender thread. The Hyde Amendment, which bars federal Medicaid funds from being used for abortion, strikes directly at the poor. The fourth circuit, in *Greenville Women's Clinic v.*

Bryant, in a 2–1 decision in 2001, approved a rigorous bundle of require-ments on clinics, ranging from the extensive and expensive training of clinic workers to the width of clinic doorways. These regulations made it so diffi-cult for doctors, few in the states governed by the circuit court will perform abortions. The fourth circuit, with a 45 percent minority population—one of the poorest in the nation—succeeded with that decision in increasing the number of back alley abortions and deaths. The very conservative court overruled the trial judge who found the procedures irrational and crafted mainly to discourage the procedure. That law stood up when the full fourth circuit affirmed it, and the statute is now a model for new statutes being passed around the country.

Abortion is still a right today only because of O'Connor. The number of reported deaths due to illegal abortions has dropped dramatically since *Roe*. Irrespective of precedent and polls, Rehnquist, Scalia, and Thomas would override *Roe* in a minute. So, too, would any nominees George W. might appoint to the Supreme Court, as well as most of his circuit court nominees. Hence, it would be unusual for *Roe* to have any real life left in it if Bush has one or two High Court appointments. If Stevens and O'Connor step down, the abortion vote switches.

Justice Scalia wants courts and legislatures to set out rules that will make life simple for courts and litigants. He believes that judges merely "find" or "discover" the law and do not ever make it. In a 1990 case, he said, "to hold a governmental act to be unconstitutional is not to announce that we forbid it, but that the Constitution forbids it." Justice White, attacking Scalia, said, "Even though the justice is not naive enough (nor does he think the Framers were naive enough) to be unaware that judges in a real sense make law, he suggests that judges (in an unreal sense, I suppose) should never concede that they do no more than discover it, hence suggesting that there are citizens who are naive enough to believe them."

The contradiction between being a believer in judicial restraint while at the same time arguing for the easy overturning of precedent, Scalia explains by saying, "I do not care how analytically consistent with analogous prece-dents such a holding might be, nor how socially desirable in a judge's view." This refusal to adhere to precedent contradicts what he has previously writ-ten elsewhere and decided in at least one concurring opinion.

While the legislature can be criticized for not producing clear statutes (as we shall see when we examine the new federalism in chapter 5), Scalia's attempted restructuring of our government is not the answer. Scalia's willingness to overrule Congress and treat it like a low-level trial court is based on his belief that congressional laws are more a reflection of lobbyists and politics than of the will of the people. In this, he is joined by O'Connor, the only justice who was a legislator prior to being on the Court. Together, they reject reliance on legislative history and legislative fact finding. Their approach, when reviewing legislation, is solely to interpret the words; since words are open to interpretation, the justices have enormous latitude.

Scalia draws a distinction between "original meaning" and "original intent." He claims to look at the words of the Constitution, not at the intent in the framers' minds. Original meaning, he says, permitted the possibility of an evolving Constitution. An original intentist would say that a provision means today exactly what it meant in 1789; if flogging were permissible then, it would be permissible now. In other words, the "Constitution is not meant to be elastic," and a court of nine judges cannot fill it up with whatever content the current times "seem" to require.

Scalia's argument for being an originalist is elegantly justified—"Our Constitution is a covenant running from the first generation of Americans to us and then to future generations. It is a coherent succession. Each generation must learn anew that the Constitution's written terms embody ideas and aspirations that must survive more ages than one." Drawn to originalism because it mandates a "rock-solid unchanging Constitution," Scalia's is, thus far, a minority voice, however; the Supreme Court does not have four other members who agree with him.

Tradition, as a source of constitutional rights, is favored most by those who see the Constitution as preservative. Rehnquist, Scalia, and Thomas have it as the cornerstone of their constitutional doctrine. In the areas of abortion or gay rights, they look to a cherished and romanticized past to decide moral issues. Scalia seems to reserve his most heated and vitriolic opinions on cases involving sex, abortion, gay rights, and moral issues that he sees as related to family and marriage.

No case demonstrates his values better than that of *Michael H. v. Gerald D.*, whose last names were omitted by the Court to save the parties involved embarrassment. Some cases have great impact; others tell you a great deal about the justices' views of the world and the values used to arrive at their decisions. Michael H.'s case does both. His daughter, Victoria, was born in 1981 out of an affair he had with Carole, who at that time was married to Gerald. Carole separated from Gerald but, after living with Michael, later returned to Gerald. Both men claimed the child as their own, although paternity tests proved her to be Michael's biological child. When Gerald and Carole refused to let Michael see his child, he brought a visitation action.

Michael lost 5–4. The Supreme Court's decision, written by Justice Scalia, makes his moral judgments and sense of tradition clear in the opening sentence. "The facts of this are, we hope, most extraordinary. California law, like nature itself, makes no provision for dual fatherhood." Of course, whether you like it or not, the facts in the case today are not extraordinary, and "dual fatherhood" is not uncommon in divorce cases. And the reference to "nature," evoking both Adam and Eve before their fall and natural law, has little to do with Michael's desire to see a child he fathered and, for a time, lived with.

Although Carole acknowledges Michael is Victoria's father, Scalia says that there can be only one father and that Michael is not it. Therefore, to give him visitation rights is impossible. Justice Scalia starts out by talking about the traditions of the American family and finds that permitting Victoria, who was conceived in adultery, to be visited by her biological father violates his view of what the family is. This leads him to propose that "when the husband or wife contests the legitimacy of their child, the stability of the marriage has already been shaken . . . allowing a claim of illegitimacy to be pressed by the child . . . may well damage an otherwise peaceful union." "Here to provide protection to an adulterous natural father is to deny protection to a marital father." This is an exaggeration that is not true; the stability of the marriage was in question when Victoria was conceived, and then for months afterward. Giving Michael rights does not necessarily give Gerald any fewer "rights."

Scalia argues that Michael and Victoria should lose because of "the historic respect—indeed sanctity would not be too strong a term—traditionally accorded to the relationships that develop within the nuclear family . . . our [decision establishing] that the Constitution protects the sanctity of the family is deeply rooted in the nation's history and traditions."

Justice Brennan's dissent, while referring to the value of tradition, rejected Scalia's reasoning and speaks instead in terms of "liberty," saying that the biological father must have the liberty to see his child. Brennan carefully explained why he would limit (not reject) the use of tradition in interpreting "the Constitution's language." In effect, both Brennan (who admits it) and Scalia (who does not) are giving the Constitution a moral reading and coming up on opposite sides. The Scalia decision made clear that the sanctity of family values prohibited the "adulterous" father from having any rights whatsoever. If "nature" does not accept Victoria's illegitimacy, then certainly the five-justices majority will not. They see this case in clear terms of right and wrong. The majority focus on the wrongdoing "adulterous" father, while the four dissenters focus on Victoria. Scalia's opinion, based on nature's law, blasts the immoral Michael. No feeling for the child is truly expressed.

Scalia's idealized worldview is as unrealistic as it is harsh; as Justice Stevens, writing the dissent said:

> We are not an assimilative, homogeneous society but a facilitative, pluralistic one, in which we must be willing to abide someone else's unfamiliar or even repellent practices because the same tolerant impulse protects our own idiosyncrasies. Even if we can agree, therefore, that family and parenthood are part of the good life, it is absurd to assume that we can agree on the content of those terms and destructive to pretend that we do. In a community such as ours, liberty must include the freedom not to conform. The plurality today squashes this freedom by requiring specific approval from history before protecting anything in the name of liberty.

The psychology and morality of each justice was at play in *Michael H.*, as it is in most cases.

When I argued before the U.S. Supreme Court, I was amazed by the psychological nuances of the process. Because you are arguing in the center of a curved bench, you are and feel physically close to the justices. It can help make the argument more like friendly conversation, an experience facilitated by the fact that the well-prepared advocate knows the position of nine justices, knows which justices are interjecting rhetorical questions to prove you right, and which are trying to prove you wrong. It is also the justices' opportunity to get their best fix on the case, which they each do in a different way. As you argue, you and the members of the Supreme Court become a small group. The justices' faces and questions display their irritation with one another, with the lawyer with whom they disagree, and with those parts of the law they feel are unjustified. Watching the Court over a relatively short period of time, you see the tensions, the idiosyncrasies, the ideologies, and the egos running up against one another.

Seeing the Supreme Court justices in action during argument tells you more about them than their biographies do. Scalia and Souter tend to dominate many arguments, although Ginsburg gets in her share of questions. O'Connor, on the bench, focuses on the facts and tries to avoid the larger philosophical issues. You can see how she thinks—she wants to have the facts totally under control before she has to look at the constitutional issues. When opinions are announced in Court, they are often not pro forma. It is the frustrated moderate dissenters, constantly losing, who most often vent their spleen. Souter, who appears off the bench to be so mild mannered, is anything but that when he reads an angry dissent in open court. Scalia, who is said to be one of the most charming people away from the Court, is not so in Court, when he is dismissive of his Republican brethren. The likelihood of his succeeding Rehnquist as chief justice has faded because of the hostility engendered from the nasty dissents that have become his trademark.

The opinions of the Court are also very personal; each justice has his or her own written style, from which you can learn much about each individual personality. Scalia's acerbic, polemical, caustic style is unique. No other Supreme Court justice writes the way he does. When O'Connor, Stevens, and Kennedy disagree in written opinions, for instance, Scalia calls their reasoning "silly," "nonsense," "incomprehensible." Scalia, in *Webster v. Reproductive Health Services*, had every reason to believe *Roe v. Wade* would be overruled; when it was not, as we saw, his fury at O'Connor, Kennedy, and Stevens jumps off the page. Then, when *Miranda v. Arizona* was not overruled in *Dickerson v. United States*, Scalia went after Rehnquist, who had written for the majority. Justice Scalia always writes with absolute certainty, as if the Constitution and the cases he reads do not permit any other view. He ignores and forgets, as Justice Robert Jackson explained it, that the Supreme Court is not infallible because it is always correct; it is infallible only because it has the final word.

That a justice's genealogy informs his or her politics is clear when we look at Sandra Day O'Connor and Ruth Bader Ginsburg. So much of what these two women do is focused on their roles as pioneers and icons. We tend not to look at them as people first, but, like the men they have succeeded and joined on the Court, they are complex products of their own very different histories.

O'Connor was born March 26, 1930, on an isolated ranch in El Paso, Texas, where the nearest neighbors were twenty-five miles away. Most of her youth was spent in isolation. Her father, a Depression veteran, an arch conservative who hated the politics of FDR and an expansive federal government, passed many of his political beliefs on to his daughter. She learned to drive at seven and could ride horses and shoot proficiently at eight. Though Sandra Day O'Connor graduated third in her class at Stanford in 1952, not one California law firm was ready to hire a woman lawyer. William French Smith, later Reagan's attorney general, agreed to hire her as a secretary. She became a prominent Republican Party activist first in the Goldwater campaign as a precinct captain; later she became a party leader in Arizona. O'Connor became an assistant attorney general, a state senator, and finally a state judge.

Her Arizona legislative record contains some contradictions. She voted against an amendment to legislation that prohibited abortions in state hospitals; voted for legislation that allowed doctors to refuse to perform abortions; and sponsored a state bill to provide comprehensive family planning services. In 1974, she left the legislature to go to the Arizona court but remained politically active.

In February 1981, Justice Potter Stewart told Vice President Bush he would announce his retirement that summer and asked him to keep the decision secret, certainly until very near the end of the term. Attorney General French Smith started to push for O'Connor even before there was a possibility of a vacancy. Ronald Reagan, he knew, supported by Nancy, wanted very much to be the first president to appoint a woman to the Court. The investigation into O'Connor's private life and legal values, including interviews with her friends and people who knew her prior to her nomination, is indicative of the background check that Supreme Court justices undergo. Very little, if any of it, is visible.

Once Stewart's impending retirement became public, a paper drafted by an internal task force led by Roger A. Clegg, a special assistant to the attorney general (and presently, a significant force on the Federalist Society), defining the attributes of a so-called ideal Supreme Court candidate, was used to evaluate candidates. Clegg's report made clear that to be a justice you had to share the politics and passions of the Republican Right.

After a month, three men's and five women's names were floated, nearly all federal circuit court judges, but the focus turned to O'Connor. Warren Burger, who had just taken a trip with state judges, including O'Connor, praised her. A deputy of Kenneth W. Starr, then counselor to the attorney general, was dispatched to Arizona to learn more about O'Connor. He spoke to political and judicial friends, read her cases, and researched her legislative history, particularly as they related to her views on abortion and law and order. Starr was satisfied. He came back with a positive rating. On June 27, Kenneth Starr and an aide flew to Phoenix to interview O'Connor. Two days later she came to Washington, privately, of course, and dined with administration officials. On July 1, 1980, she met with the president; notes taken by a member of the executive branch show O'Connor declaring she "was personally opposed to abortion and she found abortion 'personally abhorrent.'" I don't credit those who say O'Connor deliberately misled him with carefully parsed language. Imperious, willful, and always correct, she would not have stooped to do so.

O'Connor's impressive performance during her one-hour session with the president all but clinched her nomination. Reagan was persuaded by the meeting; he liked what he saw. As a legislator, O'Connor had sponsored a death penalty bill and new laws to increase penalties for drug offenders. As a jurist, she had sentenced a young Scottsdale mother of two children, found guilty of passing $3,500 worth of bad checks, to ten years, rejecting the woman's plea for mercy so she could take care of her children. Reagan's judge-vetting team concluded that she would be a good law-and-order judge, restrictive of defendants' rights and comfortable with punitive sentences; generally they were right. They also concluded her view on race in America suggested that she would oppose preferences and quotas as discrimination against whites.

But the lack of clarity in O'Connor's legislative history, and her persistent refusal to be publicly identified with the anti-abortion movement, led to a revolt by Right to Life groups even before most of the country knew how seriously she was being considered. Reagan, criticized by the Far Right, was forced to react, and on July 6, he asked Smith to make sure of her record. Smith, on Reagan's behalf, spoke to O'Connor twice that day. Starr prepared for Smith a memorandum, which in hindsight looks thinly prepared, but it convinced Smith. The following day, five months after the selection process started, Reagan announced Sandra Day O'Connor's nomination to the U.S. Supreme Court—to decidedly mixed reviews. The National Right to Life Committee called her nomination a "betrayal" because she did not seem to be totally committed to an anti-abortion position. And, indeed, during her confirmation hearing, O'Connor responded to the Congress a bit differently than she supposedly had to Reagan: she is opposed to "abortion as a matter of birth control," she told them. And many women, of course, were appalled that the first woman justice was so uninvolved in any feminist issues.

Once confirmed, O'Connor quickly found her seat on the right side of the aisle. She typically voted in opposition to Justice Rehnquist, her Stanford classmate, about 10 percent of the time (primarily on women's rights, sexual discrimination, First Amendment issues, and affirmative action matters) and opposite the liberal and moderate bloc in over 45 percent of the cases. Although she and Scalia differ sharply on many issues, they share the belief that Congress is the branch of government most likely to be controlled by interest groups and opinion polls, and that the judiciary's role is not to defer to Congress on federalism issues, but to try and roll back their power.

When O'Connor was appointed, she admits she was not prepared for the position of Supreme Court justice. "I didn't know whether I could do the job well enough. This is a hard job. I had not been a federal judge." As a hardworking politician and die-hard Republican, she was rewarded with trial and appellate court judgeships, but she was, at best, an ordinary judge, perhaps mediocre. Yet at the Supreme Court she is acknowledged as one of its hardest-working judges. At her desk at eight, working evenings and Saturdays, she reads all the briefs and she asks her clerks for a summary and a list of issues and questions for each case.

And yet she has sometimes stumbled. O'Connor's political party commitments while on the Supreme Court bench have been inappropriate. Twice she has lent her name for partisan causes, an act no federal, lower, or appellate court judge would be permitted. Both are astonishing lapses of judgment; they confirm her political persuasions are as strong today as ever. It helps persuade that in *Bush v. Gore*, and in so many other cases, her politics run deeper than her commitment to a balanced jurisprudence. First she agreed to meet privately with Republican donors belonging to a political action group called GO-PAC. Each had contributed at least $10,000 for the group's sole aim, giving the Republicans control of Congress. Two years later, she agreed to write a letter supporting a proposed Republican Party resolution declaring this country to be "a Christian nation based on the absolute law of the Bible, not a democracy." She wrote the letter on Court stationery, not personal letterhead, and claimed surprise when she was criticized for it. Stories of her frustration and pro-Bush statements on the night when Gore seemed to have won the election are believable and consistent with her partisanship.

Now, after twenty-one years on the Court, it is understood that where she goes, the majority nearly always goes, and most of the time it goes to the right. But she rarely writes broadly, and, while she contributes to the revisionist tide, she is circumspect by often refusing to join in the broad sweeps of Rehnquist, Scalia, and Thomas. Clearly, the Court would change even more radically if O'Connor stepped down and Bush got the kind of justice he wants—someone in the Thomas and Scalia mold. The Court could take cases it does not hear now. The decisions that would come from the Court could be the broad, sweeping decisions that Scalia favors, not the narrow ones O'Connor crafts.

The second woman appointed to the Supreme Court, Ruth Bader Ginsburg, like her colleague O'Connor, also believes in judicial restraint and in narrowly crafted decisions. Unlike her colleague, she shows her passion, commitment, and activism in cases including women's rights. Because the abortion cases get so much attention, her views on the other 99 percent of the cases that come before the Court get obscured—she is a moderate similar to the Republican appointees Souter and Stevens. When Justice Byron White retired in 1993, court watchers saw that Clinton was making a very safe choice, a candidate who would please everyone except the Far Right.

Born on March 15, 1933, to working-class immigrants in Brooklyn, New York, Ruth Bader attended Cornell University, graduating first in her class. There she met her husband, Martin D. Ginsburg, and two years after her college graduation, she gave birth to her first child. She then went to Harvard University Law School on scholarship from 1956–58. While there, Dean Edwin Griswold asked the women in her class what it felt like to be occupying the places of men, and she reacted sharply against the insulting question.

She, like O'Connor, was a brilliant student. Ginsburg graduated tied for first in her class after transferring to Columbia University Law School. She became the first woman hired with tenure at the Columbia Law School, where she taught until 1980 when President Jimmy Carter nominated her to the U.S. Court of Appeals. She has since remarked on the hostility to women at both of the law schools she attended.

It had been twenty-seven years since a Democratic president had appointed a Supreme Court nominee. Clinton, in describing the reason for her appointment, called Ginsburg the Thurgood Marshall of the women's rights movement, comparing her to the last Democratic appointee. The comparison of Marshall and Ginsburg was both correct and incorrect: both transformed antidiscrimination law by slowly building on the test case method, creating a solid foundation, and then going to more controversial areas. She argued six cases involving women's rights before the Supreme Court. Like Marshall, as a litigator Ginsburg was highly fact-oriented and picked her courts and judges carefully.

But Marshall earned his appointment by fighting for years in the trenches, attacked by judges in the South where so much of his practice was. He faced death threats, abuse, jailings, and contempt proceedings. His liberalism was deep-rooted. Ginsburg's is far less so. Marshall's seat on the Court was, in part, a product of his unique previous experience as general counsel to the NAACP. Ginsburg's was aided in part by a letter campaign orchestrated by her wealthy and well-connected husband, and by widespread personal lobbying to get her on the District of Columbia circuit court, a stepping-stone to the Supreme Court.

Justice Ginsburg diverged from Marshall in both life experience and in his view of race, criminal law, and judicial activism. She and Marshall also had totally different views of the Court's role. She perceived the Warren Court as an activist court, one that saw itself as carrying out the will of the people, of being a major actor in the greatest issues of the day. Her moderate view was that the judiciary should take a backseat to the elected branches of government, that the courts should not run in front of political movements. This, of course, was the position of Rehnquist, Scalia, and Thomas until they got control of the Court.

During her confirmation hearings, Ginsburg's centrist judicial record made it difficult to attack her from either side, and her Supreme Court record has the same effect now. She satisfied Senate Judiciary Republicans that she favored judicial restraint, even in the women's rights field, to which she had devoted a good deal of her professional life. Ginsburg defended her criticism of *Roe v. Wade* under questioning, expanding upon her belief that intense controversy and aggressive anti-abortion movement provoked by *Roe* had weakened the pro-choice movement. Clearly more liberal on abortion matters than Byron White, the justice she replaced (White and Rehnquist were the two dissenters in *Roe*), she was less liberal on racial matters than the other judges being considered in the nomination pool. After two days of hearings, Ruth Bader Ginsburg was seen as the best that Clinton would get through: a judicial-restraint moderate. The Senate Republicans applauded her, and following a confirmation vote of 96–3, Justice Ginsburg was sworn in on August 10, 1993.

The *New York Times*, on July 22, 1993, commenting on the proposed nomination, said that Judge Ginsburg's approach should make her a comfortable fit on the current Court, near the center now inhabited by Justices O'Connor, Souter, and, less consistently, Kennedy. The editorial pointed out her approach to judging as compatible to theirs, and that she refuses to declare the kind of broad sweeping relief that a Marshall or Scalia would do. Except for issues concerning women, she as much as any other member of the Court truly practices judicial restraint.

She has been consistent in this approach. Judge Ginsburg was, in fact, sharply criticized by abortion rights advocates for a New York University speech she gave in the early 1990s when she said the Court had moved too far, too fast in 1973 when it invalidated all the country's abortion laws with its broad ruling in *Roe*, a surprising position for her to take. This ruling, she said, had led to bitterness and divisiveness, by stepping boldly "in front of the judicial process," thereby "exposing the Court's precarious position." In that case, she went on, states could have been given more latitude to resolve the public dispute about abortion by creating their own abortion statutes, testing the Court's limits on how far they could go to restrict abortion.

Ginsburg's view that the Court's continued avoidance of a ruling like *Roe* would avoid controversy is wishful thinking. First, it would have deprived more women of choice for many years; and second, there is no reason to believe the women's movement would have subsided. There had, as well, already been criminal indictments with severe potential penalties for doctors who performed abortions, and the Court would have been forced to face the issues in those cases. Furthermore, there is good reason to question her view that the Courts should avoid controversy, and avoid alienating groups it needs for its cloak of legitimacy. Anti-abortion groups were organized and outspoken before *Roe*. What is true is what Justice Ginsburg said after *Roe*: "Poor women are not much better off than before *Roe*." Laws restricting or making abortion illegal "use public power to force women to bear children."

Justice Ginsburg, somewhat like Justice O'Connor, tends to abstain from most broad historical debates, often resorting to procedural arguments to conclude that constitutional questions should be sent back to the lower courts. And unlike the unapologetically combative Justice Scalia, she is known for emphasizing the importance of cooperation among the justices on the bench. If she ever became chief judge (an unlikely prospect), she would push the Court for more consensus, fewer dissents, and a more unified approach. Perhaps, then, it is no small surprise that Ginsburg said, in a mildly worded criticism of her five colleagues' vote in *Bush v. Gore*, that the justices should have exercised "restraint" in December and stayed out of the Florida vote recount battle. In a post-election address she began by quoting a 1980 speech by William Rehnquist on the obligations of a good judge. "He or she must strive constantly to do what is legally right, all the more so when the result is not the one Congress, the president or the 'home crowd' wants." Yet, Ginsburg said, the legal fight over the Florida recount showed "just how important—and difficult—it is for judges to do what is legally right, no matter what 'the home crowd' wants."

In an article written six years ago, Judge Ginsburg accurately saw that further social change would no longer come from the Court: "The logical progression from the 1970s litigation, it seems to me, is to another arena, not to the courts with their distinctly limited capacity, but to the legislature." She could have said, like other civil rights advocates, that the composition of the Court changed and that the courts were now the place to avoid. It was the change in the composition of courts that saw the Supreme Court, since 1986, render decisions about gay rights that were distinctly different in tone.

It was in this area of the law where one of the Rehnquist Court's earliest decisions became one of the worst in the Supreme Court's history. With Justice White's 1986 stunningly angry and dismissive opinion in *Bowers v.*

Hardwick, the Court refused to strike down a Georgia law that criminalized homosexual sodomy even when done in the privacy of a home. In order to reach this result, Justice White wrongfully rewrote the statute to say something it never intended to say. Although the statute banned sodomy whether homosexual or heterosexual, White interpreted the law to read that it prohibited only homosexual sodomy.

Under Georgia law, sodomy (defined as "any sexual act involving the sex organs of one person in the mouth or anus of another") applied to both heterosexual and homosexual conduct. The case against Michael Hardwick, a gay bartender, began on August 3, 1982, after policeman Keith Torrick burst into Hardwick's home and supposedly inadvertently saw, through a crack in the bedroom door, that Hardwick was having sex with another man. The officer had come to the house to serve a warrant on Hardwick for not paying a $50 fine for drinking in public. Torrick said he was "shocked" and "grossed out." Hardwick was charged with sodomy, a felony that carried a prison sentence of up to twenty years. But although the district attorney's office filed charges, it did not prosecute. Hardwick, who could not get the charges dismissed, then brought an action challenging the constitutionality of the law, claiming the Georgia law violated his right of privacy as articulated in *Griswold v. Connecticut*. The lower court judge dismissed Hardwick's case. Hardwick was very lucky in his draw of an appeal judge: Judge Frank Johnson of Alabama. Difficult personal rights cases always seemed to come before Judge Johnson, and many of the landmark decisions of the civil rights movement were his.

Johnson, ruling in Hardwick's favor, said, "The Georgia sodomy statute infringes upon the fundamental constitutional rights of Michael Hardwick." Pointing to "buried bones" (earlier obscure references by justices who are anticipating future issues to come before it) written by Justice Brennan, Johnson warned that the Supreme Court had not ruled that sodomy laws were not constitutional.

In framing his argument, Harvard professor Laurence Tribe, Hardwick's lawyer, relied on the 1969 *Stanley v. Georgia* case that said, "If the First Amendment means anything, it means that a State has no business telling a man, sitting alone in his house, what books he may read or what films he may watch." Hardwick claimed that sodomy could not be made criminal. The only reason for the distinction and his arrest, he suggested, was the belief of a majority of the Georgia electorate that believed homosexual sodomy is immoral and unacceptable, and that this was an inadequate basis for the law.

The justices' positions were clear from the start. Burger, White, O'Connor, and Rehnquist would vote against Hardwick. Brennan, Blackmun, Marshall, and Stevens would vote for him. The key to the Supreme Court decision was Powell. As one of Hardwick's lawyers said, the Hardwick briefs and argument were a "love song" to Powell.

Rehnquist asked Tribe, who argued that sodomy in the privacy of the home could not constitute a crime, if he also thought incest and polygamy, in the privacy of the home, should be made legal. Tribe said these laws were very different. Rehnquist battered Tribe with questions: Why, for example, shouldn't the Court let society's supposed evolution in sexual matters be expressed by legislative "majority rule"?

Justice Marshall jumped in to protect Tribe and, through a rhetorical question, made clear his view was that the *Stanley* case, relied on by Tribe, decided 9–0 by the Supreme Court, which established a man's right to privacy in his own home, must be followed and required that Hardwick should win. *Stanley* had, in fact, been the unquestioned law for sixteen years—everyone agreed. Marshall said that the state cannot restrict activity that affects no one other than two consenting adults. While twenty-four states and the District of Columbia had made sodomy between consenting adults criminal, Tribe said the fact that a majority of society finds sodomy immoral or criminal does not stop the Constitution from protecting the consenting individuals' privacy rights.

On rebuttal, Georgia's lawyer declared, "The Constitution must remain a charter of tolerance for individual liberty. We have no quarrel with that. But it must not become an instrument for change in the social order."

On April 2, 1986, at the first Court conference after the argument, Powell, the acknowledged swing vote, declared he would vote for Hardwick, making it 5–4 in favor of finding the law unconstitutional. Burger wrote him a note after the conference openly lobbying for Powell's vote. This letter is remarkable. Justice Burger, so passionate about the issue, wrote that the *Bowers* case "presents for me the most far reaching issue" of his thirty years on the bench. The letter continues,

I have never heard of any responsible member . . . of the A.P.A. [American Psychiatric Association] who recognized homosexuality as an "addiction" in the sense of drug addiction. It is simply without any basis in medicine, science or common sense. In fact these homosexuals themselves proclaim this is a matter of sexual "preference." Moreover, even if homosexuality is somehow conditioned, the decision to commit an act of sodomy is a choice, pure and simple—maybe not so pure!

The Fourteenth Amendment argument goes too far because there is no limiting principle that would allow the states to criminalize incest, prostitution or any other "consensual" sexual activity. Moreover, it would forbid the states from adopting any sort of policy that would exclude homosexuals from classrooms or state-sponsored boys' clubs and Boy Scout adult leadership. . . . The record simply does not remotely support a conclusion that sodomy is compulsive. . . . Are those with an "orientation" towards rape to be let off merely because they allege that the act of rape is "irresistible" to them? Are we to excuse every "Jack the Ripper"?

Hardwick merely wishes to seek his own form of sexual gratification. Undoubtedly there are also those in society who wish to seek gratification through incest, drug use, gambling, exhibitionism, prostitution, rape and what not. . . . As Justice [Oliver Wendell] Holmes put it, "pretty much all law consists in forbidding men to do something that they want to do." . . .

Shortly after getting the letter from Burger, Powell contacted his colleagues and told them the Burger letter was nonsense and would have no effect on the vote. But he later told his fellow justices that he had changed his mind on the law and was now voting to reverse, and to hold the statute constitutional.

Justice White wrote the majority opinion. Twenty-one years earlier, in *Griswold,* the Court had relied on "deeply rooted tradition" in finding a right of privacy. Here he found that "tradition"—the long statutory making sodomy a criminal offense—permitted this invasion of privacy. White did not treat homosexuals the way the Court had treated blacks and women, as a specially protected "suspect" class under the Constitution, entitled to a high level of protection. "[To] claim that the right to engage in such conduct," wrote White, "is 'deeply rooted in this nation's history and tradition' or 'implicit in the concept of ordered liberty' is, at best, facetious."

Blackmun, who would have written the majority opinion if Powell joined the liberal group, was deeply offended by White's opinion. Blackmun said Michael Hardwick had "the right to be left alone." "This case," said Blackmun, "is about the most comprehensive of rights and the right most valued by civilized men, the right of privacy in one's bedroom. . . . The Court's crafted reading of the issue before it makes for a short opinion but it does little to make for a persuasive one."

Blackmun saw that a homosexual was arrested although that law applies to heterosexuals as well. He attacked White's decision for its "almost obsessive focus on homosexual activity."

Blackmun said,

> The fact that a majority in a State has traditionally viewed a particular practice as immoral should not be a sufficient reason for upholding this law. Miscegenation had previously been struck down by the Court although it had a long history of legal enforcement. Second, individual decisions by married persons, concerning the intimacies of their physical relationship, are a form of liberty protected by the Due Process Clause of the Fourteenth Amendment. Although the meaning of the principle that all men are created equal is not always clear, it surely must mean that every free citizen has the same interest in liberty that the members of the majority share. From the standpoint of the individual, the homosexual and the heterosexual have the same interest in deciding how he will live his own life.

Yet four years later, Justice Powell, the critical swing vote that gave the conservatives the majority they needed, told New York University law students he "probably made a mistake" in ultimately voting the way he did. But Powell tried to minimize his error by telling his audience that *Bowers* was "a frivolous case." Powell's naïveté or innocence had surfaced during the Court's discussion of *Bowers*. He said he did not think he had ever seen a homosexual even though some of his clerks were openly gay. His clerks were astonished at his failing or refusing to see what was obvious to those around him. Little did he understand how it did, and continues to, resonate deeply with those concerned both with sexual rights and the rights of privacy; as Thomas Stoddard, executive director of the LAMBDA Legal Defense and Education Fund, put it, "For the gay rights movement, this is our Dred Scott decision."

Then, in 1996, the next major case involving homosexual rights came before the Court. In the interim, six justices had retired. Scalia, Kennedy, Souter, Thomas, Ginsburg, and Breyer took their places. Only Rehnquist,

Stevens, and O'Connor were the *Bowers* holdovers. Breyer, the most recent appointee, had, as a clerk for Justice Arthur Goldberg, drafted Goldberg's concurring decision in the 1965 *Griswold* case.

The new case, *Romer v. Evans* (1996), took place in Colorado. Boulder, Aspen, and parts of Denver had been home to the counterculture in the 1960s, and by the mid-1980s had long accepted the gay community. But other parts of Colorado did not. Allegedly espousing traditional sexual values, Evangelists and right-wing groups successfully sponsored a statewide referendum that would stop the state from extending to gays the benefit of antidiscrimination laws in the workplace, housing, education, and health and welfare services. The Right was counting on Colorado voters' belief that blacks and women could not be discriminated against, but homosexuals could.

The referendum was bitterly fought. Vast sums of money from the Evangelical Right poured into the campaign. An umbrella group, Colorado for Family Values, attempted to link homosexuals to child molestation, and put out eight hundred thousand copies of an eight-page tabloid charging that homosexual extremists wanted to legalize pedophilia, promote homosexuality in gay schools, and abolish the traditional family. But the coalition's most successful tactic was to portray the gay community as not being entitled to "special rights" that are not available to the general public by their being allowed to sue under antidiscrimination laws. In the end, 53 percent of Colorado's voters agreed; outside the state, outrage over the amendment's passage translated into a boycott that cost Colorado $40 million in convention business and tourism.

Richard Evans, a gay activist, joined by other individuals and a coalition of activist groups, sued the state governor and challenged the amendment, claiming it denied gays rights equal to other minority groups and therefore violated the Equal Protection Clause of the Fourteenth Amendment. The Colorado state court found the amendment unconstitutional and ridiculed the notion that married heterosexuals would choose to become homosexual if discrimination against homosexuals was prohibited.

Romer v. Evans was the first case argued before the Supreme Court on October 10, 1995. Once again, four moderates could be expected to vote against the referendum and three conservatives to vote for it. Evans's lawyer focused on the two swing votes, Kennedy and O'Connor.

As soon as Timothy Tymkovich, Colorado's lawyer, began his argument, Kennedy interrupted. "I've never seen a law like this. Is there any precedent that you can cite to the Court where we've upheld a law such as this? Here the classification is adopted to fence out from protection a class." As Colorado's lawyer was vainly arguing with Kennedy, O'Connor interrupted and said it seemed to her that the amendment stripped homosexuals of all legal protections. "The literal language would indicate, for example, that a public library could refuse to allow books to be borrowed by homosexuals and there would be no relief from that apparently."

The line of hostile questions continued. Then it was Evans's lawyer's turn to be drilled by Scalia. "Are you asking us to overrule *Bowers v. Hardwick*?" he asked. When the lawyer answered no, Scalia continued, "Well [in *Bowers*] we said that you could make homosexual conduct criminal. Why can't we take a step short of that and say 'we're not going to make it criminal, but on the other hand, we certainly don't want to encourage it.' And therefore, we will neither have a state law giving it special protection, nor will we allow any municipalities to give it special protection. It seems to me the legitimacy of the one follows from the legitimacy of the other."

At the first conference after the argument O'Connor initially said she wasn't sure how she would vote. Kennedy was sure he would vote for Evans. Stevens, because he was senior justice on the liberal side, had the right to assign the opinion and asked Kennedy to do it. Stevens believed if Kennedy wrote the decision this would keep O'Connor and might make it a very legitimate 6–3 decision rather than a 5–4 vote that carried less weight. He was right. On May 20, 1996, the Court struck down the amendment. O'Connor and Kennedy abandoned Thomas, Rehnquist, and Scalia.

The majority avoided their differences in *Bowers* by not mentioning it. It was like not seeing the white elephant in the corner of the room. What is clear from the records and decision is that O'Connor was not prepared to join Kennedy if he had tried to overrule or distinguish *Bowers* and make it less a precedent. O'Connor chose instead to silently join *Romer*, knowing it would make her face the wrath of Scalia, who would accuse her of inconsistency. She also knew in 1996 that Justice Powell, the swing vote in *Bowers*, later said he had made a mistake. Her resolve in *Romer* notwithstanding, had Bork been on the bench instead of Kennedy, the decision, like *Casey*, could have gone 5–4 the other way. Court clerks at the time confirm her indecision and wavering. The Court's decisions often ride on the justices' most uncertain convictions.

Kennedy was given the majority opinion to write. The majority justices had agreed to have only one written opinion in order to present a unified view and to mask their differences over *Bowers*. Kennedy opened his decision defending the individual rights of homosexuals by referring to an opinion that made clear how despicable it was to treat minorities unfairly. He harked back to Justice Harlan's famous 1896 *Plessy v. Ferguson* dissent, which said, "The constitution neither knows nor tolerates classes among citizens." The Colorado amendment not only stripped away from gays legal protections the rest of the population had, Kennedy said, it also declared that gays were unequal to everyone else while the Constitution required they be treated equally.

Commentators who say that *Bowers* and *Romer* are directly contradictory are wrong. A criminal law against homosexuals, upheld in *Bowers*, was not legally inconsistent with *Romer's* striking down of a civil law that disfavors them. But the tone of the *Romer* decision was totally different. The *Bowers* majority was furious and hostile to gays; the *Romer* decision the exact opposite. *Bowers* was not mentioned even though the language that forms the legal rationale of the two cases is very different. In *Bowers*, White implies gays are outlaws who can be singled out and criminally punished for their sexuality. In *Romer*, they are equal. Its refusal to use *Romer* to reject *Bowers* is unfortunate because it stands awaiting expansion by a more rightist Court.

In 2001, the Court heard its most recent gay rights case in *Boy Scouts of America v. Dale*, which decided whether the Boy Scouts can keep out homosexuals.

James Dale had wanted to be a Boy Scout since he was five. He first joined the Cub Scouts, then the Indian Guides, and by eleven, he was a full-fledged Boy Scout who would go on to earn twenty-seven merit badges. At eighteen, and now a Rutgers freshman, he became assistant scoutmaster of his old troop. Then on August 5, 1990, after the Scouts learned he was gay, Dale received a letter from a Scout official. His membership was revoked because the "standards of leadership established by the Boy Scouts of America . . . specifically forbid membership to homosexuals." Shocked, Dale sought a lawyer. Even so, since neither federal nor state laws prohibited antigay discrimination, Dale appeared to be without a remedy. But the following year, New Jersey amended the state's public accommodation law to prohibit discrimination based on "affectional or sexual orientation."

New Jersey superior court judge Patrick J. McCann ruled against Dale, branding him an "active sodomist" and added that the Bible considered this to be a "gravely serious moral wrong." (New Jersey had repealed its sodomy act fifteen years before.) In the New Jersey Supreme Court's earlier decision in this case, the Boy Scouts were defined as a "public accommodation," similar to a hotel, restaurant, or taxi service, and subject to the New Jersey Law Against Discrimination. Therefore, as southern restaurants could not refuse to serve an African American, the Scouts could not refuse to accept Dale as an assistant scoutmaster.

The law moves slowly. Ten years after Dale received the letter revoking his Scout membership, the New Jersey Supreme Court reversed the trial court and declared, in a unanimous ruling, that the Boy Scouts had acted wrongfully. The Boy Scouts appealed to the U.S. Supreme Court, which decided to accept the case. Dale was optimistic. *Romer*, he felt, has begun to treat homosexuals as equals under the law. But the press seized on concerns of pedophilia and child molestation that were triggered by the thought of a homosexual Scout leader around young boys.

On April 26, 2000, the argument began. George Davidson, lawyer for the Boy Scouts, observed, "This case is about the freedom of a voluntary association to choose its own leaders." Kennedy, who wrote the four-year-old *Romer* opinion, asked if Dale was expelled for trying to persuade other Scouts that being gay was permissible. Souter asked whether Dale would be excluded from a leadership position if he had simply said, "I am a homosexual." O'Connor, following up on Souter's question, asked, "What about the heterosexual Scout leader who openly espouses the view that homosexuality is consistent with Scout law and oath and is not immoral?"

Davidson answered these questions evasively, but in response to Justice Stevens's question "[If] homosexual conduct violates the Scout code . . . why is it relevant whether the man is open or not?" Davidson replied that the Scouts would oust any gay man it knew of.

By the time Dale's lawyer, Evan Wolfson, got up to argue, he believed he would win. After describing the New Jersey law, O'Connor asked whether a decision in their favor meant the Boys Scouts would have to admit girls— Wolfson said no, there was a single-sex loophole, an answer that did not satisfy either Ginsburg or Souter. O'Connor, who had been in both the *Romer* and *Bowers* majorities, let it be known that she did not think a public accommodations law could be applied to an organization like the Boy Scouts, a noncommercial association—not a good signal. Wolfson knew he had to get O'Connor or Kennedy.

Seven weeks after the argument, Dale lost in a 5–4 decision. The six-member *Romer* majority shattered, O'Connor and Kennedy this time joining the reactionary trio and holding that forcing the Boy Scouts to readmit "an avowed homosexual" would violate the Boy Scouts' First Amendment right of association.

Justice Stevens, dissenting along with Ginsburg, Breyer, and Souter, put it bluntly—the justices have decided that homosexuals are so unlike the rest of us that they are denied the Constitution's protection. Charging that the Rehnquist majority stood still while the rest of the country changed, he referred to *New York Times* reports that General Motors, Ford, and Daimler Chrysler were offering domestic partner benefits to autoworkers, that the CIA had celebrated gay pride day, that a prep school had welcomed gay parents as dorm parents, and that the AMA no longer declares homosexuality an illness.

Stevens slammed the majority's view as "astounding," "mind-boggling," and "far fetched." A close reading of New Jersey's law reveals it prohibits discrimination on the basis of sexual *orientation*, but when Dale was expelled from the Boy Scouts, the national organization said it did so because of his sexual orientation, not because of his sexual conduct. Stevens pointed out that "unfavorable opinions about homosexuals have ancient roots. . . . Over the years, however, interaction with real people, rather than mere adherence to traditional ways of thinking about members of unfamiliar classes, [has] modeled those views" and the "still prevalent" prejudices against homosexuals have "caused serious and tangible harm to countless members of the class New Jersey seeks to protect. That harm can only be aggravated by the creation of a constitutional shield for a policy that is itself the product of a habitual way of thinking about strangers."

In his opinion, Chief Justice William Rehnquist, who once compared homosexuality to a contagious disease, acknowledged that "homosexuality has gained greater social acceptance." However, he continued, the Boy Scouts are a private organization possessing a constitutionally protected right of "expressive association." Because of the Scouts' moral code, he ruled that the Scouts' constitutional rights would be violated if they had to grant a leadership role to a homosexual, Rehnquist argues that the gay lifestyle contradicts the values and the message found in the Scout oath and law and the traditions of the ninety-year-old organization. This time Rehnquist points out the value of judicial restraint: "It is not the role of the courts to reject a group's expressed values because they disagree with those values or find them internally inconsistent."

Rehnquist articulated thirty years ago what he saw, and still sees, as his burden. "Sensing . . . that there were excesses in terms of constitutional adjudication . . . that seemed to me hard to justify . . . I felt that at the time I came on the Court, the boat was kind of keeling over in one direction. Interpreting my oath as I saw it, I felt that my job was . . . to kind of lean the other way." When, and if, all his notes and memoranda are released, we shall see he has urged even more extreme views within the Court than have appeared in his public statements or in his opinions. Especially on sex, race, and "states' rights."

Author's Note: *Atkins v. Virginia* (pages 64–65) was decided on June 21, 2002, when the Supreme Court in a 6–3 decision (Thomas, Rehnquist, and Scalia dissenting), citing the "national consensus," banned the death penalty for retarded defendants. Rehnquist's angry dissent said this was jurisprudence by "opinion poll results." Scalia read his dissent in open court, claiming there was no national consensus and that should not be the reason for Atkins's victory. The majority decision did not hold out any hope that the majority would find the death penalty unconstitutional.

5

FEDERALISM AND STATES' RIGHTS

Federalism is not defined in the Constitution. It began long before the Constitution was drawn. The federalism fight is described as a battle between those who want a strong national government and those who want a weak national government and stronger state governments. But, in truth, today federalism is the battle over race, class, religion, money, and power. It is a battle between groups that have different visions of this country and different visions of the Constitution. In the judiciary, the chief player in that battle is the Radical Right. The change in the last twenty years has been the Rehnquist Court's efforts to change the balance in the area of "states' rights." The Court uses seemingly neutral language that expands and protects the individual at the expense of the federal government and diminishes the powers of Congress. In fact, the contest over states' rights has been—and continues to be—anything but dispassionate.

The federalism issue is camouflage for states stepping on people's rights. The language of the debate is eye-glazing. It sounds nonpartisan to expand state power at the expense of federal power but most often it is nothing of the sort. What really happens is that states' power is expanded and individual rights and liberties are cut back. This Court's idea of federalism means seizing rights from the people. Whereas the activist New Deal Court relied on and trusted the legislature—it trusted the people to make the democratic process work—the Rehnquist Court trusts neither the people nor democracy.

For all their patriotic grandstanding, the reactionaries are usurping the rights of the people by arguing that if the state is trying to stop the spread of killings with gun control or trying to stop rapes by giving women a day in court, the federal government cannot enact additional or different legislation to achieve the same ends. But for over two hundred years, the states and federal government each performed both separate and joint functions, though sometimes with a great deal of blurring. The states have their separate areas, their own taxing power and funding of schools and there are areas where there is both federal and state involvement, as in employment laws and discrimination suits. When the Congress decides that there are certain matters that transcend the individual states, where national standards are required for the benefit of all Americans, such as in establishing the same minimum wage and minimum health standards to protect the worker in Alabama and New York, it has the right to do so. The federalist structure is a check on local abuses of government power in matters of race, religion, and on the invasion of personal rights.

The new federalism is politically motivated. The issues that Americans care most about—education, abortion, school prayer, the punishing of criminals, environmental protections—have gone from the Congress to the courts for final adjudication. The political and religious obsessions of the right wing—abortion, homosexuality, pornography, and evolution—are in the courts. Pat Robertson, perhaps one of the most important political figures of the last two decades, tried to force the Republican Party to make the judiciary the Radical Right's private preserve in order to keep him, and the constituencies he led, within the Republican Party. The Republicans were determined to decide those battles in the courts they controlled and to reduce the power of a Congress they often did not control.

Right-wing Republicans see themselves with a clear mandate to shrink the federal government. Newt Gingrich, an architect of the new Republican majority in the 1990s, put it precisely, "We are going to re-think the entire structure of American society and the entire structure of American government. This is a real revolution." President Bill Clinton agreed with Gingrich's concept when he declared "the era of big government is over," thereby rejecting the underlying rationale of the New Deal and its courts. Most of Gingrich's "Contract with America" was passed under the Clinton administration. Most recently, in late December 2000, Justice Anthony Kennedy, sounding the same theme in *Bush v. Gore,* said the Court was reconsidering "our place in the design of the government," in changing the balance between the states and the federal government and the courts and the Constitution, because, he said, the newly placed Court cannot "admit inability to intervene when one or the other level of government has tipped the scales too far." But Gallup polls confirmed that by the 1990s, big government had replaced both big business and labor as the entity feared by most Americans.

Some commentators thought the need for a powerful central government that national crises traditionally provoke—the Civil War, the Depression, and both World Wars—would reverse this Court's weakening of the federal government. But September 11 has not had that effect—the majority of the Court still goes on its way, even though the moderate justices have warned against it.

The changing nature of the government's balance and the Court's role in government will be felt more than ever in the nomination process. As the courts, with their claim to supremacy over the Congress, become more involved in what had been considered to be political matters, the pressure for more political appointments will be felt. Blocking Democratic judicial appointments and rejecting congressional acts has already become as commonplace as bottling up bills in committee. Today's Republican appointees are being blocked by the Democratic-controlled Senate Judiciary Committee. It may be political payback time for the hundreds of installed Clinton nominations, but, at least until the courts are balanced, each time the Senate and the president are of different parties, intense political infighting will become standard.

The Founders of the country relied on what might be called a colonial or revolutionary model of federalism: "revolutionary" because of the way it drew on their experience opposing centralized authority before the American Revolution and under the Articles of Confederation. Forced to explain how states could withstand the superior legal power of the national government created under the Constitution, the Federalists pointed to the realistically superior political power of the states and argued that state governments would have real rather than formal, document-driven power in any disputes with Congress.

The reliance of Rehnquist, Scalia, and Thomas on the Founders' original intent to justify their states' rights arguments makes little sense. When today's conservatives argue with the New Deal by pointing out how much the balance of power has shifted to the federal government, how awesome it is in size, how many new areas it deals with, how much money it has, they are correct in their facts but wrong in their conclusions. Our world is very different, even from the pre–New Deal Court that tried to cut back the federal government. Since 1937, federal expenditures have risen from 3 percent of the gross national product to 21 percent. Regulatory agencies went from fifteen to forty-one, and programs receiving federal grants increased from thirty to more than six hundred. Each year the federal government transfers nearly $30 billion to state and local governments.

The fact is, we have a national economy, whether it be in guns, milk, railroads, airplanes, hotels, or securities markets. To exclude the federal government from areas they have dominated since 1937 ultimately serves negative purposes—the diminution of rights and the diminution of the economic safety net and security expanded under the New Deal. The conservative demand to use eighteenth-century standards to define today's federal balance is best answered by Thomas Jefferson. "We might as well ask a man to wear the coat which fitted him as a boy, as civilized society to remain ever under the regiment of their barbarous ancestors."

The reactionaries use the Eleventh Amendment to elevate the power states have over citizens, by forbidding citizens from suing the states over states' violations of federal law. The Eleventh Amendment provides that "the judicial power of the United States shall not be construed to extend to any suit . . . commenced against one of the States by citizens of another state [or] any foreign state." But the Eleventh Amendment's plain language only prevents a federal court from hearing a suit brought against a state by a citizen of another state or another country. The Rehnquist Court has misinterpreted the amendment's text in other significant ways. Despite the amendment's limitation to "judicial power," the Court has ruled that Congress is also powerless to subject states to lawsuits in federal court. In addition, the Court has ruled that Congress cannot require *state courts* to hear lawsuits challenging a state's compliance with federal law.

The Tenth Amendment has also been resurrected and expanded by this Court and interpreted to be an independent source of judicially enforceable limits on the exercise of congressional power. The amendment states that "the powers not delegated to the United States by the Constitution, nor prohibited by it to the states, are reserved to the States respectively or the people." The plain reading of the amendment does not take away rights from the people and give those rights to state governments. To turn the Tenth Amendment into a states' rights amendment is totally unfounded. Constitutional history does not support it. The federal government is not a government of so limited power.

Courts are necessary to protect individual freedoms—to act as an oversight agency. The Rehnquist Court's breathtakingly new interpretation of the Tenth and Eleventh Amendments to cut back on the Commerce Clause is a constitutional fig leaf meant to obscure their cutbacks on protections aimed at women, racial minorities, the disabled, the aged, and other vulnerable members of our society.

Article I of the Constitution gives the federal government a host of powers, including the power to regulate "commerce . . . among the states." Chief Justice John Marshall, who believed in a more powerful federal government and is thus called a Nationalist, gave the Commerce Clause a wide, expansive reading. The New Deal Court used his rulings to pull the country out of economic depression, as the building blocks for the Social Security legislation, for the National Labor Relations Act, and a host of other federal acts resulting in the creation of the administrative state. But the Tenth and Eleventh Amendments, the Rehnquist majority says, can actively block Congress's exercise of much of the power it got from the Marshall Court, from case law, and from the Constitution. The Congress, until the Rehnquist Court's recent decisions, freely used its commerce power to regulate not only interstate commerce but nearly any interstate activity that affects commerce. Chief Justice John Marshall said in 1824 that Congress's power "may be exercised to its utmost extent, and acknowledges no limitation other than those prescribed by Congress." The broad grant of power contained in the Constitution has allowed Congress to extend its power to protect citizens, for example the power to set minimum wage and health standards law. It is through the Commerce Clause that Congress and the courts have created this very powerful national government.

Today the courts use the Tenth and Eleventh Amendments to cut back severely on the people's (Congress's) power, and to create a wall of protection around the states and create a new constitutional order. The clash between the expansion of the Commerce Clause, traditionally used as a vehicle to protect and expand federal rights, and the use of the Tenth and Eleventh Amendments to substantially limit that, has now become one of the great constitutional debates of our time. It is a debate that is today being won conclusively by the Court's conservative majority.

The Court's majority perception is that the endless expansion of the Commerce Clause of the Constitution during the New Deal, Warren, and early Burger Court days has allowed the federal government to extend its power too far, and now it must be cut back. In the civil rights movement the Congress and the federal government used the Commerce Clause to protect the people against the states, against the governors who wanted to shut schools, and against the business owners who did not want to seat or serve African Americans.

The Supreme Court's debate on the Tenth and Eleventh Amendments often hinges on the distinct and separate views of what happened before and after the Articles of Confederation, and before and after the drafting and ratification of the Constitution. The Founding Fathers' spoken and written words are regularly questioned, argued about, interpreted, analyzed, and parsed by all nine justices as authority for different positions, to decide facts and circumstances in cases of which no one could have conceived two hundred years ago. Gun control, environmental laws, abortion, aid for the disabled and aged, workplace safety and wage standards, obscenity standards, school integration, and racial discrimination—nearly every political area that comes before the Court is the turf where profound states' rights battles are fought.

The majority's definition of federalism is different than the minority's. O'Connor talks of "discerning the proper division of authority between the Federal Government and the states within a dual system of sovereignty." She claims the New Deal Court wrongfully expanded the federal government's power. "The question is not what power the Federal Government ought to have but what powers in fact have been given by the people." The function of federalism, she and her colleagues claim, is to protect local power and to stop the federal government from creating and protecting rights that impinge on states' rights. But according to Justice William Brennan, the function of federalism was "to protect individual freedom" from local or national "repressive governmental action." Today's majority takes such a different tack from Brennan and reads the same documents in such a different way that it is hard to believe it is the same Constitution they are talking about.

The Supreme Court today asks us to trust them to figure out the boundaries of this democracy. Our forefathers, however, recognized that democracy is not a matter of faith but of constitutional guarantees and the structure of government; they emphasized that by creating a strong national government. The states, even before the Constitution was contemplated, feared nationalization could lead to state citizens identifying more with the federal government than with the state governments, thereby allowing the federal government power to tie the union together irrevocably—a result states' rights advocates did not want. It is a fear with a foundation.

Immediately after the Civil War, federalists wanted to give each state citizen the same set of federal rights—a set of rights that would stop individual states from infringing on the rights of state citizens. They hoped this would lead to a stronger federal government, with the citizen owing his primary allegiance not to his state, but to the federal government. Justice John Harlan, at the turn of the twentieth century, expressed the view, in a series of dissents, that whatever would be a violation of the Bill of Rights, if done by the federal government, was equally unlawful under the Due Process Clause of the Fourteenth Amendment, if done by the states. His formulation was that Bill of Rights amendments applied to the states by virtue of their "incorporation" through the Fourteenth Amendment, which was passed in 1868.

In chapter three we showed how the incorporation doctrine expanded individual rights. It is a key part of the federalist theory that leads courts in our day to find that citizens of every state have a right to privacy, a right to have an abortion, a right to competent counsel.

Fights over federalism parts of the incorporation doctrine flared up again during the 1950s and '60s when southern states tried to deny civil rights demonstrators and defendants some of these constitutional protections. The Warren Court extended more and more of the Bill of Rights to state citizens. And now, the politics of the Reagan, George Bush, and George W. Bush eras are resurrecting the anti-incorporation view, an argument long thought dead. They make arguments similar to those that were successful at the end of the nineteenth century; the Framers did not intend to have those federal protections applied through the Bill of Rights, for, if they had, the Constitution would have specifically said it.

There are many reasons to accept the nationalistic view of federalism over the states' rights position when they are in conflict. If separate state governments are allowed to go their own way, citizens may choose to live and work in states where they are best treated by the state government, where they are most comfortable, where their economic and personal needs and interests are similar to their neighbors'. A particular state may not tax the rich; another state may benefit the middle class; another may create a regulation-free, tax-free environment to which businesses will flock. A state may be actively pro desegregation, for the total integration of parochial and private schools, and for the equal use of funds for a dual school system. Some communities may be antigay, or antiwoman, or anti-Catholic. States may erect economic barriers against other states, pass their own economic laws, permit child labor, or deny health and safety regulations. Some may put monies into good school systems, others not; parents may then move to the states with better schools. Very different states will become separate pockets, with separate interests, contrary to the idea of a nationalized government sensitive to the diverse needs of a heterogeneous country. Migrations and competitiveness between states will occur. Originally, Alexander Hamilton feared each state would have its own armies and fight with one another. That vision was proven true in the Civil War and still exists today—only now the combatants are the special interests against the poor, the minorities against the majorities.

The Framers originally placed a high value on giving substantial latitude to the states because they were seen as laboratories in which to experiment with political innovations. It was understood that if these experiments worked out, they could be adopted by other states and perhaps by the federal government. That has not turned out to be true. Innovation rarely comes from the states; what generally comes is the deprivation of individual rights. Potential state tyranny may be more dangerous than the potential of federal tyranny, limited as it is by the Bill of Rights and the Constitution.

The opening shot in attacking Congress's interpretation of the Commerce Clause and sixty years of federalism arose from a small incident involving a high school student arrested on a minor criminal charge in Texas. That case was in many ways just as significant as *Bush v. Gore*, even though it did not settle the question of who was to be the president for the next four years. *Bush v. Gore* was a high-profile affair. *United States v. Lopez* (1995) and the cases that followed, discussed in this chapter, slipped under the radar screen, but in fact they will control much of our life for decades.

Alfonso Lopez Jr., eighteen in 1992, was a senior at Edison High School in San Antonio, Texas. He planned to join the Marines upon graduation. But on March 10, a mother called the school to report that Lopez had a gun. Jean Guzman, the boy's teacher, pulled him out of class, took him to the principal's office, and pulled an unloaded .38-caliber gun and five bullets from his pocket. Lopez told the principal that a friend had asked him to give the gun to another friend who needed it for a "gang war." Lopez said he was paid $40 to deliver the gun.

Two years before this incident, Congress passed the Gun-Free School Zones Act, which made it a federal offense to possess a firearm in a school zone. Congress relied on the authority of the Commerce Clause of the Constitution to justify passage of the legislation as a way of stemming the rising tide of gun-related incidents in public schools. It was on this charge that a federal grand jury indicted Lopez, who had first been charged with the state crime of gun possession before agents from the Federal Bureau of Alcohol, Tobacco and Firearms concluded that he had violated the two-year-old law. At the one-hour federal trial, Lopez's lawyer, John Carter, argued that Congress's law was unconstitutional because it held no hearings on the law when it was passed. Assistant U.S. attorney Pamela A. Mathy responded that the Commerce Clause protected the statute and U.S. district judge H. F. Garcia accepted her argument in a one-sentence decision: "The Gun-Free School Zone Act is a constitutional exercise of Congress' well-defined power to regulate activities in and affecting commerce and the business of elementary, middle and high schools," he said, as it "affect[s] interstate commerce."

Lopez, who never had any criminal record, expected a suspended sentence; he then planned to go on and fulfill his life's dream of becoming a Marine. But the judge, concerned about guns and killings in schools, decided to make him an example; he gave Lopez a six-month jail sentence. Lopez appealed.

It seemed like an easy case. The law was clear and simple. Although the control of street crime was generally in the hands of the states, there was abundant evidence showing that school authorities and states were unable to stop the violence; the school authorities said so themselves. There was also clear evidence showing guns in schools were interfering with the quality of education and substantial evidence showing the relationship between our ability to educate our children and its economic effect. The federal appeal was argued before a three-judge circuit court in the conservative fifth circuit. Judge Will Garwood, a Reagan appointee, and two colleagues found the law unconstitutional. When a panel of the liberal ninth circuit in a similar matter found the Gun-Free School Zones Act constitutional, the Supreme Court, seeing the conflict between two federal appeals courts, took the *Lopez* case.

For the last sixty years, going back to the New Deal, the Supreme Court had accepted that Congress had broad authority to regulate virtually every aspect of American life through the reach of the federal Commerce Clause. That should have been the end of the matter. In addition, the Gun-Free School Zones Act had bipartisan support. Moreover, the bombing of the Alfred P. Murrah Federal Building in Oklahoma City, while it occurred after passage of the Gun-Free School Zones Act, created a political environment where both the Clinton administration and Republican congressional leaders believed that the federal government had to combat individual and group terrorism and restrict the weapons they used.

Although the National Education Association (NEA) joined with the Clinton administration and various antigun groups arguing that school violence could be checked by such a law, the law's opponents, including the National Rifle Association and the conservative Cato Institute, were many and well funded. They insisted that while the goal of reducing school gun violence was laudable, Congress had failed to establish a national link between mere possession and actual gun violence, nor could they make a link between gun possession and interstate commerce. Such regulation, they argued in any case, properly belonged at the state and local level; it was simply beyond the power of Congress to regulate control over public schools. Worse, the conservative groups argued, increasing federal authority over local crimes posed a threat to the states' sovereignty.

The Gun-Free School Zones Act would surely have been upheld by every Supreme Court since 1937. But, at the November 8, 1994, argument, it was clear that this Court was ready to move boldly against it, striking down a bipartisan law that 100 senators, 493 representatives, the president, and 4 Supreme Court Justices thought was appropriate.

Speaking for the administration was the solicitor general, Drew Days III, who began to argue that there was no reason for the Supreme Court to overrule this act of Congress. He was quickly cut off by Justice Rehnquist, who said Congress's regulation of guns near schools had nothing to do with business between the states. When Days responded that the Courts should not become involved in adjudicating this legislation, Rehnquist said the court must, "if we were concerned that the original understandings and structural theories that underlay the Federal system have been so eroded [by this law] that the whole system is in danger."

When Scalia questioned whether legislation similar to this had been upheld, Days explained:

> This Court has operated upon . . . an initial assumption . . . that Congress was given the power under the Constitution to legislate directly upon private individuals, and that there are no built-in limitations on the Constitution. But what we have in this particular act is not that bold assertion by Congress. What we have is, first of all, enough evidence to meet the test that this Court has set that Congress had a rational basis for thinking that gun possession on or near school grounds affected interstate commerce. One was the relationship between violence itself and the economic activity of the country. To the extent that there is violence in certain parts of the country, it makes it difficult for institutions to function. There is the insurance consequence. Where violence occurs, insurance burdens are shared by the entire country, not just by the locale where this particular violence occurs. It interferes in the same way that this Court found in *Heart of Atlanta Motel* with respect to the travel of persons in the face of segregation in places of public accommodations. It interferes with the willingness of people to travel to certain parts of the country.

The case Days referred to, *Heart of Atlanta Motel v. United States* (1964), a landmark civil rights case, affirmed Congress's power to stop discrimination in public places on the grounds that motels, buses, and train stations were parts of interstate commerce. Because he believed it was a precedent that clearly supported his position, Days wanted to bring it to the attention of the moderate members of the Court, and he wanted the conservative members of the Court to confront it. Days understood that if the Commerce Clause argument lost here, the Rehnquist Court could reach back and cut into *Heart of Atlanta Motel*, then narrowly interpreting not only the Civil Rights Act of 1964 but also cases since then that prohibited racial and gender discrimination. Days did not want to see all that precedent undone, and he hoped painting a broader picture might persuade O'Connor and Kennedy. Days did not want to let the Court write a disingenuous opinion that would undercut *Heart of Atlanta Motel* without mentioning it. How could mere possession be the subject of interstate commerce? Rehnquist asked. . . .

"Well, I think, Chief Justice Rehnquist, that it is an easy step from possession to use," Days responded, "and, therefore, the fact that Congress might be concerned with possession doesn't mean that it wasn't concerned about use. And there also is sufficient evidence, he continued,

> in the consideration of even the Gun-Free School Zones Act that there was heightened violence on school property by juveniles, and if one looks at the findings and records with respect to earlier legislation—for example, the Omnibus Crime Control and Safe Streets Act of 1968—Congress makes specific findings between the easy availability of firearms and the level of juvenile and youthful violence and criminality. So that the connection between possession of firearms on or near schoolyards and violence and the regulation of that possession are relationships that Congress has considered in the past, and in our estimation made perfectly good sense under the Gun-Free School Zones Act.

Scalia, O'Connor, and Rehnquist took turns attacking Days. O'Connor asked how the possession of a gun near a school could be considered interstate commerce. Days said the test was not whether Congress correctly decided it was local or interstate commerce, it was whether Congress should be free to make these judgments. At one point, when Days was explaining that Congress had decided the act was required to protect students and that this Court should not interfere with Congress's judgment,

Rehnquist cut him off and not too subtly asked, "Can you tell me, Mr. Days, has there been anything in our recent history where it appears that Congress has not made a considered judgment?" The spectators burst into laughter. When Days said Congress acted rationally, Justice Scalia declared, "Benjamin Franklin said it was so wonderful to be a rational animal, that there is a reason for everything that one does. And if that's the test, it's all over."

John Carter, the attorney for Lopez, had never before argued in the Court or handled a case with significant constitutional issues; he found himself very far from arguing solely about guns or the Gun Control Act. As he spoke, Justice Kennedy cut in to ask rhetorical questions clearly meant to help Carter out. Carter sought to show that the area of gun control in schools was a local problem that the states could deal with. He was concerned that the federal law intruded on the states' laws in controlling states' problems. If the federal law supplanted the states, he made it clear, the law must be struck down. On the other hand, if the law supplemented, or helped the states, it might be appropriate.

Stevens attacked Carter by making a a statement in the form of a question and then asked Carter his view. He suggested that whether or not guns move in interstate commerce, schools' books do, the desks do, and so might the teachers. But people, he observed, "will not move to places where children are killed in schools by guns, and so if in fact the Federal Government can't do something about it, maybe the whole economy will go down the drain in a thousand obvious ways, all right." Stevens pressed on. "So that would be the argument in *Wickard v. Filburn*. If some homegrown wheat affects interstate commerce, which I guess is a borderline question economically, certainly guns in schools do really, not borderline, affect commerce." Carter reiterated that the statute spoke only of possession, and that could only be within a state.

I was present in the Supreme Court that day and with most of the other lawyers in Court saw the significance of Justice Stevens's seemingly obscure reference to wheat and to *Wickard v. Filburn* (1942). Decided in 1942, fifty-two years before *Lopez,* the case took congressional power to legislate under the Commerce Clause close to its outer limits. *Wickard* held that the Commerce Clause empowered Congress to regulate production of wheat grown solely for home consumption. The wheat never left the farmers' land. But it was held to be a commerce issue because home consumption by many farmers "in the aggregate," could affect interstate commerce prices.

The revisionists, in *Lopez,* won with a bitterly divided 5–4 decision, holding that the Gun-Free School Zones Act exceeded the bounds of the federal commerce power. It crossed the line from a principled to an unprincipled decision. As Justice Stephen Breyer argued in dissent, he could not understand why the majority would accept that Congress had the power to regulate the school environment by keeping it free from drugs and alcohol, but not from guns. Both economic and "police" objectives can underlie legislation, said the dissenters, and they charged that the conservatives had substituted their views of the Court for those of elected public officials. Indeed, until this time the Constitution was read by the Supreme Court to give Congress substantial latitude in Commerce Clause and Fourteenth Amendment interpretation.

While the Court's majority recognized that Congress is not as constrained as the Courts are from broadening rights secured by the Fourteenth Amendment, in rejecting Days's argument Rehnquist declared "that Congress's authority under the Commerce Clause" to regulate numerous commercial activities that substantially affect interstate commerce, "is not to be interpreted as broadly as prior courts had." It was a flat rejection of Justice John Marshall and of Justice Jackson's 1942 statement that Congress, if it acted rationally, must be shown deference, and any "restraints on its exercise must proceed from political rather than judicial process."

Justice Clarence Thomas, agreeing with Rehnquist, added a strongly worded concurrence that offered his history of the commerce power, supporting the argument that the New Deal, Warren, and several Burger Court decisions were wrong in saying that the courts had to approve Congress's acts based on the Commerce Clause merely because Congress acted rationally. Justice Kennedy, also concurring with the majority, acknowledged that constitutional interpretation favored the minority's view that decisions on many matters should be left to the political branches and the people but said, "It does not follow, however, that in every instance the Court lacks the authority and responsibility to review Congressional attempts to alter the federal balance."

This was the first time in six decades that the Court had invalidated a congressional statute because it exceeded the scope of the Commerce Clause, or even questioned Congress's judgment as to what affects interstate commerce. In doing so, it began a steady accumulation of self-enforcing and self-perpetuating doctrines. In *Lopez,* and the later cases we will discuss next, the Rehnquist Court ignores the fact that the Court is not a legislature—and that a legislature is not a court of law. They are two totally separate, independent branches of government. Nor is the Court a super legislature, any more than the Founders intended the legislature to be a super judiciary. That distinction today is largely unheeded by the Court's conservatives.

Alfonso Lopez and the events of his case were unknown to the general public. The genesis of the next gun case to come before the Supreme Court was John W. Hinckley Jr.'s attempt to kill Ronald Reagan. At 1:30 P.M. on March 30, 1981, the young gunman stepped forward from a crowd of television reporters and fired six shots from a Rohm R6-14 revolver, striking the president and three other people, including Press Secretary James Brady. All of Hinckley's victims survived, although Brady suffered terrible head wounds and a broken spine. He has been in a wheelchair ever since. Immediately following his hospital release, Brady began lobbying for a gun-control bill. When Hinckley's trial began, his obsession with guns, killing, and stalking people resulted in a jury finding of not guilty by reason of insanity.

Hinckley was the perfect poster boy for gun control. A college dropout and malcontent, he purchased his first gun, a .38 caliber pistol, in 1979, and attempted to kill himself by playing Russian roulette. On antidepressants and tranquilizers, the following year he bought the exploding bullets he used to shoot Reagan. He is well remembered for stalking screen actress Jodie Foster; less vividly recalled are two 1980 incidents involving President Carter. In one, Hinckley attended a Carter campaign appearance but left his gun collection, now numbering three handguns and two rifles, in his hotel room. When Hinckley flew to Nashville during another of Carter's campaign stops, he was arrested when airport security detected handguns in his suitcase. The guns were taken, and Hinckley was fined $62.50. Later, though, he bought two more .22-caliber pistols. On the morning of the assassination attempt, he wrote Foster that he was going to kill President Reagan; a few hours later, he nearly succeeded.

Congress, faced with this close call and a history of gun-generated violence with which the states seemed unable to cope, held extensive hearings, considered the danger, and sought to remedy it. The long, tortured congressional history of the Brady Bill evidenced that Congress recognized the evil early on, but until Clinton's election, it did not have a sympathetic Congress and gun-control president ready to fight the power of NRA lobbyists. On November 24, 1993, after ten years of heated debate and evidence showing the states alone could not contend with the problem because of the enormous interstate commerce traffic in guns, the Brady legislation was passed by a Democratic Congress. The statute, in addition to providing a waiting period of five days to purchase a gun, required local law enforcement to conduct background checks on potential buyers. At the time of the vote, a CNN/USA Today Gallup Poll showed 81 percent of Americans supported gun registration and that 89 percent favored mandatory safety training for handgun purchasers.

As soon as the bill was passed, two sheriffs, Jay Printz of Ravalli County, Montana, and Richard Mack, of Graham County, Arizona, backed by the gun lobby, filed suit in federal court challenging the law on the grounds that the federal government did not have the power to order state officials to help administer a gun-registration law.

The appeals court dismissed the sheriffs' case, *Printz v. United States*, but in 1997 another bitterly divided Supreme Court, aligned exactly as it had been in *United States v. Lopez*, continued the practice of striking down federal laws. The Brady law was unconstitutional, Justice Scalia said, because the federal government did not have the right or power to order state officials to help administer a federal law, for this would break down the separation between the federal and state governments. Scalia based his decision on his "historical understanding and practice, in the structure of the Constitution, and in the jurisprudence of the court." Uncertainty is not part of Scalia's jurisprudence. His argument, never made in two hundred years of constitutional history, was pulled out of thin air; it is described by Professor Kermit Hall, a Supreme Court scholar at North Carolina State University, as "one of the most remarkable assertions by the Court in favor of State authority in the history of the nation." The Court was using states' rights as a smokescreen for the right-wing goal of minimizing gun control.

Justice Thomas's decision was as stunning as Scalia's. Although the issue was not before the Court, the justice volunteered his lengthy historical view of the right to bear arms, covered by the Second Amendment. While saying that a definite understanding of the Second Amendment must wait for another day, he clearly believed every citizen had a right to a gun. Thomas was sending a message to the lower courts. He rejected the argument that only an authorized "militia" could bear arms to protect the state, and he based his decision on the rediscovered Tenth Amendment that limits Congress's power and expands the states' power. Thomas's dicta made the position presentable enough so that within two years, for the first time in our history, a lower federal court found the Second Amendment gave every citizen the right to own a gun, a ruling that was then affirmed by a conservative circuit court. A tenet of conservative jurisprudence is that you do not rule on, or even speak to, issues that are not before the Court. A hallmark of Scalia and Thomas's jurisprudence is that they do exactly that.

The dissenters' arguments were impassioned. Stevens and Souter denounced as wrong the majority's reading of American history and of constitutional documents as establishing dual sovereignty, with the states protected from such federal intervention. They referred to the text of the Constitution and the Federalist papers, in which Alexander Hamilton said that, under the Constitution, state officials could become "auxiliaries" to the federal government, obligated to help carry out law enforcement. This text, the dissent said, very specifically justified the use of state offices to help apply the Brady law. Justice Breyer, in fact, went further, noting that state aid to enforce federal regulation had always been an integral part of the law. He pointed out that the federal government had the option of having federal employees in the states carry out the federal law, and he said doing so would be seen as more of an intervention than using state employees. Yet no case made the argument better than John W. Hinckley. Without the Brady Bill's provisions, there might not be a record of what he had done elsewhere. Only a federal program could have tracked him.

Yes, continued Souter, the Constitution did seek to distinguish between interstate commerce and local commerce. But, as the New Deal Court recognized, the line is often blurred, and inflexible distinctions between what is local and what is national make no sense in modern times. He therefore distinguished three basic principles required to interpret the Commerce Clause: first, that Congress can reach local activities; second, that when deciding if commerce is "affected" (permitting federal legislation), the Court must look at cumulative acts, not single acts; and third, that the judgment of Congress is entitled to the substantial deference the Constitution provides—it should be the people, through the electoral process, and not the courts to determine if Congress has made the wrong political judgments about issues affecting the nation's health, safety, and welfare.

Having none of this, the five-member bloc, in their *Lopez* and *Printz* decisions, beefed up its authority—and its arrogance—by rejecting much of *Gibbons v. Ogden* (1824), a famous and significant landmark in American history. The *Gibbons* case was extraordinary in every way. In it, one of America's greatest lawyers, Daniel Webster, argued before one of America's greatest jurists, John Marshall, on one of the most important legal issues in our democracy. It came in the context of a fight over a steamboat monopoly. Webster's client, Thomas Gibbons, held a federal license to run boats between New Jersey and Manhattan. Robert Fulton, considered the inventor of the steamboat, had a conflicting license issued by New York State over the same waters. How broadly the Commerce Clause in the Constitution should be defined was the question before the Court. In a 6–0 decision written by Marshall, the answer was very, very broadly. Decided a month after it was argued, Marshall held for Webster's client; the federal license prevailed. The federal government, said the Court, was superior in dealing with matters of interstate commerce. Yet Justice Clarence Thomas, over 160 years later, wrote that Marshall had defined it too broadly—too broadly, he in effect says, to stop protecting presidents from future Hinckleys. By reinterpreting the *Gibbons* case, Thomas seeks to undercut its essence.

But John Paul Stevens, in claiming the Brady law was valid, said it was irrelevant whether Scalia could find authority in the documents that preceded the Constitution, that whether or not the gun laws in *Lopez* or *Printz* were appropriate in 1789 is not the question. Congress decided they are necessary now. He quoted Chief Justice John Marshall in the *Gibbons* case: "The power over commerce with foreign nations, and among the several states is vested in Congress as absolute[ly] as it would be in a single government."

Stevens's reasoning, as was John Marshall's, is obvious. If different states created their own rules of commerce, the United States would become like separate sovereignties, each potentially in conflict with another. The right of states to be totally sovereign over their own citizens could reduce the federal government to a meaningless entity. In that case, the federal government could not stop adulterated goods from being sold between states; it could not create national waterways; it could not create a national Social Security system, minimum wage laws, or national environmental regulations. Marshall's voice in 1824 was the voice of a man who had a vision of the future; he, more than anyone, helped create the architecture of the federal government.

In 1997, four years before the World Trade Center tragedy, Stevens was aware of the future consequences of the majority's decision. He said in the *Printz* case that the "threat of an international terrorist may require a national response before federal personnel can be made available to respond. Is there anything [in the Constitution] that forbids the enlistment of state officials to make that response effective?"

The *Lopez* and *Printz* decisions spurred the Court's conservative justices to start attacking Congress's many other attempts to deal with economic and social problems. Even after September 11, the gun lobby and the right wing continue to press their agenda, even though it is against law enforcement interests and is clearly against the interests of the American people. Attorney General Ashcroft, who was a vocal opponent of both the laws attacked in *Lopez* and *Printz* during his tenure as Missouri senator, refused to let the Justice Department turn over to the FBI records showing whether any of the twelve hundred people it detained after September 11 own guns. The FBI–Ashcroft fight became public on December 6, 2001, when, after two months of failed negotiations, the FBI claimed the attorney general was hampering the war against terrorism. Despite the unfavorable media coverage, Ashcroft did not back down, claiming that doing so would violate the privacy rights of gun holders. The High Court has never said gun holders have the right to keep their ownership private—on the contrary, the Justice Department kept such records with the knowledge of gun owners. The *Printz* opinion, precluding federal officials from "commandeering" state officials for gun-control purposes, can severely inhibit our war against terrorism. Congress could help the fight by specifically writing legislation that would give the federal government power to commandeer state agencies. The question is whether the Court would act against this new legislation as it did in Brady. If the no-commandeering rule is truly the future, then the only alternative to fighting domestic terrorism may be to set up a new cumbersome and inflexible enforcement bureaucracy that provides less safety than if the states could work under the federal government.

In 2000, the Rehnquist Court heard a case that asked whether Congress could give women who were the victims of rape the right to sue for damages in the federal courts. The issue presented echoed both *Lopez* and *Printz*; given the fact that the states have criminal rape laws of their own, would the Court conclude jurisdiction is "local," or an area in which the federal government should be involved.

On September 13, 1994, President Clinton signed into law the Women Against Violence Act (WAVA). This act made gender-motivated acts a civil rights violation and gave the victim the advantage of being able to file a damage suit for money damages in the federal courts. Federal laws already existed against sexual assault and harassment in the workplace, but not for crimes committed in the homes and streets. The law won bipartisan, almost unanimous support, in both houses of Congress. It authorized $1.6 billion for law enforcement, rape education, and public safety programs. Twenty-one states supported it, agreeing that federal intervention was necessary because their state's criminal justice systems did not adequately protect women. Indeed, these states welcomed the new law and looked forward to participating with the federal government to help rape victims.

Nine days after the bill's signing, Christy Brzonkala, a Virginia Polytechnic Institute freshman, attended a party at which the alcohol flowed freely. "I probably drank three or four or maybe five beers," she recalled. Back at her dormitory after the party ended, she and a friend heard "guys whistling at us from the third floor." The girls found the whistlers, Antonio Morrison and James Crawford, two freshmen football players. Christy's friend left, but Christy said she wanted to stay a few minutes longer. Though her memory of the details was admittedly vague, she says Morrison first forced her into his bed and the two men, each weighing more than two hundred pounds, raped her three times. Each said they were not using contraceptives. Before he left, Morrison warned, "You better not have any fucking diseases." "I was in shock and blanked out," Christy recalled. When it was over, she returned to her room, sat in the bathtub for hours, and told no one about the incident. Over the next weeks, she withdrew into herself. She stopped going to classes and refused to leave her dorm room. She cut her hair and slept all day. Several months later, in an April phone call to her parents, Christy blurted out the truth. Nine months and one suicide attempt after the attack, she reported the rapes to the university.

She was told not to go to the district attorney, that it would be bad for the school, and that, in any event, the state of Virginia would not prosecute because she had waited so long to tell anyone. The university, Christy was told, would take care of it. She was advised to file charges under the university's Sexual Assault Policy. Following a May 1996 hearing, Morrison, the star linebacker, was suspended for a year; charges against Crawford were dropped. Morrison appealed and lost. Christy thought that was the end of it.

But when school started, the football team needed Morrison. The school's dean contacted Christy, said they had used the wrong policy for the hearing and that another hearing would be held. After the second hearing, school officials decided the Morrison suspension would be "deferred" until after he graduated. The school never told her of the decision; Christy "accidentally" heard it when she learned Morrison was playing again.

In December 1995, Christy Brzonkala filed a lawsuit under the Women Against Violence Act in the Virginia federal court seeking damages from Morrison and Crawford, the two men who raped her, and an injunction stopping Virginia Tech from using its hearing process to prosecute future sexual assault charges. The football players claimed the act was unconstitutional, basing their major argument on the *Lopez* case. The federal appeals court, the conservative fourth circuit, wrote a 224-page opinion that threw out Christy's case.

Morrison was represented by the Center for Individual Rights, a conservative group that had previously fought the University of Texas Law School's affirmative action policy on behalf of white applicants and won. Funded by Washington law firms and the Christian Coalition, the center's motto is: "Better Living through Lawsuits."

Christy's lawyer in the Supreme Court was Julie Goldscheid, who would attempt to show the Women Against Violence Act satisfied the Commerce Clause because there is a logical connection between rape and commerce—if a woman gets raped, she does not go back to work. It was the same logic that sustained the Civil Rights Act—if travelers could not ride a bus or check into a motel because of race discrimination, then this would affect interstate commerce. And Congress here, unlike *Lopez*, had made a voluminous factual record.

The question on Goldscheid's mind on January 11, 2000, as she began her oral argument in *Morrison v. United States*, was whether O'Connor's interest in protecting women would overcome her strong belief in states' rights and her disdain for Congress. Ms. Goldscheid started her argument by summing up the nearly uncontroverted evidence Congress had reviewed when passing the bill. Calling gender-based violence "one of the most persistent barriers to women's full equality and free participation in the economy," she went on to detail the four-year bipartisan study that found it "deters women's travel interstate, restricts women's choice of jobs and ability to perform those jobs, reduces national productivity, and increases medical and other costs." The effect was pervasive and compelling; most dramatic was the evidence Congress heard from the victims of spousal abuse, "whose batterers kept their partners from working, who wouldn't let them leave home if they did work, or who inflicted visible injuries so that [the abuse victims] were afraid to go to work or were physically unable to show up."

After her opening statement, Ms. Goldscheid was attacked by the five judges. Normally the four justices who might agree with her would have come to her aid and thrown some softball questions. But the majority did not stop the attack long enough for the other justices to have a chance. And Goldscheid never again had time to give full answers.

Seth Waxman, representing the United States and prepared to argue on Goldscheid's side that the law was constitutional, was next. He was optimistic when he started but less so when he finished, after Scalia asked if the states that supported the legislation were the worst states in dealing with the problem. Waxman responded that it was not Congress's intention "to deal with the States as bad actors." Congress's finding revealed the federal courts are often not much better. When asked by Scalia if the Congress had any evidence to show that the states were discriminating against women who filed criminal rape charges, Waxman pointed to the states' briefs admitting that discrimination.

It was now Michael Rossman's turn representing Morrison. Rossman argued that the act's intention was to supplant state law and that the federal government has no jurisdiction over crimes occurring within a state. Justice Breyer, after pointing out that there were federal as well as state drug laws, asked Rossman if his "view is that if it turns out that, to use one of the Government's examples, people are in their own houses cooking up biological warfare or it turns out that in their own fireplaces, they pollute the air in a way that will, through global warming, swamp the East Coast—or, you know, use any of their other imaginative examples—Congress is powerless to act?"

Rossman started to answer, but Breyer cut in: "Well, you see my point. My point is that there are many, many, many instances of non-commercial activity, when you collect them all together, that could have overwhelming effects on interstate commerce. And so I want to know if you think in any of those myriads of examples—I won't be too far-fetched—the Congress is powerless to act simply because the cause of the major economic impact is itself not economic?"

Justice Ginsburg asked Rossman if he was challenging Congress's conclusions concerning the impact of rape on the national economy. Rossman said those findings were "broader than the aim of the statute." Ginsburg followed up by asking if there was a distinction between the Women Against Violence Act and the Civil Rights Act: "We have so many parallel legislations in public accommodations, laws, employment and discrimination. We don't say that that's a traditional area for the States just because they got there first, which they did. In both areas there was State legislation before Federal. So, if you can have harmonious legislation for public accommodations, for employment, then why not here?"

Rossman's answer tried to distinguish WAVA from the 1964 Civil Rights law. He did the opposite of what Days did in *Lopez*. "I take it we've moved back to the Commerce Clause, Justice Ginsburg. And I think the answer to your question is because this isn't commerce. The reason that there was harmonious legislation on both the Federal and State level in the examples that you described is that Congress is regulating commerce. This is not commerce. This is violence. This is interpersonal violence, the kind of thing the States have always had the exclusive province of regulating since the start of our country."

One of the differences between the *Morrison* case and the *Lopez* case was that Congress, before it passed the WAVA, did hold at least nine extensive hearings specifically related to the issue over a six-year period of time. The Congress concluded that the testimony before them showed that the incidence of rape rose four times as fast as the total national crime rate over the previous ten years; that 125,000 college women "can expect to be raped during this—or any—year"; that 41 percent of state judges surveyed believe that state juries give sexual assault victims less credibility than other crime victims; that an individual who commits rape "has only about four chances in one hundred of being arrested, prosecuted, and found guilty of any offense in the State Court"; and that almost 50 percent of rape victims "lose their jobs or are forced to quit because of the crime's severity."

Five months later, in May 2000, the Court decided the case. The factual record, the Court majority said, "is not enough to find the statute Constitutional." Rape did not have sufficient economic effects to allow the federal government to step in. Ms. Goldscheid's pre-argument analysis was correct; if she could not get O'Connor's vote, Christy Brzonkala would lose. She did not get O'Connor's vote and lost 5–4.

Chief Justice Rehnquist, who wrote the *Morrison* majority opinion, said the federal government did not justify its interfering in the states' legal process; that the people should look to the states to protect them. It was another instance of this Court's rewriting of American law. The building blocks of the American democracy were not the people, Rehnquist said, but the states, which were the authentic organs of democratic government. Thus, from a practical standpoint, according to Larry Kramer, a constitutional law expert who teaches at New York University Law School, the Court's *Morrison* explanation means that "any possibility of using the Commerce Clause to regulate what the Court defines [as] non-commercial appears doomed."

Justice Souter disagreed strenuously with Rehnquist's conclusions, fearing the Court would use *Morrison* to reverse prior cases. Alarmed, he wrote, "We live in a Nation knit together by two centuries of scientific, technological, commercial, and environmental change. Those changes, taken together, mean that virtually every kind of activity, no matter how local, genuinely can affect commerce, or its conditions, outside the State." Justice Breyer's dissent, joined by Justices Stevens, Souter, and Ginsburg, quoted from essential parts of Congress's voluminous findings:

> Partial estimates show that violent crime against women costs this country at least 3 billion—not million, but billion—dollars a year. . . . Estimates suggest that we spend $5 to $10 billion a year on health care, criminal justice, and other social costs of domestic violence. Three out of four American women will be victims of violent crimes sometime during their life. . . . Violence is the leading cause of injuries to women ages 15 to 44. . . . As many as 50 percent of homeless women and children are fleeing domestic violence. . . . Between 2,000 and 4,000 women die every year from [domestic] abuse. . . . Arrest rates may be as low as 1 for every 100 domestic assaults. . . .

Justice Breyer protested that the majority's casual disregard for Congress had the effect of upsetting the separation of powers established in the Constitution and of making the Court superior to the people's elected body. He stated that the majority, "through its evidentiary demands, its non-deferential review, and its failure to distinguish between judicial and legislative constitutional competencies, improperly invades a power that the Constitution assigns to Congress."

Breyer's remarks in the *Morrison* oral argument turned out to be prescient. He said that if you limited the federal government's power to the extent that it could not stop attacks on women because of existing state laws, how could it stop terrorists from developing biological weapons because states also had laws that made that a crime. Clearly, he said, if the states could not deal with national problems—it was up to the federal government. The federal government's attempt at gun control, rejected in *Printz* and *Lopez*, the attempt in *Morrison* to stop violence against women, and the crisis that flows from September 11, all demand a level of national coordination and expertise that only the federal government possesses. Federal officials, Breyer made clear in his remarks in the *Morrison* case, are better equipped to fight national problems. Through his questions, he urged, at argument, that the Supreme Court's federalism decisions should not be he used to prevent Congress from enlisting state and local officials to fight terrorism.

Congress's capacity to protect women from the injustice of violence and discrimination is a critical element in the defense of civil rights in the United States. The country feels differently about the cause, effect, and present harm of racial discrimination as compared to discrimination against women, and that is perhaps one of the reasons *Morrison* was decided as it was.

Some, not all, are prepared to accept the history and effect of slavery in America. We speak of slavery in the past tense, even as we recognize that the consequences of slavery are enduring, pervasive, and affect much of our present cultural landscape. But there is very little acceptance of the profound effects of centuries of gender discrimination. We rarely refer to the effects on men, women, and children of centuries of gender discrimination; of the exclusion of women by state and federal law from holding political offices, from having certain professions and jobs, from buying or selling property, from retaining their own earnings if they were working, from receiving legal protection if their husbands beat them. This long history of discrimination and often violence left behind deep injuries that courts have only recently begun to deal with. The Women Against Violence Act was

Congress's attempt to rectify some of those past failures by dealing with the future.

When the Supreme Court in *Morrison* had an opportunity to stop private acts of violence against women that do not cross state lines they had, as models, the civil rights laws that gave African Americans that protection. But the civil rights legislation was, according to the conservative members of the Rehnquist majority, forced on the South by the federal government at a time of misperceived crisis. The southern states opposed the passage of civil rights legislation and then opposed the federal government's attempts to enforce the law. Now, with *Morrison*, they could claim a "legitimate" states' rights issue, and indeed, in the decision, Justices Rehnquist, Scalia, and Thomas all chillingly questioned the constitutionality of the Civil Rights Act as previously justified by the Commerce Clause and the Fourteenth Amendment.

But this time the states were the champions of the Women Against Violence Act. Federalism was forced down their throats by the Supreme Court, as Justice Souter was to say. State representatives testified without any substantial opposition and gave statistics to Congress. Twenty-one states said that women did not get equal justice in their state systems and that they needed the federal courts. They recognized their inability to deal effectively with the problem and pledged their cooperation with federal authorities. Not one state opposed the law. The states were not arguing states' rights—only the majority of the Supreme Court was.

Another very recent case concerning Congress's right to legislate under the Commerce Clause was argued before this Supreme Court. The state of Florida wanted to initiate casino gambling but did not want to use Indian lands for it, as mandated by federal law. A look at the money involved explains why this matter, played out in *Seminole Tribe of Florida v. Florida* (1996), became such a rallying point for states' rightists.

Several states in the 1980s rushed to raise revenues by authorizing casino gambling. While gamblers were in large supply, land on which to put the casinos was not—except for the large tracts of unused land that belonged to Native Americans. It was, potentially, a win-win situation for everybody. Native Americans have the highest unemployment rate and the lowest income in the country. The vast reservations have no businesses. In 1988, Congress sought to help Native Americans by giving them access to some of the monies from the casinos. It passed the Indian Gaming Regulatory Act, permitting casinos, requiring states to negotiate with tribes, and allowing the Native Americans to file lawsuits in federal courts when the states refused to consider allowing the Native Americans to have the desperately needed casinos.

The law directed the states and the tribes to negotiate in good faith and to devise "tribal-state compacts" to regulate gambling. As could be anticipated, there were immediate conflicts over who received the gambling monies—the tribes on one side and the state governments and business interests on the other; but in any event, casino gambling in the United States became a gold rush, benefiting both, generating, by 1995, more than $4 billion a year in business, with two hundred tribes operating 126 casinos in twenty-four states.

For the Seminole Indians in Florida, the prospect of casino gambling was lifesaving. The Seminoles live far below the poverty line; their housing is substandard; and alcoholism is rampant. However, Governor Lawton Chiles opposed bringing casino gambling to Indian lands, but allowed that the Seminoles could offer on their reservations less-lucrative gambling such as card games and raffles. He did not want the state to share profits with the Indians—he wanted his casinos built on state-owned lands. When Chiles refused to negotiate with the Seminole tribe over casino gambling, as mandated under the Indian Gaming Act, the tribe took Florida into federal court, charging that the governor had failed to exercise the good faith the new statute required. Governor Chiles said that Congress could not force the states to negotiate with the tribes; that Florida did not consent to be sued and therefore the Eleventh Amendment, which says that a state could not be sued, required the dismissal of the Seminoles' suit. In the Supreme Court, the case became a major dispute over states' rights. But unlike in *Lopez, Printz,* and *Morrison,* thirty-one other states joined Florida in opposing the law. None of them wanted to share gambling revenue with the Native Americans. Florida made the states' rights argument that these matters were purely local.

The Rehnquist Court's 5–4 decision agreed. Congress, the majority said, lacked the authority, under the commerce power, to authorize Native

American tribes to sue states. It was one of the most stunning states' rights victories in jurisprudential history. The Eleventh Amendment, said the five, restricted federal judicial power and in declaring the statute unconstitutional, they overruled a case decided only seven years before in *Pennsylvania v. Union Gas Co.*, relying this time instead on a states' rights case, *Hans v. Louisiana*, decided in 1890. In the *Pennsylvania* case, the state, while excavating a creek, struck a large deposit of coal tar, a hazardous substance that polluted the waters. It was such a disaster that the Environmental Protection Agency designated this area as the nation's first emergency superfund site. The Court held Pennsylvania could be held liable for damages in the federal court; the decision in *Seminole Tribe* is in direct contradiction to the *Pennsylvania* case. Again the doctrine of standards and adherence to precedent was thrown out by this alleged judicial restraintist court. Rehnquist turns the clock back in 1996 by relying on *Hans*, decided at the end of the nineteenth century: "For over a century we have reaffirmed that federal jurisdiction over suits against unconsenting states was not contemplated by reconstitution when establishing the judicial power of the United States." This 112-year-old rejected precedent supposedly justifies the majority's ruling in the *Seminole Tribe* case. The only difference between the 1989 *Pennsylvania* case and the 1996 *Seminole Tribe* case was the change in the Court's composition. Brennan and Marshall were gone when *Seminole Tribe* was decided.

The four moderate justices vehemently disagreed with the Court's resurrecting a legal argument that had been consistently rejected for over one hundred years. Stevens, writing his own dissent said: "This case is about power—the power of the Congress to create a private federal cause of action against a State, or its Governor, for violation of a federal right." He said the majority decision was a "shocking affront to a co-equal branch of our government." Looking toward the future, he predicted that the Rehnquist Court's mission was to strip Congress of the power to let federal courts decide cases involving the environment, the regulation of the economy, and a host of other laws traditionally within their bailiwick.

The Court's decision drew a particularly furious response from the usually mild-mannered Justice David Souter. He took the very unusual step of reading his dissenting opinion aloud to the full Court. Souter, speaking clearly and authoritatively, told a packed courtroom on March 27, 1996, that the Constitution had always intended for the states to be subject to the jurisdiction of the federal courts and that, in this light, the Indian Gaming Act was entirely constitutional. His voice rose when he said, "The court today holds for the first time since the founding of the republic, that Congress has not the authority to subject a state to the jurisdiction of a federal court at the behest of an individual asserting a federal right. Throughout this century, access to the federal courts had historically always been a venue where less powerful groups could assert their rights against a State that was oppressing them. Without it the Civil Rights movement would have had an early death."

The implications of the case, emphasized Souter and Stevens, are indeed revolutionary, and cases since then have confirmed that view. Souter attacked the majority concept of immunity inherent in statehood, expanded state sovereignty, and elimination of the power of the centralized government, noting pointedly that Rehnquist's view of government had been rejected by James Madison and the majority of the fifty-five participants at the Constitutional Convention. Souter argued, futilely though memorably, that the revolutionary Framers believed that if there was a right, there must be a remedy, and the Rehnquist Court by eliminating the remedy—access to the courts—was ending that crucial federal right. His passionate appreciation of the use of federal courts to protect all Americans against powerful interest groups was apparent to everyone in the courtroom.

The elder George Bush, when considering making David Hackett Souter his first Supreme Court appointment in the summer of 1990, could never have predicted that passion or that Souter would become part of the moderate bloc. Nothing in his record, only recently vetted, was there to indicate it. After all, Bush had appointed Souter to the U.S. Court of Appeals for the First Circuit only months before. And Bush was determined to proceed cautiously and certainly not to appoint another man remotely like the one being replaced, William Brennan, a savvy politician who could persuade, lead, and guide a Court down a liberal path. Nor did Bush wish to be drawn into a nomination fight with the Senate; he was determined to be a two-term president, keeping together the coalition that elected him. No divisive Bork hearings for him. Given Souter's personality and his New Hampshire backers, the expectation was that this quiet conservative would fill Bush's job requirements admirably.

Souter was born in Melrose, Massachusetts, on September 17, 1939, the only child of a loan officer at a Concord bank and his wife. Described as churchgoing, bookish, and unathletic, he excelled academically and socially at his high school, which voted him, in 1957, "Most Literary," "Most Sophisticated," and "Most Likely to Succeed." Souter's extraordinary mind (he was once described as "135 pounds, 120 of which is brain") led him to Harvard, where again he distinguished himself. Following graduation, he earned bachelor's and master's degrees in jurisprudence at Oxford as a Rhodes scholar, having decided to become a lawyer after taking Mark De Wolfe Howe's Harvard course, The Role of Law in Anglo-American History. Howe's respect and veneration for the law, which emphasized intellectual integrity, moved the young student. Souter returned in 1963 to Harvard Law School, where he did well.

Quiet and hardworking, Souter began in private practice, then joined the New Hampshire attorney general's office as Warren Rudman's assistant, before becoming the attorney general himself when Rudman left. Souter also served five uneventful years as a trial judge. Then, because of his relationship with Governor John Sununu and now Senator Rudman, he was named in 1983 to New Hampshire's highest court. State Court decisions rarely touch on the issues that appear before the U.S. Supreme Court, so although Souter was a long-time state judge, he had left no paper trail. His first circuit court tenure still brief, Bush relied only on Sununu and Rudman when making Souter's High Court appointment, for no one else knew him. Apparently Souter's conservative flashes satisfied them.

Souter is an intensively private man, and not even his former colleagues had very much to say about him. I suspect, from what I have read, that his friends would be surprised by his words in the *Seminole Tribe* case. The New Hampshire Supreme Court judges who had sat with him respected his legal ability and joked about his frugality. Charles Douglas, a former aide who had become a congressman said of Souter, "When his electric bill got over thirty dollars a month, we all heard about that. Some of us were even shocked that he had electricity."

Doubts about Souter's candidacy were raised, predictably, at both ideological ends. Ann F. Lewis, a contributing editor of *Ms*, wrote on July 25, 1990: "Are Senators prepared to accept an almost blank slate as a record of substance, and will they accept Judge Souter's relative lack of experience as evidence of suitability for the nation's highest court? Or will they use their authority to develop a record on which this nomination can be judged." Judith Lichtman, president of the Women's Legal Defense Fund (WLDF), was unimpressed by Souter's responses before the Senate Judiciary Committee. She told them, "Judge David H. Souter has put the country in an untenable position. He is asking the American people to support his nomination to the Supreme Court without assurances that he will protect our rights once on that court. . . . Judge Souter's nomination must be denied." Faye Wattleton, president of Planned Parenthood, equally disappointed and frustrated, said, "After days of evasive answers and filibusters, we know nothing more about Judge Souter's views on reproductive rights than we did before the hearings began." Nonetheless, Bush pressed on. When the Senate Judiciary Committee voted for affirmation, only Senator Edward Kennedy voted no. The Senate confirmed him on October 2, 1990, as the nation's 105th U.S. Supreme Court justice.

Souter's doubters also thought he would be overawed by the job, and would appear retiring and docile during contentious argument. Yet there is a will of iron beneath the deferential manner. Once he was on the Court, it was clear he was not intimidated by any of his fellow justices; he has, in fact, become one of its most persistent questioners, sometimes seeming to fight with his good friend Scalia to get his questions, answers, and views into the argument. He asks precise questions, and, if he fails to get responsive answers, he pushes the question again. Lawyers soon learned that Souter was and remains a relentless questioner who allows lawyers no chance of honorable evasion. Souter, off the bench, maintains the simple bachelor lifestyle with which he arrived. He brings to work every day his own lunch, consisting of apples and yogurt, and lives in an undecorated apartment. During the summer breaks, he returns home to New Hampshire, where he enjoys walks in the woods.

Unlike Thomas, Bush's second appointee, Souter has become an important part of the Court process, and his decisions can at times be described as eloquent—a rarity on this Court where the text decisions rarely rise above the commonplace. His centrist leanings were originally shown by his unprecedented twenty-four similar votes with Justice O'Connor. But as the Court has drifted further and further to the right, his reliance on moderate values has displeased his backers, Republican presidents, senators, and especially the Right, where NO MORE SOUTERS buttons began to appear regularly at Federalist meetings.

Justice David Souter's appointment to fill William J. Brennan's seat dramatically changed the White House judicial selection and nomination process. He, like Brennan, barely known and chosen initially for political considerations and anticipated votes, could be the leader of the Court's moderate majority (if there ever is one) while he is on the bench. Souter's independent, unpredictable forays, as in *Rust v. Sullivan* and *Atwater v. City of Lago Vista*, are disturbing, but, as time goes on, they may occur only in those rare and unusual cases that seem to touch some eighteenth-century part of his life. It may be that in *Seminole Tribe of Florida v. Florida* his decision was powered by his concern and sadness for the trodden-upon Indians. His passion, at times like Brennan's, often evokes the liberalism of the past. But no longer will either Democrats or Republicans flirt with, much less bed, an enigma—no longer will the White House rely on politicians not sufficiently versed in the delicacy of the law. No longer will White House and Justice Department interviewers fail to get definitive answers to questions directly aimed at politics and ideology. Souter alone justifies the Federalists' claim that they should be involved in every part of the judicial nomination process.

Some commentators said, after *Bush v. Gore*, that the somewhat chastened Supreme Court was stepping back from expanding its judicial revolution. That was wrong. After *Bush v. Gore*, the Supreme Court's conservative bloc continued using its one-vote majority to extend its assault on congressional power. Two cases decided in 2000 illustrate how indifferent the majority has become to traditional notions of the separation of powers, fidelity to constitutional, statutory text, and—most ironically—to their own rhetoric about judicial restraint. Once again, the winners were the advocates of a judicially active Court and states' rights. This time, the losers were the aged, the disabled, and nearly five million state employees across the nation.

In 1995, Patricia Garrett was diagnosed with breast cancer. Fifty-five years old and the nursing director at a University of Alabama hospital, she had a lumpectomy and underwent chemotherapy. Then, like many people who are treated for cancer, she tried to keep working. But Garrett, who worked in a division handling high-risk pregnancies, says she was pressured by her boss at the medical center to quit and then was demoted. She later testified that a colleague had told her the boss didn't like "sick people" and tried to get rid of them. "I loved to work," Garrett says now. "It was so demoralizing. To just be told to go home was terrible."

Milton Ash, also of Alabama, was a prison guard who had asthma. Assigned to work in an asbestos area, he asked to be moved to another location where he could still perform the same work. The state refused and fired him. Ash's and Garrett's separate lawsuits seeking money damages under the Americans with Disabilities Act were soon after joined. Their briefs to the High Court argued that the history of this nation's treatment of people with disabilities have been previously described as grotesque, and that this case, *University of Alabama v. Patricia Garrett and Milton Ash* (2001), more so than *Lopez* or the *Seminole Tribe* case, dealt with Congress's power to protect the minorities it has traditionally protected. If ever legislation was similar to the aim of New Deal legislation, this was it.

As civil rights laws showed, often the most effective way of stopping an illegal action and of making sure it doesn't happen again is to allow money damages. Garrett and Ash said: "The fact is, society's vital quest for equality, integration, and dignity of the disabled has never been about money damages. . . . To the extent the disabled have ever asked for anything more than the government already provides all citizens, it has always been about the forward-looking objective of removing barriers to access, not the backward-looking objective" of damage lawsuits.

In a highly unusual bipartisan act, the GOP and Democratic congressional leaders who wrote the Americans with Disabilities law asked for permission to file a brief on behalf of the claimants and against the state of Alabama. The Court permitted it. Then, former president George Bush, for whom the ADA represented a major accomplishment of his administration, also asked to file a brief; his request, too, was granted. Bush's brief argued that before the ADA, laws protecting the disabled were enacted in a piecemeal fashion. He explained that the goal of the law was to cover "all aspects of American life, including our workplaces, our communities and our schools, and other public services."

At issue were two seemingly opposing constitutional guarantees. Garrett and Ash argued that Section 5 of the Fourteenth Amendment authorizes Congress to enforce rights guaranteed therein by "appropriate legislation," of which the Americans with Disabilities Act would be an appropriate example. The state of Alabama argued that the Eleventh Amendment protects the state from unreasonable interference in its business by the federal government, and stops the use of the Fourteenth Amendment enforcement process.

The *Lopez* claim, that the evidence given to Congress was not sufficient when it passed the gun law, could not be made here. Congress, both with respect to the aged and disabled, held extensive hearings to see if there was massive state discrimination over a period of years. In fashioning its ADA legislation, Congress held thirteen hearings in Washington, created a task force that held additional hearings in all fifty states, and took testimony from thousands of witnesses. There were at least three hundred acts of alleged discrimination by the states. Educated by testimony and hearings, Congress found that discrimination and maltreatment against the disabled was so widespread that it pervaded every aspect of our society, and that private companies as well as state and local governments were all responsible. The act was passed by the legislature specifically to stop that nationwide discrimination.

Michael Gottesman, who is now a Georgetown University law professor, was an experienced litigator who had argued nineteen cases before the Supreme Court. He knew when he was asked to represent Pat Garrett and Milton Ash that he had a difficult road ahead. A year earlier, the Court, in yet another 5–4 ruling, had voted to deny a Florida State University physics professor, J. Daniel Kimel, from filing an age-bias suit against the university. The Court said it is constitutional for the state to discriminate against the aged if the state has a rational reason for the discrimination, even if it "is probably not true that those reasons are valid in the majority of cases." In addition, prior to *Garrett*, in six decisions after 1993, the conservatives also ruled in a string of decisions, over angry dissents by the other justices, that damage suits against a state are barred by the Eleventh Amendment.

Gottesman's concern that these decisions and the *Kimel v. Florida Board of Regents* rationale might cover his case was justified. The Supreme Court, indeed, relied on its decision against Kimel in its 5–4 vote: disabled people like Garrett and Ash could not sue a state in any court to enforce a right created by a federal statute. Rehnquist found the Eleventh Amendment trumped the enforcement clause of the Fourteenth Amendment. The Court said that the Fourteenth Amendment—stating that no state may "deny to any person the equal protection of the laws" and that "the laws of the United States shall be the supreme law of the land . . . the laws of any state to the contrary notwithstanding"—were not violated. Nor did the Court find that states are required to make special accommodations for the disabled. "They could quite hard-headedly—and perhaps hard-heartedly—hold to job-qualification requirements which do not make allowance for the disabled," said Rehnquist. Moving in for the kill, he added that even if all the statistics did show a pattern of discrimination, Congress hadn't proved that the discrimination was "irrational," and in so doing he brazenly brushed aside all Congress had heard and saw and all the conclusions it had reached. Disingenuously, the chief justice said, Congress had put together only "minimal evidence of unconstitutional state discrimination." This conclusion, denigrating Congress as being incapable of evaluating what it heard, and rejecting its judgment, brings us back to the early twentieth century, when the Court refused to allow Congress to decide if child labor laws were needed. With this opinion, the five conservatives substituted their judgment for that of the senators and representatives of Congress who had passed the bill and of the president who had signed it.

Once more, Justice Souter expressed his opposition. The Eleventh Amendment, adopted in 1794, and enacted to stop the states from being bankrupted with suits over debts from the Revolutionary War, he explained, "is inapplicable to the claims of Garrett and Ash. Rather, that amendment merely denies federal courts the authority to hear suits against a state by residents of another state. The conservative majority has, however, interpreted the amendment to incorporate the ancient and now-discredited notion that 'the king can do no wrong.'" As a result of the Rehnquist Court, he continued, "State governments do not have to pay their victims when the states do what Congress has prohibited." No matter how egregious the violation, Souter said the state can now disregard the Fourteenth Amendment and discriminate because of the new, wrongful use of the Eleventh Amendment.

As a consequence of the *Garrett* and *Kimel* cases, much of the federal statutes protecting the aged and disabled against discrimination have been thrown into the wastebasket. Significantly, states can now violate congressionally created rights for the elderly, pregnant women, the mentally disabled, the mentally ill, and others with impunity, for they know they won't have to pay anything if they are sued. Hypercritically, O'Connor claims the laws were vague because they were not as carefully written as a group of law professors might have written the statutes. But for the past 200 years, congressmen, after compromise and negotiations, were the ones to write laws, not law professors.

Soon after Pat Garrett's case against Alabama, the Supreme Court was faced with another claim that tested the reach of the Civil Rights Act of 1964. Alabama was sued on behalf of Martha Sandoval and other Spanish-speaking residents who protested the state's switch to offering the written part of the driver's license exams in English only. Just as Justice Souter had predicted, the logic of the *Seminole Tribe* case and of the *Garrett* and *Kimel* cases could destroy parts of the civil rights laws.

Jeffrey S. Sutton, hired by the state to argue its case, and now a Bush nominee to the federal appeals bench, described Alabama as "a co-equal sovereign" with the United States. As an equal partner, the state should not be subjected to discrimination suits brought under federal law. The Justice Department, conversely, argued that civil rights law barred agencies receiving federal funds from adopting policies that "have the effect of subjecting individuals to discrimination" because of their race or national origin.

Alabama won the 5–4 decision in *Alexander v. Sandoval* (2001), written by Scalia, who said the federal civil rights law covers only "intentional" discrimination, not policies such as the English-only driver's exam that have a harsher effect on racial or ethnic minorities.

Finally on May 28, 2002, the Supreme Court, in another 5–4 decision, said that *sovereign immunity* means that federal agencies cannot hold hearings in a proceeding brought by a private party complaining that a state has violated a federal law. As Cass Sunstein, professor at the University of Chicago Law School said, the Court in *Federal Maritime Commission v. South Carolina Port Authority*, notched judicial overreach to a new high level. We will see the day when a state violating your federal rights will be nearly totally immune before administrative agencies that were created since the New Deal days, as well as before the federal courts.

The clash between the Rehnquist bloc and the moderate members of the Court over whether citizens should be able to sue federal and state government officials over violations of their constitutional rights is of great meaning. The difference is more than the interpretation of specific statutes or constitutional clauses, or questions of who has standing to sue. It is based on two very different views of our democracy, on how the government is to be run, and on what values shape the Constitution.

Conservatives believe that the government cannot run if its managers, police officials, and welfare agencies are constantly defending themselves in court. The government was created by the Constitution to be run by those elected officials, but the conservatives argue if each discretionary act by an official could lead to a constitutional claim, the government would come to a halt. Within this context Rehnquist sees many sexual and racial harassment suits as frivolous. Distrustful of litigation, plaintiffs, and a litigious society, Rehnquist feels that clogging the courts with an infinite number of claims will lead to a government, run by judges, that would become paralyzed. The Supreme Court's basic purpose, he believes, is to resolve disputes that have significant impact and are of broad general concern.

The liberal view starts from the assumption that the people should hold the government accountable under the Constitution. When a citizen's rights have been trampled upon, citizens have the right to sue welfare officials, prison officials, even school board members, and all manner of public employees who are accused of deliberate rights violations.

Liberals tend to see the Court as inbred with a sense of justice and fairness and will, according to the conservatives, stray more often from the literal reading of the law. The law is rarely clear-cut, and that is why politics and personal feelings play such a large role. By the time the case has come to the Court, numerous judges in the federal and state trial and appellate systems have attempted to interpret the law. If a case travels up the federal ladder and a full appellate court hears it, as many as twelve to fifteen judges may have different views of how the laws should be applied. Then the Supreme Court decides it 5–4.

The conservative media and partisan extremists have consistently urged the present Court to become even more activist, striking down laws of Congress that impinge on big business and bring on multimillion-dollar punitive-damage awards against oil polluters and tobacco companies. It is a course upon which the present Court, and the one to follow, are already set: The *Wall Street Journal* applauded the Supreme Court's May 14, 2001, opinion that said appellate courts were not bound by a jury's ruling on punitive damages, that the judges could look anew at the record and were relatively free to set aside people's verdicts. With future appointees likely to be antigovernment–free-market ideologues sympathetic to business, this decision is but a taste of things to come.

Rehnquist, during the Warren Court period, railed that the least dangerous branch, the judicial, was becoming the most dangerous branch—and that the Constitution's separation of powers would be frustrated by the Court, an unelected undemocratic elite. He has fulfilled his prophesy—that is exactly what his Court has done. Although the Warren Court was accused of arrogance and of refusing to pay attention to any branch of government other than itself, it can't come close to the disdain the Rehnquist Court shows to Congress and federal agencies. First, the Rehnquist Court strikes down a law passed by Congress. Then, Congress passes a new law to fix the defects in the old one the Court found objectionable. Next, the Supreme Court strikes down that new law. Between our elected legislatures and the Supreme Court rages a war to an extent never before seen. Today, separation of powers exists conceptually, though not in reality. The Court overrules the Congress nearly whenever it wishes.

The ultimate hypocrisy of the Right's attack on federalism may be seen in John Ashcroft's assault on the doctor-assisted suicide under Oregon's Death with Dignity Act, overwhelmingly passed by voters during a 1997 referendum. Ashcroft has placed himself, and the Drug Enforcement Administration, between Oregon physicians and their dying patients. He announced he would make it a federal crime for a doctor or patient to collaborate in assisted suicide and that the doctor's license would be revoked.

While the U.S. Supreme Court has so far refused to strike down the Oregon law, opinions in two earlier related cases suggest the Court may be poised to interfere with a law that Oregon voters passed. Commenting on the attorney general's action, Oregon senator Ron Wyden, a Democrat, said: "They've tossed the ballots of Oregon voters in the trash can. They're frustrated by the inconvenience of the democratic process." For the moment, at least as of this writing, the attorney general's hands are tied. On November 13, 2001, a federal judge issued a four-month temporary restraining order and then later a permanent injunction stopping Ashcroft in his tracks.

Yet, if and when the Supreme Court decides to take the Oregon case, it will be interesting to see if the Court uses its familiar states' rights analysis to uphold the legality of legislation a majority of the justices morally oppose. One has to wonder how true to its own intellectual constructs this Court will be. As we saw in *Morrison v. United States,* the Court has already decided that Congress lacks the power to permit rape victims to sue their attackers in federal court because the issue is "local," and that Congress, in *United States v. Lopez,* could not outlaw the carrying of guns near schools, or require the registration of guns, because the issues are "local." The results in both of these cases were supported by Ashcroft.

As I pointed out in chapter 2, the Founding Fathers had hoped to keep the Supreme Court out of politics. They did all they could to avoid a party system where the Court's main body of work was to referee political and economic wars. Factions, they understood, would form around certain disagreements, but they hoped there would not be permanent political parties. But very quickly, as political parties inevitably began to form early in the Washington administration, national leaders reached out for support to state and local leaders and overrode states' rights. Ultimately, it was the party system that made federalism work.

If the Founders were appalled by the prospect of parties, they were, at least in part, quite justified. They were not naive, and they recognized self-interest. When men of the eighteenth century spoke of "parties" and "factions," they had in mind interest groups, each group looking out for the interests of its constituency. No one could foresee that the extensive organizations we have today are able to appeal both to interest groups and the public at large, with a broad general philosophy that was the foundation for party workers, party programs, and party control of government. This circumstance had never before existed.

Times were changing, and the concept of democracy as set forth in the Constitution was new and unique. Our new democracy rejected titles and inherited social standing and (other than with African Americans) supposedly tried to create a society built upon the common man. Its economy, overwhelmingly agrarian, was dynamic and market-driven; the United States was, at the time, "perhaps the most thoroughly commercialized nation in the world."

Most significant was how its size was governed; the states' righters did not believe a government as far away from the players as a federal capital could understand or identify with the people in individual states. They ferociously denied that this central government could ever get "the confidence of the people." But, Alexander Hamilton told the New York Ratifying Convention, "The confidence of the people will easily be gained by a good administration. This is the true touchstone."

In truth, states' rights and federalism issues are always bent for political purposes. When it suits our fickle leaders, they are in favor of broad federal powers, as in the 1996 and 2001 antiterrorism bills; when it does not, they claim states' rights. When Jefferson was not in office, he supported states' rights against Federalist Alexander Hamilton. When he got into office, he tried to expand federal power. James Madison did the same thing. When southerners ran the government, New Englanders who opposed the War of 1812 muttered about secession.

As the South was losing control to an industrializing North, they hit upon the primacy of states' rights, and how it might be manipulated to serve their changing needs. Illinois senator Stephen Douglas believed in federal power to build railroads but not to limit slavery in federal territories. As a Senate candidate in 1858, Abraham Lincoln vowed to protect Illinois's right to prohibit slavery. As president, he reversed course when he prevented Missouri from voting to secede.

The Bush administration's new push to change the balance of powers between the three branches of government continued after the World Trade Center tragedy. But fighting terrorism in a democracy requires an exquisite balancing of our architecture of government.

Commentators argue that the events of September 11 will stop the Court from using the Tenth and Eleven Amendments as assault weapons against the federal government. September 11 confirms that federal actions, whether antiterrorism legislation, new cabinet level agencies seeking to protect our homeland, or massive relief funds, are critical in terms of meeting a national emergency, and that Congress needs the broadest discretion to protect us. As Jeffrey Rosen, a professor at Georgetown University, put it in the January 2002 *New Republic*, the Court will have to change its path because "anti-Federalism may have seemed quaint before the Twin Towers fell, but the possibility that the Court might hamper Congress' responsibility to a serious threat is no laughing matter."

6

CAPITALISM AND THE FREE MARKET:
Rolling Back the Clock to the 1900s

On March 28, 2001, the Federalist Society sponsored a panel in Chicago called Rolling Back the New Deal: Judicial Review of Economic Regulations; the panel featured, among other speakers, the University of Chicago Law School professor Richard Epstein. The program brochure said, "Since the New Deal, the Supreme Court has taken a hands-off approach to economic regulations. If an economic regulation had any rational basis, it was generally deemed constitutional. Now however . . . the Court has begun to look more closely at legislation to determine if it unconstitutionally takes property from businesses or individuals. If a law requires a business to pay for activities that occurred long ago, the retroactive liability may violate the Takings Clause of the Fifth Amendment."

The Takings Clause provides, "[N]or shall private property be taken for public use, without just compensation." According to Epstein, that one sentence in the Constitution covers virtually any governmental "interference" with an owners' right to possess, use, and dispose of property. That one sentence says a great deal, but whether or not it can be put to the radical use that Epstein wants is in the hands of our nine justices. Traditionally called the power of eminent domain, this clause allows the government to physically take one's property, even under protest, for a public use—a park, a hospital, a dam, a public highway, in exchange for just compensation.

The discussion that took place that evening articulates the Right's desire for deregulation and the legal argument that supports it. It is an effort that is driven by a simple desire to protect the free-market business. Even though one of the most public corporate economic disasters America has suffered, the Enron bankruptcy and the damage it has done to all Americans, can be traced to deregulation, the Right still pushes its agenda before the Courts and the legislature.

This panel and others like it pulled together the chief theorists of the reactionary movement as they announced their view of how the law in the economic sphere had changed over the past twenty years and would continue to change over the next twenty years. They claimed that five- and six-year-old Rehnquist Court decisions eviscerating congressional power are now treated as "settled law," and that the body of new law that has been created gives the Supreme Court the building blocks to "deregulate society and restore property rights to its proper place." Professor Epstein and the Federalists pointed out that the Supreme Court majority is incrementally and relentlessly moving forward. The Court's having established its supremacy in limiting individual freedoms, and having rolled back much of the Warren and Burger Court's advances, Epstein still found the Court lacking because so much of the New Deal law was still on the books. The deregulation of business—in part achieved by striking down federal child labor, minimum wage, and maximum hour laws—was essential to get the benefits of the free market. His free-market views extend into every area of the law—from approving voucher programs, financial aid to parochial schools because it gives parents "choice" and because it reduces public school monopolies (as discussed in chapter 9) to claiming that desegregation should end because the costs are too high and the method too invested with governmental control. His positions, not all yet accepted, are the harbinger of the future. What Epstein urges is nothing less than a betrayal of constitutional values most of us believe in.

Epstein's panel resurrected legal and political arguments successfully made between 1890 and 1916. That period is known in legal culture as the Lochner era. To evoke it is to evoke a time long past, a time of strikes and sweatshops, low wages and long hours, tenement living and economic tumult. The federal and state cases that came down during this time reflected the benefits and costs created by the industrial revolution. With money flowing into capital expansion, the Court was prepared to accept the brutal price of that growth.

In 1895, as a result of new progressive forces and the beginning of unionism, New York State passed legislation to regulate sanitary conditions as well as to reform working conditions and reduce work hours. Ten years later, the Supreme Court, in the 5–4 *Lochner v. New York* decision, invalidated the New York regulation. Justice Rufus Peckham said that New York's attempt to regulate hours of labor in (in this case) bakeries "necessarily interfered with the right of contract between the employer and the employee." Denying there were valuable economic reasons for the state regulations, Peckham held that the liberty protected by the Fourteenth Amendment included the right to purchase and sell labor. Any statute interfering with it would be invalid "unless there are circumstances which exclude that right"—slavery being one such circumstance. *Lochner* stands for the judiciary thwarting the will of its elected officials, for the judiciary overruling legislative judgments. The case is a symbol of unrestrained judicial activism of a Court asserting its supremacy over the legislature and undermining the legislature's constitutional responsibility to respond to economic and social problems. When given a chance, the Rehnquist Court now asserts that same authority to help big business at the expense of the people.

Lochner, the case we saw referenced a half century later by Hugo Black in *Griswold v. Connecticut*, is well known for its two dissents by Justices Oliver Wendell Holmes and John Harlan. As the latter argues, the New York legislature had sound reasoning for the passage of the law:

> The labor of the bakers is among the hardest and most laborious imaginable, because it has to be performed under conditions injurious to the health of those engaged in it. It is hard, very hard work, not only because it requires a great deal of physical exertion in an overheated workshop and during unreasonably long hours, but [also because the] constant inhaling of flour dust causes inflammation of the lungs and of the bronchial tubes [and the] long hours of toil to which all bakers are subjected produce rheumatism, cramps and swollen legs. [Nearly] all bakers are pale-faced and of more delicate

health than the workers of other crafts . . . they seldom live over their fifti-
eth year.

Yet with the exact same information that Harlan had before him, Peckham reached the exact opposite factual conclusion. "It is manifest to us that
the [law here] has no such direct relation to and no substantial effect upon
the health of the employees as to justify us in regarding the section as really
a health law."

Justice Holmes's famous dissent started with one of the most memo-
rable phrases in American legal writing. "The Fourteenth Amendment
does not enact Mr. Herbert Spencer's Social Statics . . . a constitution is
not intended to embody a particular economic theory, whether of paternalism and the organic relation of the citizen to the State or of laissez faire. It
is made for people of fundamentally differing views, and the accident of
our finding certain opinions natural and familiar or novel and even shocking ought not to conclude our judgment upon the question whether
statutes embodying them conflict with the Constitution of the United
States. General propositions do not decide concrete cases. The decision
will depend on a judgment or intuition more subtle than any articulate
major premise."

For many years thereafter the Supreme Court, because of the *Lochner*
rationale, continued to reject state wage and safety laws. The child labor
legislation, also declared unconstitutional, was seen by the 5–4 majority in
Hammer v. Dagenhart (1918) as something that could put an end to "all
freedom of commerce . . . and thus our system of government [would] be
practically destroyed." It is the logic of Scalia, Rehnquist, and Thomas: that
government ought not interfere with the free market; that the benefits of
the free market will flow down to the employees; and that there is a greater
danger from regulation than from potentially benevolent employees. Governmental paternalism is the great danger.

But if any side could be charged with "interference," it would be
Lochner and *Hammer*, the dissenters said, where the Court substituted its
views over those of elected officials. Indeed, the Court, headed until the
Great Depression by Chief Justice (and former president) William Howard
Taft, invalidated state and federal regulatory laws in greater numbers than
any previous Court until the Rehnquist Court. The free market was made
freer. Taft's Court created new rights for the benefit of business so that it

would be unhampered by the government. The right of contract, not found in the Constitution, was established by this conservative Court, in the same way, today's right-wing conservative jurists argue, that the Roosevelt, Warren, and early Burger Courts created rights not found in the Constitution.

In truth, even before 1932, the Supreme Court was starting to shift away from its role as a protector of business. The New Deal Court did not discover, and was not the first Court to try to protect, individual rights against business interests. Some Court decisions in the late 1920s were critical of the extent to which the legal system was protecting laissez-faire capitalism at the expense of individual rights.

When, after Franklin D. Roosevelt's election, the Democrats began to experiment with national economic regulation, the Supreme Court responded in 1934 and 1935 by striking down much of the New Deal. After Roosevelt's 1936 landslide reelection, he denounced the Court for imposing its own views of laissez-faire economics for those of the people, and he sought ways to remove the Court as an obstacle. The Court was composed of aged railroad lawyers and business executives. He proposed in 1937 to expand the court if any of the existing justices remained on the bench after the age of seventy, in order to dilute the power of the "nine old men" who were stopping progress. Even though the court-packing plan failed in the Senate, the political pressure forced the justices to remove themselves as obstacles to the New Deal. The Court's "switch in time saved nine," as it changed from a posture of judicial activism to one of judicial restraint, giving the president and Congress broad deference to regulate the economy in an increasingly interdependent world.

But it was not until 1941, in *United States v. Darby Lumber,* when the Supreme Court, in a 9–0 decision, upheld Congress's right to set minimum wages and maximum hours for all employees who worked on goods shipped in interstate commerce, that finally, *Hammer,* the child labor law case, was totally rejected. Justice Harlan F. Stone invoked "the powerful and now classic dissent of Mr. Justice Holmes," in the *Lochner* case, to uphold Congress's nearly unreviewable power to interpret the Commerce Clause.

Epstein claims the "Marxist view" that "minimum wage laws, for example, can boost the least fortunate workers' share of the gain to a larger, and more just, proportion" is wrong. Instead, he says, minimum wage laws for adults and children "induce some employers to reduce their work forces, others to change non-wage terms of the contract. It will narrow the gap between lower and higher skilled employees and thus reduce workers incentives to invest in their own human capital." "The higher the minimum wage," he says, "the more likely that some firms will exit from the market."

His concern, and the concern of today's right-wing jurists, is to value property rights over personal rights. One of the most important cases in the New Deal's judicial revolution, *United States v. Carolene*, decided in 1938, is, according to Epstein, wrong. *Carolene* established a different and higher level of protection for personal rights than for property rights. *Carolene*, the underpinning for the next sixty years of law, is today being rejected by much of this Court and will firmly be entombed if one or two more right-wing jurists are appointed.

Justice Harlan F. Stone, who later became chief justice, wrote the opinion in *Carolene* upholding a federal law, justified by the Commerce Clause, prohibiting the shipment of "filled" milk (skim milk mixed with nonmilk fats) as an exercise of its national police power to protect the citizens of all states. Refuting the minority argument that the Congress did not have the authority to expand the Commerce Clause to achieve that result, Stone said laws "effecting ordinary commercial transactions" were to be presumed constitutional and struck down only if lacking "some rational basis within the knowledge and experience of the legislators." He added his famous "first freedoms" footnote, suggesting that there may be a stronger case for holding a law unconstitutional: if the laws are aimed at the political process, at free speech, religion, privacy, "they are subjected to more exacting judicial scrutiny" than laws dealing with economic matters.

Because of the *Carolene* case and other New Deal court decisions, American law since 1938 has been to let Congress be the laboring oar in deciding what is right and wrong for the country on economic matters, with respect given to the judicial system as the government branch charged with protecting individual rights against federal or state intrusion. It has been an understanding uninterrupted until 1996; the Supreme Court had not struck down one congressional regulation. Since then, some of it, not all the present Court majority, through a variety of both new constitutional strategies and the reinterpretation of old established principles, has virtually consigned this important New Deal legacy to mothballs. The concepts behind *Lochner* are being resurrected, and *Carolene* has been firmly, though not explicitly, rejected. The test going forward is what is best for the free market and not what is best for the people.

One argument for the preferred freedoms doctrine is that we cannot be a free people without the Court's aggressively protecting freedom of speech, press, and religion, but we can be a free people without the courts being as zealous in their protection of economic rights. The Bill of Rights explicitly contains political rights, while many economic rights rest on creative interpretations of the due process clause. In this way, we are able to justify a greater protection to freedom of communication than to freedom of contract.

Professor Gary Lawson of Boston University, writing in the 1994 *Harvard Law Review*, speaking for himself and a large body of conservative scholars, says: "The post–New Deal administrative state is unconstitutional." He has no difficulty overruling *Carolene*. The judiciary is the sole interpreter of the Constitution, he believes, and there is no need to defer to Congressional fact-finding or conclusions, both of which are irrelevant. Precedent, he writes, is in general not required by the law. Because judicial deference need not be paid to judicial meaning, nearly any case can be overruled. Lawson, as well as voluminous conservative literature and certain appellate judges, justify the resurrection of *Lochner* and *Hammer*, validate the attack on the post-1937 Court, and support *Epstein*, as well as the decisions in *Lopez, Kimmel*, and *Garret*, discussed in the previous chapter.

Since 1986, Rehnquist, Scalia, and Thomas, whenever they can, go back to the logic of *Hammer* and *Lochner*. The 1938 Fair Labor Standards Act (FLSA), which set minimum wage and maximum hours standards, was the last major piece of New Deal social legislation. The act was expanded in 1974 to include state and local governments; but in a 5–4 1976 decision, *National League of Cities v. Usery*, the Supreme Court struck down that wage extension for encroaching on the states' "traditional functions and their ability to function effectively." Writing in dissent, Justice Brennan declared the Court was overreaching, ignoring a carefully considered decision of Congress. Calling it a "catastrophic judicial body blow at Congress['s] power under the Commerce Clause," he pointed out that the logic of the Court could undo much of the New Deal achievement. He saw it as the rehabilitation of *Lochner*. Nine years later, in 1985, another 5–4 decision, the *Garcia v. San Antonio Metropolitan Transit Authority* case, overruled *Usery*. States, the Court now said, were not immune from following national overtime and minimum wage requirements. Garcia, the appellant, would henceforth receive his overtime pay because one of the majority justices in *Garcia*, Harry Blackmun, who'd voted with the *Usery* majority, had now changed his mind. Like a Ping-Pong ball being paddled back and forth, the law can be changed repeatedly. Blackmun is long gone, and today's Court is different. If a case close to *Usery* and *Garcia* came to the Court now, the result would be the same as *Usery* with the likelihood of an unequivocal resurrection of *Lochner*.

Both sides in *Lopez v. United States*, *Printz v. United States*, and *Morrison v. United States*, referred in their briefs to *Wickard v. Filburn*, the 9–0 1942 Supreme Court case. Justice Stevens, as I pointed out in the previous chapter, mentioned the 1942 case during oral arguments in *Lopez*. For me, one of the marvelous aspects of our law is the use of precedent, often in cases with totally different narratives decided generations ago. The *Wickard* reference in those arguments, evoking the long-ago struggle to give Congress the power necessary to help govern the country—reminds us that the line defining interstate commerce is often difficult to draw. Congress and the Roosevelt court recognized that formal, previous distinctions were not helpful, and that it was more important to look at the reality of each situation.

For the Court, the *Wickard* case turned out to be the high-water mark of its expansive view of Congress's ability to determine the limits of the Commerce Clause. It best indicates how completely the Supreme Court had come in agreeing that federal intrusion is necessary for the country to function. Reading *Wickard* in the context of *Lopez* and *Morrison* shows how a legal system such as ours, built on precedent, develops and operates. The history of the Commerce Clause in this century is bookended by a $120 fine imposed in the *Wickard* case and by Christy Brzonkala's failed damage claim.

The specific question in *Wickard* was whether Congress's Agricultural Act seeking to enforce wheat quotas could be applied, under the Commerce Clause, to wheat that never left the farm and supposedly never went into interstate commerce. This was the same legal principle as in the *Lopez*, *Printz*, and *Morrison* cases. Is the activity involved in interstate commerce? Does it affect interstate commerce in a substantial way, or is it purely or primarily a local matter? In deciding that early case, the court had to look at the same part of the Constitution the Warren Court later looked at when it upheld the constitutionality of the Civil Rights Act of 1964, and the same part of the Constitution the Rehnquist Court looked at in deciding *Lopez* and *Printz*.

When Roscoe Filburn's challenge of his $120 fine reached the Court in 1942, it was a body that had been dramatically restructured by President Roosevelt's new appointments. Had the case gotten to the Court in the early 1930s, Filburn would have won; the Court would have concluded that Congress interpreted the Commerce Clause too widely. Instead, the entire Court agreed that Filburn's tiny 239 bushels of wheat consumed but not marketed still had an effect upon interstate commerce and thus could be regulated. In the early 1940s, more than 20 percent of all the wheat grown in the country never left the farm. By consuming their own grain, Filburn and thousands of farmers like him cut the overall demand and depressed the market price of wheat. Their actions taken together clearly affected interstate commerce and were, the Court agreed, subject to federal regulation.

The 9–0 ruling in *Wickard* rejected formality in the interpretation of the Commerce Clause and deferred to Congress's view of reality. *Wickard*, *Lopez*, and *Morrison*, over a half century apart, talk to each other and to us. Judge Souter, referring back to *Wickard* in the *Morrison* case, said that the five conservative judges' attempt to circumscribe the commerce power "can only be seen as a revival of similar efforts that led to near tragedy for the Court."

Christy Brzonkala's lawyer and the government lawyers in *Lopez* and *Printz*, as well as the Court's dissenting judges, believed *Wickard* set the contours for the law. If you could regulate homegrown and home-consumed wheat because it affected interstate commerce and therefore the nation, so, too, could you uphold federal laws that give a raped woman a claim for damages and one that penalized gun possession near a school. But when the composition of the Court changed in the early 1990s, with Brennan and Marshall gone and Clarence Thomas present, the Court started to relentlessly strike down congressional laws using the Commerce Clause to protect the personal rights of individuals.

The majority decision in *Lopez* told us the Court was rethinking all of the Commerce Clause cases and preferred freedoms cases, decided by the New Deal Court. For the first time it told us, starkly and most clearly, that any federal legislation, whether it be about guns or child labor, would be examined very closely—and that if Congress passed maximum hours and minimum wage laws, such as existed in the *Usery* case, the Court would now rule as it had then. *Garcia* would be a dead letter. As Justice Stevens said, the present Court's logic "would undermine most of [the Court's] post–New Deal Commerce clause jurisprudence."

At the same time that Reagan became president, the Chicago School of Economics, along with the University of Chicago's School of Law, gave rise to the law and economics movement, providing a new rationale for limits on legislative decision making. That movement is today one of the most powerful forces in changing the law's direction and completing the legal revolution. It is the application of economics to an ever-increasing range of legal fields. Free-market legal theory sought to empty legal doctrine of socially binding moral content and aspirations by reinstating the primacy of the individual or business, who must be free to do whatever it, he, or she wants, unless it, he, or she is paid for any legal constraints put on that freedom by the government. In other words, if the government wants to regulate, it will have to pay such a heavy price that it will be encouraged or, in fact, forced to deregulate.

Richard Posner is the seminal influence in the law and economics movement. Few jurists have been more important and, for many valid reasons, more respected than he. A graduate of Harvard Law School, a clerk for Justice Brennan, a law professor at Stanford and then University of Chicago, he was then appointed in 1981 by Ronald Reagan to the U.S. Court of Appeals for the Seventh Circuit. Because Posner has written so much, has been so provocative, and is over sixty, it is unlikely he is a candidate for the Supreme Court. But Posner's relentless decisions and prolific writings dominate the circuit court he sits on, which has jurisdiction over Illinois, Michigan, Indiana, and Wisconsin. Indeed, the Supreme Court and some circuit courts have in a number of cases referred to his economic analysis of law, giving it added legitimacy.

The Posnerian analysis furnishes support to the New Right in areas besides pure economics. His is a worldview that admittedly "manifests a conservative political bias." In his scheme, capital punishment has a deterrent effect; legislation designed to protect consumers frequently ends up hurting them; no-fault automobile insurance is probably inefficient; and securities regulation may be a waste of time.

Posner seeks to reject much of the law developed after 1937. In his book *Economic Analysis of the Law* (1993) he says, "The pre–New Deal Courts were on solid ground when [they] refused to enforce agreements to join unions, enjoined picketing, and enforced yellow dog contracts." Posner says that health, welfare, and safety laws enacted by the state and federal governments are not necessary because "the employer has a selfish interest in providing the optional level of worker health and safety." Posner argues that the employer will look out best for his workers' benefits; that paternal employers rather than a paternal government will lead to efficiency and wealth for all and is achieved best by the invisible hand of Adam Smith. The administrative state is to be dispensed with, as are all safety nets like Social Security and subsidies.

For Posner, the goal of law, as of economics, is efficiency; and efficiency is defined as wealth maximization. The law should intervene "to reprehend only that which is inefficient," and even then the law's role should be limited since the "market punishes inefficiency faster and better than the machinery of the law." To Posner, the New Deal Court's rulings "were attempts to suppress competition under the guise of promoting the general welfare." The acceptance of this doctrine would result, as Posner rightly says, in a "seismic constitutional change."

Because all legal rights have costs, he articulates and promotes a cost-benefit analysis (CBA) of the law. In fact, Posner's cost-benefit analysis has had remarkable success in tort law and is now being applied to constitutional law. It is a strategy that asks the courts to decide cases on an economic basis—to put a dollar figure on the cost to society of protecting individual rights and then to ask if it is worth it. He and Epstein agree that large amounts of money should not be spent on desegregation efforts, or on propping up the public school system by denying governmental monies to parochial schools that precludes them from competing. Posner even looked at the decision in *Bush v. Gore* (of which he approved) through a cost-benefit analysis and determined that the Supreme Court was correct largely because, had the Supreme Court not quickly rushed in, the costs of the imminent constitutional crisis would have been greater. In a December 2001 article in the *Atlantic Monthly,* he argued for the constitutionality of the antiterrorism law arising out of September 11 using a cost-benefit analysis: individual rights "should be curtailed to the extent that the benefits in greater security outweigh the costs in reduced liberty."

Posner's cost-benefit analysis reduces law to dollars and cents. If the financial benefits of regulation are exceeded by its costs, then there should be no regulation. He says that if requiring low emissions standards or other environmental protections outweigh cost-benefit analysis, then environmental protection laws should not be upheld. He argues that air quality is not a value to be used in considering the validity of environmental law.

Posner applies his efficiency standards to argue that juries are an unnecessary expense because there are judges presiding at both nonjury and jury trials. He recalls fondly the income tax cases of the nineteenth century, where the Supreme Court ruled invalid the 1894 federal income tax law. He wants the free market to triumph over regulation. To the Chicago School of Economics, the law's role should be limited, and he himself has done much to translate his market theories into legal doctrine.

Posner's analysis of the law is of a kind with his other empirical studies. To him, all aspects of life are on a balance sheet. He has argued that a higher proportion of black women than white women are fat because the supply of eligible black men is limited, thus black women find the likelihood of profiting from attaining an elegant figure too small to compensate for the costs of dieting. Posner, ever aware of the reputation he cuts, described himself to Larissa MacFarquhar in a December 2001 *New Yorker* profile: "I am cold, furtive, callous, snobbish, selfish and playful, but with a streak of cruelty." He has rewritten the Golden Rule to mean we should "be kind to the kind and unkind to the unkind." Justice, to Posner, is helping your friends and harming your enemies.

The right wing in legal thinking supports the right wing in the economic arena. Political argument has been transformed into constitutional argument, and the battle over economics and the future of the administrative state has moved into the courts and away from Congress.

Like his former colleague at the University of Chicago Law School, Richard Epstein sees a half-century of protective regulation as harming friends and helping enemies. Laura Ingalls Wilder's *Farmer Boy*, Epstein claims, shows that "The children in the factories were certainly not as well off as we would like, but they were probably better off than they would have been back on the farm, or than if they had been left in the city without any opportunity to sell their labor. Their families had voted to leave the farm or the old country with their feet, as a matter of life and death. . . . Laws limiting child labor should be reversed because they may well have been misguided initiatives that inflicted harm upon the very persons they were ostensibly intended to benefit."

Some of Epstein's harshest rhetoric is directed against welfare and government entitlement programs. He, like Posner, has been deeply critical of the humanity driving *Goldberg v. Kelly*, a 1970 6–3 Supreme Court decision, called by Justice Brennan one of his most important cases, "the opening shot in the modern due process revolution." Today, that case—little known except to legal specialists—has been undercut by procedural obstacles. Brennan, in *Goldberg*, found that welfare benefits could not be terminated without giving the recipient a chance to oppose that termination. Prior to that decision, welfare recipients were arbitrarily cut off from aid, often for no reason at all—often just to reduce the cost of welfare.

In the *Goldberg* majority opinion, Justice Brennan described what happened after two of the five plaintiffs had their benefits terminated:

> Angela Velez and her four young children were evicted for nonpayment of rent and all forced to live in one small room of a relative's already crowded apartment. The children had little to eat during the four months it took the Department to correct its [termination] error. Esther Lett and her four children at once began to live on the handouts of impoverished neighbors; within two weeks all five required hospital treatment because of the inadequacy of their diet. Soon after, Esther Lett fainted in a welfare center while seeking an emergency food payment of $15 to feed herself and her family for three days.

The amount of monies to be gained by the Velez and Lett families were trivial as compared to the cost of the hearing. Due process be damned, say Epstein and Posner. By Posnerian logic, the costs and injustices of the hearings required by due process can be judged solely by a cost analysis. If the cost of the injustices are less than the cost of obtaining justice, the hearing should be cut back or ended.

Prior to *Goldberg v. Kelly*, due process was required only where personal or property rights were adversely affected by governmental action. Brennan extended that due process right to anyone who had a "statutory entitlement" to benefits, and said the decision can be seen as expressing the importance of attention to the concrete human realities at stake in governmental conduct. From this perspective, *Goldberg* can be seen as injecting common sense into a system mired in abstraction, as can another Supreme Court case, *King v. Smith*, which I argued in 1968. That case said that the welfare benefits of single mothers and their children had been wrongfully denied under an Alabama statute aimed at punishing women for having extramarital relationships. Finding the state had disregarded the economic needs of the children, the Court here, as in *Goldberg*, attempted to protect the vulnerable from the unregulated free market. These cases draw the harshest anger from Epstein.

The Supreme Court, a prime player in effecting a transition from the free market to the safety net times of the New Deal, is now trying to turn the country back toward the laissez-faire state. A few more conservative justices on the court, and the fight will be over. As one federal court said, "Of the three fundamental principles which underlie government, and for which the government exists, the protection of life, liberty and property, the chief of these is property."

Richard Pipes, now a professor at Harvard, and formerly a Reagan National Security Council advisor, supports Epstein's analysis and commitment to property rights over personal rights. "The assault on property rights is not always apparent," he says, "because it is carried out in the name of the common good—an elastic concept, defined by those whose interest it serves." For instance, Pipes asserts that minimum wage laws do not "bring wage earners the material benefits which is their purpose"; rather "[they outprice] the labor of persons with little education, especially black youths, making some of them unemployable, and thus, unintentionally, [discriminate] against them." As he writes in *Property and Freedom*:

> Thus the modern government not only "redistributes" the possessions of its citizens, it also regulates their use. It invokes environmental laws to limit the use of land and housing. It interferes with the freedom of contract by . . . enforcing "affirmative action" hiring practices. It imposes rent controls. It interferes with virtually every aspect of business, punishing any action that looks like price-fixing, setting rates for public utilities, preventing the formation of trusts, regulating communications and transport, pressuring banks to lend to designated neighborhoods, and so on.

Pipes says, "The right of property in and of itself does not guarantee civil rights and liberties. But historically speaking, it has been the single most effective device for ensuring both, because it creates an autonomous sphere in which, by mutual consent, neither the state nor society can encroach: by drawing a line between the public and the private, it makes the owner co-sovereign, as it were. Hence, it is arguably more important than the right to vote."

Professor Bernard Siegan, the rejected Reagan appointee to a federal court of appeals judgeship, has written extensively in the law and economics area. Without property rights, says Siegan, the Framers knew personal rights would have no meaning and would be devoid of practical content. Until nearly half a century ago, he points out, property predominated in the trilogy of rights protected by the Constitution.

According to Professor Siegan, the Court should sit as a super legislature. If a law is based upon what the judge considers an unsound economic theory, the judge should, Siegan believes, hold the law contrary to due process. Siegan concludes: "Judicial withdrawal from the protection of economic activity violates" the Constitution: "The evidence is very persuasive that *Lochner* was a legitimate interpretation. . . . Full rehabilitation may be in order"—and that means unregulated markets.

Newt Gingrich may be gone, but his legacy is with us today. The Contract with America endorsed by the majority of Americans in 1994, enjoying wide popular support, contained a clause calling for compensation of property owners whenever government regulations reduced their value. The resulting Private Property Rights Bill, passed by the House of Representatives in March 1995, called for compensation if government actions caused a property's worth to decline by 10 percent or more. The proposal has not as yet been enacted into law, although a bill with those provisions is submitted each year. But what Congress refuses to do through legislation, the Court may do through decisions.

The doctrine relied on by both Epstein and the Court's reactionary members, "that a regulation on the use of land may cause a taking of property," comes from a 1922 decision—*Pennsylvania Coal Co. v. Mahon*—striking down a Pennsylvania statute that prohibited the mining of coal from underground land owned by the coal company. In it, Justice Holmes said that a land use regulation can become a taking if it went "too far" in restricting the use of land and thereby diminished its value.

Holmes's decision, rarely cited after 1922, is now incorrectly cited as the foundation for Epstein's argument. Even the Burger Court, contrary to Epstein and some present members of the Rehnquist Court, said: "The denial . . . of one's traditional property right does not always amount to a taking. At least where an owner possesses a full 'bundle' of property rights, the destruction of one 'strand' of the bundle is not a taking because the aggregate must be viewed in it entirety."

Indeed, the Fifth Amendment is one of the best known and most celebrated amendments, woven into the fabric of American history. Thousands of cases have interpreted it. The Supreme Court has many times referred to the Fifth Amendment, but rarely to the eminent domain clause. It is not a surprise that few have paid attention to this last, nearly lost clause.

The Meese Justice Department laid the groundwork for Gingrich's justification of the Takings Clause's use through a number of important measures. They convened conferences on "economic liberties" to discuss the strategies for reinvigorating the clause; they drafted a takings executive order, requiring government decision makers to "evaluate carefully the effect of their administrative, regulatory, and legislative actions on constitutionally protected property rights"; and, most important, they helped appoint takings activists to spots on the three federal courts—the Supreme Court, the Circuit Court of Appeals for the District of Columbia, and the Court of Federal Claims—that mainly control the direction of federal takings law.

This Takings Project is long term, and is still gathering momentum. Several of the right-wing foundations have fueled intensive programs to further takings cases. At least twelve active organizations, with combined budgets in excess of $15 million, litigate such cases on behalf of developers. The Federalist Society and others recruit and train an army of private practitioners to assist in shepherding these cases through the legal system. And groups such as the Foundation for Research on Economics and the Environment (FREE) host all-expenses-paid seminars in resort locations for federal judges, educating them in how to strike down environmental protections in takings cases.

There could be something to be said for the Takings Clause if we were all just recently removed from a state of nature. Certainly, long ago, if we owned adjoining pieces of land, and mine was saddled with governmental regulations, your land would be more valuable than mine. But today, if I buy a business or a piece of land, the market in nearly every transaction has already discounted the restriction the new owner faces. If I buy acres of land near the sea, which prohibits me from building a factory or restricts me to building a small private house, the price I pay will reflect that. To suggest that our forefathers, in enacting the Takings Clause, believed that if the government sets up land use regulations or environmental controls the owner should be fully compensated for his loss, finds very little authority.

There is almost no constitutional history of the Takings Clause. The federal Bill of Rights, with the Fifth Amendment and the Takings Clause, was the work of James Madison. His draft, shown to the House of Representatives on June 8, 1789, was the basis for the amendments passed by the First Congress. The Takings Clause then read: "No person shall . . . be obliged to relinquish his property, where it may be necessary for public use, without a just compensation." Reading the clause, it seems clear Madison intended that it apply only to the direct, physical taking of property for public use, not for cases in which the owner still keeps it, even though it is hampered by regulation.

Miller v. Schoene, decided by the Supreme Court in 1928, is a case that ignites Epstein's fury and puts his argument in its best light. Rust-infected red cedar trees in Oregon threatened to destroy neighboring apple orchards by contamination. Apple growing was a major part of the state's economy, and Oregon had a statute permitting the destruction of infected trees that could wipe out other farmers. As a consequence, the red cedar trees were cut, the apple industry was saved, and the owner of the infected trees was not compensated even though he totally lost his property. So far as the cedar tree owner was concerned, Epstein says it was no different than losing his trees through eminent domain, and therefore he should be paid.

The unanimous *Miller v. Schoene* decision, written by Justice Harlan F. Stone, Epstein tells us, "is wholly inconsistent with any theory of property rights. . . . In the absence of any wrong by the owner of the cedar trees, the decision not to compensate is nothing more than authorization to transfer property illicitly from one class of citizens to another, as the owner of the cedar trees is left with neither the thing nor its value, when he has done no wrong."

But this decision is logical. The state took the property under its legitimate police power, in order to protect the welfare of the people. Every regulation gives preference to governmental interest over the right of the property owner. Justices Scalia, O'Connor, Thomas, and Rehnquist approve of much of Epstein's argument. Kennedy is not yet there. One or two more justices can make for a solid majority view that will see regulation and taking as synonymous. How far the new conservatives will take the Epstein argument is still unclear.

Taxation, Epstein tells us, is taking. "With a tax, the government takes property in the narrowest sense of the term, ending up with ownership and possession of that which was once in private hands." Thus, all taxes and subsidies, every part of the safety net—even unemployment benefits and workers' compensation—are takings that require compensation.

As Bernard Schwartz, former professor of law at New York University, has said, Richard Epstein's conception of the Takings Clause would effect the most radical change in public law that has ever taken place. "The Takings Clause would become the center of a new constitutional cosmology, with its rays protecting property to a hitherto unheard-of extent. Property rights would be immunized against the police power and redistributive taxation. Public power would be reduced to a power to proceed by purchase."

Various opinions in the five recent cases from the Supreme Court agree with Professor Epstein's concept that "takings" and "regulations" may be synonymous.

In the first of these, the 1987 case *First Lutheran Church v. Los Angeles County*, Chief Justice Rehnquist speaking for the Court said a regulation can amount to a taking requiring the owner to be paid even if the regulation is withdrawn after a successful court challenge. The First English Evangelical Lutheran Church of Glendale owned buildings destroyed by floods, but an ordinance prohibited the rebuilding on the flood plain area where the church had been. Following a successful Court challenge, the ordinance was withdrawn. The church was permitted to rebuild—and the Supreme Court said that holding up the rebuilding required the government to pay a compensation.

And in a 1988 California case, *Pennel v. City of San Jose*, Justice Scalia applied the Takings Clause to rent control. Although the majority of the Court decided not to decide the case because it was premature, Scalia, joined by Justice O'Connor, dissented, stating that they would decide and would hold that the Takings Clause was violated. In his opinion, Scalia agreed with the landowner that the hardship provision underlying rent guidelines is aimed at the problem of poor tenants, and that landlords are being compelled to subsidize those who cannot pay reasonable rents. Scalia declared that rent regulation is being used "to establish a welfare program, privately funded by those landlords who happen to have 'hardship' tenants." Scalia's logic applies to every part of the safety net and calls into question all economic regulation that affects wealth transfers, including other comparable regulatory measures, such as those providing for price control and wage and hour regulation.

A high point in the Radical Right's revision of taking laws and their attack on government regulation was in the *Lucas v. South Carolina* 1992 case. David H. Lucas paid $975,000 for two lots of land along the South Carolina coast. In twenty of the forty years prior to the time Lucas bought the land, all or part of the land was part of the beach or flooded twice daily by the ebb and flow of the tide. Between 1963 and 1973 the shoreline was 100 to 150 feet onto Lucas's plots.

Lucas knew when he bought the land both that it had been under water for a long period of time and that for many years prior to the date of purchase, both the federal and South Carolina governments had been seeking to protect the beach from erosion. Nonetheless, when the state refused him permission to build on the land, he claimed the land was wrongfully taken from him.

The Supreme Court agreed in a 6–3 decision. Scalia wrote the opinion of the Court. Agreeing with him were Thomas, Rehnquist, O'Connor, Kennedy, and White. Blackmun, Stevens, and Souter dissented. Scalia rejected the claim that South Carolina had the power to prevent, without compensating Lucas fully, the use of property the state found harmful to the coastline. Again, relying on Justice Holmes's decision in the 1922 Pennsylvania coal case, Scalia said South Carolina had rendered Lucas's land valueless, and thus he was entitled to compensation.

Blackmun's dissent contradicted Scalia's history of the Takings Clause. Relying on *Miller v. Schoene*, the 1928 case that justified the burning of some trees to save others, Blackmun claimed that Holmes's earlier 1922 decision had been consistently taken out of context to form the basis for Scalia's takings theory. Homes, said Blackmun, regarded economic injury as only one factor to be used in evaluating if there was a takings. Holmes did not say that once there was an economic injury it necessarily followed that the landowner must be paid the full value of the damage.

Stevens argued that the *Lucas* case showed again that the majority was returning to the *Lochner* era—that laws of Congress and the State of South Carolina were being rejected because the Court was substituting its own judgment on what was the best way to protect the environment. Later in the *Lake Tahoe* case (*Lake Tahoe Preservation v. Lake Tahoe Regional Planning*) Scalia, Thomas, and Rehnquist lost when they tried to extend *Lucas* to cover an instance where landowners were temporarily blocked from building developments along the Nevada lake.

The next case, *Dolan v. City of Tigard* (1994), shows how Epstein's theories became even more firmly embedded in American jurisprudence after Clarence Thomas joined the Court. Frances Dolan owned an electrical and plumbing supply store in the central business district of Tigard, Oregon, a Portland suburb. Business was good. She asked the Tigard City Planning Commission for permission to more than double the size of her building; they agreed to give her the permission if she gave to the city a strip of her land for bicycle and pedestrian use and if she gave to the city a piece of her land on a flood plain so the city could better protect itself against floods. In response, Dolan sued to allow her to build and to require the city to pay for any land it took. The Land Use Appeal Board, the Oregon trial court, and the Oregon Supreme Court all decided against her.

Rehnquist, writing for a 5–4 majority, ruled in her favor. In reversing three prior decisions, he dusted off the Takings Clause, saying it "was as much a part of the Bill of Rights as the First and the Fourth Amendments" and should not "be relegated to the status of a poor relation." Economic liberties are worth at least as much protection as personal liberties, he says. Any diminution of property values requires as much protection as any diminution of personal rights; thus, in battles between landowners and the government's "takings," the government loses.

Stevens and Souter, in dissent, said this decision was predicated upon a radical departure from the law, weakening in crucial ways the government's ability to protect its citizens. The dissenters warned that the unrestrained majority could now crack down on minimum wage and maximum hour legislation by reaching back to the *Lochner* result through a Takings Clause theory.

Another high-water mark in the Court's use of the Takings Clause was in

1998 when Justice O'Connor's swing opinion in the *Eastern Enterprises v. Apfel* case was based on Epstein's view of the clause's intent. The roots of this case reach back to the 1940s, when labor and management were at odds and Harry Truman seized the coal mines in order to keep them running. Shortly thereafter, the disputes were settled and agreements between the unions and the owners were entered into.

Eastern, a very successful coal company that began in 1946, agreed to give health benefits to its miners. By 1965 the corporation called Eastern had stopped mining coal, but its wholly owned subsidiary continued making substantial profits until 1987. Eastern totally owned the holding company for twenty-two years, took 100 percent of the profits of the coal mining operation, as they did before ($100 million from 1965 to 1987), shared offices with the holding company, and had the same officers, indicating clearly that it was only a corporate facade paper company that Eastern owners were using to try to insulate themselves from liability.

The case arose when the company challenged a 1992 federal statute requiring coal operators to retroactively provide health benefits for miners. The question before the Supreme Court in 1998 was how to interpret those contracts—the first of which was finalized in 1946—when so much time and history had intervened.

The Supreme Court argument took place on March 4, 1998. After reviewing the history of the contracts and labor struggles, Peter Buscemi, arguing on behalf of the miners, said, "I think it's easy in the midst of the argument to lose sight of the human dimension in the problem." Under questioning, he rejected Scalia's argument that Eastern's liability should be passed to the consumer: "Neither fairness nor justice should permit Eastern to avoid all financial responsibility for its coal industry retirees and to have these costs shouldered by the general public." Fourteen hundred employees and spouses would be covered if the Court ruled against Eastern, although no hard numbers were known on the total cost to Eastern.

Eastern argued that the Supreme Court could not "pierce the corporate veil"; namely, the fact that they sold the mining company to one of their own subsidiaries cut the company's liability off in 1965, the date of the transfer, even though the subsidiary continued to operate the mine and make substantial profits. Additionally, Eastern claimed that to make them pay the miners' benefits would so diminish the company's value that the government must reimburse it.

Justice O'Connor observed during the argument that "Eastern sold the coal mining company to a wholly owned subsidiary . . . and then there was cross management. I mean some of the same managers were also managers of the subsidiary corporation." She then asked if the original coal mining company had agreed, as a condition of the transfer, to repay the subsidiary if a court found that subsidiary must pay the miners benefits. Eastern's counsel tried to avoid the question. O'Connor pursued it, and the attorney finally answered yes, the original coal mining company would bear the entire burden, for it had agreed, as part of the sale, to indemnify the parent. These answers should have persuaded O'Connor to go along with the moderates. She looked behind the corporate structure and saw that it was form over substance. But it was not to be so.

The case was decided with the usual 5–4 split on the Court. The coal miners lost; the corporation won. Justice O'Connor's separate opinion in *Eastern* refused to require the company to pay the unpaid benefits, claiming any order to require Eastern to pay substantial monies, between $50 and $100 million, would be wrongfully "taking" the company's money: You cannot ask a company, she said, that stopped doing business in 1965 to pay thirty years of benefits more than thirty years later. O'Connor describes her test for implementing the Takings Clause. One must look at the financial impact on the company, and the extent to which the regulation interferes with the company's expected profits.

Eastern, once you look at reality and pierce the corporate veil, was a profitable company operating until 1987, and was trying to renege on an agreement that gave it substantial profits. Justice Breyer said the coal company earned substantial profits until 1987: "For many years Eastern benefitted from the labor of those miners. Eastern helped to create conditions that led the miners to expect continued health care benefits for themselves and their families after they retired." Justice Stevens saw that the sickness and early deaths of coal miners led to an understanding that the miners would put themselves at risk in exchange for lifetime benefits. The coal company had gone through quite a bit of corporate manipulation, he cited, not all driven by the desire to get rid of the miners, but having that effect anyway.

The moderates did not emphasize the cost to the 1965 company—the company they were writing about was making profits in 1987. The way the majority and minority saw facts differently helped justify their very different decisions. The extent to which the different fact finders deviate from a "true" reading of the record tells the reader how result-oriented is the decision. Previous to the *Eastern* case, five federal circuit courts that had looked at the issues similar to those presented in this case; all decided against Eastern's position.

In their *Eastern* dissent, the four minority justices claimed the Takings Clause was totally inappropriate, applying only when the government physically takes over property; the clause was never intended to reallocate funds of two private warring parties. The government itself took nothing in this case, they noted, and yet the Court was striking down a congressional act, passed after extensive hearings. Congress said in passing the law, "retired coal miners have legitimate expectations of health care benefits; that was the promise they received during their working lives and that is how they planned their retirement years. That commitment should be honored." Echoes of *Lochner* and *Hammer* could be heard in the Court's decision.

Most important, the dissenters concluded that the Takings Clause could drastically alter the constitutional landscape by giving greater recognition to economic rights. An expansive reading of the clause, warned Justice Breyer, could be raised whenever government assessed taxes or imposed any burden on certain parties.

The Supreme Court has fueled takings activism in the last fifteen years by ruling in favor of developers and other property owners in an unbroken string of cases. Although these rulings are relatively narrow, they reflect an untoward eagerness to overcome procedural obstacles in order to uphold takings claims.

Another way the Supreme Court can limit personal rights and protect economic interests is to stop an individual from going to court to sue. "Standing," the right to stand in court for a constitutional violation, is not just a mere technicality; it goes to the heart of the Constitution. If you don't meet the legal requirements for standing, you can't sue. For plaintiffs to satisfy the standing requirements and get into Court, they must prove they have suffered a real injury; that the injury is the result of an act forbidden by law, and that the Court can provide relief. What this means is that if I don't have a remedy—a place to enforce a right given to you by law—then you don't have the right. It's that simple.

The Warren Court opened the doors to the courthouse, expanding access to the federal courts because it saw that the state courts were not enforcing Constitutional rights. Justice Douglas was in favor of giving the widest access to "private attorney generals" to challenge laws the people believed were unconstitutional rather than have to wait, often in vain, for elected officials to do so. Expanding standing would dramatically change the kinds of cases the federal courts would hear.

In a 1968 Warren Court decision, *Flast v. Cohen*, the Court held by 8–1 that under limited circumstances taxpayers could sue in federal courts to challenge federal spending. Even though the plaintiffs suffered no economic harm, the concept of opening the courts to citizens for limited purposes brought nearly all nine Supreme Court justices together. Two years later, with only the change of chief justices, Burger replacing Warren, the Court upheld and expanded *Flast*, giving standing to anyone who claimed an actual injury to some recognized interest, be it economic, environmental, aesthetic, or otherwise.

At last, children denied access to schools had access to federal courts to enforce their rights to attend integrated schools. Demonstrators denied the right to assemble went to federal courts to protect their right to do so. But after Rehnquist and Powell replaced Black and John Harlan II, the Court clamped down and began to close the courthouse door. In 1974 the Court in a 5–4 decision recognizing the new conservative power refused to allow a taxpayer to make public the CIA's expenditures because the taxpayer "is seeking to employ a federal court as a forum in which to air his generalized grievances about the conduct of government." Justice Burger, who wrote the majority opinion, and Justice Powell, who wrote a concurring opinion, blasted *Flast*.

The Court, through a variety of legal strategies, including standing, joined the elder Bush's support of corporate interests who attack the environment. The limitation on standing is especially significant in environmental protection cases, where the question of who has been injured by the pollutant companies is directly relevant to who can challenge them in Court. Justices Rehnquist, Scalia, Kennedy, O'Connor, and Thomas have already used their positions as part of 5–4 majorities to undermine the ability of citizen groups to bring lawsuits in their efforts to enforce environmental protections. It is a major weapon. In the recent environmental case, *Friends of the Earth v. Laidlaw*, we can see how a court adopting the dissenting views of Scalia and

Thomas would weaken or nullify some important environmental laws. Here, a waste disposal company repeatedly released toxic pollutants, including mercury, into a river in South Carolina, a direct violation of the company's permit to operate a wastewater treatment plant. The trial found that Laidlaw had violated the mercury limits on 489 occasions between 1987 and 1995.

But the Supreme Court majority opinion refused to authorize citizen lawsuits to enforce the antipollution law that the company was charged with violating. Scalia and Thomas, ridiculing the dissent, first argued there was no proof that the illegal release of mercury and other pollutants into the waterway actually harmed the environment. They also claimed that citizen suits should not be allowed at all, that only the individuals damaged could bring suit.

Individuals, of course, rarely have the resources to sue large corporations. And yet, when they do, the individual challenging the government is routinely denied standing. These cases do not even get to the Supreme Court, for the Court denies review. The nearly physical revulsion many conservatives feel for environmental groups and values, and their reflex action to protect business being encroached upon, threaten to wipe out all the gains that preceded this Court. Raw political partisanship that sees the Court side with business interests is most apparent in environmental cases. The courts are in lockstep with the Right's attempts, outside the courts, to weaken the enforcement of environmental laws.

Minorities have run into a near impenetrable wall of "standing" law when they bring discrimination claims. The Rehnquist Court, building on the later part of the Burger Court, has raised the toughest standing hurdles in cases where minorities challenge racial or gender bias zoning practices that keep minorities out of new or previously white areas. Poverty plaintiffs are barred from challenging the tax-exempt status of hospitals that deny them emergency services. In 1996, Thomas and Scalia, joined by Chief Justice Rehnquist, in *M.L.B. v. L.J.*, indicated they would even permit states to prevent poor parents from appealing the termination of their parental rights by imposing high appeal and other fees, contrary to the majority's ruling. A portion of the dissent that not even Chief Justice Rehnquist would join showed that a Scalia-Thomas Court would overturn forty years of Supreme Court cases. One ruling they sought to overturn is a 1956 *Griffin v. Illinois* case, where the Court held for the "proposition that a State cannot arbitrarily cut off appeal rights for indigents while leaving open avenues of appeal for more affluent persons." If that case were overruled, high fees would even be allowed to prevent appeals by indigent criminal defendants facing the possibility of long prison sentences. On the other hand, standing requirements are relaxed when sustaining the unconstitutionality of federal subsidies for the nuclear power plant industry, for upholding offshore leasing policies, and for affirming tax credits to private schools.

In *Bragg v. Robertson*, a 2001 case, homeowners joined an environmental group in West Virginia to sue state surface-mining officials for routinely issuing permits allowing the environmentally devastating practice of mountaintop-removal coal mining. Just as the name suggests, under this practice, the tops of mountains are literally blown up and removed and thousands of tons of rock and debris are dumped in adjacent valleys. These "valley fills" level forests, bury streams, and pollute the rivers fed by these streams. This causes flooding, dust, noise, and vibrations severe enough to crack the foundations of nearby houses. The federal appeals court, in its zeal to seal off traditional state responsibilities from federal law and injured plaintiffs, said the state was immune from suit. The Supreme Court denied review.

It is hard to imagine how such a practice could be permitted under the federal Surface Mining Control and Reclamation Act (SMCRA), which is charged with protecting society from such adverse effects. Nonetheless, for years West Virginia surface-mining officials have routinely and expeditiously granted permits to do just that. Striking a deaf ear, too, has been the District of Columbia Circuit Court. In the last few years, it has struck down or hindered a long list of critical environmental protections ranging from wetland protections Superfund site designations, to guidelines on the treatment of petroleum wastewater.

Early on in his career, Justice Rehnquist said the values jurists bring with them informs how they judge. In the economic area the mind-set of the majority justices helps them see economic issues through personal lenses that are politically influenced. They are not familiar with or sympathetic toward the group in society that most bears the brunt of a free market. None of them were elected to political offices—they have not had to listen, see, work with, or apprehend the other. Whether O'Connor and Kennedy, acting in good faith, let their constitutional interpretations lead to the same result as Rehnquist, Scalia, and Thomas or whether, as some commentators have suggested, they delude themselves into thinking that the malleable Constitution parallels their politics, ultimately matters very little to the people affected. The result—and the defiling of our constitutional heritage—is the same.

7

RACE, GENDER, AND ETHNICITY

The defense of white privilege has primarily been carried out on the state level. At the time the Constitution was signed, every state except Massachusetts permitted slavery. A little-read section of the Constitution provides at Article I, Section 9 that the slave trade cannot be abolished until 1808. Had it said that after 1808 slavery must be prohibited, our history might have taken a far different course, for the South made clear it would not join the Union with an explicitly stated prohibition against slavery.

When Benjamin Franklin and Quaker abolitionists petitioned the House of Representatives in 1790 to end slavery, they were met by the resistance of the South and the complicity of the northern states, especially New York and New Jersey, which relied on slaves. A compromise resolution was thus prepared that read, "The Congress shall have no authority to interfere with the emancipation of the slaves, or in the treatment of them within any of the States; it remaining with the several States alone to provide any regulation therein, which humanity and true policy may require."

James Madison, who more than accepted the resolution as necessary to keep the Union together, explained that the Constitution made it unconstitutional to pass a law abolishing slavery. Neither he nor Thomas Jefferson rose to oppose the House resolution.

The Declaration of Independence and the U.S. Constitution, among the most imaginative documents ever written, are both deeply stained by the cancer of slavery. Our Founding Fathers' "self-evident truths" were anything but that when they dealt with race. The fifty-five members of the Constitutional Convention were elite property owners, not necessarily representative of the noble image meant to be conveyed by the phrase "We the People." The blacks paid a heavy price to solve a political problem thought necessary to create and preserve the Union. Indeed, the United States was the next to last Western nation to abolish slavery. Abraham Lincoln, the father of the Emancipation Proclamation, shared the belief of most Americans of his era—that free blacks could never live harmoniously with whites. On one occasion, he even remarked that his first impulse would be to "free all the slaves and send them back to Liberia, their own native land." The abolitionist leader Frederick Douglass unsuccessfully lobbied the president to declare that the Civil War was an antislavery battle.

The draft of the Emancipation Proclamation contained a provision that would have sent some blacks abroad or isolated them in black areas of the country; that provision was dropped from the final version because Lincoln could not gather support for it. The final proclamation, more a practical political document than an articulation of morality, indicated that freedom would follow the movement of Union armies—slaves behind Union lines would be liberated, set free. Neither truly a privilege nor a right, liberty came instead as a warning to southern combatants that further resistance would result in emancipation and, thus, further loss of property. The strains and resentments of two races are still with us. It is no wonder why states' rights and race remain on the forefront of the Supreme Court docket.

The Supreme Court from 1873 until the 1930s, with one exception, dismantled the Civil War amendments passed to enact into law the newly enhanced status of blacks, in ways that left them without equal protection. That trend, reversed by the important gains of the New Deal and Warren Courts, has been reinvigorated by a Rehnquist Court that is determined to deny blacks and other minorities an education, opportunities to better their economic condition, and the right to a meaningful vote.

This Court's race jurisprudence, including affirmative action and school separation, is based on a sleight of hand. It interprets Justice Harlan's use of the words "color blind" to stop segregation in his 1896 *Plessy v. Ferguson* dissent, to prevent or set back integration today. The Court's major rulings, which set back race-based litigation, are often procedural rather than substantive, but their effect is no less pernicious. Discrimination cases that now require evidence of a specific "discriminating intent," the new standard we saw articulated in the *Alexander v. Sandoval* case, make the enforcement of rights of African Americans, women, and other minorities almost impossible.

For example, in a 1981 case, *City of Memphis v. Greene*, the city of Memphis erected a traffic barrier between an all-white community and an all-black community, claiming it was a traffic safety measure. The city then widened the barrier twenty-five feet and closed the strip to the public. The black community had difficulty gaining access to a previously segregated park and zoo, and their property values were reduced. The Court accepted Memphis's explanation that the barrier was needed to control traffic and to preserve the residential character of the neighborhood. Justice John Paul Stevens, considered by some a liberal on today's Court because the Rehnquist Court has swung so far to the right, said the African American complainants presented "no evidence" of purposeful discrimination. This means that a governmental agency can do nearly what it wants unless racist motivation is specifically mentioned as a reason for an action, which no government would admit.

In a 1989 case, *Patterson v. McLean Credit Union*, Justices Rehnquist and Scalia, thinking they had the votes, tried to attack *Jones v. Mayer Co.* and *Runyon v. McCrary*, two landmark civil rights cases decided over one hundred years later by the Warren and Burger Courts. The *Patterson* decision does not give a hint either of the Court struggle or the reasons why Rehnquist and Scalia failed more than they succeeded. Of course, Thurgood Marshall was still on the bench in 1989; today, with a different Court that includes Thomas, the result would be different.

The history of prior cases is necessary to put the *Patterson* case in context. In 1968 the Warren Court held, in a 7–2 decision, in *Jones v. Mayer*, that the civil rights law enacted during Reconstruction prohibits racial discrimination in the sale or rental of property. Thus a private company could not refuse to sell a house to a black buyer. In 1976, one hundred years after the 1866 law was passed, the Burger Supreme Court, in another 7–2 decision, said, in *Runyon v. McCrary*, that the civil rights law prohibits racial discrimination in the making and enforcement of private contracts. A private school could not refuse to enter into a contract with black parents in order to keep the black child out of school. Both these cases seemed obvious and were seemingly established beyond attack.

Not, however, according to Rehnquist and some of his conservative colleagues. They tried to use *Patterson* to restore the law to the days prior to the passage of the 1866 Civil Rights Act and Reconstruction. Rehnquist and White had been the sole dissenters in *Runyon v. McCrary*, but by 1989, both the Court and the times had changed. Rehnquist eagerly seized on *Patterson* as the vehicle to move his minority position to the majority.

The chief justice's history on race issues is significant. At the time of the *Brown v. Board of Education* argument, Rehnquist, then clerking for Supreme Court justice Jackson, thought *Plessy* was correctly decided and *Brown* wrongly decided. Rehnquist's constitutional vision, and that of most of the justices on this Court who support him, resembles the politics of the post–Civil War northern Democrats, who were hostile to Reconstruction. Once slavery was abolished, they believed there was nothing left to reconstruct, and that no further restrictions should be imposed on the southern states in their dealings with their former slaves. By contrast, the Radical Republicans, led by such fighters as Thaddeus Stevens and Charles Sumner, believed that the war had been fought over the denial of civil rights by oppressive state governments, of which slavery was only the worst example. The Reconstruction amendments were to herald a new day, a new constitutional order under which state sovereignty would be limited by federal civil rights protection.

The Supreme Court, in 1873, in the Slaughterhouse cases, which involved a Louisiana law that dealt with the butchering of animals, ultimately interpreted the new amendments in accordance with the view that Reconstruction was a mistake and that the states had free rein to do what they liked with the new freedoms. Many of the rights of blacks were undercut. Ten years later, in the *Civil Rights Cases* in 1883, the Court held the Civil Rights Act of 1875 unconstitutional because it made blacks "the special favorite of the law." The Court had to decide if the civil rights amendments abolished only the structure of the past or if it also meant that blacks were now as free as whites. If they were as free as whites, they were entitled to have their rights protected against any future violation by state or federal governments. Another post-Reconstruction case struck down federal laws aimed at stopping the activities of the Ku Klux Klan on the grounds that they needlessly interfered with state sovereignty.

The *Patterson* case, at first look, does not appear to be a major decision, but when the case went up the federal judicial ladder twice, each time finishing in the Supreme Court, it became clear that more was at stake.

Brenda Patterson, a college graduate, spent ten years doing clerical work for the McLean Credit Union in Winston-Salem, North Carolina. She took a great deal of verbal racial abuse from the white supervisor and was given demeaning tasks (dusting, for example) not assigned to white workers. As the work piled up and relentless criticism by her white supervisors worsened, Brenda Patterson's health began to deteriorate. Marshall Patterson watched his wife, whom he described as ebullient and effervescent, be transformed into a nervous and depressed woman who frequently burst into tears when she told him about her difficulties at work. Although she was the only one of the ten employees at McLean who was black, the Pattersons had expected that Brenda would advance when she accepted the job there as accounting clerk. Instead, she saw her career go downhill over the course of a decade. "Blacks are known to work slower than whites by nature," her supervisor, Robert Stevenson, said when she asked about a promotion, according to Patterson's allegations. Stevenson denied this and said Patterson was judged on her performance rather than her race.

Harvey Kennedy, Brenda Patterson's lawyer, filed suit under the 1866 Civil Rights Act rather than the 1964 act, because the older statute gave Brenda Patterson the right to a jury trial for punitive damages and back pay beyond the two-year statute of limitations established in the new act.

On February 29, 1988, Penda Hair, the Legal Defense Fund attorney representing Patterson for the Supreme Court, began her argument by telling the justices that if on-the-job harassment is legally permitted, an employer "can say to a [black] worker: 'We'll hire you but only if you submit to [being] humiliated and demeaned because of your race.' That type of condition is exactly the badge of inferiority that the Thirteenth Amendment [abolishing slavery] and Section 1981 were designed to prohibit." Rehnquist challenged her, saying that losing a job because of race and being harassed on the job were two totally different situations with different legal consequences.

In response, Penda Hair replied that the contract of employment, under the act, prohibited the employer from racial discrimination in hiring. Rehnquist argued that if there was no discrimination in hiring and firing, Patterson should lose. But Penda Hair fought back with the argument that "the right to make and enforce a contract has to include the right to perform that contract free of racial discrimination."

At the judicial conference on March 2, 1988, Justice Brennan said Brenda Patterson should win because there was racial discrimination and it did not matter if it was after she got the job or if it was the reason she was denied the promotion. But that wasn't enough for the chief justice, who sensed this case was merely bait for a bigger kill. And so he put the earlier cases, the landmarks, *Runyon v. McCrary* and *Jones v. Mayer*, squarely on the table. He knew he had White and Scalia, and he thought he had the newly appointed Kennedy and O'Connor, all of whom now voted to reconsider *Runyon*. He hoped to get votes from Blackmun, who had written a decision while on the federal appeals court negating the argument that the 1866 act covered private discrimination, and from Stevens, who had written a previous Supreme Court opinion that led Rehnquist to believe he, too, could be persuaded.

But Stevens immediately told the conference he would join Brennan and Marshall to vote against reconsidering *Runyon*. O'Connor said she agreed with Rehnquist. Then Blackmun joined the liberal group, leaving it up to the newest judge, Anthony Kennedy, who, after reading White's attack on Brennan's opposition, switched his vote and joined the majority to consider overruling *Runyon* and *Jones*. Rehnquist had won. Kennedy wrote a note to Rehnquist saying, "I am in full agreement with your position and the arguments of those who oppose you do not sit well with me, and are most disappointing."

The liberals were shocked. Justice William Brennan attacked Rehnquist's attempts to reinterpret the 1866 act and pointed to a long string of Supreme Court cases that would have to be reversed. He said *Runyon* and *Jones* were not only correct, but precedent required the justices stay with them unless they were clearly wrong. Brennan pointed out that the 1866 act was passed in response to the Black Codes, by which the Confederate states imposed severe restrictions on the freed blacks in order to replicate the effects of slavery. He reminded his colleagues that the Thirty-ninth Congress had passed the 1866 act because they knew that blacks would be as vulnerable to private discrimination as they were to state discrimination, and they were determined to stop it. Blackmun, the Nixon appointee, in turn bewailed what the new majority was trying to do. "I am at a loss to understand the motivation of five members of this Court to reconsider an interpretation of a civil rights statute that so clearly reflects our society's commitment to ending racial discrimination."

Two months after the argument, the Court requested reargument on *Patterson* and asked the lawyers to focus on whether *Runyon v. McCrary* and *Jones v. Mayer* should be overruled. This was a rare event made even rarer because the lawyers knew that the validity of *Runyon* and *Jones* had not been challenged and had not been briefed by either side on the *Patterson* case. Shock waves went through the civil rights community.

Emboldened by recent appointments, Rehnquist was now drawing his line in the sand. It was, Rehnquist hoped, a clear signal to minorities that the new Court intended to rewrite civil rights law. The order setting the case down for reargument created an uproar. Amicus briefs from historians, attorneys, constitutional scholars, and civil rights groups flooded the Court. The departure from the established law was so dramatic, and the potential harm from a reversal so great, that the order for reargument became a media event. Even more significant than Brenda Patterson's case was that Rehnquist, three years into his new job, was exploiting his majority to try to reject settled laws that had led to substantial racial progress. One reason he gave for the reversal of *Runyon* was that it would substantially cut down on the number of cases filed in the federal courts—an argument he repeatedly advanced against environmentalists, criminal defendants, poor people, and those who opposed the drug, chemical, and tobacco companies.

The second *Patterson* argument before the Court was very different from the first. The courtroom was packed, and the tension between the justices was visible. With much more at stake, the Legal Defense Fund chose Julius Chambers, a very experienced counsel, to represent Brenda Patterson. He told the Court, "And as we look at the legislative history [of the 1866 law] we see a Congress that saw blacks, freed blacks, harassed in the workplace, denied pay, and that's the kind of conduct this Congress was trying to reach. We're not working the farms now—we're working in the credit unions. The type of discrimination may differ, but the conduct, the discrimination, the enslavement, the badges of slavery are the things we are trying to reach."

On October 14, 1988, at the conference days after the second argument, White, Scalia, and O'Connor deserted Rehnquist, saying *Runyon* was wrong but should not be overruled. Scalia said "public reaction" to overruling it would be too great.

It took eight months after the argument for the Court to reach a decision. Kennedy had originally, at the October conference, voted with the moderates and thus would have represented the fifth member of a majority vote for Brenda Patterson. But when he changed his mind to join Rehnquist, Rehnquist assigned him the opinion for the new *Patterson* majority (Rehnquist, White, O'Connor, Scalia, and Kennedy), an unusual choice, since Kennedy had not yet completed a full term on the Court. Important opinions generally are given to more seasoned justices. But in *Patterson*, the chief needed Kennedy's vote, and the assignment could help reinforce the junior justice's commitment. Morever, if Rehnquist had given the assignment to Justice Scalia, he might have risked losing Kennedy once again.

On June 15, Kennedy read the decisions in *Patterson v. McLean Credit* to a courtroom filled with civil rights activists and media. Outside, demonstrators were challenging the Court's right to wipe out one hundred and thirty years of law. Kennedy announced two separate rulings: the first, 9–0, and the second, 5–4. The Court, he said, would uphold, by unanimous vote, its past rulings of *Jones v. Mayer* and *Runyon v. McCrary* that extended what remained of the 1866 Reconstruction law to racial discrimination by private employers. A sigh of relief was audible in the courtroom. Rehnquist had made an embarrassing tactical blunder; he had shown the less attractive side of himself and gotten slapped in the face for it.

The second 5–4 decision said only discrimination in hiring, not racial harassment on the job or the denial of a promotion, was covered by the law. Kennedy's last paragraph could have led a reader to conclude that Patterson had won. "Discrimination based on the color of one's skin is a profound wrong of tragic dimension," Kennedy said. "Neither our words nor our decisions should be interpreted as signaling one inch of retreat from the nation's commitment to eradicating racial bias." The decision "is entirely consistent with our society's deep commitment to the eradication of discrimination based on a person's race or the color of his or her skin." Kennedy said that if the white supervisor had called blacks "slower" than whites and constantly looked over Brenda Patterson's shoulder, "this type of conduct [is] reprehensible," but it does not violate the terms of the 1866 law; Patterson was not denied the right to "make and enforce a contract" because of her race, so she cannot claim her rights were violated under this law.

The four dissenters were furious, not only at the result, but at the difference between the rhetoric of the opinion and the opinion itself. Brennan said he was chagrined and puzzled by Kennedy. How could he say the Court had not retreated "one inch" on ending racial discrimination, while refusing to go along with an opinion making illegal racial harassment that was "severe and pervasive"? Brennan's fury can be seen in the language at the beginning of his *Patterson* draft. "What the Court declines to snatch away with one hand, it *steals* with the other," he wrote. "The Court's fine phrases about our commitment to the eradication of racial discrimination disappear," said Brennan, when the law is to be applied, because the Court truthfully does not want discrimination eradicated.

The decision was both a victory and a defeat. It left *Runyon* and *Jones* intact, and it refused to consider racial harassment as a violation of the statute. Penda Hair called Kennedy's opinion an "underhanded way to erode a settled civil rights law. We're left with a shell of a law." Ralph Neas, then executive director of the Leadership Conference on Civil Rights, pointed to the string of recent reversals. "We've lost more in two and a half weeks than we had in the previous two and a half decades," he said.

Now that the Court had spoken, the battle over civil rights and job discrimination moved across First Street to the Capitol. "Congress must not let these decisions stand," said Senator Edward Kennedy. Because the rulings interpreted federal law, Congress could reverse the decisions by rewriting the law. It did so by passing the Civil Rights Act of 1991.

The *Patterson* decision immediately cast the light on Anthony Kennedy. Kennedy, the newest justice who decided *Patterson*, was President Reagan's third choice for Justice Lewis Powell's seat. Kennedy in 2001 voted more with Rehnquist than any other justice.

After Robert Bork's embattled Senate confirmation hearings and the withdrawal of the even more conservative Douglas Ginsburg because of revelations that he had smoked marijuana while a student and that he had also exaggerated his court experience, attention focused on Kennedy. In fact, Anthony Kennedy's most important asset was that he was neither Bork nor Ginsburg. The "third choice," as Kennedy refers to himself, is a devout Roman Catholic, close to Edwin Meese, to whom he owes his appointment.

Kennedy was born on July 23, 1936, in Sacramento, California, the son of a successful lawyer and powerful lobbyist. A graduate of Stanford University and Harvard Law School, Kennedy practiced law for fifteen years (six of those as a solo practitioner), until his father's death changed his career path. He returned to Sacramento and took over his father's law practice with its heavy lobbying component.

Kennedy was a successful lobbyist who presented the case for favorable legislation for his clients while at the same time working hard within the Republican Party. He knew where he wanted to go. He gave lavish parties, donated large sums of his money to the Republican Party, and persuaded some of the bigger California corporations to do the same. Not long after, when Ed Meese, then Governor Reagan's chief advisor, was looking for a Republican lawyer to draft a state referendum proposition that would limit state spending through taxation, he chose Kennedy. The referendum lost, but Kennedy gained entrée into California's Republican inner circle. In 1975, at thirty-nine, he became one of the youngest federal appellate judges in the nation; he wrote more than four hundred opinions, all exhibiting judicial restraint. Like Ginsburg and Breyer, he wrote scholarly, narrowly crafted, fact-based decisions that were difficult to reverse. He did not have a bad paper trail.

By the time Kennedy entered the historic paneled Senate Caucus Room on December 14, 1987, for his confirmation hearing, his nomination was secure. His reputation had been carefully built on a long record of steady and cautious personal and professional achievement. Democrats Joseph Biden and Edward Kennedy praised Judge Kennedy. Chairman Biden praised Kennedy "for not having any ideological briefs in your back pocket. You are an extremely honorable man." Asked if he possessed an overriding constitutional philosophy, Kennedy replied, "I do not offer myself as someone with a complete cosmology of the Constitution."

Senator Arlen Specter asked Kennedy if he could reconcile *Brown v. Board of Education* with the "original intent" of the Framers of the Fourteenth Amendment (a question that had been Bork's downfall). "I do not think the Fourteenth Amendment was designed to freeze into society all of the inequities that then existed," Kennedy replied. Kennedy's answer pleased Democratic senator Howard Metzenbaum. A skillful witness, Kennedy assured the committee that it was entirely appropriate for them to seek assurances that "a nominee to the Supreme Court is sensitive to civil rights. We simply do not have any real freedom if we have discrimination based on race, sex, religion or national origin." With this, on February 18, 1988, Kennedy succeeded to Justice Lewis Powell's seat, with the unanimous vote of the Senate.

Richard Willard, Attorney General Meese's assistant, and Meese, along with Grover Joseph Rees, a Reagan judge picker, had assured the right wing of the Republican Party that Kennedy "would not disappoint conservatives on prayer, abortion and other social and moral issues." But the justice was seen as a turncoat when he subsequently refused to vote to overturn *Roe v. Wade* and voted against school prayer. *Human Events*, in a 1996 article entitled "Justice Anthony Kennedy: Surely Reagan's Biggest Disappointment," accused Kennedy of having "gone with the flow of liberal opinion"; *Washington Times* columnist Don Feder, a right-wing activist, put it bluntly in 1996, in a column in the form of a "memo addressed to the next president." Feder wrote, "Be damned sure you are putting a Scalia clone on the bench and not another Kennedy."

Although both Kennedy and Stevens were appointed by Republicans, they disagreed with each other nearly all the time. According to the November 2001 *Harvard Law Review*, which each year examines voting alignments, Stevens disagreed with Rehnquist more than any other justice. Kennedy and Stevens voted together 34.5 percent of the time, as compared to Rehnquist and Kennedy who, in 2001, voted together 89.5 percent of the time. The sharp difference between Stevens and Kennedy can be seen in *Patterson*. Stevens cannot justify banning discrimination before the making of the employment contract but not after. Stevens said: "A contract is not just a piece of paper. Just as a single word is the skin of a living thought, so is a contract evidence of a vital, ongoing relationship between human beings." Kennedy's opinion ignores the human element.

Like his predecessor, William O. Douglas, Stevens is iconoclastic and highly individualistic, not a coalition builder. He voted against Kennedy's position in *Patterson* and against the Court's sending the case down for reargument to reconsider *Runyon* and *Jones*. Plucked from the U.S. Court of Appeals for the Seventh Circuit by President Gerald Ford to replace William Douglas, the most liberal member of the Roosevelt-Warren-Burger Courts, Stevens was considered a respectable conservative. Ford wanted a noncontroversial justice who reflected his views and would sail through the nomination process. Stevens filled the bill.

Born on April 20, 1920, to a wealthy Chicago family, Stevens graduated first in his class from Northwestern University School of Law, where his grades were the highest on record. His extraordinary intelligence and achievement earned him a clerkship with Supreme Court justice Wiley B. Rutledge, a legal scholar who refused to allow technical obstacles to interfere with his sense of justice. Justice Rutledge was a model for Stevens; his opinions were often long, meticulous, and fact-based.

After his clerkship, Stevens practiced law and taught at the University of Chicago and Northwestern University law schools. Appointed to the seventh circuit court of appeals by President Nixon in 1970, he continued to establish his reputation as a formidable intellect, with opinions similar to Rutledge's—detailed and careful.

Many Republicans thought that Stevens and O'Connor would be the swing votes on the Rehnquist Court, turning it to the right. But Stevens often refused to join in either minority or majority opinions, choosing instead to write his own view of the case and often showing a fresh, unique perspective. What a law clerk once said of Douglas applies to Stevens: "Douglas was just as happy signing a one-man dissent as picking up four votes." Stevens remarked in a 1986 speech, "The audience I most frequently address does not always seem to be listening to what I have to say." Douglas might have said the same thing.

Stevens votes today in much the same way on most issues as he voted at the beginning of his career. As the Rehnquist Court moved toward the Right during the Reagan and the elder Bush presidencies, Stevens stayed where he was.

Indeed, Stevens has proved consistently inconsistent and thus interesting to watch. The statistics kept by the *Harvard Law Review* each year evaluating where the justices stand on the liberal-conservative spectrum shows he was the justice at the center of the Burger Court when he joined it in 1975, disagreeing equally with the justices at the liberal and conservative poles, and was, years later, still in the middle, disagreeing with Judge Rehnquist in 35 percent of the cases and with Justice Brennan 32 percent. During the 2001 term of the Court, he was the leading dissenter and the justice who voted least with Rehnquist. According to that year's *Harvard Law Review* analysis, he voted less with Scalia, Thomas, and Rehnquist than did the other moderates. Stevens is a bloc in himself; he voted less with Ginsburg, Souter, and Breyer than they did with each other. He reminds me of Morarji Desai, the former prime minister of India, who, when asked what party he belonged to, said, "I am a party of one and I generally dissent from it." A law clerk once described Stevens as a "unique mix of radicalism and restraint." Today he votes most often with the moderate bloc, although his legal positions have not greatly changed. He has not been reborn—the Court has.

The year 2000 saw a further and substantial evisceration of the civil rights law by the conservative majority. We already saw in the *Alexander v. Sandoval* case that the Court upheld an Alabama law requiring an applicant for a driver's license to pass an English literacy test—a statute clearly aimed at non–English-speaking minorities. But even moderates are becoming impatient with Spanish-speaking-only classes in our publicly financed school systems (i.e., in California and New York), which appear to coddle new immigrants and delay their assimilation. *Alexander* is a powerful precedent that can help destroy bilingualism.

English-only laws have always been supported by Evangelicals and other groups that are part of the Republican Right. It was a platform plank in Pat Buchanan's 1992 presidential campaign. Robert Dole in 1996 supported the English-only movement to protect "national unity." Newt Gingrich proclaimed that bilingualism threatened "the very fabric of American society." Language differences, he said, fostered "linguistic and cultural isolation" that could cause tension and unrest. The Washington Legal Foundation, one of the litigation arms of the Federalists, argued in a case supporting Arizona's English-only law that the statute making English that state's official language was consistent with the hopes of those who wrote the Constitution and the Mayflower Compact. And when the 1997 census revealed that Hispanics were the majority minority, John Tanton, the founder of a national advocacy group called U.S. English, warned of a "Latin onslaught." "Mongrelization" of America became one of his favorite images. In this atmosphere, a seemingly minor case like *Alexander* became a 5–4 decision to be used in severely limiting civil rights protection for the benefit of America's white majority.

More important than the English-only driver's license test upheld by the Court was the new test the Court imposed on those seeking to prove dis-

crimination. An individual citizen previously could claim that a job requirement that appeared to be innocuous on its face was, in fact, a requirement
meant to discriminate. For example, if all of California's and Alabama's rural
street cleaners had to have high school diplomas, a requirement totally
unrelated to the job, most minorities might be excluded. Similarly, a driving
rule linked to literacy in California might prohibit licenses, and thus jobs,
for non–English-speaking minorities, a substantial part of the population.

The federal appeals courts had allowed private plaintiffs to sue using the
"results" standard of proof for three decades. But Scalia, as we saw, writing
the majority opinion in *Alexander*, said suits could be brought only for
intentional discrimination on the basis of race and national origin, and not
over policies that have a discriminatory impact. His ruling severely limited
one of our most potent civil rights laws.

The *Alexander* decision restricted Title VI, a critical component of the
Civil Rights Act of 1964, one of the most important of the 1960s legislation
and acknowledged by Lyndon Johnson as his major achievement. Section
601 of that law provides that no person shall, on the grounds of race, color,
or national origin, be excluded from participation in, be denied the benefits
of, or be subjected to discrimination under any federally funded program.
The law supports disparate discrimination claims, from discrimination in
education and health care programs to bank red-lining of poor neighborhoods. Previously, both private individuals and the government could sue,
but now a new standard prevails.

The *Alexander* decision is part of the Court's proposed blueprint. The
Civil Rights Act was passed to stop blatant discrimination and to try to
anticipate clandestine methods of discrimination, some that already existed
and some that were sure to be created. The conservatives had failed in cases
such as *Patterson* to make sweeping changes, and they were aware, as Scalia
said, that the public would stand for only so much change. They voted not
to overrule the civil rights law but instead tried to pick it to death.

In his dissenting opinion in *Alexander*, Justice Stevens said that "it makes
no sense" to differentiate for the purposes of private lawsuits between intentional discrimination and discriminatory impact. "There is but one private
action to enforce Title VI, and we already know that such an action exists."
Stevens, speaking for himself, Souter, Ginsburg, and Breyer, said, "Today in a
decision unfounded in our precedents and hostile to decades of settled expectations," the Court reverses twenty-seven years of law effectively "underlying

the majority's dismissive treatment of our prior cases," in both a "flawed analysis" and "uncharitable understanding" of the intent of the Civil Rights Act. In *Alexander*, as in other cases, the majority refused to look at Congress's intent in passing the civil rights law, a practice that was uniformly observed prior to the Rehnquist Court. It was just another example—like *United States v. Lopez, Kimel v. Florida Board of Regents*, and *Morrison v. United States*— of disregarding Congress. As Justice Stevens put it, "The settled expectations of the Court undercut today's decisions not only from judicial decisions, but also from the consistent statements and actions of Congress."

Previous case law shows how radical the Supreme Court's *Alexander* ruling was. Of the twelve federal appeals courts, nine had addressed the issue and all nine had found that suits for discriminating impact could be filed under Title VI. But *Alexander* is a significant damper on other federal laws as well, for example, on those that prohibit sex discrimination in programs that receive federal money. Women who bring private lawsuits will be required to prove intentional discrimination. Scalia's *Alexander* decision affected the rights of many millions; far fewer claims are being filed, many of which are determined to be precluded from Court review, and of those that do go to trial, many more lose.

Scalia's majority decision, arguing that the case changes little, is misleading. All *Alexander* means, says Scalia, is that an individual who is discriminated against cannot sue unless he shows intentional discrimination directly aimed at him, but that the government can sue on his or others' behalf. However, little federal money exists to fund such suits, and Republican administrations are not apt to rush to court to challenge laws such as these.

This problem becomes particularly acute, for example, when environmentalists want to attack a Department of Transportation regulation that they claim is discriminating, such as when companies that create pollutants are found in minority areas. According to Scalia, only the government can make the disparate impact claim, but there is no likelihood of a Republican Department of Justice bringing suit against a Republican Department of Transportation carrying out Republican policy.

Scalia's decision is strewn with language that can destroy other parts of the Civil Rights Act. Because few federally financed programs are overtly discriminatory, suits for intentional discrimination are rare, while lawsuits alleging discriminatory effects represent the biggest category of cases under Title VI. The law authorizes federal agencies to issue regulations that bring their own programs into compliance with Title VI, and many regulations go beyond intentional discrimination also to bar the use of federal money in programs with discriminatory effects. But, as we know, a private citizen can hardly win under those regulations.

Justice Stevens criticized the majority not only for its decision, but also for taking the case in the first place, as there was no conflict among the lower federal courts on the issue. While the newly conservative and right-wing circuit courts increasingly agree with one another, the Court, with more space on its docket, will continue to reach out, as it did in *Eastern* (discussed in the previous chapter) and in *Patterson* and *Alexander*, to change decisions and laws that it doesn't like, that are not before it, or that need not be before it. The conservative principal of judicial restraint— judges decide cases narrowly and do not decide cases that are not before them—is totally ignored by this Court. In *Bush v. Gore*, the Court majority, like in *Alexander* and *Patterson*, claimed they were obligated to decide the issues they felt were forced on them. This is nonsense; it's merely another example of an established outreach pattern. No other Court has done this in such a systematic way and has been so disingenuous about its actions. The justice primarily responsible for this change in policy is Chief Justice William Rehnquist.

During a legal career spanning forty years, Chief Justice Rehnquist has moved from being an often isolated dissenter (he dissented alone fifty-four times, a Court record) to the commander of the majority. He succeeded, beyond what must have been his wildest imagination when first appointed to the Court, in fulfilling his self-described mission to clean up the legal and political errors of past Courts and chart the Court's new path. He will be remembered as one of its most influential justices.

Although Rehnquist and the conservatives flail at the New Deal and Warren Courts, many of the cases that bother them most were decided during the early years of the Burger Court. Warren Burger's seventeen-year reign in many instances expanded the Warren Court. *Roe v. Wade*; the *Furman v. Georgia* case, knocking down the death penalty; *Goldberg v. Kelly*, Brennan's favorite case dealing with due process; and a leading church-state case, were all argued on Burger's watch.

Burger, who did not have either the political skills or the intellectual force necessary to lead the Court, retired early, stepping down in 1986. By then members from both aisles of the Court had had enough of him. Rehnquist, his successor, led the Court through a seismic transition in political ideology. No other justice has played such a large part in that transition. He had the ambition, intellect, and political skills to support it, and now—sitting forty years—the longevity.

Rehnquist, a brilliant student, was Phi Beta Kappa at Stanford, then earned a master's degree in government at Harvard before attending Stanford Law School. He graduated in 1952 at the top of his class and soon became a law clerk to Justice Robert Jackson. Rehnquist, not shy about his views, told Justice Jackson that he believed the long delay in executing the Rosenbergs was wrong and asked why "the highest court of the nation must behave like a bunch of old women every time they encounter the death penalty." David Savage of the *Los Angeles Times* reported that Harvard Law School professor Donald Troutman, who clerked with Rehnquist on the Supreme Court, said, "He had no sympathy for criminal defendants. None. When you talked about the problems of the cities or the poor or blacks, it was clear he had no understanding. It was a universe he didn't comprehend."

Rehnquist's time on the Court drove him even further to the right. He sought to crack the wall of separation between church and state; supported official prayers in schools and opposed school desegregation; opposed the Equal Rights Amendment for women, saying it would "turn holy wedlock into holy deadlock" and "hasten the dissolution of the family"; and argued that the Constitution's "equal protection guarantee" did not forbid sex discrimination because the Fourteenth Amendment was designed to protect blacks, not females.

As a young lawyer in Phoenix in the mid-1950s, active in Republican politics, Rehnquist denounced the "left-wing philosophers" on the Warren Court who were showing "extreme solicitude to Communists and other criminals." During Barry Goldwater's 1964 presidential campaign, he denied the charge that he acted illegally in obstructing black and Hispanic voters by challenging their eligibility—a practice then routinely accepted and used against minority voters in Arizona and many other parts of the country.

David Savage, in his fine book, *Turning Right*, reported that when, on June 15, 1964, the Phoenix City Council was considering a citywide "public accommodations" law that would forbid discrimination against customers based on race, color, or religion, Rehnquist opposed it. "I oppose the ordinance because I believe that the values it sacrifices are greater than the values which it gives," he declared. The issue as he saw it was "freedom" of an individual against heavy-handed government interference. Later he wrote, "The Founders of this nation thought of it as the 'land of the free' just as surely as they thought of it as the 'land of the equal.' . . . The ordinance summarily does away with the historic right of the owner of a drug store, lunch counter, or theater to choose his own customers."

Rehnquist argued that no law, in fact, could remedy the racial problem, because it "stems from the state of mind of the proprietor . . . unable to correct the source of the indignity to the Negro, it redresses the situation by placing a separate indignity on the proprietor. It is as barren of accomplishment in what it gives to the Negro as in what it takes from the proprietor. The unwanted customer and the disliked proprietor are left glowering at one another across the lunch counter." Despite Rehnquist's rhetoric, the measure passed by an overwhelming vote. Later, as the top legal theorist of the Nixon administration, Rehnquist defended the government crackdown on Vietnam War and civil rights protesters along with initiatives such as wiretapping, "no-knock" searches, and the FBI's surveillance of private citizens. When a later case came before the Court challenging the very surveillance practices in which Rehnquist was involved, he refused to recuse himself.

Nixon nominated Rehnquist to the Supreme Court in 1972. Judiciary Committee members heard from witnesses concerning the allegations of voter obstruction. During Senate deliberations on his nomination as chief justice, witnesses opposing his confirmation again raised such charges. One witness described a "shoving match" involving the nominee that erupted at a Phoenix polling place when a black voter became angry because Rehnquist, the witness claimed, challenged the voter's credentials. James S. Brosnahan, a highly respected former federal prosecutor in Phoenix, who by 1986 was a senior partner in a San Francisco law firm, testified that he had gone to a polling place during one election to investigate allegations that Republican workers were harassing minority voters. Until 1964, Brosnahan noted, it had been legal to challenge voters if there was reason to believe they were illiterate, but not to stop persons in a voting line without reason, which is exactly what Rehnquist did.

Memoranda he wrote to Justice Jackson that surfaced during the confirmation hearing make clear that the then law clerk was no friend of the minorities, first railing at "the liberals" who were breaking down segregation in the South, then expressing his belief that the Court was wrong in deciding *Brown*. Rehnquist first laid out his philosophy on this point in a 1952 memo to Justice Jackson, advising the justice to "reaffirm" the separate but equal doctrine of *Plessy v. Ferguson* because it "was right." Rehnquist wrote:

> To those who would argue that the "personal" rights are more sacrosanct than "property" rights, the short answer is that the Constitution makes no such distinction. To the argument made by [plaintiff Brown's attorney] Thurgood, not John, Marshall that a majority may not deprive a minority of its constitutional right, the answer must be made that while this is sound in theory, in the long run it is the majority who will determine what the constitutional rights of the minority are. . . . I realize that it is an unpopular and unhumanitarian position, for which I have been excoriated by "liberal" colleagues but I think *Plessy v. Ferguson* was right and should be re-affirmed.

When the *Plessy v. Ferguson* memo initialed "WHR" resurfaced during the 1986 hearing on Rehnquist's nomination to be chief justice, Senators Metzenbaum and Biden hammered at the use of the "I" in the memorandum, trying to get Rehnquist to concede he was expressing his own views and not Jackson's, as he was steadfastly maintaining. Senator Carl Levin of Michigan told the Senate:

> We now have had a better opportunity to examine the evidence relating to this memo than the Senate had in 1971. . . . [I]t is very difficult to conclude anything other than that the memo does not contain Justice Jackson's views, and must therefore have been either an expression of law clerk Rehnquist's views or an attempt on the part of law clerk Rehnquist to provide Jackson with the pro-*Plessy* point of view. In either case, the evidence casts serious doubt on Justice Rehnquist's account of the nature of his memorandum.

Senator Robert Dole, arguing in Rehnquist's favor, said that "the people voted for Ronald Reagan by landslide proportions in 1980 and 1984" and "they expect the President to carry their mandate all the way to the Supreme Court." After the hearings ended, the Republican-controlled Congress and the president's extensive lobbying led to a 65–33 victory. It was the most votes ever cast against a chief justice nominee.

In 1988, two years after the hearing, Professor Bernard Schwartz found further evidence bearing on Rehnquist's candor and view on *Plessy*. He was given access to Justice Jackson's concurring draft opinion in the *Brown* case, which was never issued. The draft showed that Jackson clearly believed that school segregation was unconstitutional. Schwartz concluded logically: "It is hard to believe that the man who wrote the sentences holding segregation invalid in his draft held the view only a few months earlier attributed to him by Chief Justice Rehnquist—'that *Plessy v. Ferguson* was right and should be re-affirmed.'"

The majority's theme in the school segregation, discrimination, and affirmative action cases is that the injury to minorities has been sufficiently rectified and, if not, the Court should no longer try to redress the injury. As Justice Scalia proudly said in justifying the conservative view, "We are all Americans." From the Right's viewpoint, we have passed too many laws to protect individuals from racial discrimination, unfair legal systems, and indifferent educators.

Their legal view is based upon a fundamental misreading of the Fourteenth Amendment. Clause 5 reads: "nor shall any State deprive any person of life, liberty, or property, without due process of law; nor deny to any person within its jurisdiction the equal protection of the laws." The operative questions are: How does one define liberty in the first part of the sentence? Does liberty in other parts of the document's first section mean something broader, narrower, or the same, as liberty in the Due Process Clause? These words have been fought about since the amendment was enacted, for their implications shape our understanding of how far the Due Process Clause of the Fourteenth Amendment may go in limiting state power. Today's majority thus finds the Court's minority interpretation of the Fourteenth Amendment extravagant: they claim that the liberals' definition of the words *liberty* and *due process* have gone too far in expanding individual rights and in narrowing economic rights.

The Rehnquist Court gave this interpretation its own spin when it stopped federal trial courts from enforcing school integration.

The Supreme Court was hostile to most claims filed by African Americans until the mid-twentieth century. The legendary *Brown* case began in 1950 when young students from Kansas, South Carolina, Virginia, and Delaware said that they had been denied admission to schools open to whites because they were black. When reached in 1954, the decision signaled that a new era of protection had begun. *Brown*, which was Earl Warren's first case, had been argued originally in 1952 before he was appointed to the Court by the NAACP's lawyer, Thurgood Marshall, who was later to become Warren's colleague. The Court was then divided on the decision and on how to enforce it against school systems throughout the country. Had it been left to the then Chief Justice Frederick Vinson, the result would have been totally different. The plaintiffs could have lost, and even if they won, it most probably would have been a split decision with a narrow ruling. When Vinson died and Earl Warren came in as chief justice, the case was reargued. Extraordinary politician that he was, Warren persuaded the Court to issue a unanimous moral statement, a clarion call to America.

Prior to *Brown v. Board of Education*, an estimated one-quarter of the South's black population was illiterate. Investment in school plants was four times higher for whites than for blacks. Segregated states spent $86 million on white colleges, $5 million on black ones. There were twenty-nine accredited medical school for whites, one for blacks, forty law schools for whites, one for blacks. The burden of school-integration cases, which we turn to now, are commonly thought to rest on the belief that the Court found that the Framers intended the Fourteenth Amendment's Equal Protection Clause to be applied to school segregation. But that was not the basis of the Warren Court's decision.

Before the reargument before the new Warren Court, many of the justices had concluded that the legislative history of the Fourteenth Amendment was chaotic—that you could not say that the Thirty-ninth Congress, which passed the amendment after the Civil War and voted to submit it to the states for ratification, either had, or did not have, an intent to outlaw segregation in the schools. In fact, given that Washington, D.C., where the Framers lived, always had segregated schools and they never made any attempt to desegregate them, the better argument, the Right says, is that the Framers had no intention to stop the practice of all-black and all-white schools and therefore we now cannot stop segregation.

But the Warren Court, in its 1954 decision, treated the Constitution as a living organic document: "We must consider public education in the light of its full development and its present place in American life throughout the nation. Only in this way can it be determined if segregation in public schools deprives those plaintiffs of the equal protection of the laws." The manner in which that Court arrived at the decision also distinguished precedent. When Justice Oliver Wendell Holmes declared that "the life of the law has not been logic; it has been experience," and that the law must decide "what is expedient for the community," he, too, spoke to the living, changing Constitution that drove the *Brown* decision.

There were, in fact, two *Brown* decisions, both landmarks. The first said school segregation was unconstitutional. The Court waited a year to see the reaction to the decision and to decide how to implement it. The second decision, called *Brown II*, directed the South to make a "prompt and reasonable start" and a transition "with all deliberate speed" to integrate schools.

The Supreme Court justices recognized how long, bitter, and costly the fight for integration would be. Justice Hugo Black predicted only "glacial movement" toward desegregation in the South. At first, the cost was borne by the NAACP, whose clients were the children trying to go to school. The Department of Justice knew the multimillion-dollar legal work for the desegregation plans could not be borne by the underfinanced, overworked, and overcommitted NAACP, and so the Department of Justice, to continue the cases, took up much of the burden. President Eisenhower admitted he himself did not agree with *Brown* and did no more than promise to obey the law of the land until the situation got so ugly he was forced, against his will, to use troops to protect the black schoolchildren.

Some states totally ignored *Brown*; some fought back. Virginia was a leader of that resistance; many Virginia counties tried to avoid complying with *Brown* by abolishing their systems of public schools and substituting state financing of "private" schools. The images of that era—James Meredith walking past a jeering, threatening gauntlet in order to get to the Oxford campus of the University of Mississippi; southern governors standing on schoolhouse steps; federal marshals escorting children to school—are forever etched in the minds of millions who watched the events on television. And yet *Brown* was itself nullified for over ten years: very little was done actually by the courts to further desegregation. "With all deliberate speed" meant infinite delay. Justice Black, in later talking of the *Brown* victory, said, "The original plaintiffs have doubtless all passed high school age, but they were still not able to attend white high schools."

Brown II had left it to the lower courts to enforce *Brown*. But because of the states' fierce opposition and the lower courts' hesitancy, very little was happening. Few federal judges would fight the communities they lived in over segregation, an issue they did not believe in. Because the *Brown* Court did not lay down specific guidelines, a very serious mistake, the federal judges could avoid enforcement responsibility in their communities by claiming the Supreme Court had not given them a specific order or decree. It was not until the Supreme Court buckled down and actually tried to enforce *Brown* that the opposition would go beyond name-calling and into the incidents of physical resistance we all remember that compelled Presidents Eisenhower and Kennedy to call in federal troops.

When it became clear that the federal government, and particularly the federal judiciary, could not, or would not, enforce *Brown*, the civil rights movement joined the battle. Martin Luther King Jr. helped organize a nonviolent movement that finally led to the passage of the Civil Rights Act of 1964, supported earlier by John F. Kennedy and then Lyndon Johnson. Title VI, which denied federal funds to schools practicing racial discrimination, was used by the federal government to compel compliance by threatening to withhold the monies.

Two Supreme Court decisions, *Green v. County School Board of New Kent County* and *Swann v. Charlotte-Mecklenburg Board of Education*, started to make desegregation a reality. In *Green*, a 1968 case, the Warren Court struck down, in another 9–0 decision, the state of Virginia's "freedom of choice" plan as a transparent evasion of *Brown*. Virginia decided in 1965 to fight to protect a new plan that allowed black and white students the right to choose one of two schools, the formerly all-black Watkins School or the formerly all-white New Kent School. After three years, no white students had registered at the black high school, and an inconsequential number of blacks were attending the white school. Fourteen years after *Brown*, Virginia still had a dual school system.

School districts and the state, under *Green*, were "charged with the affirmative duty to take whatever steps might be necessary" to eliminate racial discrimination, "root and branch." The lower courts were not free, *Green* said, to approve a plan and not see its implementation. The decision

required the courts to stay involved "until it is clear that state-imposed seg-
regation has been completely removed." Warren privately wrote Brennan,
"When this opinion is handed down the traffic light will have changed from
Brown to *Green*. Amen."

Professor Lino A. Graglia, of the University of Texas School of Law,
wrote that *Green* "worked a revolution in the law of segregation comparable
to, indeed more dramatic than *Brown*." The impetus of *Brown* and *Green*
and the Court's composition carried over to the beginning of the Burger
Court. Justice Warren stepped down on June 23, 1969, and the *Swann* case
was argued the following year. Graglia, the outspoken opponent of school
busing and affirmative action, whose name was withdrawn by the Reagan
administration for an appeals court position, termed *Swann* "the *Dred Scott*
of the Twentieth Century."

Burger wanted, in *Swann,* to emulate Warren by getting a unanimous
decision. He succeeded. The 9–0 decision approved busing to disperse a
highly concentrated black student body—thirteen thousand students—at
an annual operating cost of more than $500,000 and a start-up cost of $1
million. But the case said, "Once the affirmative duty to desegregate has
been accomplished and racial discrimination through official action is eliminated from the system," neither the school authorities nor the courts are
required to stay involved. This opened the door to the Court's continued
involvement in school-related segregation issues.

A pattern developed in many of the integration cases. The determination
of the facts, motive, and intent were decided in the first instance by the trial
courts. Many of the decisions ruled against the school boards in favor of the
children. But first the late Burger Court and then the Rehnquist Court
started to reverse those cases, finding that the trial courts had made the
wrong factual determinations. Normally, an appellate court gives great deference to the fact finder, and especially so in school cases, which are often
long, sometime decades old, complex, and bitterly disputed. But now, as
with Congress's "fact-finding" in such cases as *Printz* and involving the
Brady Bill, the Supreme Court was taking it upon itself to make its own factual determination. In doing so, the Court showed as little respect for federal trial and appeals court judges as it did for Congress, and the lower
courts got the message. No court likes to be reversed—so their fact-finding,
and the atmosphere of the lower courts, totally changed.

It started slowly, in the *San Antonio School District v. Rodriguez* case;

the Court in 1973 recognized that disparities in state funding of schools based on property taxes lead to black schools and white schools, and good schools and bad schools; nevertheless, they said, the Court should not intervene, for poor students were not a protected class, education was not a federally protected constitutional right, and thus, the Courts should do nothing.

By 1974, four years after the unanimous *Swann* opinion, the composition of the Supreme Court was substantially altered. Black and Harlan II had left, replaced by Powell and Rehnquist. Once the Warren Court was gone and President Nixon had the opportunity to appoint four justices, the Court was positioned to limit the reach of desegregation remedies. When the Court was asked to consider *Milliken v. Bradley*, a desegregation case involving busing in, pointedly, a northern city (Detroit), where the officials had drawn up a school plan that encouraged white flight resulting in white suburban schools and black urban schools, the decision showed the Supreme Court's continued dramatic retreat.

On July 25, 1974, the new Nixon judges, Powell and Rehnquist, joined with Burger to help form a 5–4 majority that reversed the lower courts, who, relying on *Brown, Green*, and *Swann*, had approved a busing plan. It was wrong, the Court now said, to bus white students from suburban "innocent" school districts to wrongfully created urban districts. How quickly a 9–0 decision is forgotten. With the change in judges, the conservatives began to form a permanent political bloc that was consistently stronger than the liberals'. While it was not until years later that the Court had a solid working majority, the *Milliken* case, with the seating of Powell and Rehnquist, signaled the turn of the Burger Court and the beginning of conservative limits on its and on the Warren Court's protection of individual rights.

Then the Rehnquist Court tried to close the door and dramatically alter the school-integration landscape. Rehnquist saw school-desegregation cases as nitpicking the law and threatening to overwhelm the courts, with the federal courts acting where they should not have been in the first place. The opposition on the Court and in the community to school integration broadened as the Court went from *Brown* to *Green* to *Swann*.

The Rehnquist Court expressed anger in its school-integration decisions, not at the states who continued to resist the federal courts, but at the judges seeking to enforce orders, and at the judicial process itself. The Court's decisions were a total reversal of the *Brown, Green*, and *Swann* philosophy, and it affected not only the cases before the Court but also cases before other trial and appellate courts.

The Supreme Court, in 1991, in *Board of Education of Oklahoma City v. Dowell*, at 5–3 (Souter did not participate), made clear it was fed up with school segregation cases. The Court's interest was in a final resolution of the desegregation cases by returning complete control of school boards back to school districts and claiming all that could be done was done. The retreat had turned into a rout. Prior to *Dowell*, there was some hope that the Court would retain some control over districts that had been found to be noncompliant. The frustration, unhappiness, and sadness in Justice Marshall's dissent helps tell us one of the reasons (his health and age were other reasons) he left the Court the following year, notwithstanding his promise to hang on until a Democrat was in office.

The facts of the case are undisputed. Oklahoma's constitution when it gained statehood in 1907 mandated separation. For the next sixty-five years the school board maintained separation, and when, after *Brown*, nothing happened, parents of African Americans filed suit in 1961. By 1972, eleven years after the suit, with the school board firmly resisting integration, the black schools became worse. The board finally adopted a plan in 1972, and three years later the district court stepped out of the case, saying the board had complied with *Brown*.

When the case came to the Supreme Court, thirty-three of sixty-four elementary schools had student populations of greater than 90 percent African Americans. The racial mix in most of the other thirty-one were little better. Marshall, in 1991 in his dissent, recounted the thirty-seven years of Court decisions since *Brown* and declared that the continuing stamp of inferiority placed on African American children was now a "self-perpetuated phenomenon." Then in 1992, with a Court edging even more dramatically toward the right, it decided in *Freeman v. Pitts* that federal judges should stop supervising pupil assignments in school systems where African American children were isolated, if the isolation resulted from demographic shifts and resistant school officials.

The case took a long, circuitous route as it made its way to Washington. DeKalb County, Georgia, a major suburban area of Atlanta, has a school system of seventy-three thousand students, making it one of the nation's largest. In 1976—twenty-two years after *Brown*—one-tenth of 1 percent of the students were participating in an integration plan, a figure a federal court found unacceptable and about which it agreed with the parent who had filed the suit seeking school integration.

With the situation still unchanged a decade later, school officials moved for a dismissal of the 1968 lawsuit. The lower court granted it, finding that DeKalb had done all it could, and that demographics were the problem. The federal appeals court, however, said that the lower court judge was wrong to dismiss the case and ordered the federal court back in.

Justice Kennedy's 1992 opinion, distancing himself from the commitment to integration reflected in the Burger Court's early decisions, agreed with the state of Georgia and reversed the appeals court. He sets forth in *Freeman* the nearly forty years of history in Georgia since *Brown*, acknowledges the fact that this lawsuit was now twenty-four years old, and describes the impossibility of asking courts actually to carry out the mandates of *Brown*, *Swann*, and *Green*. Kennedy, sympathetic to the school authorities, says they need not take "heroic measures" when the imbalance is at least partially attributable to district demographics. The fact that the lawsuit is twenty-four years old is a "fact" held against the schoolchildren and against the "efficacy" of the judicial process, rather than against the contemptuous school boards and state. Although there is a victim, the fault does not lie with the state; there is no wrongdoer, and the state is helpless to right the wrongs that may exist.

Kennedy agrees with the *Brown* decision that segregated schools hurt black children. "A sense of inferiority affects the motivation of a child to learn. Segregation with the sanction of the law, therefore, has a tendency to retard the education and mental development of Negro children and to deprive them of some of the benefits they would receive in a racially mixed school system." But while Kennedy goes to great lengths to talk about population shifts throughout the country and how, according to evidence, blacks prefer to live in mixed neighborhoods and whites in mostly white ones, he does not point out what the appeals court found—that DeKalb, Georgia, never made any attempt to create one school system for blacks and whites. Rather, the five justices agreed DeKalb County had acted in good faith and did all it could. Courts should no longer be in the desegregation business anyway. It decided to settle for partial integration, which then became token integration.

The Rehnquist Court, led by a consistent dissenter against school-desegregation law, adopted the assumptions that the damage of discrimination had been cured as much as possible, that enough had been done so that the Court-ordered initiatives should be ended, and that there was a serious danger of discrimination against whites if civil rights requirements were to continue. Rehnquist and Scalia had always opposed enforcement of *Brown*. But it was not until Justice Thomas joined the Court that Rehnquist had the needed majority to turn it back.

Three years after *Freeman*, in 1995, the state of Missouri asked the federal courts to stop supervising the Kansas City public schools. In an unusual twist, the Kansas City school board argued against the state, claiming that the schools were still racially discriminatory. The lower federal court agreed with the school board, as did the appeals court, which implied the federal courts should supervise the school system until standardized test scores had improved to the level of national standards.

The Court in the 1995 *Missouri v. Jenkins* case was different than the Court in 1992, and the new hope was that the constant reversals of the trial and appeal courts would stop. Ginsburg and Breyer were there now to join Stevens and Souter. The moderates needed only O'Connor or Kennedy to find a majority. But six months after the argument, it was clear that the two justices would add their votes to the Rehnquist bloc to help form the majority and again reverse the lower court. The 5–4 decision, written by Rehnquist, again harped at the cost of the litigation, at how much time it took, and at how much money the state would have to spend to improve the black schools. The state could do nothing, he said; it was not the state's fault that whites would not go to black schools. In rejecting the school board's argument that money to improve the black schools would come only if they were attended by white students, he said separate was equal, and all the school board had to do was give more money to black schools—a fact that Rehnquist knew was a political impossibility. In this he was joined by Justice Thomas, who sharply attacked the school board argument that blacks must solve their problems by having whites in their schools. Declared Thomas, "It never ceases to amaze me that courts are willing to assume that anything that is predominantly black must be inferior."

Professor Lino A. Graglia said the integration program forces vast amounts of state tax revenues into lavish expenditures in one school district while the educational needs of other children, black and white alike, suffer from comparative neglect. He claims desegregation, as well as affirmative action plans, are restitution where none is deserved because "today's school children bear no relationship to the black children in that district whom segregation might have shortchanged."

Chief Justice Rehnquist ordered the case back to the trial court, with the observation that the court "should consider that many goals of its quality education plan already have been attained." He also said time had passed by *Brown, Green,* and *Swann,* and that the court must "restore state and local authorities to the control of a school system that is operating in compliance with the Constitution." Rehnquist believed that whether or not the schools were integrated was not the issue, but rather whose fault it was. But unlike Justice Ginsburg, who looked at Missouri's forty-two years of opposition to integrated schools and insisted the state had an obligation to do something about it, he refused to place the fault at the state's doorstep.

The conservatives in this and in other cases have adopted a new meaning for the Fourteenth Amendment. Totally disregarding how it came to life, the Court now interprets it to apply to both blacks and whites. "Racial discrimination" is barred; "equal protection" for "any person" is guaranteed. The Court's refusal to look at the facts, past and present, and claim instead to rely on "logic" is a result-oriented rationale.

In *Missouri v. Jenkins,* as in *Freeman v. Pitts,* a winning argument was that one could not distinguish whether resistance to segregation had created all-black and all-white schools, or whether demographic factors were to blame. The argument continues, claiming that school desegregation has no beneficial effects on students and that the courts, because of their limited impact, did not truly affect integration. But studies indicate otherwise.

A July 1, 2001, report, "Schools More Separate: Consequences of a Decade of Resegregation," by Harvard University's Civil Rights Project, describes a return to segregation even in the face of growing support for integration. The most important reasons for the reverse shift, the study concludes, are the present Court's limiting and reversing desegregation orders, along with sharp reductions in federal funding, a decrease in political support for desegregation in schools and in housing, and demographic changes.

The Harvard study, which analyzed educational and census data, found that 78 percent of black children attended predominantly minority schools in the 1998–99 academic year, dramatically up from 66 percent just a few years before. Minorities were most likely to attend school with whites in the South, although integration was also unraveling most quickly in the South.

The July 2001 report also said that more evidence exists now than did at the time of *Brown* that desegregated schools both improve test scores and dramatically change the lives of students, that more schools are today isolated both by race and poverty, and that they are in no way even remotely equal. Because of the "dramatic reversal of *Brown's* spirit by the Rehnquist Courts, there was little the Clinton administration did do to reverse the demise of integration. . . . There has been little or no positive political leadership on this issue for a generation . . . and the courts have made a dramatic turn around in decisions about desegregated schools. . . . Citizens in some communities, such as Charlotte, N.C., have elected school boards committed to integration only to have their will blocked by a federal court forbidding any conscious effort to achieve or maintain segregation," states the report. There is still a good deal of *Brown*-inspired litigation throughout the country. There are more than two hundred consent orders currently being enforced (twenty-six in Alabama), and in 2001, a Louisiana judge in Fayetteville, Arkansas, took control of the schools after he learned that a school board had intentionally disobeyed an order. Although the Legal Defense Fund has as many lawyers involved in the cases today as it did fifteen years ago, the federal government is no longer as active as before.

James Madison warned, "If a majority be united by a common interest, the rights of the minority will be insecure." The tyranny of the majority requires safeguards to protect "one part of the society against the injustice of the other part." Majority rule and democracy are not the same thing. What is good for the 51 percent majority is not necessarily good for everyone. People of color can improve their lives only through their political power. Over the years, poll taxes, literacy tests, all-white primaries, grandfather clauses, and violence surrounding elections have led to the disenfranchisement of minorities. The disenfranchisement of blacks in Florida by the violence and obstruction that surfaced in *Bush v. Gore* in 2001 occurs regularly in the South. The NAACP keeps voluminous records of years past, and in one of my previous books I described some of the ways blacks were stopped from voting by being beaten up, having their cars ticketed on their way to the polls, and being threatened with the loss of either welfare or jobs. Although the Fifteenth Amendment, which was ratified on February 3, 1870, prohibited the denial of every citizen's rights to vote "on account of race, color or previous condition of servitude," it is not yet fully operative.

Many of the Warren Court's decisions, and the Voting Rights Act of 1965, with its 1982 amendments, tried to eliminate racial discrimination in voting and to protect minorities from being overrun by majority rule. The decisions and law tried to ensure that Hispanics and blacks not only got one vote per person, but also tried to ensure that their one vote had the same power and effect as that of a white voter. The Voting Rights Act and its amendments immediately doubled the number of black and Hispanic majority districts throughout the country.

Resistance to giving up voting power was formidable. The Court regularly struck down laws and regulations that sought to frustrate the Voting Rights Act. By lowering barriers to the right to vote, and making sure each vote counted, the Warren Court decisions helped the blacks and the poor, both primarily Democratic voters. The Rehnquist Court, on the other hand, uses the color-blind test and the language of reverse discrimination to strike down Warren Court concepts; their concern is for the majority, who are only being asked to share voting power equally.

Its reversals in the voting rights area are directed not at the states, who resisted and continue to resist, but at the minorities, who come to court to protect their right to vote. This Court wants out of voting litigation, just as they want no further part of the school litigation. Pervading all these decisions is the thought that we have now achieved equality, an America without racism—and an America defined only by the vision of the majorities, a concept that Madison found so dangerous.

In 1980, President Reagan's first year in office, the Burger Court could not find racial discrimination in voting when African Americans, who composed over a third of the population of Mobile, Alabama, challenged an at-large electoral scheme that, combined with regular bloc voting by whites, consistently resulted in an all-white city commission and a white mayor. Racial opportunism is the rule not the exception when legislatures redistrict. The Court in one of the cases said, "The Constitution does not entail the right to have Negro candidates elected" and denied that "their freedom to vote has been denied or abridged by anyone." This is a theme that continues. The recent Supreme Court is trying to justify the *New York Times* headline of March 25, 2002, "Why Republicans are shamelessly in love with the Voting Rights Act." In *Presley v. Etowah County Commission* (1992), for example, the Court ruled that blacks may enjoy the right to vote, but that does not necessarily include the right to govern. They overrode the intent of a statutory scheme Congress extended three times over an eighteen-year period.

A more recent case concerns the districts of Representatives Eva Clayton and Mel Watt, both Democrats elected in 1997 and the first blacks ever elected to Congress from North Carolina. Their districts were newly drawn after the 1990 census to meet federal standards designed to increase the chances of minority candidates.

Under the guidelines of the 1965 Voting Rights Act and the directive of the elder Bush's Department of Justice, North Carolina doubled its number of black and Hispanic majority districts from twenty-six to fifty-two. Of these new districts, however, none had an odder history and a stranger shape than the twelfth, which Representative Watt served. Except for a few bulges and detours, the Twelfth Congressional District ran along Interstate 85 for about 160 miles, from Durham to Gastonia; in some instances, the district was no wider than the interstate highway that it followed. North Carolina initially had been gerrymandered to keep blacks out of office, but the Department of Justice said two districts must be created in order that the state's 22 percent African American population be sufficiently represented in Congress.

Even after North Carolina's redistricting, the majority white population continued to control ten of the twelve districts, while it constituted only 70 percent of the state's population. But Ruth Shaw, a white Democrat, and four other residents of her district, brought suit against North Carolina and the United States, in *Shaw v. Hunt*, claiming the cutting up of districts for the benefit of black voters violated the Equal Protection Clause because the districts had been divided by race and whites were proportionally underrepresented. Such racial redistricting, they argued, discriminated against whites and insulted blacks because it implied that they could not work together. As a result, the plan threatened to balkanize North Carolina into competing racial factions and entrench racial-bloc voting. It was precisely such gerrymandering, Shaw said, that discriminated against blacks in the South during the first half of the twentieth century and led to the Voting Rights Act.

The Democratic plaintiffs, however, were haunted by another political reality. By consolidating the black vote, a process called max black, which had historically been Democratic, the Republican Party was better able to make inroads in "bleached" white districts. The federal government and the state of North Carolina argued that they had done in the Twelfth District exactly what the Voting Rights Act required—used race to establish districts with majority black voting blocs where there had been voting discrimination. Even though white voters had now lost one historically white district, the government argued, blacks were still disproportionally underrepresented in Congress. Moreover, the court of appeals agreed: such redistricting was appropriate because of North Carolina's long history of discrimination in creating voting districts. After the appeals court said that if racial gerrymandering were not permitted, North Carolina would never have an African American congressman, the case went to the Supreme Court.

In a 5–4 decision reversing the lower court, the Supreme Court held that the Voting Rights Act of 1965 did not allow for race-based districting. Invoking the language of individual rights, Justice O'Connor, writing for the majority, said voters had a right to participate in a color-blind election. "It is unsettling," O'Connor continued, "how closely the North Carolina plan resembles the most egregious racial gerrymanders of the past," and it "bears an uncomfortable resemblance to political apartheid." The Warren Court had said that "preference for pleasingly shaped districts" should not be used to justify the denial of voting rights for blacks. But O'Connor rejected the Warren Court's reason and criticized the odd shape of the Twelfth District, whose residents "may have little in common with one another but the color of their skin." O'Connor said that racial classification can only lead to larger social harms, such as the balkanization and politicization of racial groups. She and the majority said the state would have to show a compelling interest that required it to treat some of its citizens differently from others based on race in order to find this, or any future redistricting plan, acceptable—a test she understood the state could not meet.

Justice Byron R. White, on his last day in the Court, disagreed that white voters in North Carolina had been hurt by the redistricting plan. The benefit of the Equal Protection Clause of the Fourteenth Amendment belonged on the side of the minority voters, not the majority white voters. The state's effort to get at proportionality in voting could not, he said, violate the Fourteenth Amendment.

Then, in an April 19, 2001, decision, Justice Sandra Day O'Connor justified a different position as she switched sides. The 5–4 vote this time was won by the moderates. In another North Carolina case, *Hunt v. Cromartie*, she concluded that politics, not race, was the predominant factor in drawing the districts. The swing vote for the Right in the *Shaw* case, she now became the swing vote for the moderate bloc, holding that it was permissible for district lines to be drawn along race lines, if that was not the sole motivation. She claims she is not contradicting herself. Some commentators described her vote as part of the *Bush v. Gore* aftermath: O'Connor trying to show her more moderate side, her freedom to disagree with the conservative four. Justice O'Connor now acknowledged that gerrymandering on racial grounds is also gerrymandering on political grounds, because the black southern vote is predominantly Democratic. Her view is that the Constitution generally forbids the government from making decisions based on race, but there is no such legal bar on making decisions based on political or partisan grounds. Therefore, shifting African American voters into a new district to create a Democratic stronghold could be justified as a political decision, not a racial one.

Stephen Breyer, writing in the majority, emphasized that because African Americans in the state register and vote Democratic more than 95 percent of the time, it was hard to distinguish a legislature's effort to create a majority black district from a legislature's effort to create a safe Democratic one. And because white-registered Democrats more frequently cross over to vote Republican than African American–registered Democrats do, a legislature trying to secure a safe Democratic seat could plausibly include more heavily African American precincts for political, not racial, reasons. "Race in this case correlates closely with political behavior," Justice Breyer concluded, reasoning that judges should therefore give legislatures leeway to balance racial and political considerations without assuming one was predominant over the other.

Justice Thomas, the strongest opponent of race-based decision making, wrote the opinion for the four dissenters: "Racial gerrymandering offends the Constitution whether the motive is malicious or benign and it is not an excuse that the legislature merely may have drawn the district based on the stereotype that blacks are reliable Democratic voters."

While blacks vote 95 percent Democratic, white voters are more split. Thus, by reducing the number of blacks in an area, they will win; and by putting more blacks in contested areas with a previously white majority, Democrats can win. While a very small percentage of blacks will, given the choice, vote against a black Democrat, a substantial percentage of white voters will vote for black candidates. An Emory College study published in the *Emory Law Journal* found that in many states, including southern states, black congressional candidates "always got at least one white vote in five." Professor Charles Bullock III of the University of Georgia, the coauthor of the Emory study said, "The white electorate is increasingly willing to vote for black candidates."

After the April 18 decision, courts in both the South and the North began to uphold racial redistricting, calling it partisan redistricting when the legislators' motive was to create partisan redistricting. Racial redistricting, according to the Rehnquist Court, violates the Fourteenth Amendment, but partisan redistricting does not.

The political nature of voting cases was best shown in a recent Mississippi case. On March 1, 2002, Justice Scalia, showing disregard for judicial ethics, and affirming his commitment to bullying politics rather than the law, rejected an emergency appeal in a voting rights case in Mississippi.

Mississippi, losing one of its five seats in Congress, redistricted the state. Both the Justice Department and a trial judge approved a plan that would favor the Democrat incumbent Ronnie Shows rather than the Republican incumbent Charles Pickering Jr. Ashcroft intervened, and the Justice Department reversed itself. Shows appealed to a three-judge Republican Court, which included Pickering's father, that reversed the trial court. When Shows sought an emergency appeal to the Supreme Court, Scalia denied it.

Pickering Sr., then a Bush nominee to the circuit court of appeals, should have recused himself. Another one of the three judges, Henry Wingate, had actively supported Pickering Sr.'s proposed nomination to the circuit court. Scalia, a close friend of Pickering Sr.'s, who spent social time with his family in Mississippi and then personally administered the oath to Pickering Jr. when he was sworn in to Congress, refused to disqualify himself on the case. The "Guide to Judiciary Policies and Procedures" declares that "a judge shall disqualify himself or herself in a proceeding in which the judge's impartiality might reasonably be questioned." Each judge decides for himself whether he should sit or not. Scalia's and Pickering Sr.'s rulings were clearly improper.

On March 13, 2002, Senator Patrick Leahy sent a letter to Ashcroft urging an inquiry into the Pickering Jr. case. He was stonewalled. Today, four justices make it clear they would never allow districts to be drawn in order to consider the voting strength of racial minorities. Four moderate justices make it clear they would allow these districts to be drawn. Every voting district in the country that has litigation must wait for O'Connor's small fact-based decisions. Rehnquist, Thomas, and Scalia's view, that the law should be settled so that individual government and private entities will know how to act, is defeated by O'Connor's approach.

Justice O'Connor, the only former state legislator on the High Court, has played the key role in all these decisions. "On these cases, the Court is O'Connor," said Columbia University law professor Sam Issacharoff, a voting rights expert. "She has shown a distrust for racial politics. But if she is convinced that politics is driving the process, she is comfortable with that."

In *Shaw*, and in the cases that precede it and flowed from it, the Court is creating a white constitutional right not to be represented by an African American as a result of redistricting under the Act, thereby going a long way toward invalidating the Act.

This Supreme Court has rejected Justice Harry Blackmun's conclusion in the 1978 *Regents of the University of California v. Bakke* case that we must look at the country's long history, for, he said, the present reality of discrimination requires that "in order to get beyond racism, we must first take account of race." The problem is that this Court does look back—but it looks too far back—before *Brown*, before the civil rights movement, before much of this century. As a result, the effect of their decisions is very much like that of the nineteenth-century courts that tried to deconstruct the gains of the Civil War by interpreting the civil rights amendments to permit oppression in a form not very different from slavery. Education, job protection, and voting rights for African Americans are low on this Court's priorities, and thus America is again moving quickly toward two separate societies. Nowhere is this more true than in the affirmative action battle.

8

AFFIRMATIVE ACTION:
Putting the Nail in the Coffin

Affirmative action followed the perceived success of *Brown v. Board of Education* and the success of the nondiscrimination law in the 1960s. The Republican Party, under Richard Nixon, originally pushed for affirmative action both for good reasons and because conservatives saw it as a "beautiful wedge issue which would fracture the Democratic party's old coalition of labor, Jew and Blacks." Angry white males gave Reagan his crushing victories. A 1986 Gallup Poll showed 87 percent of American men were opposed to affirmative action. By 1996, even though Bill Clinton said "mend it, don't end it," most Americans were opposed to racial preferences. That November, California voters passed Proposition 209, which eliminated most public affirmative action programs, although the closer margin of 54 to 46 percent indicates that voters feel enormous moral ambivalence over this issue and that the answers to the polls depend in large part on how the question is framed. Recent polls are inconclusive but lean toward rejection.

Affirmative action programs in school admissions and job hiring make a "positive" out of factors so long considered negative in this country—race and gender. President John Kennedy first used the term affirmative action in 1961. After the passage of the civil rights law of 1964, at the time when the country was committed to forbidding considering race and gender as a justification for discrimination, affirmative action programs began to bloom.

President Lyndon Johnson saw that more needed to be done. In a speech to Howard University's 1966 graduating class, he said, "But freedom is not enough. You do not wipe away the scars." He observed, "You don't take a person who, for years, has been hobbled by chains and liberate him, bring him up to the starting line of a race, and then say, you're free to compete with others and believe that you have been competing fair." But it would fall to the administration of his successor, Nixon, to add teeth to affirmative action programs by introducing actual numerical quotas and target goals for minority hiring. The Reagan backlash just four years later changed everything. Charles Fried, Reagan's solicitor general, tried to enlist the courts to "end the drift to a quota society and end government-imposed racial preferences" both in schools and on the job.

For Reagan supporters, the trouble with quotas is that they "dangerously aggrandize government"; they give the federal government a power to make decisions that the federal government should not have and, as a result, give government improper hold over schools. Never mind that the majority of colleges were voluntarily choosing quota systems, for they saw benefits of racial diversity in classes and believed that quotas were essential if blacks were going to have a chance to compete in business and the professions. America's past history, they argued, required redress. Fried argued that quotas lead to a "sinister" politicization, where jobs are handed out not according to market pressures or individual will but "according to membership in a group that has managed to attract political power." Those seeking jobs would come to rely on politics rather than their own capabilities—as if the white society had not done exactly that.

Preference programs have been a polarizing issue throughout the country. They have often split moderates and liberals. Even Justice Douglas, one of our great liberal justices, said in *De Funis v. Odegard*, an early affirmative action case, that "there is no constitutional right for any race to be preferred." The lower and appellate federal courts, in urban and rural areas, the South or the North, were each under different pressures as the courts have struggled, for the last three decades, to evaluate local, state, and federal programs in our fifty states. The pressure to stop these initiatives—with their grants and subsidies for educational and work programs running into the billions—is intense and remains a key issue for many Americans.

It is one thing to oppose affirmative action because of the cost; it is another to refuse to recognize obvious bias. *Color blind* is the phrase used today by the Rehnquist Court to deny minorities the benefits of affirmative action and preferential programs. Rehnquist's legal hijacking of words, first used by Justice John Harlan in 1896, is astonishing. Justice Harlan's dissent in *Plessy v. Ferguson*, attacking discrimination by saying the law must be color blind, has now been inverted by the Rehnquist Court to attack laws seeking to help minorities. The words *color blind* have been a gold mine for the Rehnquist Court in every race-conscious case. The Rehnquist Court continues to twist language in striking down affirmative action programs by saying they are "reverse discrimination" cases. Now, by treating the white population as the victims of reverse discrimination, they argue they are only being consistent, in their application of the law, by stopping any and all kinds of discrimination wherever they find it. These two magic, misused phrases, *color blind* and *reverse discrimination*, are part of the Right's sleight of hand to disguise reality and obscure the varied purposes of racial preference programs.

In *Plessy*, the majority said the Louisiana law, requiring separate railroad cars for black and white passengers, does not discriminate because it allows each race equally to have private cars. Justice Harlan's rejoinder was "But [everyone] knows that [the law] had its origins in the purpose, not so much to exclude white persons from railroad cars occupied by blacks, as to exclude colored people from coaches occupied by or assigned to white persons." The Rehnquist Court's idea of reality is similar to the *Plessy* Court's. They are *willfully* color blind.

The ideal of the integrated society and the importance of education and job opportunity to that ideal has been continually attacked by this Court, often with Justice O'Connor as the swing vote. Her rhetoric, more temperate than her colleagues', often reaches the same result on the same theory. She, like them, claims to be trying to stop reverse discrimination as she defends the white majority and strikes down minority affirmative action programs. Many Americans reject the argument that the African American community, uniquely among minorities, has been victimized by our nation, and reject the notion that the law should help Hispanics and women to get a level playing field.

The Rehnquist Court is driving its agenda forward in a series of predictable 5–4 decisions. Before, blacks were the victim class being protected; now, under Rehnquist, whites are the victim class being protected. Two cases to be decided in the term starting in October 2002, one dealing with undergraduate racial preferences and another with graduate school preferences, can help undo the entire gamut of affirmative action programs. We can expect bad decisions, ones that will get worse over time as the Court's composition continues to change.

We begin in 1972 during the early time of the Burger Court. Allan Bakke, a white student, then thirty-two years old, was rejected by the University of California Medical School at Davis. Bakke was one of 2,664 applicants for 100 entering positions at the school; 84 applicants came through the regular admissions program; 16 were minority students entering through a preferential program created in 1970 because so few nonwhite students were enrolling. Bakke's grades and test scores were better than those of the minority students accepted.

After being rejected for a second time, Bakke filed a lawsuit declaring that the medical school's practice of setting aside positions for minorities made him a victim of racial discrimination, which violated Title VI of the Civil Rights Act of 1964, and also denied him equal protection of the law under the Fourteenth Amendment. The university agreed that its program was race-conscious and that race-conscious classifications, while always suspect, must be considered in light of the past. Yes, the Equal Protection Clause and the Civil Rights Act prohibited discrimination, and yes, they agreed, Bakke was being discriminated against, but it was consideration for past history of discrimination against blacks. You could not, they argued, ignore history. This redressing of past wrongs, they admitted, had a cost. But the pure goal of meritocracy, the university said, is outweighed by the social goal of having more blacks in colleges, medical schools, and law schools. (Davis's first class, in 1968, contained three Asian Americans and no other minorities.) Furthermore, an increase in minority students would provide needed medical services for underserved medical communities. Minority doctors were both role models and better able to relate to the patients of their own race. Until the early 1970s, less than 2 percent of America's doctors, lawyers, and medical and law students were members of minorities. The school wanted this changed.

The state trial court and state supreme courts agreed with Bakke. The case was decided by the Supreme Court six years after Bakke first sought admission. The university appealed to a Burger Court that, in 1978, had five new Republicans on the Court: the so-called law and order "Minnesota Twins," Warren Burger and Harry Blackmun; Lewis Powell, the conservative former head of the American Bar Association; the unabashedly partisan William Rehnquist; and the newest appointee, John Paul Stevens, who joined the Court in 1975, three years before *Bakke* was argued. The conservative Court had coalesced, and both Brennan and Marshall believed their days of winning were over.

Reynold H. Colvin, Bakke's lawyer, argued that his white client, individually, was being asked to pay for many of America's past racial sins. He argued against any race-conscious balancing and any quota system, no matter how favorable to minorities. When pressed by the Court, Colvin stood his ground; leaving even one school admissions opening for a minority candidate would be unconstitutional, he said.

Justice Thurgood Marshall leaned over, and in an angry voice, roared: "You are arguing about keeping somebody out and the other side is arguing about keeping somebody in."

"That's right."

"So it depends on which way you look at it, doesn't it."

Yes, it "depends on which way you look at the problem."

"You are talking about your client's rights. Don't those underprivileged people have some rights?"

"They certainly have the right to compete."

"To eat cake."

Archibald Cox, the law professor and former Watergate special prosecutor, arguing for the preference programs, said that a school could have a number of undifferentiated programs for diversity, such as ones trying to get students from rural areas. Cox began with a powerful statement of the importance of the case:

> This case . . . presents a single vital question: whether a state university which is forced by limited resources to select a relatively few number of students from a much larger number of well-qualified applicants, is free, voluntarily, to take into account the fact that the applicant is black, Chicano, Asian or native American to increase the number of those minority groups trained for the educational professions and participating in them, professions from which minorities were long excluded because of generations of pervasive racial discrimination.

The answer the Court gives will determine, perhaps for decades, whether members of those minorities are to have the kind of meaningful access to higher education in the professions which the universities have accorded them in recent years, or are to be reduced to the trivial numbers which they were prior to the adoption of minority admissions programs.

As he tried to make the point that the sixteen-place program was not a quota, Cox was interrupted by a question from Justice Potter Stewart. Stewart asked, "It did put a limit on the number of white people, didn't it?" Cox replied, "I think that it limited the number of non-minority and therefore essentially white, yes. But there are two things to be said about that: One is that this was not pointing a finger at a group which had been marked as inferior in any sense; and it was undifferentiated; it operated against a wide variety of people. So I think it was not stigmatizing—in the sense of the old quota against Jews was stigmatizing—in any way."

Then Justice Harry Blackmun asked if it was the same thing as an athletic scholarship, "since most institutions seek athletic prowess."

"Well," replied Cox with bemusement, "I come from Harvard, Sir . . . and I don't know whether it's our aim, but we don't do very well." Following that observation, the intense mood of the courtroom was punctuated by a burst of laughter from the justices and the packed spectator section.

During the postargument conference, Marshall urged Brennan to try to dispose of *Bakke* on procedural grounds, feeling the "Nixon Four" and Byron White would totally reject quotas or affirmative action. He suggested there was a "standing" defect in the case, the strategy we now know is used regularly today by the conservative Court to avoid dealing with hosts of cases attacking social problems. White indeed agreed there were procedural grounds for not hearing the case. Regardless of the affirmative action policy, Allan Bakke was unlikely to be admitted because there were more than a dozen students ahead of him with higher ratings. But the majority of the Court, assuming the result was foreseen, wanted to decide the case. The result was unexpected.

A sharply divided 5–4 Court, issuing six separate opinions but guided by Justice Powell's critical opinion, said racial preferences can be justified to aid diversity but not for compensation of past injury. The Court rejected the California program, but also ordered Bakke admitted. White and Powell joined those in favor of his admission. The first paragraph of Justice Marshall's decision reverberates today:

It must be remembered that, during most of the past 200 years, the Constitution as interpreted by this Court did not prohibit the most ingenious and pervasive forms of discrimination. Now, when a state acts to remedy the effects of that legacy of discrimination, I cannot believe that this same Constitution stands as a banner.

And Justice Blackmun:

I yield to no one in my earnest hope that the time will come when an affirmative action program is unnecessary and is, in truth, only a relic of the past. I would hope that we could reach this stage within a decade at most. But the story of *Brown* [suggests] that this hope is a slim one. At some time, however, beyond any period of what some would claim is only a transitional inequality the United States must and will reach a stage of maturity where action along this line is no longer necessary. Then persons will be regarded as persons and discrimination of the type addressed today will be an ugly feature of history. . . .

Justice Powell agreed with the eight other justices on some issues and disagreed with them on others. His historic declaration was that "diversity is a constitutionally permissible goal for an institution of higher education" and that universities could consider race as one of several positive factors in selecting applicants. It is this one sentence since 1978 that pervades all education preferential decisions, one sentence by one justice that has been a pivot since *Bakke* was decided.

One of the underlying concepts of Powell's solitary *Bakke* opinion was that to have different races in a class enriched the lives and education of all students, because different races had different viewpoints, different perspectives. Powell believed that while racial diversity may make minimal difference in a mathematics class, it will make a significant contribution in contemporary American literature or American history. But Powell said that it is in the school's intellectual, cultural, and social life outside the classroom where most of the benefits occur. Even on those campuses where the races tend to stay together more than to integrate, he accepted California's argument that diversity was a value in itself and must be protected. In addition, in reviewing its conclusions, the majority Court adapted a strict scrutiny test for affirmative action programs. As we saw in chapter 4 when we discussed *Webster v.*

Reproductive Services, the Missouri abortion case, this test, the most rigorous of all constitutional tests, when applied, often results in a finding that the program is unconstitutional. In order for affirmative action to pass muster, the reasons for it must be compelling and narrowly defined. The Court found California's program failed to meet that test. Had there been a long history of past instances of specific discrimination at the twenty-year-old institution, the program might have passed the test. But that was not that medical school's history. It was too new. That is why Bakke was ordered to be admitted.

The Court's view in *Bakke* can be seen as Solomonic because both Bakke and affirmative action programs appeared to win. The 154 pages of opinion please neither side entirely. Yet the decision generated an enormous amount of confusion because of the multiple decisions and, what seemed to many, inconsistent results.

The dissenting judges Stevens, Burger, Stewart, and Rehnquist said Justice Powell's *Bakke* opinion violated the civil rights statute and its "broad prohibition against the exclusion of any individual" on racial grounds from a publicly funded program. A second group, however, consisting of Brennan, Marshall, White, and Blackmun, found that, absent a stigmatizing intent or effect, one "drawn on the presumption that one race is inferior to another," or one that places "the weight of government behind racial hatred and separation," the preference should be upheld so long as the state can demonstrate an important purpose and the means do not unduly burden "those least well represented in the political process." In other words, race-conscious remedies to help people who had suffered racially motivated injuries were constitutional.

After *Bakke,* universities believed they could accomplish the results they sought by utilizing different criteria that ultimately worked in favor of minority students, and they were correct. Justice Lewis Powell agreed with Stevens's plurality on the illegality of California's racial quota system, and also agreed with Brennan's plurality view on the permissibility of racial considerations in admissions. Powell said that because Allan Bakke had been "totally foreclosed" from competing for the sixteen special positions, he had been denied equal protection. Racial *quotas,* Powell's opinion made clear, are allowed only when there was a past constitutional or legal violation identified by a properly authorized governmental body. But at the same time, Powell could find justification for affirmative action programs in the First Amendment's guarantee of academic freedom, finding that in a truly competitive process, racial considerations could be taken into account as part of the university's interest in promoting a "diverse student body."

Bakke was one of the most criticized decisions in Court history. Alexander Bickel, a distinguished professor at Yale University School of Law, said we always believed that discrimination was wrong and now that must "be unlearned [as] we are told that this is not a matter of fundamental principle but only a matter of whose ox is gored." Yet even Republicans who oppose affirmative action recognize the need for racial and gender diversity in judicial appointments, and have benefitted from it. Sandra Day O'Connor and Clarence Thomas—who protests he was not appointed for his race, but was nevertheless given Marshall's chair—owe their seats to it. And now, with the new power of the Hispanic vote, the current Bush administration is looking for Hispanic conservatives to go on the High Court as well as on the federal appeals courts.

As Archibald Cox (who represented the University of California in the *Bakke* case) wrote in a paper he presented the year before he argued *Bakke*:

> The first and most obvious truth is to recall that after the Civil War and the abolition of slavery, black people suffered still another century of systematic discrimination, partly private and partly governmental. The result was two Americas. Socially and economically, black communities were isolated and disadvantaged. All but a very few extraordinary individuals were excluded from the mainstream of opportunity in American life. In 1968 only 2 percent of the medical doctors in the United States were blacks. There were only 216 black medical students who were attending schools other than the all-black Howard and Meharry. One saw scarcely a black face in the ranks of business executives. The skilled trades in the building and construction industry and in manufacturing establishments were closed to blacks.

Many opponents of affirmative action argue that nondiscriminatory access is appropriate. But preferences in education, Cox believed, are critical to an integrated society. The majority's "color-blindness" test is a determined disregard of the context in which the cases are decided—a variation of Scalia's textualist myopia. Black representation in higher education, with the use of preferences, in half of American universities is still less than half (6 to 7 percent) their numbers in the general population (15 to 20 percent). Without racial preferences, Nathan Glazer, professor of sociology at Harvard, predicted, in 2001, that the figure would drop to less than 2 percent of the student body. The loss in the universities and professional schools of minority students would put the finishing touches on the concept of a racially equal country. It may be that irrespective of what the Courts and voters do at referendum time, colleges, through a variety of means, will continue to fashion ways of securing racial preferences, and the conservative Court is waging a battle that may be useless.

In 1978, the same year *Bakke* was decided, Congress passed the Public Workers Employment Act of 1977 that said 10 percent of federal funds granted for local work projects should be set aside for businesses owned or controlled by minorities. The 1977 act was the first federal statute since the Freedman's Bureau Act of 1866 to contain an explicitly benign race-conscious classification. At the time it was passed, blacks, Hispanics, and Asians constituted 16 percent of the population but formed only 3 percent of the nation's 13 million businesses and produced less than 1 percent of gross business receipts. A white company working in heating and air-conditioning brought suit in *Fullilove v. Klutznick* (1980), claiming that even if it put in the best bid for a contracting job, it would lose to a minority bidder solely because of race. But the *Fullilove* case saw the plaintiff lose 6–3, with the majority paying deference to Congress's fact-finding. Warren Burger, writing the majority opinion, said, "We reject the contention that in the remedial context the Congress must act in a wholly color blind matter." Joining Burger were Marshall, Brennan, Powell, White, and Blackmun, in the majority; Stewart, Rehnquist, and Stevens, in the dissent. Again, Burger disappointed the conservatives—again, Brennan managed not only to pull together a winning coalition but also to have the chief justice on his side.

Justice Stevens, who opposed "quotas" in *Bakke*, saw the worst kind of partisan politics at play—the legislative history of the act made him see the act as legislation created by, written by, and passed by blacks. Contemptuously, he wrote, "There is a group of legislators in Congress identified as the Black Caucus and [the] members of that group argued that if the federal government was going to provide $4,000,000 of new public contract business, their constituents were entitled to 'a piece of the action.'" In fact, it was a coalition of blacks with liberal allies such as Representative Dan Edwards of California and Speaker of the House Thomas "Tip" O'Neill.

Describing the 10 percent figure set aside as "special reparations," "patronage," and a payoff to voters, Stevens warned, "In the long run any rule that authorized the award of public business on a racial basis would be just as bad as one that awarded such business on a purely partisan basis." His dissent was remarkable both for its bitterness and because he later changed his mind. Stevens went to great lengths comparing racial distinctions in affirmative actions to the Nuremberg laws. He said in a footnote to *Fullilove*:

> . . . If the National Government is to make a serious effort to define racial classes by criteria that can be administered objectively, it must study precedents such as the First Regulation to the Reichs Citizenship Law . . . "Article 5, 1. A Jew is anyone who descended from at least three grandparents who were racially full Jews. Article 2, par. 2, second sentence will apply. 2. A Jew is also one who descended from two full Jewish parents, if: (a) he belonged to the Jewish religious community at the time this law was issued, or who joined the community later; (b) he was married to a Jewish person, at the time the law was issued, or married one subsequently; (c) he is the offspring from a marriage with a Jew, in the sense of Section 1, which was contracted after the Law for the protection of German blood and German honor became effective . . . (d) he is the offspring of an extramarital relationship, with a Jew, according to Section 1, and will be born out of wedlock after July 31, 1936."

Rehnquist's dissent joined in by Stevens and Stewart focused on the fact that the statute's practical effect elevated one class of citizens over another. He totally ignored history by relying on an idiosyncratic reading of the Fourteenth Amendment, aimed at making sure blacks would be treated equally. He claimed that affirmative action to help blacks disenfranchised whites, and thereby violated the amendment's equal protection intent. Here again, Rehnquist drew on Justice Harlan's *Plessy v. Ferguson* dissent, claiming that one race should not benefit at the expense of others. His minority view was soon to become the majority view in affirmative action cases.

The last words of the fading Burger Court in 1980 were in favor of affirmative action in the workplace. Nine years later, with Rehnquist in control, before Thomas joined the Court, Brennan was still able to eke out a 5–4 affirmative action decision. But starting with 1989, with Kennedy in place, though still not yet Thomas, the new majority went to work. First to go, in a 6–3 shift, was a Virginia state affirmative action law, where the new Court announced that the Court's previous approval of a federal preference program did mean that state and local preference programs were constitutional.

The 1989 case, *Richmond v. J. A. Croson Co.*, evolved following an ordinance passed by the Richmond City Council, whose members numbered five blacks and four whites. O'Connor said this fact required the Court to look very closely at their actions, something O'Connor had never said when whites were in control of the legislative process. An angry and offended Thurgood Marshall responded, "Such insulting judgments have no place in constitutional jurisprudence." Marshall then noted the city council's thorough review of that city's admitted history of discrimination in the construction area—minority businesses had received virtually no city contracting dollars and rarely, if ever, belonged to trade associations—and that various studies submitted by the defense showed that blacks were excluded from the construction industry.

> The members of the Richmond City Council have spent long years witnessing multifarious acts of discrimination, including, but not limited to, the deliberate diminution of black residents' voting rights, resistance to school desegregation and publicly sanctioned housing discrimination. Numerous decisions of federal courts chronicle this disgraceful recent history.

The eighty-two-year-old justice, more cantankerous than ever, barely hanging on to his seat while vowing to stay on the Court until he died or until he could see a liberal justice replace him, argued that the affirmative action program was critically necessary. "The more government bestows its rewards on those persons or businesses that were positioned to thrive during the period of racial discrimination," he said, "the tighter the deadhand grip of prior discrimination becomes in the present and future."

Justice Blackmun, one of the three dissenters, said the Richmond plan did not give minorities an unfair advantage. All it did was seek some level of proportionality, less of an advantage than society provided to Irish, Italians, or Germans, who for a while were the police and firemen of the city: "I never thought I would live to see the day when the City of Richmond, Virginia, the cradle of the Old Confederacy, sought on its own, within a narrow confine, to lessen the stark impact of persistent discrimination, but Richmond, to its great credit, acted. Yet, this Court, the supposed bastion of equality, strikes down Richmond's efforts as though discrimination had never existed or was not demonstrated in this particular litigation."

The constitutional test the Court used by O'Connor to kill the Richmond program was strict scrutiny. The test the Court could have used, less harsh than strict scrutiny, is intermediate scrutiny. Also called "semisuspect scrutiny," under this test the law to be upheld must be "substantially" related to an important government interest. "Closely related" and "compelling" are the key words in the first test, "substantial" and "important" are the key words in the second test. This is the level of scrutiny given to government actions based on sex, a lesser degree of scrutiny than is given to race.

Justice O'Connor and Justice Stevens, still an opponent of affirmative action, who agreed with her, found the Richmond law failed the strict scrutiny test. The more lenient intermediate test, Marshall argued, was the correct one because even though such law is unarguably race-conscious, it promotes important governmental interests. Affirmative action laws designed to help minorities are totally different than laws that promote segregation, he said. Here, the three justices were not just indulging in legal sparring: all understood what was at stake. For clearly, if the holding of this case, beyond the Richmond program itself, were that strict-scrutiny laws were to be used to decide the constitutionality of all affirmative action laws, that would be the end of affirmative action because they clearly are race-conscious claims.

Affirmative action programs, begun in the 1950s, dramatically grew during the civil rights movement, and then, after the Supreme Court permitted them, they expanded enormously. By the early 1990s, federal programs totaled $11.5 billion. Building on the *Fullilove* decision, which upheld the 10 percent set-asides in rewarding public-works contracts, federal agencies—from the Small Business Administration to the Department of Transportation—had all become involved.

The most important affirmative action decision of the Rehnquist Court was *Adarand Constructors, Inc. v. Pena*, decided in 1995. The background case to *Adarand* was *Metro Broadcasting v. FCC*, decided 5–4 in 1990, before Thomas and Souter came to the Court. In upholding a federal program designed to increase black ownership in the media, the Court said that Congress had far more latitude than state and local governments to use "benign racial classifications," reasoning that Congress "as a national legislature that stands above factional politics . . . is unlikely to be captured by minority racial or ethnic groups and used as an instrument of discrimination." The Court held that the licensing preference was justified by the goal of programming diversity.

In the 1990 *Metro Broadcasting* case, where we saw the proponents of affirmative action claim that increasing the diversity of broadcast viewpoints served a very important state interest, Brennan cobbled together a majority that included Stevens. In dissent, Justices O'Connor, speaking for herself, Kennedy, Scalia, and the chief justice, said, "Modern equal protection has recognized only one [compelling state] interest remedying the effects of racial discrimination. The interest in increasing diversity of broadcast viewpoints is clearly not a compelling interest. It is simply too amorphous, too insubstantial and too unrelated to any legitimate basis for employing racial classification." That dissent states todays' majority view of what is, or is not, "a compelling interest." Since that decision, Thomas has, of course, replaced Marshall, making for a solid majority.

Five years after *Metro Broadcasting*, when *Adarand* arrived, the Court had changed dramatically. Randy Pech, the white owner of Adarand Constructors, a Colorado construction company, sued Federico Pena, the Secretary of Transportation, when he lost the contract to construct a guardrail in the San Juan National Forest to a Hispanic-owned company even though his was the low bid. Pech claimed he failed to win the project because of his race. After losing in the lower and federal courts, he appealed to the U.S. Supreme Court, which had been less than clear in its previous decisions when talking about federal programs. The Supreme Court reversed the two lower courts—and as it did, it announced the death knell of federal affirmative action programs. The federal programs, Justice O'Connor said for the Court, had to meet the same test as state programs in the Richmond case, the strict scrutiny test. The case was remanded back to the lower court to see if the statute passed that test. Since then the case has been back to the Supreme Court twice (it was finally mooted out when a new program was passed), but its 1995 decision remains constitutionally significant.

The *Adarand* 5–4 decision said that for an affirmative action program to be upheld, it had to apply to individuals who were victims of past discrimination rather than simply helping any and all minorities. In dissent, Justice Ginsburg said the courts should not constantly interfere with Congress's decision to pass federal affirmative action programs, and that Congress could draft laws to get past the *Adarand* strict scrutiny test. Stevens, who had voted with Rehnquist in *Bakke* and *Fullilove,* and now, voting against Rehnquist in the *Adarand* minority, said that in view of past injustices, the government was required to enact programs to remedy that past.

It may seem hard to believe that Stevens, who so vehemently opposed affirmative action in *Fullilove* that he cited the Nuremberg laws, had now switched. It is explainable. He never believed that past racial injustice no longer existed as did the conservatives. He never believed the playing field was now level; his change, I believe, was in reaction to the complacent callousness of the Rehnquist bloc, and he was offended by it.

Dramatically rejecting color blindness in *Adarand,* Stevens found "no moral or constitutional equivalence between a policy that is designed to perpetuate a caste system and one that seeks to eradicate racial substitution: Invidious discrimination is an empire of oppression, subjugating a disfavored group to enhance or maintain the power of the majority."

O'Connor, in sending *Adarand* back to the trial court, was doing so, she said, on procedural grounds. She argued the same test should be applied to a law that discriminates against blacks as one that favors blacks and that antidiscrimination laws in the employment field could accomplish what affirmative action programs were trying to do. This is, she says, true color blindness. "Not so," disagreed Scalia, who consistently overrules procedural objections when it suits his agenda. The federal program was not, he said, valid, and there was no point in asking the lower court to look at it. "In the eyes of the government, we are just one race here," and thus no minority should be given special treatment. He easily disposed of the *Metro Broadcasting* precedent as being wrongly decided, and he rejected the argument that overturning such recent precedent violated the concept of *stare decis. Stare decis* is a conservative doctrine. It seeks to have the justices look to past decisions and respond in a manner consistent with precedent. But in *Adarand* and a host of other cases, this Court has relatively little trouble ignoring *stare decis* and directly overturning cases it chooses to, the mark of an activist Court. Scalia's legacy, like that of the *Dred Scott v. Sandford* chief justice, Roger Taney, will not be whether he is a judical restraintist or how he rules on procedural matters. Taney's reputation rests on his vote for slavery, and Scalia's on the substance of his decisions. Scalia wanted the Court in *Adarand* to clearly state that any affirmative action program violates the Constitution. Government can never have justified racial classifications, even if it is shown there was discrimination in the past. He warned that "benign" use of racial preferences reinforces prejudice.

Scalia, joining Thomas, argued that to pursue the concept of racial entitlement—even for the most admirable and benign of purposes—is to reinforce and preserve for future mischief the way of thinking that produced race slavery, race privilege, and race hatred. While *Adarand* means the death of most affirmative action programs, it leaves a window in the difficult case to prove programs aimed at specific discrimination.

Thomas's condemnation in *Adarand* of the programs that helped get him to the Supreme Court was consistent with his pre-Court views. "Government sponsored racial discrimination based on benign prejudice," he had said, was "just as noxious as discrimination inspired by malicious prejudice." He charged that Stevens wanted to create "a racial paternalism exception to the principle of equal protection" and that "so-called benign discrimination teaches many that because of chronic and apparently immutable handicaps, minorities cannot compete with them without their patronizing indulgence. These programs stamp minorities with a badge of inferiority and may cause them to develop dependencies or to adopt an attitude that they are entitled to preferences perhaps indefinitely."

Clarence Thomas was bitter, angry, and very much the victim even before his public life began. He has been manipulative and ambitious. When he was thirty years old he left the Democratic Party to become a Republican because, as he admitted, a black conservative could go far in national politics. That same year, he told a reporter from the *St. Louis Dispatch* that he "wanted to be on the Supreme Court" and started to groom himself as Thurgood Marshall's replacement. Now that he is there, he has vowed to sit until the second quarter of the twenty-first century. He is an immovable block on the Court, one whose influence continually grows in the arch-conservative world as he leaves Scalia's shadow.

Born in Pinpoint, Georgia, on June 23, 1948, Thomas grew up with poverty and loss—his father abandoned him when he was two, and his mother, even though she worked long hours as a maid, received money from church charities to supplement her income. At seven, after his house burned to the ground and his mother remarried, he was sent off to live with his grandmother, Myers Anderson, in Savannah. Anderson was strict and kind. She taught Thomas discipline, and if Thomas strayed, he was whipped with a thick leather belt. Educated at a Roman Catholic school, he first attended seminary to become a priest but left, he claimed, because the white students were guilty of bigotry. He attended Holy Cross College and the Yale School of Law under affirmative action programs, programs he began to attack immediately after graduation from Yale in 1971.

After graduation Thomas worked for Senator John Danforth, and prominently displayed a Georgia flag, which included the stars and stripes of the Confederacy. During that time he met and was befriended both by Strom Thurmond and the black conservative Thomas Sowell, and he became committed to a belief in free-market economy with as little government regulation as possible. A flair for self-promotion brought Thomas to the attention of Ronald Reagan in 1980. Thomas refused to work in the civil rights area and at first turned down Reagan's offer to join the Equal Employment Opportunity Commission. "When I was asked to go to the Department of Education as well as come here [the EEOC], you're dang right I was insulted. What other reason beside the fact that I was black." He ultimately became chairman of the commission, working against the goals the commission stood for. Thomas's initial assessment was correct; the EEOC was and remains a black person's position, and when he took it, Thomas knew he got it primarily because of his color and politics. At the EEOC, he eased pressure on corporations to comply with Court orders, timetables, and numeric goals; he ended the use of class action suits that relied on statistical evidence of discriminatory effect; and he refused to enforce standards on corporate owners. The American Association of Retired Persons (AARP) accused Thomas of neglecting to stop discrimination of the elderly. Of course, it was also his color and politics that saw him nominated for Thurgood Marshall's seat.

During his Supreme Court confirmation hearings in September 1991, Thomas was questioned in the famous Caucus Room of the Old Senate building, where a good deal of wrangling and bitter accusations had gone on before by senators in political battle. Thomas either lied, or was very uninformed, or both. A good law student would have known the answers to the questions he missed. To prepare himself, he had watched tapes of the Souter hearings, and some of Thomas's answers, especially on abortion, were unabashedly lifted, nearly word for word, from them.

Although *Roe v. Wade* was decided while Thomas was a law student, and he knew one of the primary reasons for his appointment was his opposition to it, when asked by Senator Patrick Leahy whether he ever had a discussion of the *Roe* decision, Thomas replied, "If you're asking me whether or not I've ever debated the contents of it, the answer to that is no, Senator." When asked if he ever debated the issue, he said no. He denied having an opinion on *Roe* "this day." The press misrepresented his cagy and misleading answers as saying he had never discussed *Roe v. Wade* with anyone. Long after the hearings, it came out he had extensive discussions about the case long before the hearing and stated flatly he was against it. Attorney Michael Boscourt, Thomas's colleague at Danforth's office, was working on a number of cases in which the state of Missouri was defending statutes restricting the right to abortion. He recalls his own ambivalence about the cases and Thomas's clear anti-abortion views. Still later, less than ten years before his nomination to the Supreme Court, Brad Reynolds, a member of Reagan's inner circle, recalls Thomas saying how little he thought of *Roe*. The arch-conservative Paul Weyrich remembered that he and Thomas had discussed abortion and that he'd found Thomas's lack of candor at the hearing "disingenuous" and "nauseating." Other professional colleagues such as Armstrong Williams recalled similar comments.

The print media published a report, never challenged, that then Judge Thomas drafted an unpublished opinion for the federal appeals court in Washington that would overturn a preference for women in broadcast licensing, and he held it up pending his confirmation hearing. The Supreme Court case *Metro Broadcasting*, as we saw, had held otherwise. When asked in his confirmation hearings whether he agreed with the *Metro Broadcasting* decision, he dodged: "I have had no basis as a judge to disagree with it." The senators did not pursue the question. It is clear the answer was deceptive. He knew he issued an opinion to the contrary and held it up after he knew of his nomination. Since Thomas has been on the Court, affirmative action has been the subject of his most passionate writings. "It is irrelevant," he said, "whether a government's racial classifications are drawn by those who wish to oppress a race or by those who have a sincere desire to help those thought to be disadvantaged." In 1988, three years before he came to the bench, Thomas wrote that Congress is an irresponsible institution of "little deliberation and even less wisdom," which "no longer deliberates or legislates in a meaningful manner" and "is out of control." He "overruled" Congress long before he got to the Supreme Court.

Even Leahy's noncontroversial questions drew unbelievable answers: "Just tell me, to help us know how you think, what you would consider a handful of the most important cases that have been decided by the Supreme Court since you became a law student twenty years ago." Thomas did begin to discuss cases, and he was wrong about the facts or decisions as often as he was right. And then there was Anita Hill. Thomas was both revolting and brilliant in playing the race card, characterizing that hearing as "high-tech lynching for uppity blacks." Thomas, never mentioning his accuser was also black, spit out that he was being "lynched, destroyed, [and] caricatured by a Committee of the United States rather than being hung from a tree." His confirmation vote, breathtakingly close, did not end the controversy. Polls showed later that most people in the country believed that he was lying and that Hill was telling the truth, and they were sorry he had received the nomination. Yet that seemed to leave little residue at election time. He was not a major issue when Clinton opposed Bush in 1992.

Thomas's involvement in oral argument can be compared unfavorably to his fellow justices'. Even though they have all been on the bench many more years, they each come prepared, ask hard questions, have read the briefs, and know where they want the argument to go. They frequently help the lawyers choose positions they agree with and batter the lawyers on the other side. On the bench ten years, Thomas rarely asks a question because he believes the argument is of little significance. He acts totally uninterested in the arguments, his hands cover his eyes, he looks up at the ceiling, rarely at the opposing counsel, and little seems to move him. His totally predictable decisions are based as much on history as on law. He could mail in his decisions for the year at the beginning of the term.

Thomas has the power on the Supreme Court to get back at groups like women and African Americans who denigrate him. When Thomas gave an address at a judicial conference last year at the Adam Marks Hotel, he refused to answer the question of why he was speaking at the hotel while it was being boycotted by the NAACP because it discriminated against blacks.

Nearly all of his talks during the last ten years evoke his "high-tech" lynching claim, his victimization mentality, the transgression of him and his drive to survive. All agree he never got over the pain inflicted on him during the hearings. He never wants the world to forget the price he paid to get on the Supreme Court, and he continues to repeat the story of his life, which his wife describes as "good triumphing over evil."

Although he has been repeatedly criticized for it, Thomas, since his appointment, has spoken in more public forums than any judge other than Scalia. Religion, morality, and hellfire and brimstone run through Thomas's speeches before Federalist groups and the American Enterprise Institute. The darling of the conservative lecture circuit, he has done what federal and trial judges are prohibited from doing. The Judicial Code of Conduct prohibits a judge from "being a speaker or guest of honor at an organization's fund-raising events or making speeches for political organizations." He speaks at numerous fund-raisers, sits on daises where money is raised for causes, and gives his name to fund-raising groups. The Supreme Court does not ban this practice; it was assumed such a law directed at the High Court was unnecessary.

Thomas has written of his agreement with much of Richard Epstein's takings jurisprudence and the economists of the Chicago School. "I believe," he said, "that individual freedom finds tangible expression in property rights," and that the protection of those rights is "central to our heritage."

Bakke did not finally resolve affirmative action in education. Without Powell's vote there would have been a deadlock, and now Powell is gone. Much of the *Bakke* bench is gone. New justices have yet to be heard from. The circuit courts feel free to accept it or disregard it.

The fifth circuit court of appeals, sitting in Atlanta, in the 1996 *Hopwood v. State of Texas* case, said that subsequent decisions had overtaken Powell's *Bakke* opinion and that it was no longer precedent. The appeals court was thus free to invalidate the affirmative action plan at the University of Texas, which had used the goal of achieving diversity as a justification for its program. The Supreme Court refused to review the case, implying that *Bakke* is not the law in the territory covered by the fifth circuit.

Two cases from Michigan that appear to be directly contradictory most probably will arrive in the Supreme Court in the year 2003. The cases are being closely watched. A federal judge in Detroit ruled on March 28, 2001, that the race-conscious admissions system of the University of Michigan's law school is unconstitutional, contradicting a December 2000 ruling in a parallel case that upheld the same university's affirmative action policy for undergraduate students. On December 6, 2001, the circuit court heard both cases. Most of the lengthy argument focused on Justice Powell's *Bakke* decision. The lower courts' split decisions in the Michigan cases are surprising because the undergraduate admissions' system uses race more blatantly than the law school, and therefore it seemed more vulnerable to attack. In admitting freshmen, for example, the university gives black and Hispanic applicants a 20-point boost on a 150-point scale; the law school's approach is more subjective, with only vague guidelines that speak about the importance of having a "critical mass" of minority students. Most schools that want to admit minorities use language similar to Michigan's.

While white students have been more likely to gain admission to the law school than their minority counterparts—38 percent of white applicants were accepted in 2000 compared with 35 percent of African Americans—a comparison of students with similar grades and test scores shows the advantage given to African Americans. In 1995, for example, all four African American applicants with an undergraduate grade point average between 2.75 and 2.99 and scores on the Law School Admissions Test (LSAT) of 161 to 163 were accepted, while none of the fourteen white applicants in those ranges were admitted. Among those with a GPA between 3.25 and 3.49 and LSAT scores of 154 or 155, four of five African Americans were admitted, compared to just one of fifty-one white applicants, evidence that the judge, Bernard A. Friedman, said proved the heavy emphasis the law school places on race in making its admissions decision. "All racial distinctions are inherently suspect and presumptively invalid," wrote the judge, clearly disputing Justice Powell's reasoning in *Bakke*, that diversity is compelling interest. Lawyers for the university's law school, on the other hand, sought to show that Powell's opinion had a factual basis. Psychology professor Patricia Gurin's studies concluded that students of different races who take ethnic studies courses and attend race-awareness workshops are "better prepared to become active participants in our pluralistic, democratic study." Most scientific studies show that students who live and learn in a racially diverse school have the greatest academic and intellectual growth. The judge in the earlier undergraduate admissions case accepted these findings. Friedman rejected Gurin's studies. "The diversity rationale is not among the governing standards to be gleaned from *Bakke*," he said.

In rejecting both the constitutional and factual arguments, Judge Friedman also dismissed lengthy sociological testimony of the discrimination minorities had experienced in poor inner-city high schools, in poverty-stricken neighborhoods, in white-dominated colleges, and in taking standardized tests. While all this is true, Friedman said, "the effects of general, societal discrimination cannot constitutionally be remedied by race-conscious decision-making." The law school's admissions system is illegal because it is "indistinguishable from a straight quota system."

The issue in the Michigan appeals is whether the school may use race as a plus or as a predominant factor, or it may decide that, in schools, as in the workplace and in the voting booths, there can be no racial preference, however disguised.

While the Michigan case was being considered in the sixth circuit, a Georgia case was decided by the fifth circuit.

In September 2001, when the fifth circuit court of appeals, sitting in Atlanta, referring to *Adarand Constructors, Inc. v. Pena* and the *Hopwood v. State of Texas* cases, struck down the University of Georgia's affirmative action program, the university's lawyers decided not to ask the entire fifth circuit court for reargument and rehearing and not to try to go to the Supreme Court. Instead, the university went back to the drawing board, trying to draw a plan to help minorities that would not run afoul of the federal courts.

Clearly, the university, which had relied on the Powell standard in *Bakke* to correct a long tradition of racial exclusion until 1961 followed thereafter by token minority admissions, understood its affirmative action plan would now not withstand the legal action filed by three white students denied admissions.

Former University of Georgia president, Charles Knapp, defending Georgia's policy, testified that having blacks in Georgia's formerly all-white classes increased diversity in the classroom. Although there was no evidence to contradict Knapp's testimony, the trial court rejected it out of hand, deriding it as "amorphous," and found that rather than seeking diversity, the university was trying to manipulate its black-white population to reflect the same ratio as that in the population at large. The appeals court agreed. Judge Stanley Marcus, who wrote the appeals court decision, said if the university wanted to create a diverse community, a white applicant from rural Appalachia might contribute more to the student body than a non-white applicant from suburban Atlanta. Citing the Rehnquist Court affirmative action and voting cases' decisions in affirmative action cases, the court said the assumption that "members of a particular race think alike, share the same political interests and will prefer the same candidates at the polls," is racial stereotyping that violates the Constitution.

Here we see the appeals court anticipating the Supreme Court's view even though the High Court has not spoken.

Any other decision, they understood, would be reversed. If, in fact, the courts agree and pronounce *Bakke* dead, not allowing our universities to diversify, America and the movement for civil rights will have been dealt a terrible blow.

Less than a year after the fifth circuit decision, the sixth circuit, in the Michigan law school case, on May 14, 2002, came to the opposite conclusion. Judge Friedman's decision was reversed. A full nine-judge circuit court split 5–4 and said it agreed with, and was bound by, *Bakke*. The majority decision was written by Boyce F. Martin Jr., a Democrat; the minority decision by a Reagan appointee, Judge Denny F. Boggs. Five Democrats constituted the majority; three Republicans and one Democrat constituted the minority.

In the meantime, the differing decisions of the federal court, sitting in Michigan, make the point, not just in affirmative action but in nearly all cases, that the lower and circuit courts have great latitude in interpreting Supreme Court decisions, especially those that have multiple opinions.

The critical rule of law in the affirmative action arena is now clear; racial classifications, in view of their cruel and invidious history, are always suspect. Their use—though we are told they are not absolutely excluded—must be very solidly justified; any government program that treats races differently will be subject to a very high standard of review. Most preference laws will fail. O'Connor denies that "strict scrutiny is fatal in fact." Any use of racial classifications by an arm of government in order to be justified must be shown both to serve a compelling state interest, and to be "narrowly tailored" to serve that compelling interest. Narrowly tailored means the remedy must fit the wrong. It must surgically attack the problem and not infringe on anyone's other rights.

Whether or not the Court takes the Michigan cases or some other one, and the question of who wins and how, will be largely decided by who then sits on the Court. Four votes are needed to take a Supreme Court case. Four of today's justices would surely jump on any opportunity to finish off affirmative action. Most likely, O'Connor's vote may be the deciding one, and she will vote on racial preferences the same way she votes on job preferences.

Notwithstanding the Supreme Court and the lower and appellate rulings, academic institutions are still trying to consider race a plus factor. Universities that want to admit lower-scoring minorities try to do so by reducing the influence of test scores and developing vaguer criteria. In February 2001, the chancellor of the University of California, who favors using racial preferences however they are disguised, called for the abolition of SAT. Bans on race-conscious college admissions in California and Texas in the late 1990s led to dramatic declines in minority enrollment. The number of new black students on California's Berkeley campus, for example, fell from 562 to 191 (out of a total of roughly 8,000 students) in 1998, the first year of the ban. In 1997, the year the University of Texas ended its race-based admissions, the law school enrolled only 4 black students in its entering class (of a total 468 students), compared with 31 in 1996 (of a total of 488). These statistics encouraged other universities to seek different formulations to get the same result. In July 2001, the University of California Board of Regents approved a new policy intended to admit more blacks, Hispanics, and good students from poor, i.e., black high schools.

Starting in the fall of 2003, Californians who graduated with grades that placed them in the top 12.5 percent of their high school class would be assured of a place at one of the university's eight campuses, a significant step forward but not one the board thought would pass constitutional muster. Such a program would ensure that communities that never sent anyone to college would now do so. And so in November 2001, the regents moved toward adopting a new policy they hope will broaden the factors considered in selecting students. Among the new factors will be a student's success in overcoming economic and educational disadvantages. The policy, known as comprehensive review, has been criticized as a covert way of reviving race as a factor in admissions, which is banned by state law. But supporters maintain that the new policy looks at how all students, not just poor ones, met challenges and therefore is race-neutral.

Scalia, Thomas, Rehnquist, Kennedy, and O'Connor hide behind Harlan's towering reputation and idea of a color-blind constitution as an argument against affirmative action, school segregation, and other race-conscious policies. Reality contradicts.

The Thirteenth, Fourteenth, and Fifteenth Amendments, passed immediately after the Civil War, were themselves race-conscious amendments, freeing blacks from slavery, protecting all citizens from abuse, and giving all citizens the right to vote. The Rehnquist Court's language, and its inability to see today what is in the United States, is evocative of the Supreme Court's contemptuous statement in the 1883 Civil Rights cases, when the Court made clear that special protection for the slaves was no longer necessary. "When a man has emerged from slavery, and by the aid of beneficent legislation has shaken off the pressures of the state," stated Justice Joseph P. Bradley for the majority, "there must be some stage in the progress of his elevation when he takes the rank of a mere citizen and ceases to be the special favorite of the laws."

Opponents of affirmative action believe their day is here. The University of Georgia, by not pursuing other legal remedies at this time and by deciding to redraft its admissions policy, is one of many examples of civil rights groups and public institutions ducking the courts that appear so clearly to be inhospitable. In Piscataway, New Jersey, to cite another such situation, a coalition of civil rights groups joined with the local school board to pay damages to a white schoolteacher who had been laid off on the grounds that maintaining an equally qualified black teacher on the staff was necessary for purposes of racial diversity and in keeping with affirmative action goals. The civil rights groups believed that if the justices had heard the case, they would almost certainly have decided against the school board and the concept of voluntary affirmative action.

And yet, even now, affirmative action, the nation's much-debated answer to generations of racial injustice, is showing surprising resilience after years of attack by courts and politicians and by conservative-led efforts to overthrow it at the polls. The Michigan and Georgia university disputes have led educators nationwide to declare their support for affirmative action and have drawn a surprising, vigorous defense from business giant General Motors and from former President Gerald Ford. "A few years ago there was a feeling that an anti-affirmative action wave was sweeping the country," Columbia University president Lee Bollinger has remarked. "There's much more support for ethnic and racial diversity now." Indeed, polls show rising support for affirmative action. More people today (56 percent, up from 49 percent in 1995) say such programs are needed to counter bias against minorities and women. But what may ultimately prove more persuasive to the Court is a White House wary of how an assault on affirmative action would be viewed by the rapidly growing Hispanic population, which the GOP considers key to its expansion.

Robert Bork, in a *Wall Street Journal* article, called supporters of affirmative action "the hard-core racists of reverse discrimination." For now, O'Connor's pattern appears to be that she is more likely to uphold affirmative action for women than for blacks. O'Connor makes distinctions that permit her inconsistent legal thinking in this area because it is all based on how you select the facts you need for your decision. She distinguishes between a "numerical goal"—a quota—and a plan that addresses blatant discrimination and societal discrimination. These are labels she applies to get the results she wants. A program that was enacted to remedy specific instances of past discrimination, with measurable goals and a precise timetable to achieve those goals, might pass muster with her. If she is replaced by a Republican president, he will surely seek a candidate who will gut affirmative action. It is unlikely even her test will satisfy Bush's Supreme Court nominees.

If Bush gets one appointment from a Stevens or O'Connor step-down, then affirmative action, part of America since the early days of John F. Kennedy, is entirely gone. A promise of the civil rights movement and legislation will have been reneged on. The effect, in minority communities, will be catastrophic.

9

RELIGION

Pat Robertson's resignation as head of the Christian Coalition in December 2001 "confirmed the ascendence of a new leader of the Religious Right in America." It seems to be George W. Bush. Quoting the religious conservative Gary Bauer, Dana Milbank of the *Washington Post* reported, "Robertson stepped down because the position has already been filled." Christian publications shower George W. Bush with praise, preachers from the pulpit testify to his faith and point to his memoirs, describing his discovery of God with the help of Billy Graham. "Reverend Graham planted a mustard seed in my soul, a seed that grew over the next year. He led me to the path, and I began walking. It was the beginning of a change in my life." The Christian movement is no longer on the outside, or merely a player on the inside. The Religious Right is dominant in matters of church and state, and in parochial schools, morality, abortion, school prayer, and a host of other issues. John Ashcroft, who detests nonbelievers, considered running for president in 2000 as the candidate for the Religious Right. Most of the men and women being nominated for the bench share these views. This was exactly what the writers of the Constitution did not want.

Religion was one of the most important motivating factors in the settlement of America. The Puritans and other settlers were refugees from religious wars that ravaged England. Following John Locke's influence, the

Founders created a separation of church and state, ensuring there would be protection for everyone to freely exercise nonorthodox as well as orthodox religions. The First Amendment clauses dealing with religion come out of our own early experiences.

In America during the eighteenth century, primarily prior to the Revolution, religious organizations controlled politics. Churches were the first political parties. Even though they knew of the long history of powerful state-supported religions suppressing minorities, many of those coming to America, oppressed by the British government support of the Church of England, set up their own churches and pushed hard to make them the official religion of the state. Congregationalists in New England and related Presbyterians in other regions—dissenters to the British crown—with traditions of hostility to the crown that reached back to the Puritan revolution, tried to keep the church out of government. The Quakers, powerful in Pennsylvania government and politics, were persecuted. James Madison and his colleagues at the first session of Congress put their religious concerns in the first of the Bill of Rights amendments.

The First Amendment contains two separate clauses dealing with religion: "Congress shall make no law respecting an establishment of religion, or prohibiting the free exercise thereof." These two clauses, elegantly and concisely written, exist in dynamic balance with each other. They and the interpretations given them, until very recently, have been remarkably effective in creating a balance that the Founders wanted.

The Establishment of Religion clause of the First Amendment means at least this: Neither a state nor the federal government can set up a church. Neither can pass laws that aid one religion, aid all religions, or prefer one religion over another. Neither can force nor influence a person to go to or to remain away from church against his will or force him to profess a belief or disbelief in any religion. No person can be punished for entertaining or professing religious beliefs or disbeliefs, or for church attendance or nonattendance. No tax in any amount, large or small, can be levied to support any religious activities or institutions, whatever they may be called, or whatever form they may adopt to teach or practice religion.

Americans believed that individual religious liberty would best be achieved by denying the government the power to tax, support, or assist any or all religions, for they "had a vivid mental picture of conditions and practices which they fervently wished to stamp out in order to preserve liberty."

Starting in 1785, Thomas Jefferson and James Madison led a successful fight against a tax to support Virginia's established church. Madison argued that a true religion did not need the support of the law and that no person, either believer or nonbeliever, should be taxed to support a religious institution of any kind, while the rejection of the tax bill led to Jefferson's famous Virginia Bill for Religious Liberty. The bill's preamble declares that "to compel a man to furnish contributions for money for the propagation of opinions which he disbelieves, is sinful and tyrannical."

A few of the founding generation feared this would lead to a collapse of religion. But, on the contrary, it led to one of the most vibrantly religious societies in the West. More Americans evince a belief in God and church than those in any other Western nation. But America has always had a deep puritanical streak and, in this century, a deep fundamentalist streak. As a result, the clear division that fostered both religion and political freedom is under sharp attack both from the Supreme Court and from powerful conservative coalitions.

Often each particular incident seems small and nonthreatening. Having a one-minute meditation, saying a prayer at graduation, busing both public and parochial schoolchildren from home to school, allowing the state to pay for an interpreter for a child in parochial school, using public facilities for parochial schools, placing a creche in a public building—all seem non-threatening. But the larger picture is fearsome, and that is why Jefferson spoke of a wall of separation.

The amount of monies involved in parochial school aid plans, in just one state, New York, is in the many hundreds of millions. Multiply that by plans in other school districts in other states, and we are speaking of billions of dollars. The Framers and the Supreme Court have always recognized the divisiveness and political potential of state and local religious programs. Once the wall is breached, the pressure for more and more funds for church-related activities will find its way into the halls of the legislatures, where lobbyists—since available money is limited—will argue for allocation of funds on behalf of their religious groups at the expense of the others. Inevitably voters will align with their faiths, and political parties along religious lines will develop and become formidable, one of the principal evils the Framers said the First Amendment was meant to protect.

Today, many see the Republicans as the party of God and church—it is there that the Christian Right and the Evangelists have found a home. Mainline Protestants, particularly the most committed, are also within the

Republican Party, while less committed white Protestants, black Protestants, Jews, and seculars tend to be Democratic. Committed Catholics tend to vote Republican, and less committed Catholics tend to vote Democratic. It is no accident that the religion clauses are in the First Amendment; the Framers were stating their priorities.

Religious battles reach levels of passion and anger not often found in other debates. Nowhere have we seen more clearly how conservative politics are transformed into constitutional politics than in the area of religion. The extreme right wing today seeks to hold hostage moderates in the Republican Party with the abortion case and by insisting the party's commitment be to breaking down the wall of separation. When the South was uniformly Democratic, nearly all of today's evangelical voters were in the Democratic Party. But Ronald Reagan, in breaking the back of the southern Democrats, appealed to the Christian Right by claiming his party would best protect God and country. Patriotism and a commitment to religion became the special preserve of the Republican Party. The threat of a right-wing independent political party gave the Right in 1988, and Pat Robertson today, a prominent voice in the selection of justices for the Supreme Court, the area where many morality and church-state issues are finally resolved.

Until recently, the notion of an impenetrable wall of separation was an article of faith. The Supreme Court, from the late 1940s to the middle of the Burger Court, was resolute in not restricting the free exercise of religion and in condemning any activity that could be seen as establishing any religion. The doctrine of strict separation between church and state reached its high point in the 1960s and '70s. The 1962 Court prohibited virtually all state aid to parochial schools and banned official prayers in the public schools on the grounds that it was coercive, a position opposed in a Gallup Poll taken at the time by 79 percent of American people. The ruling created an uproar.

"How can we be so blind and naive as to sacrifice . . . prayer like this," asked a Chicago man, in order "to appease a few agnostics and atheists." A Methodist bishop argued, "It's like taking a star or stripe off the flag." Evangelist Billy Graham, whose 1972 virulent anti-Semitic remarks recently surfaced, declared, "The Framers of the Constitution meant we were to have freedom of religion—not freedom from religion," while former presidents

Dwight Eisenhower and Herbert Hoover joined the chorus criticizing the Court's actions.

The Rehnquist Court, in the years since, has dramatically reversed the tide of those rulings—either overruled, distinguished, or ignored them—and developed new theories of their own. The chief justice, a sharp critic of the separationist view, and the other majority justices maintain that "neutrality" is the key principle. Government cannot favor or disfavor religion but must be neutral, they say. For example, if a school funds activities of different groups, then under the neutrality principle it must also support religious activities. But with the guise of neutrality, the funding bar can be cast aside. Justice Thomas, speaking for Rehnquist and Justices Scalia and Kennedy, wrote last year that the government can offer aid to "a broad range of groups without regard to their religion" as long as the "principle of neutrality" is followed.

So deep are the passions that, in 1993, we saw Congress, the president, and the Supreme Court go head to head over religion. As important as the decisions were in the religious area, it was as important in reexamining the balance of power that existed between our elected officials and the Supreme Court.

It began in April 1990, in *Employment Division v. Smith*, when the Supreme Court handed down a decision seen to limit the free exercise of religion. It prompted a legislative response. A few years later, on November 16, 1993, the president signed a bill, which Congress passed, that the Supreme Court saw as a challenge to its authority, making it more difficult for the courts to limit the rights of unorthodox religions. The Supreme Court in the later 1997 case *City of Boerne v. Flores* then rejected Congress's legislation.

The 1990 case concerned Alfred L. Smith and Galen W. Black, who were working as counselors in a drug rehabilitation center in Oregon. Both men are of Native American descent, and they are members of the Native American Church. A condition of employment at the rehabilitation center was that employees not use illicit drugs. Smith and Black participated in a sacramental ceremony of their church in which they ingested peyote, a mildly hallucinogenic drug forbidden under Oregon law. The amount taken by each man was not enough to produce any hallucinogenic effect; however, they were fired for "work-related misconduct."

In challenging their dismissals, the men contended their constitutional right to the free exercise of religion had been violated. The Oregon Supreme Court agreed, ruling that although peyote was an illegal drug under Oregon law, the Constitution's free-exercise guarantee barred prosecution for the religious use of peyote. The Supreme Court heard argument in this highly controversial religious-freedom question twice, first on December 9, 1987: "Don't you have to convince us your clients had a constitutionally protected right to such conduct?" Justice John Paul Stevens asked Suanne Lovendahl, a Roseburg, Oregon, lawyer representing the two fired counselors. Yes, she said, and she suggested the men were put in a situation where they had to choose between obeying rules of employment and "adhering to their faith."

Urging the Supreme Court justices to reverse that ruling, Deputy Attorney General William F. Gary argued that the state has a "compelling interest" in combating drug use that should override the religious rights that Black and Smith seek to protect. "The dangers imposed by peyote are indifferent to the motivation of the user," he continued. "Once made lawful for some purposes, the problem of controlling drug trafficking is significantly compounded." Stevens called the freedom-of-religion question "the key to this case." Justice White asked Ms. Lovendahl to name a previous High Court decision that sanctioned illegal conduct in the name of religious freedom.

She responded by citing the court's 1972 ruling that allowed Amish parents to evade Wisconsin's compulsory school attendance laws by teaching their young children at home. She added that the peyote sacrament "is an ancient religious practice that dates back before this practice was made criminal. If this were a majority religion in this country, this practice would never be illegal."

Speaking through Justice Antonin Scalia, five members of the Court (including Justice Stevens) held that Oregon's ban on peyote did not violate the Native Americans' right to free exercise of religion. The law was a criminal law of general application to all citizens equally; it was not aimed at the Native American Church in particular; it had nothing to do with religious beliefs. The Court adopted a less rigorous test than that the state must have "compelling interest" test to uphold the limitation for the Free Exercise clause; the lesser test permitted the ban on the peyote use in the free exercise of religion. Concurring in the judgment but dissenting from everything else was Justice Sandra Day O'Connor, who felt the Scalia-led majority had departed from well-settled positions on the Free Exercise

Clause. In her view, Oregon must prove that in effectively banning a religious ritual, its ban on peyote serves "a compelling interest" of the state. Otherwise, it amounts to an unconstitutional burden upon the free exercise of religion.

The history of free exercise at the time of the drafting of the Bill of Rights strongly suggests acceptance, according to O'Connor, that government should, when possible, accommodate the rights of conscience.

But on October 27, 1993, the Senate, seeking to have future Supreme Court cases on the Free Exercise Clause come down on the side of the Smiths and Blacks, completed legislative action by voting 97–3 for the Religious Freedom Restoration Act (RFRA) of 1993. It passed in the House by unanimous consent.

The act sought to change future decisions in the free exercise area by making it more difficult to uphold government regulations that banned certain religious practices, undermining *Smith*. The act directed the High Court to restore the compelling interest standard used by the Court prior to *Employment Division v. Smith*, which invalidates a law that "substantially burdened" one's religious exercise. Under that standard, Smith and Black would have won.

The act was then challenged by the city of Boerne. Situated on a hill in the city of Boerne, Texas, some twenty-eight miles northwest of San Antonio, is St. Peter Catholic Church. Built in 1923, the church's structure replicates the mission style of the region's earlier history. The church seats about 230 worshipers, a number too small for its growing parish. Some forty to sixty parishioners cannot be accommodated at some Sunday masses. In order to meet the needs of the congregation, the archbishop of San Antonio gave permission to the parish to plan alterations to enlarge the building.

A few months later, the Boerne City Council passed an ordinance authorizing the city's Historic Landmark Commission to prepare a preservation plan with proposed historic landmarks and districts. This is called a law of general applicability; it is aimed at the entire public. Under the ordinance, the commission must preapprove construction affecting historic landmarks or buildings in a historic district. Soon afterward, however, the archbishop applied for—and was denied—a building permit to enlarge the church. City authorities pointed to the preservation ordinance designating the historic district, which, they argued, included the church. The archbishop immediately brought suit.

The litigation focused on the constitutionality of the broadly supported RFRA. While all agreed that a ruling of the Supreme Court can be overturned only by a constitutional amendment, the liberal dissenter in the *Smith* case said the Religious Freedom Restoration Act was not meant to overrule that decision but was merely setting new standards for the Court to use when examining laws affecting religion. It was looking to the future, not the past.

During the February 19, 1997, oral argument in *City of Boerne v. Flores*, the city's attorney, Marci A. Hamilton, argued the case was not about religious freedom; rather, it was about federal power. Hamilton, a former law clerk to Justice O'Connor, minced no words in denouncing Congress as "the branch most likely to be controlled by interest groups and by opinion polls," that led to a "a hostile takeover of the Free Exercise Clause of the First Amendment." The Religious Freedom Restoration Act, she continued, was "a brazen attempt to reinterpret the Free Exercise Clause and to impose that reinterpretation on the courts, on the States, and to shift the balance of power between church and State dramatically in favor of the churches." It was, she concluded, an example of legislative overreaching violating "the fundamental structural constitutional guarantees, the separation of powers, Federalism, and separation between church and State."

Jeffrey Sutton, representing those states that supported the act, also attacked Congress and said that there was no record that supports Congress's findings that such a law was necessary. He said the Court should not defer to Congress. On this he was interrupted by Justice Breyer, who observed: "Mr. Sutton, it seems to me you overestimate the sturdiness of this institution. We have here a statute unanimously passed by Congress. There was virtually no dissent, and you want us to say it's no good and to judge future statutes on the basis of such ineffable principles as the etiquette of Federalism."

The attorney representing the archbishop agreed with Breyer: "Congress cannot overrule the Court," while Justice O'Connor contributed to the argument saying "there's some indication that that was what Congress was all about here, if you read the Purpose Clause. Does that concern us at all? Do we have to address that concern? Now, you admit, I suppose, that Congress cannot come in and overrule a decision of this Court it doesn't like by legislation."

In the end, the city of Boerne won in a 6–3 vote. The 6–3 Court found the federal act unconstitutional. Justice Kennedy, writing for the majority, said the act was passed to overrule the legal standard used in the *Smith* decision, and that Congress, in trying to decide what laws were and were not constitutional, was stepping out of bounds. The Supreme Court said it refused to let Congress define the constitutional standard by which to judge the Free Exercise Clause. The government argued it was not interpreting the Constitution but was enforcing the Constitution, exactly as Section 5 of the Fourteenth Amendment required them to do. *Boerne* can also be seen as creating the groundwork for the federalism attack, setting the discourse that finally leads to *Kimel v. Florida Board of Regents* and *University of Alabama v. Patricia Garrett*, discussed earlier in the Federalism chapter.

In reaching his conclusion, Kennedy relied on two constitutional principles—the separation of powers principle and, a favorite with this Court, federalism. Kennedy wrote that in the former, the Congress had impinged on the Court's role to determine conclusively what the Constitution means, while upholding the federal law that would make it difficult, if not impossible, for states to exercise their traditional authority to regulate the lives of their citizens, and thus had violated his concept of federalism. Justice Sandra Day O'Connor, writing on behalf of Justices Breyer and Souter, said she was not abandoning her level of nondeference to Congress, but reiterated her belief that *Smith* was wrongly decided, that the Court should have overturned it and allowed the Religious Freedom Restoration Act to stand. The Free Exercise Clause, she wrote, is not merely "an anti-discrimination principle that protects only against those laws that single out religious practice for unfavorable treatment"; it is, instead, "an affirmative guarantee of the right to participate in religious practices . . . without . . . government interference."

Justice Stevens is acutely aware of the inordinate power of established religious groups to lobby Congress and get their own legislation through. Stevens came down against the church and said this law of general applicability does not violate the Free Exercise Clause simply because they prohibit or burden religious practices. More important, *Boerne*, he said, overruled three decades of precedent.

If the historic landmark on the hill in *Boerne* happened to be a museum or an art gallery owned by an atheist, it would not be eligible for an exemption from the city ordinances that forbid an enlargement of the structure. Because the landmark is owned by the Catholic Church, it is claimed that RFRA gives its owner a federal statutory entitlement to an exemption from a generally applicable, neutral civil law. Whether the Church would actually prevail under the statute or not, the statute has provided the Church with a legal weapon that no atheist or agnostic can obtain. This governmental preference for religion, as opposed to irreligion, is forbidden by the First Amendment.

Until the Rehnquist Court started dealing with religion, a landmark Burger Court decision had, it seemed, settled many of the church-state issues. The 1971 case *Lemon v. Kurtzman* was the clearest attempt to interpret fairly the Establishment Clause of the First Amendment. Rhode Island and Pennsylvania passed laws that allowed their states directly to supplement teachers' salaries to teach nonreligious subjects in parochial and other nonpublic schools. This would be a very substantial aid to the development of parochial schools; but more fearful was the assumption that once the churches got a foot in the door, there would be state and church competition for funds. Large sums of money would presumably flow, and parochial schools would flourish at the expense of public educations.

Chief Justice Burger sought for unanimity in *Lemon* as Warren had in *Brown*. The Court's opinion, by a vote of 7–0, (White, joining in, also wrote an opinion, dissenting from a small part of the opinion) carrying with it the full force of the Court, was a masterpiece of compromise in a dangerous area. The Supreme Court held the law unconstitutional because of a fear that a parochial school teacher, in teaching a secular subject, might intermingle faith and morals with teaching of nonreligious matter. The Court also said that to allow the Rhode Island and Pennsylvania laws to stand, the government would continuously have to inspect parochial school classes to see if the spiritual matter was being taught, an involvement that would create an excessive entanglement between church and state.

The unanimity of the vote, with all seven justices voting together for the result under the Republican chief justice, led observers to believe the *Lemon* decision, and the constitutionality test it established, could be the basis for church-state decisions for the next several decades. It seemed so much to embrace the spirit and letter of the Establishment Clause. Under the three-part *Lemon* test, government would be seen to violate religious freedom and neutrality when its action has a primarily religious reason, when its action has the primary effect of advancing or inhibiting religion, or when its action results in excessive government entanglement with religion.

A breach of any of the three prongs required a declaration of unconstitutionality. (It was this third part that the Rhode Island and Pennsylvania law were said to breach.) Although *Lemon* itself has been applied inconsistently by the Supreme Court and has been criticized by a number of justices and commentators, it was the law, and the concept of the law that existed until the Rehnquist Court came into existence.

The James Madison view, the distrust of anyone who has power, is reflected in the First Amendment's Establishment Clause and Free Exercise Clause. Government cannot aid and support religion, and religion cannot aid and support government. If it were otherwise, Madison feared we would have religious-dominated parties. The drafting of the Religious Clause in the First Amendment is eloquent and precise, and the way it has worked is equally miraculous. The *Lemon* test— "no entanglements"— seems to carry out exactly not only the Framers' intent but also the essential ingredients for a society in which religions free of governmental control can flourish.

If the conservative wing of the Court today had its way, the *Lemon* principles would be disregarded entirely and replaced by a much more permissive "coercion" test, which would allow government involvement in and promotion of all but the most invasive religious activities. In 1990, the Rehnquist Court upheld the rights of high school students to meet on campus before or after classes for prayer or Bible study.

The last decisions of the Burger Court, and the first decisions of the Rehnquist, began a full retreat from the separationist view. Direct payment of public funds to religious schools, state-paid legislative chaplains, and a publicly sponsored native creche were all permitted by the Supreme Court in the 1980s and early '90s. The accommodationists had won all those cases.

The 1985 *Wallace v. Jaffree* case laid out Rehnquist's theories at length. Alabama passed a law providing for a moment of silence that students could use for prayer or meditation at the beginning of the school day. Kennedy and Thomas were not yet on the Court; Brennan and Marshall were. President Reagan's Department of Justice helped mobilize seven groups, including the Moral Majority and the Christian Legal Foundation, to both file briefs and argue, with the states, the *Wallace* case. But Rehnquist's argument for *Wallace*—that the Constitution requires neutrality between religions, not neutrality between religion and irreligion; that neutrality in church-state matters need not mean absolute prohibition—would have to make its presence felt another day. Powell and O'Connor were in the majority in *Wallace*, and Rehnquist lost 6–3.

In a 1992 case, *Lee v. Weisman*, the Court, in a 5–4 decision, struck down religious prayer at a public school graduation ceremony. Deborah Weisman, who was Jewish, filed her complaint after a rabbi offered an invocation and benediction at the Providence, Rhode Island, school that she attended. As she had in other establishment cases, O'Connor again joined the moderate four to make a majority. Justice Scalia, writing for the four dissenters, argued this clause should not apply to state promotion of religion unless the state forces participants to attend by imposing a penalty. His sarcastic, angry dissent scolded the majority for distinguishing the use of prayer to open a legislative session and a prayer in a school setting. Answering him, the majority found that adults attending the former could not be realistically compared to schoolchildren, whose susceptibility to peer, parental, and social coercion are more manifold.

Scalia mocked his colleagues for worrying about the mental state of adolescents who, he said, probably ignored the prayer. Indeed, in Scalia's view, the Constitution would permit a wide range of government-sponsored religious activities. In the public schools, officials could require that the school day begin with sectarian devotionals; teachers could proselytize to their students; and student religious majorities could determine what religious service or which religious leader to have at school events, regardless of the beliefs of religious minorities, so long as objecting students faced no formal punishment. In other contexts, a coercion test would allow government-erected symbols of a single faith to appear on public buildings and in public spaces, and judges, military officers, and government employers could proselytize to those under their supervision.

The elder Bush's administration had seen the *Weisman* case as an opportunity to reverse *Lemon*; the Court's refusal to revisit that decision was a significant disappointment. The ruling caught the Right off-guard. It had expected the Court, with its preponderance of Republican appointees, to finally validate the school prayer issue that many saw as an important piece of its family values campaign. O'Connor and Kennedy were again assailed by the Right. But in 1993, the Court upheld a Christian group's right to hold in a high school auditorium evening meetings to discuss morality and values. When, the following year, in *Zobrest v. Catalina Foothills School District*, parents who had enrolled their deaf child in a religious high school and claimed that federal law required the state of Arizona to provide a sign-language interpreter for the child, the Court's conservative majority held the Establishment Clause did not bar a state from providing such. This time, the Court said, filtering of government funds through "private choices" of individual parents meant it was not the government's role that was supporting religious schools, despite the fact that such "choice" is made possible only through public financial assistance provided by the government. Rehnquist could not deny that the reliance on "private choice" could open the floodgates to massive government funding of religion.

But the *Lemon* test was severely wounded, weakened but not yet dead. Scalia's view of *Lemon*'s viability was vividly set forth in *Lambs Chapel v. Center Moriches School District*, a case decided in 1993, in which the Court held that the school could not deny access to the church and its facilities when it made those same facilities available to other groups. Justice Scalia's dramatic description of his frustration in killing the *Lemon* test is clear from his concurring opinion. He likens the *Lemon* case to Dracula. "Like some ghoul in a late-night horror movie that repeatedly sits up in its grave and shuffles abroad, after being repeatedly killed and buried, *Lemon* stalks our Establishment Clause, jurisprudence once again, frightening the little children and school attorneys . . . over the years . . . no fewer than five of the currently sitting justices have, in their own opinions, personally driven pencils through the creature's heart." But Scalia offers his solution: "the secret of the *Lemon* test's survival, I think, is that it is so easy to kill. It is there to scare us (and our audience) when we wish it to do so, but we can command it to return to the tomb at will."

In 1995, *Rosenberger v. University of Virginia*, another significant church-state case arose, this time at the University of Virginia, the institution founded by Thomas Jefferson, the father of the term the "wall of separation between church and state." The *University of Virginia* case reimbursed expenditures by student groups through a Student Activities Fund, but it refused to reimburse the expenses of the student newspaper *Wide Awake*, which was dedicated to expressing Christian perspectives and beliefs, on the ground that to do so would be promoting these beliefs. Religious conservatives were pitted against civil libertarians.

Pat Robertson's American Center for Law and Justice and the Christian Legal Society asked that *Lemon* be directly overturned and that the plaintiff, Ronald Rosenberger, win. The American Jewish Congress and the liberal National Council of Churches asked that *Lemon* be upheld and that relief be denied to him.

Rosenberger won. Chief Justice Rehnquist and Reagan-Bush appointees Kennedy, O'Connor, Scalia, and Thomas, in a 5–4 decision, struck down the school's refusal to fund religious student publications as unconstitutional. Some of the media claimed it was a victory for free speech. While the Court focused on free speech concerns, the Court's decision was a significant expansion of public support for religious activities. The potential religious consequences of the *Rosenberger* case was recognized by Justice Souter, one of the four dissenters who saw that the Court's reasoning "would commit the Court to approving direct religious aid beyond anything justifiable for the sake of access to speaking forums."

Then, in 1997, the Court was asked to look at a case that directly challenged a 1985 case that the liberals won. Twelve years before, in a New York case under the same federal funding law, the Supreme Court, in *Aguilar v. Felton*, said that the presence of public school teachers in parochial schools, even if they voluntarily gave of their time, amounted to an "unconstitutional entanglement" of public and parochial education in violation of *Lemon* and the Establishment Clause. In New York City, where *Aguilar* originated, public officials responded by spending more than $100 million in federal education funds to provide, among other actions, leasing vans that were then parked on public streets just outside the religious schools. These mobile classrooms served more than twenty thousand students a year and required parochial school students and public school teachers to leave their classrooms and meet on seemingly neutral ground. It was a bald effort to navigate *Lemon*'s intent.

Now in *Agostini v. Felton*, the Court faced the decision whether formally to bury the excessive entanglements test of *Lemon*. Justice Blackmun, one of *Lemon*'s strongest advocates, was now gone. In 1994, the Court in the *Board of Education of Kiryas Joel Village School District v. Grumet* case said they would like to reconsider *Aguilar*. In order for the Right to win and ignore or overrule *Aguilar*, both O'Connor and Kennedy would have to vote with Thomas, Scalia, and Rehnquist. Since the Court had been proclaiming its commitment to precedent in the church-state area, and since *Aguilar* was only twelve years old, it was not clear that O'Connor would switch. She did.

Justice O'Connor's opinion speaking for the majority, overruled *Aguilar*. Justice Stevens, the only justice still sitting who was a member of the

Aguilar majority, was now in the minority. First, the Court rejected the *Aguilar* view, indeed the view of most of the religion cases, that all government aid directed to the educational function of religious schools is unconstitutional. O'Connor said school boards were competent to erect administration guidelines that would ensure that teachers performed in a neutral fashion without resorting to excessive monitoring and, hence, there would be no entanglement of church and state. Public money could be made available to all students for secular purposes without violating the Establishment Clause, she held, and it was also entirely possible for on-premise programs conducted by public school teachers to be free of religious connection. Finally, according to O'Connor, there was no reason to believe that the parents of secular school students would conclude that the presence of public school teachers in sectarian classrooms meant that the New York City Board of Education had placed its stamp of approval on religious education.

Precedent and *stare decis* were again thrown out the window. So, too, was judicial restraint. The Court's new ruling, as Souter said, could authorize direct state aid to religious institutions on an unparalleled scale in violation of the Establishment Clause's central prohibition against religious subsidies by the government. The following years saw the 5–4 tilt chillingly to the right in two 6–3 decisions when Breyer bolted and joined the Rehnquist majority.

In *Mitchell v. Helms* on December 1, 1999, Michael McConnell, on behalf of the state of Louisiana, argued to uphold a state law that permitted the state to lend computers and schoolbooks to parochial schools. Barbara Underwood, Clinton's assistant solicitor general, argued the lending was improper.

> This Court has articulated the money or aid not be itself directly used for religious instruction—when the aid is sufficiently substantial as to in effect support the whole operation of the school, when without it the school couldn't operate, then the fact that the dollars can be by—by accounting assigned only to secular functions isn't sufficient to remove the appearance and the understanding and the fact that the government is in effect subsidizing this school in totality.

Underwood referred back to the *Lemon* case, arguing that the government should not be in the school on a daily basis in the position of having to see if its materials are being used for religious teaching or secular teaching. That would be an excessive entanglement, prohibited by a majority of the Court.

Justice O'Connor asked: "What if you have a lectern, you know, and you can put a secular book on it or you could put a very religious book on it? That—that doesn't meant that the lectern needs to be monitored, does it?"

Underwood replied: "Well, I think if lecterns were provided—there might well be a restriction that they not be used in the theology classroom or, for that matter, the pulpit of the chapel—when worship services were engaged in."

McConnell relied on the neutrality concept:

This Court should take cases one at a time, and when the Congress passes a statute that provides secular, neutral, non-ideological equipment and material for children on a neutral basis, that not only is not a constitutional threat, Your Honors, that is something which is in the finest tradition of the First Amendment because it leaves people free to be able to make educational choices for themselves.

The government then is not subsidizing and it is not favoring religion, but on the other hand, it is not in the rather illiberal position of denying basic technological tools of the 20th century to some children because their parents have chosen religious schools.

The state of Louisiana won a 6–3 decision, Breyer voting to form a six-person majority bloc. Building on *Agostini*, Thomas wrote the judgment of the Court in an opinion joined in by Rehnquist, Scalia, and Kennedy. O'Connor and Breyer wrote a separate opinion joining the other four for a 6–3 decision. Thomas said that the state of Louisiana's law is not a law establishing a religion merely because the private school's receiving aid is religiously affiliated; that if there is any indoctrinational religion because of this program, it is not the government that is doing it. He does not deny that the program does indoctrinate and that this decision shows the "degree to which our Establishment Clause jurisdiction has shifted." He called part of the dissent "offensive" and said that "hostility to aid to pervasively sectarian schools has a shameful pedigree that we do not hesitate to disavow."

Thomas's opinion, said Breyer and O'Connor, "announces a rule of unprecedented breadth for the establishment of Establishment Clause challenges" to school aid programs.

Breyer and O'Connor, agreeing with Thomas's result but refusing to join the majority opinion, saved the country from an extreme and near earth-shattering change in the law. A one-vote change in the Court will make Thomas's view the majority in the church-state area and those 6–3 decisions may become 7–2.

Souter, Stevens, and Ginsburg, passionate and, at times, intemperate in this dissent, noted how this decision changed the law of the last fifty years. The dissenters saw their arguments characterized as "bigoted and irreligious" by the majority. They pointed out the danger that "religious schools could be blessed with government funding as massive as expenditures made for the benefit of their public school counterparts, and religious missions would thrive on public money."

The second religion case where Justice Breyer joined the majority to make it 6–3 came down on June 2, 2001. The local Good News Club, an evangelical group with 622 chapters nationwide, asked school authorities in Milford, New York, if their group could meet in its public school as soon as it ended during the week. Reverend Stephen Fournier and his wife, Darlene, said since the Girl Scouts and 4H Club were permitted to meet there, so, too, should the Good News Club.

Good News Club meetings include classes that open and close with prayer. Children are instructed that "the Bible tells us how we can have our sins forgiven by receiving the Lord Jesus Christ. It tells us how to live to please Him." The lesson plan instructs the teacher to "lead a child to Christ," and when reading a Bible verse, to "emphasize that this verse is from the Bible, God's Word" and that it is "important—and true—because God said it." Teachers are reminded of their responsibility to give the "unsaved" children in their class an opportunity "to respond to the Gospel." But the heart of the meeting is the "challenge" and "invitation," which are repeated at various times throughout the lesson. During the challenge, "saved" children who "already believe in the Lord Jesus as their Savior" are challenged to "stop and ask God for the strength and the 'want' . . . to obey him," while the "unsaved" children are invited "to trust the Lord Jesus to be your Savior from sin. . . . Please bow your heads and close your eyes," they are told: "If you have never believed in the Lord Jesus as your Savior and would like to do that, please show me by raising your hand. If you raised your hand to show me you want to believe in the Lord Jesus, please meet me so I can show you from God's Word how you can receive His everlasting life."

When school officials refused the club's request, saying school facilities are not open to commercial activities, partisan political gatherings, or for religious purpose, the Good News Club filed suit. In March 2001 the justices of the Supreme Court heard the argument.

Thomas Marcelle, representing the club, presented its case as a free-speech issue. "We're not asking for special access, just equal access," he said. Frank Miller, the school board's lawyer, responded that "religious worship" was not an appropriate activity in a public school building, even after classes had ended: "You would be permitting a school to be used as a house of worship. We don't think that's consistent with the mission of the school system." Doing so violates the Establishment Clause. The case tested whether the same free-speech principles applied with young children in an elementary school as with older children. There had been a bright line that had been alive for decades. In the past, the Court has said it was more worried about the susceptibility of very young children than high schoolers or college students to religious proselytizing.

Justices Scalia and Kennedy saw an opening and sharply criticized Miller for what they referred to as "censorship" of religion. "You are worried about kids being infected" with the religious message, Scalia said mockingly. Kennedy questioned why school authorities would think they must "purge" the religious message from groups that want to meet at school. And then Breyer surprised the Court attendees by asking whether the school's exclusion of religious groups was even legal. "Why isn't it discrimination against religion in violation of the First Amendment?" he asked.

Only Justice Souter skeptically questioned the lawyer for the Christian group. "This is like Sunday school, isn't it?" he asked Marcelle. Children meet with a minister to sing and pray, Marcelle noted. Suppose the church said it wanted to have its Sunday morning worship service in the school building. Or perhaps in city hall. Must the government agree? asked Souter. Yes, said Marcelle, the lawyer for the Christian group, as long as the city does not actually "endorse" the particular religion involved.

The written decision in *Good News Club v. Milford Central School* showed how differently justices can interpret the exact same facts. The Good News case adopted a new test that neutrality is a factor in deciding whether government action violates the Establishment Clause. While Justice Thomas described the Good News Club as teaching character and values from a religious point of view, the three dissenters—Souter, Ginsburg, and Stevens—all said the activity consisted of worship and evangelizing. The tender ages of the children invited made it possible they could be unduly pressured to join a church group that met at school. "It is beyond question that Good News intends to use the public school premises not for the mere discussion of a subject from a particular Christian point of view," Justice Souter said, "but for an evangelical service of worship calling children to commit themselves in an act of Christian conversion."

Thomas, breaking down the wall with linguistic tricks, says, "We disagree that something that is quintessentially religious or decidedly religious in nature cannot also be characterized properly as the teaching of morals and character development from a particular viewpoint. . . . We see no logical difference between the invocation of Christianity by the Club and the invocation of teamwork, loyalty or patriotism by other associations to provide a foundation for their lessons." Scalia, concurring in a separate opinion, went further than Thomas. Breyer, apparently uncomfortable with the company he keeps, tried to separate himself from some of Thomas's more extreme statements.

The majority's bland language to describe the club's active religious recruitment activities, Justice Souter correctly complains, "ignores reality." But, he says, it cannot obscure the decision's impact in establishing "the remarkable proposition that any public school opened for civic meetings must be opened for use as a church, synagogue, or mosque."

Justices Souter and Ginsburg, in dissent, dealt with reality. "It is beyond question that Good News intends to use the public school premises not for the mere discussion of a subject from a particular Christian point of view, but for an evangelical service of worship calling children to commit themselves in an act of Christian conversion. The majority avoids reality only by resorting to the bland and general characterization of Good News acting as teaching of morals and character from a religious standpoint."

Breyers justified his vote in *Good News* by his First Amendment sensitivity. But his switch to help form a 6–3 majority in *Mitchell v. Helms* is a far more dangerous precedent. Many future cases will deal with material and cash aid to parochial schools. Breyer's switch makes "material" cases a foregone conclusion.

The *Good News Club* decision is only the latest to give religious groups a free-speech right to use public buildings or to participate on an equal basis in government-funded programs. While the Court draws accolades as a body very sensitive to the speech clause of the First Amendment, it often does so at the expense of the Establishment Clause. David Savage, reporting in the *Los Angeles Times*, pointed out that "in southern Orange County, where land is scarce and new churches booming, 60% of campuses in the Capistrano Unified School District become religious sanctuaries on Sundays." During Easter and Christmas when attendance balloons, even more campuses are rented out. "Some churches were found to drape their own banners over the school's sign."

Like *Rosenberger*, the *Good News Club* drew support from a wide spectrum of religious organizations, including the National Council of Churches and the American Jewish Congress. When the decision came, reaction to the decision was swift. All observers understood instantly the long-term implications in the Court's opinion that no constitutional crisis is involved when religious institutions are afforded the same treatment as secular organizations. Edwin Darden, senior staff attorney for the National School Boards Association, said the *Good News Club* decision placed local school boards in a difficult position, both threatening local control and "setting up a competition between different religious groups trying to gain the religious fidelity of children." He said the option of closing elementary schools to all outside groups, while permissible under the ruling, would not prove practical or attractive. True enough. By opening the school door to some groups, you are just as well opening a church door. Religious worship in the school building cannot be far behind.

As we saw, Breyer joined the other side of the aisle in some church-state areas. Breyer's initial conversations with Clinton and his staff had failed to impress. They found him ambitious, very bright, self-centered, and so guarded that it was impossible to know what he really believed. Religion is one area in which Breyer now often parts company with the moderates, but another may be in the economics area. A more humane Richard Posner, Breyer, who wraps economics and the law together, may be more of a pro-business ally than other moderates when some of the New Deal decisions are revisited. Passed over by Clinton for the seat that went to Ruth Bader

Ginsburg because, according to the president, he was too cold, oversold himself, and was "without heart," Justice Breyer's record, prior to his Supreme Court elevation, was that of a moderate.

Born on August 15, 1938, of well-to-do parents in San Francisco, California, Breyer attended Lowell High School, a magnet public school where he competed against Jerry Brown, the future governor of California, and other high achievers. Designated "most likely to succeed" by his high school class (as was Souter), he first went to Stanford and then to Oxford, where he won the prestigious Marshall Scholarship and developed an interest in economics that helped lead him as a lawyer into the areas of government regulation and economics.

A distinguished record at Harvard Law School, where he edited the law review, led to a clerkship with Justice Arthur Goldberg for the 1964–65 term. There, he helped Goldberg draft the privacy opinion in *Griswold v. Connecticut*. In 1967, he married Joanna Hare, the very bright and wealthy daughter of a British lord.

After a teaching stint at Harvard, Breyer went on to the Judiciary Committee in 1974, where his singular achievement was his work on airline deregulation and criminal-sentencing guidelines, leading Breyer to garner accolades from corporate officers and Republicans. He was someone both sides could work with. As Georgetown University professor Jeffrey Rosen wrote, "Each morning Breyer would meet for breakfast with his Republican counterpart, the chief counsel for Senator Strom Thurmond, and that experience convinced him that when legislative staff meet, rather than being prisoners of ideology, both sides are often trying to achieve practical results that will help the country. While recognizing that Congress wasn't prefect, Breyer concluded that it worked pretty well, and he left the job even more optimistic about the possibilities of bipartisan legislative cooperation than when he began. He is not blind to the deficiencies in Congress—he has seen it first-hand, but on balance, he is clear that is where the power ought to reside."

In 1980, Breyer was nominated to and approved by a GOP-controlled Congress to the U.S. Court of Appeals for the First Circuit, sitting in Boston. Breyer's primary interest on that court was in the areas of antitrust and business law.

Both he and Ruth Bader Ginsburg—who in some ways are seen as the equivalent of Nixon's "Minnesota Twins," Burger and Blackmun—arrived at the circuit court the same year as Carter appointees. Their records there were similar, as were their educational and religious backgrounds—elite schools with high achievement. Both are Jewish; Breyer married an English Anglican, whose daughter, an Episcopalian priest, later wrote a book about her training in a seminary. Ginsburg and Breyer actively lobbied for their Supreme Court jobs, and at the time they were selected, each were living lives of privilege.

Before offering Breyer the seat being vacated by Justice Harry Blackmun, Clinton, remembering his first view of Breyers, started looking elsewhere. He offered the job to the former New York governor Mario Cuomo, because he thought the Court suffered from "the lack of any member of the Supreme Court who had played a prominent role in the life of the nation before coming to the Court." After Cuomo turned him down, Clinton considered then Interior Secretary Bruce Babbitt, along with a host of others. Clinton was hoping to lure someone with stature to be a leader of the Court's minority bloc. Clinton failed, and rather than spend more time on the matter, he chose Breyer.

Breyer's 1994 confirmation hearing was even less eventful than Ginsburg's. He lectured the Judiciary Committee on economics and the law; he quoted Oliver Wendell Holmes's famous aphorism that law reflects not so much logic, as history and experience; and he described the important role played by government in helping to deregulate the airline industry. Like Ginsburg, Breyer sought to present himself as a centrist. But just as her moderate views had prompted concern among abortion advocates, so now did what some perceived as Breyer's probusiness attitude. As one acquaintance, University of Texas law professor Thomas O. McGarrity, said, Breyer's nomination could be "hazardous to our health." Professor McGarrity compared Breyer's free-market views and hostility to regulation as parallel to those of the prominent Reagan appointees Scalia and Bork. But his critics may be seeing his views as overly sympathetic to business when in fact they are instances where he deferred to Congress and administrative agencies. Those supporting Breyer deflected McGarrity's hard words, calling Breyer a pragmatist and a flexible jurist who would rely on "tradition, on people, on conscience." Orrin Hatch, a long-time supporter from Breyer's Judiciary Committee days, called him an excellent nominee. Once sent to the floor, Breyer's nomination as the 108th Supreme Court justice was quickly confirmed by an 87–9 vote.

Unlike Stevens, Scalia, and Thomas, who write expansive opinions, Jus-

tices Ginsburg and Breyer each try to write the narrowest decisions possible. Breyer, in large part because he saw that Congress does work, strenuously opposes the majority's federalism decisions. He believes deference to
Congress promotes democratic participation. "Federalism," he wrote,
"helps to protect liberty, not simply our modern sense of helping the individual remain free of restraints imposed by a distant government, but more
directly by promoting the sharing among citizens of governmental decision-
making authority." While not an instinctive civil libertarian, Breyer believes
wholeheartedly in democratic participation. He is against judges who claim
to be experts in all things, overruling those qualified experts who testify
before Congress, helping the elected representatives to fashion legislation.

None of the four-justice minority are liberals in the mold of Brennan,
Marshall, or Douglas, and none of them have the political skills of Brennan, who actively pushed his agenda with other justices and often came out
with surprising victories. Ginsburg and Breyer, the only two Democrats in
the minority, do not lead it, and on some issues they come out to the right
of Souter and Stevens. Justice Breyer is, in fact, on many issues, to the
right of the justice whom he replaced, Harry Blackmun, a Nixon
appointee. After Blackmun left the bench, he prophesied the conservative
tenor of the Court would continue well into the middle of the twenty-first
century. Breyer may help fulfill that prophesy sitting on a Court where he
is part of an ever-shrinking minority, helpless as the Court veers to the
right.

The Court's move to the right comes at a time when it will soon be considering Bush's faith-based initiative. The Religious Right is determined to
throw the massive weight of the federal government behind religious
groups. "Problems like addiction and abandonment and gang violence,
domestic violence, mental illness and homelessness—we are called upon by
conscience to respond," Bush said last year as he signed the executive order
creating the new Office of Faith-Based and Community Initiatives. "As long
as there are secular alternatives, faith-based charities should be able to
compete for funding on an equal basis and in a manner that does not cause
them to sacrifice their mission," he said.

As a policy initiative, this is a drastic policy change. For more than a
century, the Supreme Court has said that church-run hospitals can receive

government aid because these facilities are providing medical care, not promoting religion. But forcing taxpayers to subsidize church-based programs and bringing more of these programs into public institutions, such as prisons, hospitals, and schools, is qualitatively different. It is akin to forcing taxpayers to put money into the collection plates of churches, mosques, and synagogues.

In the first legal challenge to Bush's faith-based initiative, a Wisconsin federal judge ordered the government to stop giving money to the Faith Works drug and alcohol addiction program that relies on Christian spirituality in its approach to treatment.

Judge Barbara C. Crabb ruled that giving "unrestricted state funding" to Faith Works was government-sponsored religious coercion. "I conclude that the Faith Works program indoctrinates its participants in religion primarily through its counselors," the judge wrote in her January 7, 2002, decision. "Religion is so integral to the Faith Works program that it is not possible to isolate it from the program as a whole.

But many states feel they cannot contest the actions of church groups. Federal funds in parochial schools can lead to government monies being misused in extraordinary ways. State officials in Missouri were distressed in early 2001 when they received a complaint that a religious boarding school in the rural town of Bethel was punishing students by forcing them to muck out deep pits of manure. The state was unaware such a practice was going on. But there was no reason it should have known; in Missouri, residential schools and homes for troubled youths are exempt from virtually all state regulation if they are run by religious organizations. "They have no obligation to even make themselves known to us," said Denise Cross, director of the Missouri Division of Family Services. "There is no regulatory body for those facilities."

President Bush's proposal to increase federal financing for charitable works of religious organizations would have allowed religions that receive federal money for charitable work to continue hiring solely within their faith. Such organizations could have refused to hire Jews, blacks, or Catholics. Under current law, religions are allowed to impose such a hiring restriction because they use private money. Had the Democratic-controlled Senate not made passage of the Bush bill conditional upon the removal of this employment provision, we would have seen federally financed discrimination in hiring. Even so, the newly passed initiative is an open invitation for mischief making. Because the government always regulates what it finances, and regulation means control, the government can audit a church's books or prohibit a synagogue, mosque, or church from using funds in ways the government feels is wrong. The Bush faith-based federal handout, its critics point out, would also lead to competition between religions for funding, a result that would have appalled James Madison.

Justice Thomas is already on record in favor of abolishing the prohibition against supporting pervasively sectarian organizations with public funds; Justice Scalia, in a 1989 case, said he supported allowing tax exemptions for religious books and periodicals, even if nonreligious publications were denied the same benefit. The Texas law in question, he claimed, did not improperly favor religion. Everything we take for granted in church-state relationships is today being put in play.

The Supreme Court is now closely divided on whether compelled tax dollars may be diverted to religious uses through such means as school vouchers. The solicitor general, on July 6, 2001, looking at the Supreme Court landslide, asked the justices to review and then uphold an Ohio program that offers Cleveland parents tuition assistance to send their children to private schools, including religious schools. In a case like this, it is unusual for the solicitor general's office to file a Supreme Court brief until the justices either agree to hear the case or ask for the solicitor general's view on whether they should hear it. Filing a brief at this early stage is a way for the administration to put its position on record and to send a signal to the court about the high priority the administration attaches to the issue. Theodore Olson's brief said the district court's ruling, based on a 1973 Supreme Court decision that struck down a tuition-reimbursement program in New York, was "at odds with" and "out of step with" the Supreme Court's more recent interpretations of the First Amendment's Establishment Clause. Policies that "benefit religion only indirectly as a result of the private choices of the program's beneficiaries" are constitutional, Olson wrote to a Court already predisposed to the solicitor's overall positions. Olson said that it was "in the nation's interest" for the court to take up the case, that policy makers needed to "know, without further delay, whether such programs are a constitutionally permissible option for expanding education opportunity for children enrolled in failing public schools across America, or whether other solutions must be sought for this critical national problem."

The Supreme Court agreed to hear the voucher case. It is the most important case of the 2001–02 term. When I began writing this book, I did not know the Court would hear the Ohio voucher case, and, of course, I did not know it would be one of the last cases the Supreme Court would decide this term. Remarkably, it weaves together the many themes of the Rehnquist Court. Vouchers come about because of the resistance of suburban schools to integration, their refusal to take inner-city students, and the failure of the courts to integrate urban schools, leaving, in many cities, bad schools that are really all black. Vouchers come about because many see public schools failing and want privatization and the end of a government monopoly on education. Vouchers are a theme that pull together diverse conservative groups, free marketers, the Religious Right, and those who want to become free of a central government that intrudes too much into people's lives. The voucher case combines an unprecedented assault on the establishment of religion prohibition that can reduce the clause to be nearly meaningless and the views of the free marketers who want the privatization of the education system. The Ohio vouchers case, *Simmons-Harris v. Zelman*, gives "preference to students from low-income families," defined as families with incomes that are less than 200 percent above the poverty line. "Scholarships may be awarded to students who are not from low-income families only if all students from low-income families have been given first consideration for placement." Over 60 percent of the children receiving scholarships in the program are from families with incomes at or below the poverty line.

But nearly all of the pupils receiving aid previously attended parochial schools, making it clear that the Ohio program was assisting people already out of the public school system. This makes suspect the claim that it is for the benefit of the poor. While there are other voucher programs in the country, the Ohio program is more beneficial to parochial schools than any other program presently operating. Although the amount of aid per child is small compared to private school cost, it is relatively large and therefore more significant to the cheaper parochial schools.

If the Supreme Court gives the green light to the Ohio program, other states will create similar programs and open the floodgates to state funding. If, on the other hand, the Ohio program is struck down as being too extreme, it will still leave life in programs presently alive in existing states. There then will be a push-push situation, as in the abortion area—the states will keep passing voucher laws that are just under the bar of unconstitutionality, to get as close to the Ohio program as they can.

During the 1999–2000 school year, fifty-six schools registered to participate in the Ohio program; forty-six (82 percent) of those participating are church-affiliated. Under the voucher plan, the participating schools are permitted to use funds made available under the program for whatever purpose they deem appropriate, without restrictions. Government was quite literally handing sectarian education a blank check, the Ohio District Court decided, when it struck down the plan.

> The alleged choice afforded both public and private school participants in this program is illusory. . . . To approve this program would approve the actual diversion of government aid to religious institutions in endorsement of religious education, something in tension with the precedents of the Supreme Court, *Mitchell v. Helms*. We find that when, as here, the government has established a program which does not permit private citizens to direct government aid freely as is their private choice, but which restricts their choice to a panoply of religious institutions and spaces with only a few alternative possibilities, then the Establishment Clause is violated. We conclude that the Ohio scholarship program is designed in a manner calculated to attract religious institutions and chooses the beneficiaries of aid by non-neutral criteria.

The appeals court reversed, and the state of Ohio went immediately to the Supreme Court. The argument was on February 20, 2002.

This is how voucher supporters described the issues in a leaflet handed out in front of the Supreme Court at the time of argument.

> We've almost grown numb to complaints: Students dropping out. Students graduating barely able to read. Crowded, undisciplined classrooms. Violence. Is it time to put massive new resources into America's troubled public schools? Or time to pour resources into alternatives such as charter schools, private management companies, and vouchers?

Justice O'Connor started out asking Judith French, arguing for Ohio, whether the state's position would require the Supreme Court to overrule its leading church-state precedent on tuition assistance, a 1973 decision of the Burger Court, the *Committee for Public Education v. Nyquist* case. In

Nyquist, the Court, relying on the *Lemon* case, struck down, in a decision with many different opinions, a New York program of tuition assistance to families with children in private schools, most of which were religious schools. *Nyquist* "certainly points the other way, doesn't it," Justice O'Connor commented, wanting to have that case distinguished.

Ms. French's argument, and brief, was a direct appeal to O'Connor. Ms. French declared that the Ohio program met the objections the Court had to the New York program. The voucher program is not tailored only to private schools, she said, the Ohio program offers Cleveland parents the option of remaining in the public schools and receiving extra money for tutoring or transferring to other schools within the public system. O'Connor seemed satisfied.

Justice Souter interjected, trying to persuade O'Connor to join him in the vote against the program, and argued that "what bothers me and Justice O'Connor" was that despite those differences, the Ohio program appeared to have the same effect as the New York program.

"At the end of the day, a massive amount of money went to the religious schools in Nyquist, and a massive amount of money goes to the religious schools here," Justice Souter said, trying to persuade O'Connor that *Nyquist* controls. "That's the sticking point."

"We don't agree," French enforced, directing her response to O'Connor's concerns that the money flowed not as "the result of government action" but because "that's what the parents have chosen." Ohio's is a "neutral program that offers a true private choice to parents," she said.

Scalia made clear in his questioning that, consistent with the Richard Epstein line, he believes public and private schools should compete in the marketplace—there should be no public monopoly, in large part because public education has failed in so many urban areas.

One of the most moving moments in Court history occurred during the voucher argument. Former federal judge Marvin Frankel, dying of cancer, fought his doctors and hospital so he could go to Court to argue, on behalf of the National Teachers Association, that vouchers violated the Establishment Clause. Released that morning in a wheelchair, he argued, with a doctor sitting behind him, that the reason Ohio public schools were found to be inadequate was because the Ohio state court previously found the schools were terribly underfunded. He argued the state could not bootstrap that argument into a justification for then putting money into parochial schools. Weak before the argument started, and weak after it ended, he was dramatic, eloquent, and forceful for the brief time he argued. Two weeks later, he died.

Robert Chanin, an experienced advocate, who argued on behalf of the National Education Association against vouchers, was brutally buffeted by the Court and gave one of the least effective arguments the Court has seen. He insisted on defending public education to a Court that believed public schools had failed. Undeterred by the Court's questions, he stuck to his script. The Court's hostility and lack of respect toward him was clear. When he sat down, it was an awkward moment—the courtroom was silent.

As of this writing, the decision in the Ohio case has not come down. It is clear, however, that vouchers, along with the faith-based initiatives, would dramatically change the nature of education and the ability of religion to proselytize. Vouchers do not go to capital costs; they go toward the ongoing expenses of running a school. Hence the flow of public monies will favor already established parochial schools and established religion.

Voucher advocates failed twice in California. They claimed the first loss in 1997 was due to lack of money and so, in 2000, with heavy financial backing this time, they again put it on the ballot. Over $30 million was spent on the initiative and again it was soundly defeated. In Michigan, where the voucher initiative was focused on children who did poorly, its proponents, early on, claimed victory. It had the support of some black ministers, the Catholic Church, and the Michigan Chamber of Commerce, all of whom substantially outspent the local teachers union and Republican suburbanites who organized to defeat it. On Election Day, less than one-third of the voters supported the measure. Church groups also failed in Colorado, Oregon, and Washington. Surveys by the Carnegie Foundation for the Advancement of Teaching, Gallup, and NBC/Wall Street Journal polls confirm nationwide that the public opposes voucher programs. One of the reasons these initiatives fail, it may be speculated, is that not one single study shows that a voucher system leads to consistent improvement.

This is the Religious Right's time to act. They have a solid five-justice majority behind them on most issues, and at times a sixth. In the last few years, several cases reached the Court involving various approaches to assisting parents with private school tuition, any one of which might have provided a reason for the justices to address the question of "school choice," as proponents of the voucher program usually refer to it. The Clinton administration, aware of the Court's composition, did not seek to have the voucher cases heard.

No matter how favorable, likely, or hopeful the opponents of "school choice" may be, they know the probabilities are that O'Connor will be the swing vote. She may find the law constitutional because the parents seemingly make the choice, not the state, even though the overwhelming preponderance of the parents take the cash and go to parochial schools. This is direct financial aid, and her possible agreement with it will revolutionize church-state law. The Court has previously made clear its sympathies for the voucher program in Ohio by permitting lower court provoucher cases to stand, thereby allowing voucher programs to run in a number of states.

In 1998, for instance, the justices permitted a voucher program in Milwaukee to remain in effect without reviewing the Wisconsin Supreme Court decision that had upheld it. The Cleveland program now involves children already attending private and religious schools who would lose their voucher money and very likely have to leave their classrooms—a most sympathetic posture for voucher supporters.

As our country turns more religious and with the increasing involvement of church groups in politics, the incremental cracks in the wall will become a gaping hole. The numbers may tell the story. Eighty-three percent of Americans in a June 2001 poll identified themselves as Christian. Nearly 50 percent of Christians described themselves as Born Again. Nearly all Evangelicals believe there should be prayer in the school and financial aid to religious schools. Over the years the greatest amount of mail received by the Supreme Court concerns church-state issues and abortion. The single case that drew the most mail was the one prohibiting prayer in school.

Churches more than ever openly provide forums for discussions of political issues and formalize political agendas. Billy Graham's speech to the Republican Party convention and Pat Robertson's presidential campaign are the tips of the iceberg. The Christian Coalition claims to have provided 75 million voter guides for the 2000 presidential election. The storm over Monica Lewinsky and President Clinton's morals gave the fractious Evangelical Right a chance to become cohesive. Theologian Michael Novak sees the next century as "the most religious in five hundred years."

Within that context, the Rehnquist Court and its successful interweaving of politics, law, and religion will surely continue to show insensitivity to minority religions, will keep various forms of prayer in, and will increase funding to parochial schools. Even before he took the bench, Rehnquist fervently supported these goals.

The chief justice's analysis is based on his readings of Madison's original intent in writing the Religion Clause in the First Amendment and particularly in the clause's redrafts. Some of the other justices have more nuanced positions. Justice Kennedy, a devout Catholic, is in favor of aid to parochial schools, but since he was brought up feeling the power of Protestantism and the minority status of Catholics, he opposes school prayer. Justice Stevens, an ardent separationist, is against institutions, including the institutional church and the power it wields. O'Connor is a swing vote in some of the church-state issues, but now, at times, is joined by Breyer. Ginsburg consistently votes with the dissenting moderates.

Reagan successfully galvanized Evangelicals and church groups by speaking out for government sponsorship of religion, endorsing school prayer and aid to parochial schools. The Rehnquist Court has already done much to fulfill that charter.

A court freshly stocked with more Scalia and Thomas conservatives would let these incremental gains turn into a court-assisted avalanche, thoroughly rewrite the Establishment and Free Exercise Clauses, permit vouchers, legalize state grants to parochial schools, and put prayer and religious ceremonies back into the public schools. On October 10, 2001, the Supreme Court threw out a lower court decision that said cities could refuse to provide free equipment for a National Day of Prayer celebration at a municipal park. The ruling requires the lower court to look again at the city of Tucson's policy of excluding religious groups from a civic events fund. It is another sign of how the Rehnquist Court is open to more government involvement with religion. The justices invalidated a ruling by the U.S. Court of Appeals for the Ninth Circuit that said Tucson was rightly respecting the separation of church and state. On December 16, 2001, the

Supreme Court refused to review a case permitting student prayer in a state university.

The Fundamentalists and Evangelicals hurt themselves when Jerry Falwell and Pat Robertson reacted to the September 11 terrorist attack by lashing out, claiming the World Trade Center was destroyed because the country has embraced church-state separation, legalized abortion, allows Internet pornography, and condones materialism.

Robertson said: "God is lifting his protection from us. The Lord is getting ready to shake this nation. We have not felt His judgment on America. This thing that happened in New York is child's play compared to what is going to happen. It was a great tragedy when we saw that suffering but a wake-up call from God." Robertson later announced that he had received a congratulatory telegram from Ashcroft because of his statements.

Robertson and his Fundamentalist allies constantly repeated this refrain and stood up for Jerry Falwell's statement: "I really believe the pagans and the abortionists, the feminists, and the gays and lesbians that are trying to make that an alternative lifestyle, the ACLU people, People for the American Way, all of them who have tried to secularize America and point the finger in their face and say you helped this happen." Two days later a group of Fundamentalist leaders said: "It is now easier in many schools to bring a weapon than a Bible. Commandments are out and condoms are in." After Falwell's and Robertson's failed attempts to refine their statements, they apologized.

Professor Marci Hamilton, who argued *Boerne* before the Supreme Court in 2001 and has written extensively in church-state matters, recently said, "The United States is in the midst of the greatest wealth transfer from government to religious entities in its history. The shift has been incremental and has occurred on a number of distinct fronts, and therefore has not been apparent to the casual observer." The pressure to crumble the wall is increasing.

10

CONCLUSION:
COURTING DISASTER

Justice William J. Brennan Jr. called "the rule of five" the most important principle of American law. This principle, he said, is not taught in law school. Brennan would hold up his hand, palm open, fingers outstretched, and say, "You can do anything you want at the Supreme Court with five votes."

The five votes today, as often in the past, are based more on political power and less on legal reasoning. The Court's composition is determined by politicians and in an increasingly polarized society, there is little the appellate court and Supreme Court do that is entirely free of politics. Of the eight rulings on civil rights and job discrimination handed down in the 2000 term, all were decided 5–4 in favor of the conservative majority. One-third of last term's cases (26–79) ended in 5–4 rulings, the highest percentage of 5–4 rulings in a decade. Nearly all were conservative decisions, with the same 5–4 conservative majority. One liberal judge could help reverse them all. One more conservative could reverse some of the liberal decisions we most cherish today. *United States v. Lopez, Morrison v. United States, Garrett University of Alabama v. Patricia Garrett, Kimel v. Florida Board of Regents, Seminole Tribe of Florida v. Florida*—most of the cases discussed in this book—are 5–4 decisions. Today's Court is making changes in nearly all areas of the law, some by degree and some in large bites. One change in the Court's composition, either way, can reverse the law as we know it.

In May 2002, Olsen again told the Supreme Court that the Solicitor General's office would no longer necessarily defend all congressional legislation against constitutional attack. Traditionally, the Solicitor General's office, representing the government, defends congressional legislation and argues for constitutional interpretation that increases congressional flexibility. Now, that office says it can pick and choose which legislation to defend.

Lifelong appointment to our nation's judiciary has tended to mean just that. Hugo Black, appointed in 1937, stayed thirty-four years; Felix Frankfurter, appointed in 1939, stayed twenty-three; William O. Douglas, appointed in 1939, stayed thirty-six. In more recent times, Harry Blackmun and Thurgood Marshall stayed twenty-four years. The median length is fifteen years. Justice Rehnquist has been there for thirty-two years; Justice Stevens for twenty-seven years; Justice O'Connor for twenty-two. Antonin Scalia, only forty-seven years old at the time of his appointment, has already served seventeen. These appointees long outlasted those who appointed them. The circuit courts of appeals, and many of the federal trial courts have judges with comparable lengths of service.

The new Republican presidents, too heavily influenced by the right wing, will, when they can, appoint justices in their thirties and early forties. That means not only will important cases be lost now, but they may continue to be lost for the next thirty to forty years. We are not talking about losing *Roe* for ten to fifteen years—we are talking of losing *Roe* for the life of your ten-year-old daughter. At present, seven of the twelve circuit courts are anti-abortion. Abortions have been effectively banned for many impoverished women who live in those jurisdictions. The conservatives intend to have all anti-abortion circuit courts; all anti-federalist circuit courts; circuit courts devoted to fulfilling the Radical Rights' agenda on race, religion, class, money, morality, and power. If George W. Bush becomes a two-term president, he will appoint the judges who will certainly try to make that happen.

In the first two hundred years of the Constitution, 128 acts of Congress were struck down, thirty of them alone since 1995. Not since before the New Deal has a bare majority been so intent on reining in the Congress and resisting encroachment on state prerogatives. The acts it held unconstitutional not coincidentally denied claims involving individual's rights. The church-state balance eroded and *Brown v. Board of Education*, *Miranda v. Arizona*, and *Roe v. Wade*, were eviscerated to the point where the "freedom" and "liberty" they stood for became nearly meaningless. The Court is now determined to impose its own political preferences over that of elected federal officials. The constitutional agreement that governed the Supreme Court for the past six decades, that gave space to Congress—the primary role to protect and balance our personal and economic liberties—has been broken.

Over the next decades, the Scalia-Thomas dissents can become the law of the land in the same way the Rehnquist dissents from the 1970s and '80s are the law of the land today. The case-by-case approach employed by O'Connor, Stevens, and sometimes Kennedy will no longer be possible. Instead of incremental fact-specific decisions, the conservatives will write with bolder, broader strokes. The Court's mission definition will continue to come from the Right.

Let us take inventory. The 2000 *Stenberg* case reaffirmed *Roe v. Wade* in a 5–4 decision. In *Planned Parenthood of Southeastern Pennsylvania v. Robert P. Casey*, the last important reproductive rights case preceding it, that majority was 6–3—with three of the six able to find no better reason to affirm than the authority of precedent and the need for this Court to retain its credibility and the public's respect. Today, the "undue burden" test and laws making it increasingly difficult for physicians to perform abortions can end abortion rights. The Bush administration is busy at this moment trying to move abortion cases up to the Supreme Court first to reverse *Stenberg* and then ultimately to reverse *Roe*. The figures we have show that, from 1974 to 1997, there were 390 abortions out of every 1,000 births; we do not know in how many of these abortions the mother's life was at stake. Reversing *Roe* would cause untold damage to our country and especially to those who can least afford further harm.

There is now a solid court majority for the death sentence. Our president, who presided while governor over 144 executions in six years, believes not mental handicap, nor youth, nor the possibility of innocence, nor the lack of competent legal representation should interfere with the biblical injunction of an eye for an eye, positions his Republican-appointed justices, his attorney general, and his solicitor general agree with.

School-desegregation cases, affirmative action, and much of the racial and gender discrimination law have already been reshaped by the conservative bloc. The Court claims it is color blind and gender blind, but quite often it seems simply to refuse to see, or do anything about obvious bias. The speculated retirements of O'Connor and Stevens would make certain that the demise of affirmative action is upon us. Rehnquist's retirement would lead to a more conservative justice in the Scalia-Thomas mold.

There is irony, contradiction, and ultimately tragedy in Thomas's becoming the point man on race. Thus it is not surprising that Senator Strom Thurman, who built his career on resisting integration, is one of Thomas's most ardent supporters. That Thomas is blind to the truth of his own history discredits the history he uses to reach his decisions. Rehnquist and Scalia, too, are disrespectful of the law, though they rely less on history and more on constitutional analysis. The academics, jurists, and other public officials that the current Bush administration has warming up in the bullpen share Thomas's, Rehnquist's, and Scalia's radical views. Adding them to the Court at this time in history would be catastrophic.

Gerrymandering, giving minorities the right to vote but making the vote meaningless, is the future the Rehnquist Court has laid out in order to undercut the one-man one-vote cases. Employers will find it much easier to fire employees; plaintiffs suing for on-the-job sexual harassment will lose under statutes that would require them to prove "hostile" or abusive work environments; victims of job-related injury will have to prove a much harder case. Students are not as protected against sexual violence by other students.

Segregated schools, caused by white flight to the suburbs, by the collapse of urban economies, or by changing housing patterns will be permanently placed beyond the reach of the legal system, while supporters of the NRA will have unprecedented access to it. The principles of *Printz* and *Lopez*, both 5–4 decisions, would never be overruled before a right-wing Court and would, as part of the law, become a firm footing for the gun lobby. Thomas's Second Amendment argument giving all citizens the right to bear arms can establish precedent to reject any restrictions on gun control. Circuit courts have already referred to it. On May 7, 2002, the Department of Justice and the Attorney General, reversing federal policy that stood for sixty years, told the Supreme Court that the Constitution "protects the rights of individuals to own firearms." They attacked a 1934 case, *United States v. Miller*, which was the basis of the government's policy. Ashcroft and Olsen reversed the government's view of the Second Amendment even though in 1999, the most recent year for which statistics are available, 28,874 Americans were killed by guns. The NRA, one of the administration's bigger financial supporters, immediately applauded this tragic change of position. In the summer of 2001, the NRA featured a picture of Ashcroft on the cover of its magazine, calling him "a breath of fresh air to freedom loving gun owners."

Advocates for free speech correctly praise many of the Court's free-speech cases, but a closer reading of the cases shows a more complex and subtle picture. The First Amendment is being upheld in order to permit tobacco companies to display billboards, and to strike down a federal law barring pharmacies from advertising "mixed-to-order drugs" that have not gone through the usual safety screening, to stop doctors from advising patients about abortion. Most important, in church-state cases, free speech is used to trump the wall of separation that protects our religious freedoms.

The Supreme Court is preparing to meet the legal issues to be generated by the war on terrorism. O'Connor, following a visit to Ground Zero, bleakly predicted, "We're likely to experience more restrictions on personal freedom than has ever been the case in this country." After Rehnquist agreed with O'Connor, Ginsburg struck back, "If we gave up our freedom as the price of security, we would no longer be the great nation we are."

During periods of war, it takes a very strong Court not to bow to the fears of the time. Benjamin Franklin's admonitions that "those willing to give up liberty for security are deserving of neither" will not become this Court's precept.

One more justice in the Thomas-Scalia mold can seriously impair privacy rights for decades to come. The Court makes moral value judgments that are often appalling. The trajectory of *Griswold* stands waiting to be cut back each time the Court is faced with a new privacy situation. There are today at least three justices solidly supporting the criminalization of homosexuality based on the concept that gays are not "morally straight" and "clean."

Property rights triumph over personal rights. Congress is virtually unable to pass laws in the public interest once the Court decides they are noneconomic matters. This Court, and the Court to follow, if packed with Scalias and Thomases, will continue to conclude that Congress's fact-finding and conclusions are simply irrelevant. Instead of seeing the Constitution as an engine for promoting democracy, this Court sees the Constitution as giving disproportionate power to the judiciary. This Court's special agenda is to change the structure of government.

To be sure, some kinds of discrimination claims have fared well in recent years. In a series of sexual harassment cases, the justices have sided with victims. For example, O'Connor joined with the four moderate justices in June 1999 to rule that school officials can be sued when they know a student is being sexually abused in school and do not act to stop it.

It is unclear how far O'Connor and Kennedy will embrace the radical activism of Scalia and Thomas and Reagan circuit court judges like Richard Posner, Frank Easterbrook, Harvie Wilkinson, and Michael Lustig. Some members of the right-wing's presumptive "board of review" see William Rehnquist as a failure; *Roe, Miranda, Lemon v. Kurtzman, Brown*, and *Regents of the University of California v. Bakke* may still have some life. Federalists are not looking for the future Justice Rehnquists, and neither are their presidents. They itch to move on to the next battleground and want a better court.

At stake is nothing less than the constitutional and legal framework that will govern the next generation of Americans. Many battles have already been lost, but the war is not over. Because circuit court nominees do not get the consistent attention Supreme Court nominees get, it is safe to say that within the next decade our federal courts of appeal may all be conservative. The project that Reagan started in 1980, and which was relentlessly pursued thereafter, has succeeded. The Right blocked, delayed, and stalled nearly all of Clinton's liberal nominees as well as many of his moderate choices; now they will try to break the ninth circuit into two or three appellate divisions, expand the number of judges on those courts, and then appoint conservative loyalists to them. Decent federal judges with lifetime tenure are losing interest—some are leaving. It is frustrating and demoralizing to be so constrained, to see your work reversed time after time.

Ideology (Radical Right), politics (*Bush v. Gore*), and current events (September 11) have combined to give this results-oriented Court an immense and frightening antidemocratic power. Today's Court has assumed the role of both legislature and court. It will continue to do so and expand the areas in which it acts. No court has ever subjected Congress to such a strict judicially created evidentiary standard; nor has any court so upset the traditional constitutional balance between the political and judicial branches. The legislature can no longer afford to cede its authority; the confirmation process is where they may begin to reclaim it.

We are heirs to a judiciary in pieces, and we must try to balance the judiciary, beginning with the nomination process. The conservatives have been clear and specific in wanting partisans, while moderates and liberals too often reach for what is at the present, and in the immediate future, unattainable. Where, they ask, are the Holmeses, the Brandeises? The answer is that they are there, in ever decreasing numbers, but for now we shall not have them in the courts. There are now primarily two criteria as the Republicans have shown us—youth and politics. The judiciary has become more like the civil service—jurists making their way up a professional ladder—outsiders not wanted. There is little commitment to merit appointments, just as this Court, and the one to follow it, has little commitment to either justice or equality. Politics has replaced law, and politicians, who have not been important political figures, have to a great extent replaced jurists in the legal system. Their cases send a message to the circuits, especially the nine conservative ones, and to the state legislatures, that the Supreme Court will literally turn a winking blind eye on to itself so these other institutions can make decisions even more conservative than the Supreme Court.

If the endless 5–4 power-seizing decisions that come down from the majority confirms that many of its judicial interpretations are explained by a look at the justices' "politics" and "motivation" to reflect the intellectual framework these men and women carry with them onto the bench—like philosophical or ideological baggage—that they unpack and use to fashion their opinions. Many scholars believe the meaning of the Constitution can be "found" if we can only figure out the best method to do so. The Constitution becomes like a religious text, and "truth" supposedly is determined by the path the constitutional scholar—or jurist—chooses. The originalists find it in a close analysis of the text or the original intention of its Framers. But the Constitution was a collaborative effort so originalists must do more than understand one author using one word. Determining the meaning of words written in the historical, cultural, and social context of the late eighteenth century, as the rabidly conservative do, is too limited. It's impossible to look at 1789 and see how the Founders felt about affirmative action, or busing for school desegregation, or laws for cyberspace. We, and today's jurists, live in a rapidly changing world and our Constitution, vibrant and timeless, properly interpreted can truly fulfill the promise of liberty and justice for all.

With the Supreme Court taking fewer and fewer cases, the circuit courts' decisions increasingly become the law of the land. When the U.S.

Court of Appeals for the Fourth Circuit upheld a South Carolina statute that effectively ended abortion in that state, we saw the Supreme Court deny review, rendering that decision for all practical purposes not only the law of South Carolina, but also a guide to other states in the circuit (Virginia, North Carolina, Maryland), suggesting to them the kind of anti-abortion legislation that will be upheld.

Political philosophy and ideology plays a large role in Court decisions. But there is a difference between political philosophy and a radical revision of the law fueled by ideology and partisan politics. The Roosevelt Court was, in fact, a cautious Court, deferential to Congress. The Court believed it was carrying out John Marshall's mandate in giving power to Congress. It certainly did not see itself, as the Rehnquist Court does, as the pivot of government. The Courts in the 1940s and '50s were timid and only treading water. The Warren Court, seen as revolutionary, had its decisions expanding individuals' rights firmly rooted in the Constitution. Many of the most controversial expansions of individual rights came during the early Burger Court, which gave us both *Roe* and *Furman v. Georgia*, the decision striking down the death penalty (which the Warren Court declined to do); *Bakke*, upholding racial preferences; and the aggressive expansion of *Brown*.

The John Marshall Court (in its affirmation of nationalism), the New Deal Court (in its affirmation of Congress's control over commerce and protection of individual rights), and the Warren Court (in its affirmation of equality) all had political agendas and practiced judicial activism. So, too, does the Rehnquist Court but in a totally different way. They limit Congress, make the states "kings," repudiate precedent, cut back Congress's role in dealing with the general welfare, seek a return to laissez-faire Darwinian economics, and try to put racial minorities back where they were fifty years ago.

The Senate has the power to refuse to consent to a presidential appointment, and it also has power to provide "advice" to the president. The Constitution's Framers specifically intended the Senate's "advice and consent" role to provide "security" against what they greatly feared: an overreaching president seeking to dominate the judiciary. There are 179 authorized circuit court positions; 32 are now vacant. There are 662 lower court positions; 70 are now vacant. Bills presently before Congress seek the appointment of

52 new judges. Balance on the federal courts can occur only if we fight for each of those seats. The Senate for now and the future should refuse to approve any appointments until the courts are more balanced. In addition, the public must try to influence their elected representatives, through voting, e-mails, and letter writing, and let members of Congress know they are affected by appointments, even those outside of their geographical area. The right wing of the Republican Party claims 17.5 million votes in the last presidential election. A substantial percentage of those voters focused directly on the Supreme Court. Far fewer Democrats or moderate Republicans were as focused—Ralph Nader persuaded millions that the Supreme Court was far less significant than it is.

A permanent counterforce to the Fundamentalists and Federalists must be created. It must function in the political, public, and legal arenas. The conservatives have a twenty-year advantage. They used their time and their advantage very well. Several private organizations, working diligently in the past, going outside the Democratic Party, now hope to coordinate efforts to keep senators under constant pressure when the time comes to vote on judicial nominations. There is a long way to go.

Democrats, moderate Republicans, and even true conservatives must take the reins and become unabashedly and overtly political in their opposition to right-wing federal judicial nominees. Senators John McCain, Jim Jeffords, and their present and future colleagues want more centrist justices who reflect the moderate wing of the Republican Party. It is in their interest to loosen right-wing control of the judiciary. For unless they do so, many of the values they stand for will be defeated.

We are in a partisan battle and should treat it as such. Whatever is done in politics, hardball or softball, should be done, beginning with the nomination process. Filibuster, stallings, trade-offs, the force of interest groups, are political tools that must be used in judicial fights. We ought not deny the judiciary is political. We should embrace that fact and learn how to deal with it. We must have a say in how the Constitution is interpreted. What we are fighting over is too important for each of us not to look squarely at the Court's face. Only when the courts are again balanced can we consider judicial bipartisanship.

I have tried to show the need for constitutional change, change that is a long, slow, incremental process. Corporations, libertarians, and the Evangelical Right have organized and effected dramatic constitutional change over the last twenty years. If we do not come together to reverse or redirect these charges, we leave a legacy that will create a cruder, harsher America, that will haunt not just our children, but our grandchildren, and perhaps even for decades thereafter.

The people are at one end of the democratic process, the justices at the other. It can now be our turn. We can change the law that governs us by changing the governors. We must use the power of our vote, as well as the power of the expression of our opinions and ideas. We know that at least some of the justices are sensitive to shifts in the public mood. We also know which candidates reflect our principles, our sense of what democracy is. If we vote for that candidate and he is elected, it becomes our duty as voters to stay involved, to make the candidate honor his commitments.

We have power. We can vote for constitutional change. So let us begin today—to reclaim the great gifts of the Founding Fathers: "There is no time to lose, for as the great Judge Learned Hand said: "Liberty lies in the hearts of men and women. When it dies, no constitution, no law, no court can save it."

Balancing the Court will take many years. It is a continuing struggle, and we must now commit ourselves fully to it.

NOTES

I have chosen to cite only the more important authorities.

Epigraph
George T. Curtis, "A Memoir of Benjamin R. Curtis, LL.D.," 1879, cited in 4 Green Bag 419 (2001).

1: The Unmaking of American Law
1. *Bush v. Gore* 531 U.S. 98 (2000).
2. Denver Area Educational Telecommunications Consortium, Inc., 518 U.S. 727 (1996).
3. Jack Balkin and Sanford Levinson, "Understanding the Constitutional Revolution," 87 Virginia L. Rev. 1045 (2001).
4. Patricia Cohen, "Judicial Reasoning Is All Too Human, *The New York Times,* June 30, 2001, p. B7.
5. Larry Kramer, "The Supreme Court, 2000 Term: Forward: We the Court." 115 Harvard L. Rev. 4 (2001).

2: The Right's Twenty-Year Attack on the Federal Judiciary
1. Edwin Meese, address before American Bar Association, July 9, 1985, in *The Great Debate: Interpreting Our Written Constitution* 9 (1986).
2. Lani Guinier, *Tyranny of the Majority* (Free Press, 1994).
3. David Alistair Yalof, *Pursuit of Justices: Presidential Politics and the Selection of Supreme Court Nominees* (Chicago: University of Chicago Press, 1999).

4. Herman Schwartz, *Packing the Courts: The Conservative Campaign to Rewrite the Constitution* (New York: Charles Scribner's and Sons, 1988).

5. Sheldon Goldman, *Picking Federal Judges* (New Haven: Yale University, 1997).

6. See, for example, Kozinski, "It Is a Constitution We Are Expounding: A Debate," 1987 Utah L. Rev. 977, 978; Kozinski, in *Economic Liberties and the Judiciary* xi (Dorne and Manne, eds. 1987).

7. Graglia, "Racially Discriminatory Admission to Public Institutions of Higher Education," 9 Southwestern University L. Rev. 583 (1977).

8. *The New York Times,* July 15, 1988, p. A12; Bernard H. Siegan, *Economic Liberties and the Constitution* (1981); Bernard H. Siegan, *The Supreme Court's Constitution* (1987); Siegan, Rehabilitating *Lochner*, 22 San Diego L. Rev. 453 (1985).

9. Sheldon Goldman, *op. cit.*

10. Evan Thomas, "Washington's Quiet Club," *Newsweek*, March 9, 2001.

11. Associated Press, "Scalia Takes on Church," *The New York Post*, February 5, 2002; Anne Thompson, "Scalia and Capital Punishment," *The Washington Post*, February 26, 2002.

12. Alfred Ross, Lee Cokorinos, and Julie Gershik, "The Federalists Society and the Challenge to a Democratic Jurisprudence," Institute for Democratic Studies, January 2001; Nina Easton, "The Gang of Five" (New York: Simon and Schuster, 2001).

13. Evan Thomas, *op. cit.*

14. Sheldon Goldman, *op. cit.*

15. Ibid, no. 5; Sheldon Goldman, Elliot Slotnick, Gerard Gryski, and Gary Zuk, "Clinton's Judges: Summing Up the Legacy," *Judicature* Vol. 84, No. 5, March–April 2001, p. 228.

16. Richard L. Revesz, "Essay: Ideology, Collegiality, and the D.C. Circuit: A Reply to Chief Judge Harry T. Edwards," 85 Virginia L. Rev. 805, August 1999; Richard L. Revesz, "Environmental Regulation, Ideology and the D.C. Circuit," 83 Virginia L. Rev. 1717 (1997); Harry T. Edwards, "Essay: Collegiality and Decision Making of the D.C. Circuit," 84 Virginia L. Rev. 1335, October 1998; Arons Weiss, "Hostile Environment Alliance for Justice," 2001.

17. Terri Jennings Peretti, *In Defense of a Political Court* (Princeton: Princeton University Press, 1999).

3: Crime and Punishment

1. Amsterdam and Brunner, "Minding the Law," Harvard University Press, 2000.

2. *Furman v. Georgia* 408 U.S. 238 (1972).

3. *Gregg v. Georgia* 428 U.S. 153 (1976).

4. *McCleskey v. Kemp* 481 U.S. 279 (1987). See also, *McCleskey v. Zant* 111 S. Ct. 1454 (1991).

5. Ibid, no. 1.

6. *Johnson v. Santa Clara County* 480 U.S. 616 (1987).

7. *Stanford v. Kentucky* 492 U.S. 361 (1987).

8. *Wainwright v. Sykes* 433 U.S. 72 (1977).

9. *Brecht v. Abrahamson* 507 U.S. 619 (1977).

10. *Beazley v. Pennsylvania* No. 90-6444, 499 U.S. 954 (1991); National Public Radio (NPR), *All Things Considered,* Host, Noah Adams, Professor Jeffrey Rosen, Texas Death Row Case of Napoleon Beazley, August 14, 2001.

11. *Gideon v. Wainright* 372 U.S. 335 (1963).

12. *Penry v. Lynaugh* 492 U.S. 302 (1989). See also *Penry v. Johnson* 532 U.S. 782 (2001).

13. *Atkins v. Virginia* 122 S. Ct. 982 (2002).

14. See *Batson v. Kentucky* 476 U.S. 79 (1986).

15. The final case taken by the Supreme Court for its current calendar is a death case. It will be one of the last of the seventy-six decisions the Court is expected to render this term. It could affect the death sentences of 796 men on death row but it is most likely that the Court, through a variety of strategies, including not letting its ruling apply retroactively, will let it affect as few death sentences as possible. In that case, death penalty laws in nine states are being challenged where judges rather than juries decide the final punishment stage of trial, the claim being that juries should make the life or death decision. What happens in most cases is that juries recommend life and judges overrule their decisions and opt for death. I know, as does most every other criminal lawyer, that a defendant would most often prefer to have a jury rather than a judge decide the punishment. Statistics show that juries treat defendants more leniently than do judges, so that fewer defendants may face death if judges are finally denied final authority and are no longer free to ignore jury recommendations of mercy.

16. *Miranda v. Arizona* 384 U.S. 436 (1966).

17. *Dickerson v. United States* 122 S. Ct. 136 (2001).

18. Yale Kamisar, "Foreward: From Miranda to Sec. 3501 to Dickerson to . . . ," Michigan L. Rev., March 2001; Charles D. Weisselberg, "In the Stationhouse after Dickerson," Michigan L. Rev., March 2001; Welsh S. White, "Miranda's Failure to Restrain Pernicious Interrogation Practices," Michigan L. Rev., March 2001; Richard A. Leo, "Questioning the Relevance of Miranda in the Twenty-First Century," Michigan L. Rev., March 2001; William J. Stuntz, "Miranda's Mistake," Michigan L. Rev., March 2001; Stephen J. Schulhofer, "Miranda, Dickerson, and the Puzzling Persistence of Fifth Amendment Exceptionalism," Michigan L. Rev., March 2001; Paul G. Cassell, "The Paths Not Taken: The Supreme Court's Failures in Dickerson," Michigan L. Rev., March 2001; Mandy DeFilippo, "You Have the Right to Better Safeguards: Looking Beyond Miranda in the New Millennium," 34 J. Marshall L. Rev. 637; George M. Dery III, "The Illegitimate Exercise of Raw Judicial Power: The Supreme Court's Turf Battle in Dickerson v. United States," 40 Brandeis L. J. 47; Yale Kamisar, "Williard Pedrick Lecture: Miranda Thirty-Five Years Later: A Close Look at the Majority and Dissenting Opinions in Dickerson," 33 Arizona State L. J. 387; Laurie Magid, "Deceptive Police Interrogation Practices: How Far Is Too Far?" Michigan L. Rev., March 2001.

19. *Hudson v. Thomas* 510 U.S. 831 (1992).
20. *Atwater v. Lago Vista* 532 U.S. 769 (2001).
21. *Vernonia v. Acton* 515 U.S. 646 (1995).
22. *Adamson v. California* 332 U.S. 46 (1947).

4: Morality and Values: Sex, Abortion, and Women's Rights

1. *Roe v. Wade* 410 U.S. 113 (1973).
2. *Griswold v. Connecticut* 381 U.S. 479 (1965).
3. See Patterson, The Forgotten Ninth Amendment (1955); Randy E. Barnett, ed., *The Rights Retained by the People: The History and Meaning of the Ninth Amendment*, 1991; Berger, The Ninth Amendment, 66 Cornell L. Rev. 1, 2–3 (1980).
4. *Brown v. Board of Education* 347 U.S. 483.
5. *Plessy v. Ferguson* 163 U.S. 537 (1896).
6. *Webster v. Reproductive Health Services* 492 U.S. 490 (1989).
7. *Rust v. Sullivan* 500 U.S. 173 (1991).
8. *Planned Parenthood of Southeastern Pennsylvania v. Casey* 505 U.S. 833 (1992).
9. *Stenberg v. Carhart* 530 U.S. 914 (2000).
10. *Hope Clinic v. Ryan* 195 F.3d 857 (7th Cir. 1999).
11. Linda Greenhouse, "U.S. Supports Bid to Uphold Ohio Limits on Abortions," *The New York Times*, February 7, 2002.
12. Robin Toner, "Administration Plans Care of Fetuses in a Health Plan," *The New York Times*, February 1, 2002, p. A23.
13. *Greenville Women's Clinic v. Bryant* 222 F. 3d 157 (4th Cir. 2000); *Greenville Women's Clinic v. Bryant* 66 F. Supp. 2d 691 (D.S.C. 1999); *Greenville Women's Clinic v. Bryant* Nos. 99–1319, 99–1710, and 99–1725, Denying Petition for Rehearing and Rehearing En Banc (4th Cir. Sept. 25, 2000).
14. *Michael H. v. Gerald D.* 491 U.S. 110 (1989).
15. Sandra Day O'Connor and H. Alan Day, *Lazy B: Growing Up on a Cattle Ranch in the American Southwest*, 2002.
16. Alan Dershowitz, "Simple Injustice," Oxford Press, 2001, at p. 246, for 66; Edwin M. Yodeer Jr., "Justice O'Connor's Unfortunate Letter," *Washington Post*, March 19, 1989; "The 'Christian Nation' Fallacy," *St. Petersburg Times*, March 17, 1989; and Al Kamen, "Justice O'Connor to Brief GOP Donors at High Court; ABA Code Bars Speeches to Political Groups," *Washington Post*, May 1, 1987; Alan M. Dershowitz, "Justice O'Connor's Second Indiscretion," *The New York Times*, April 2, 1989.
17. *Bowers v. Hardwick* 478 U.S. 186 (1986).
18. *Stanley v. Georgia* 394 U.S. 557 (1969).
19. *Romer v. Evans* 517 U.S. 620 (1976).
20. *Boy Scouts v. Dale* 530 U.S. 640 (2001).

5: Federalism and States' Rights

1. See *Bush v. Gore* 531 U.S. 98 (2000); Jack M. Balkin and Sanford Levinson, "Legal Historicism and Legal Academics: The Roles of Law Professors in the Wake of *Bush v. Gore*," The Georgetown L. J., Vol. 90, No. 1, November 2001.
2. *United States v. Lopez* 514 U.S. 549 (1995); Joseph Calve, "Anatomy of a Landmark," The Connecticut Law Tribune, August 14, 1995.
3. *Wickard v. Filburn* 317 U.S. 111 (1942).
4. *Printz v. United States* 521 U.S. 98 (1997); John Mintz, "In Bush, NRA Sees White House Access," *Washington Post*, May 4, 2000, A1.
5. Kermit Hall, ed., *Oxford Companion to the Decisions of the Supreme Court*, (New York: Oxford Press, 2000).
6. See S. Waxman, "Defending Congress in the Courts," Keynote Address at 7th Circuit Judicial Conference (May 1, 2000), pp. 1–2.
7. *Gibbons v. Ogden* 22 U.S. 1 (1824).
8. *United States v. Morrison* 529 U.S. 598 (2000).
9. Transcript of Argument in *United States v. Morrison*, January 11, 2000, p. 2.
10. *Seminole Tribe of Florida v. Florida* 517 U.S. 44 (1996).
11. *Pennsylvania v. Union Gas* 491 U.S. 1 (1989).
12. *Hans v. Louisiana* 134 U.S. 1 (1890).
13. *University of Alabama v. Patricia Garrett* 531 U.S. 356 (2001).
14. *Kimel, et al. v. Florida Board of Regents* 528 U.S. 1110 (2000); E. Palmer, "Supreme Court Favors States in Age Bias, Gender Cases," *Congressional Quarterly* (Jan. 15, 2000), p. 80 (quoting A. E. Dick Howard, professor of law at University of Virginia).
15. *Alexander v. Sandoval* 532 U.S. 275 (2001).
16. Sam Howe Verhovek, "Federal Agents Are Directed to Stop Physicians Who Assist Suicides," *The New York Times,* November 7, 2001, p. A20.
17. *Cruzan v. Director, Missouri Department of Health* 497 U.S. 261.

6: Capitalism and the Free Market: Rolling Back the Clock to the 1900s

1. See Richard Epstein, "Against Redress," *Daedalus*, Winter 2002.
2. *Lochner v. New York* 198 U.S. 45 (1905).
3. *Hammer v. Dagenhart* 247 U.S. 251 (1918).
4. Richard Epstein, *op. cit.*
5. Richard Epstein, *op. cit.*
6. *United States v. Carolene Products* 304 U.S. 144 (1937).
7. *National League of Cities v. Usery* 426 U.S. 833 (1976).
8. *Garcia v. San Antonio Metropolitan Transport Authority* 469 U.S. 528 (1985).
9. *Wickard v. Filburn* 317 U.S. 111 (1942).
10. Richard Posner, *Economic Analysis of Law*, 3rd ed. (Boston: Little, Brown & Company, 1986).
11. Richard Posner, "Deadlock" (Chicago: University of Chicago Press, 2001).

12. Richard Posner, "Security vs. Civil Liberties," *Atlantic Monthly*, December 2001.
13. Larissa MacFarquhar, "The Bench Burner," *New Yorker*, December 10, 2001.
14. *Goldberg v. Kelly* 397 U.S. 254 (1970).
15. Richard Pipes, *Property and Freedom* (New York: Alfred A. Knopf, 1999).
16. Bernard H. Siegan, *Economic Liberties and the Constitution* (1981); Siegan, *The Supreme Court's Constitution* (1987); Siegan, Rehabilitating *Lochner*, 22 San Diego L. Rev. 453 (1985).
17. See Richard Epstein, *Takings: Private Property and the Power of Eminent Domain* (1985); see also Treanor, The Origins and Original Significance of the Just Compensation Clause of the Fifth Amendment, 94 Yale L. J. 694, 711 (1985); see Large, The Supreme Court and the Takings Clause: The Search for a Better Rule, 18 Environmental Law 3, 11–12 (1987).
18. *Miller v. Schoene* 276 U.S. 272 (1928).
19. *First Lutheran Church v. Los Angeles County* 482 U.S. 304, 329 (1987).
20. *Pennell v. San Jose* 485 U.S. 1 (1988).
21. *Dolan v. City of Tigard* 512 U.S. 374 (1994).
22. *Eastern Enterprises v. Apfel* 524 U.S. 498 (1998).
23. Antonin Scalia, "The Doctrine of Standing as an Essential Element of the Separation of Powers," 17 Suffolk L. Rev. 881 (1983); Steven L. Winter, "The Metaphor of Standing and the Problem of Self-Governance," 40 Stanford L. Rev. 1371 (1988); Louis L. Jaffe, "Standing to Secure Judicial Review: Public Actions," 74 Harvard L. Rev. 1265 (1961); Raoul Berger, "Standing to Sue in Public Actions: Is It a Constitutional Requirement?" 78 Yale L. J. 816 (1969); Richard J. Pierce, "Is Standing Law or Politics?" 77 North Carolina L. Rev. 1741 (1999).
24. *Flast v. Cohen* 392 U.S. 83 (1968).
25. *Friends of the Earth v. Laidlaw* 528 U.S. 167 (2000); *Bragg v. Robertson*, 2001 WL 410382 (4th Cir. 2001).
26. I am indebted for much of this analysis to the annual report, People for the American Way.
27. Richard L. Revesz, "Environmental Regulation, Ideology and the D.C. Circuit," 83 Virginia L. Rev. 1717, 1766 (1997).

7: Race, Gender, and Ethnicity

1. *Plessy v. Ferguson* 163 U.S. 537 (1896).
2. *City of Memphis v. Greene* 451 U.S. 100 (1981).
3. *Patterson v. McLean Credit Union* 491 U.S. 164 (1989).
4. *Jones v. Alfred H. Mayer Co.* 392 U.S. 409 (1968).
5. *Runyon v. McCrary* 427 U.S. 160 (1976).
6. *Brown v. Board of Education I* 347 U.S. 483 (1954); *Brown v. Board of Education II* 349 U.S. 294 (1955).
7. Slaughterhouse cases, 83 U.S. 36 (1983); Civil Rights Cases, 109 U.S. 3 (1883).
8. David G. Savage, *Turning Right: The Making of the Rehnquist Supreme Court* (New York: John Wiley & Sons, 1992).

9. James F. Simon, *The Center Holds: The Power Struggle Inside the Rehnquist Court*. (New York: Simon and Schuster, 1995).

10. The percentages vary depending on whether we include unanimous opinions or just refer to split opinions.

11. *Alexander v. Sandoval* 532 U.S. 275 (2001).

12. See *South Camden Citizens in Action v. N.J. Department of Environmental Protection,* 2001 U.S. App. Lexis 26822 (December 2001).

13. *Green v. County School Board of New Kent County* 391 U.S. 430 (1968).

14. *Swann v. Charlotte-Mecklenburg County Board of Education* 402 U.S. 1 (1971); see Schwartz, Swann's Way: The School Busing Case and the Supreme Court 35 (1986).

15. Lino Graglia, *Disaster by Decree: The Supreme Court Decisions on Race and the Schools* (Ithaca, N.Y.: Cornell University Press, 1976); Graglia, When Honesty Is "Simply . . . Impractical" for the Supreme Court: How the Constitution Came to Require Busing for School Racial Balance, 85 Michigan L. Rev. 1153; J. Harvie Wilkinson III, *From Brown to Bakke* (New York: Oxford University Press, 1979).

16. *San Antonio School District v. Rodriguez* 411 U.S. 1 (1973).

17. *Milliken v. Bradley* 418 U.S. 717 (1974).

18. *Oklahoma City Board of Education v. Dowell* 498 U.S. 237 (1991).

19. *Freeman v. Pitts* 503 U.S. 467 (1992).

20. *Missouri v. Jenkins* 515 U.S. 70 (1995), 495 U.S. 33 (1990).

21. See Brent Staples, "Yonkers Shows How Not to Desegregate a School District," *The New York Times,* January 11, 2002.

22. *Presley v. Etowah County Commission* 502 U.S. 491 (1992).

23. *Hunt v. Cromartie* 532 U.S. 1076 (2001). See also, *Shaw v. Reno* 509 U.S. 630 (1993), *Shaw v. Hunt* 517 U.S. 899 (1996).

8: Affirmative Action: Putting the Nail in the Coffin

1. *Regents of the University of California v. Bakke* 438 U.S. 265 (1978); See Schwartz, Behind *Bakke:* Affirmative Action and the Supreme Court 71 (1988).

2. *Fullilove v. Klutznick* 448 U.S. 448 (1980).

3. *Richmond v. J. A. Croson Co.* 488 U.S. 469 (1989).

4. *Adarand Constructors v. Pena* 515 U.S. 2000 (1998).

5. *Metro Broadcasting, Inc. v. Federal Communications Commission* 497 U.S. 1050 (1990); Tinsley E. Yarbrough, *The Rehnquist Court and the Constitution* (New York: Oxford University Press, 2000).

6. *Scott v. Sanford* 19 How. 60 U.S. 393 (1857).

7. *Hopwood v. Texas* 78 F.3d 932 (1996), (Fifth Circuit).

8. *Grutter v. Bollinger* 188 F.3d 394 (1999).

9. *Johnson v. Georgia* 263 F.3d 1234 (2001) (Eleventh Circuit).

10. Civil Rights Cases 109 U.S. 3 (1883).

9: Religion

1. Dana Milbank, "Religious Right Finds Its Center in Oval Office," *Washington Post*, December 24, 2001, p. A02.
2. *Employment Division v. Smith* 494 U.S. 872 (1990).
3. *City of Boerne v. Flores* 521 U.S. 507 (1997).
4. Ibid., 3.
5. Marci Hamilton, Transcript of Argument, 1997 U.S. Trans. Lexis 17, February 19, 1997.
6. See Michael W. McConnell, "Comment: Institutions and Interpretation: A Critique of City of Boerne v. Flores," 111 Harv. L. Rev. 153, 156 (1997).
7. *Lemon v. Kurtzman* 403 U.S. 602 (1971).
8. *Wallace v. Jaffree* 472 U.S. 38 (1985).
9. *Lee v. Weisman* 505 U.S. 577 (1992).
10. *Zobrest v. Catalina Foothills School District* 509 U.S. 1 (1993).
11. *Lambs Chapel v. Center Moriches School District* 508 U.S. 384 (1993).
12. *Rosenberger v. University of Virginia* 515 U.S. 819 (1995).
13. *Aguilar v. Felton* 473 U.S. 402 (1985).
14. *Agostini v. Felton* 521 U.S. 203 (1997); 117 S. Ct. 1332 (1997).
15. *Mitchell v. Helms* 530 U.S. 793 (2000).
16. *Good News Club v. Milford Central School* 533 U.S. 98 (2001).
17. Jeffrey Rosen, "Modest Proposal: Stephen Breyer Restrains Himself." *The New Republic*, January 14, 2002.
18. Ibid., 17.
19. See also, Joan Biskupic, "High Court Allows Graduation Prayers," *USA Today*, December 11, 2001.
20. *Harris v. Zelman* 234 F3d 945 (2000), 528 U.S. 983 (2002).
21. *Committee for Pub. Educ. & Religious Liberty v. Nyquist* 413 U.S. 756 (1973); Joan Biskupic, "High Court Allows Graduation Prayers," *USA Today*, December 11, 2001.
22. Helen T. Grey, "Religious Leaders Respond to Questions after Terrorist Attacks," *The Kansas City Star*, September 27, 2001; Tom Hartman, "Falwell and Robertson Were Way Off About September 11," *New York Newsday*, October 3, 2001; Tom Hartman, "No One—Not Falwell, Not Robertson—Can Presume to Know God's Will," *New York Newsday*, October 7, 2001; William F. Buckley, "Invoking God's Thunder," *National Review*, October 15, 2001.
23. Marci Hamilton, "Free? Exercise," William and Mary L. Rev. 823, 825, March 2001; Richard Berke, "Falwell Is Raising Money to Press Conservative Agenda," *The New York Times*, December 14, 2001.

10: Conclusion: Courting Disaster

1. See also Cass R. Sunstein, "Tilting the Scales Rightward," *The New York Times*, April 26, 2001; Cass R. Sunstein, "When Conservative Judges Turn Activist," *San Diego Union Tribune*, June 3, 1999, p. B15.

BIBLIOGRAPHY

Ackerman, Bruce. *We the People: Foundations*. Cambridge: Belknap/Harvard University Press, 1991.

Ackerman, Bruce. *We the People: Transformations*. Cambridge: Belknap/Harvard University Press, 1998.

Allen, Francis, Edward L. Barrett Jr., et al. *The Supreme Court and the Constitution: Essays on the Constitutional Law from the Supreme Court Review*. Chicago: Phoenix Books, University of Chicago Press, 1965.

Attorney General of New Jersey, Interim Report of the State Police Review Team Regarding Allegations of Racial Profiling (April 1999).

Bailyn, Bernard, ed. *The Debate on the Constitution* (2 vols.). Library of America, 1993.

Bailyn, Bernard, ed. *The Federalist Papers*. Washington, D.C.: Library of Congress, 1998.

Balkin, Jack M. *What Brown v. Board Should Have Said*. New York: New York University Press, 2001.

Bass, Jack. *Taming the Storm: The Life and Times of Judge Frank M. Johnson, Jr. and the South's Fight Over Civil Rights*. New York: Doubleday, 1993.

Bickel, Alexander M. *The Morality of Consent*. New Haven: Yale University Press, 1975.

Bickel, Alexander M. *Politics and the Warren Court*. New York: Harper & Row Publishers, 1965.

Bickel, Alexander M. *The Supreme Court and the Idea of Progress*. New York: Harper & Row Publishers, 1970.

Black, Charles L., Jr. *A New Birth of Freedom: Human Rights, Named and Unnamed*. New York: Grosset/Putnam, 1997.

Bork, Robert H. *The Tempting of America: The Political Seduction of the Law*. New York: Free Press, 1990.

Brant, Irving. *The Bill of Rights*. New York: Bobbs-Merrill, 1965.

Brinkley, Alan. *Liberalism and Its Discontents*. Cambridge: Harvard University Press, 1998.

Buccino, Dowling, et al. *Hostile Environment*. Washington, D.C.: Alliance for Justice, 2001.

Burns, James MacGregor. *The Crosswinds of Freedom*. New York: Alfred A. Knopf, 1989.

Calabresi, Guido. *A Common Law for the Age of Statutes*. Cambridge: Harvard University Press, 1982.

Chang, Nancy. "Racial Profiling." Paper delivered at American Bar Association 2000 Annual Meeting.

Cole, David. *No Equal Justice: Race and Class in the American Criminal Justice System*. New York: New Press, 1999.

Cox, Archibald. *The Court and the Constitution*. Boston: Houghton Mifflin, 1987.

deTocqueville, Alexis. *Democracy in America*. Perennial Classics, 1969.

Douglas, William O. *The Court Years: The Autobiography of William O. Douglas*. New York: Random House, 1980.

Dworkin, Ronald. *Freedom's Law: The Moral Reading of the American Constitution*. Cambridge: Harvard University Press, 1996.

Dworkin, Ronald. *Law's Empire*. Cambridge: Belknap/Harvard University Press, 1986.

Easton, Nina J. *Gang of Five: Leaders at the Center of the Conservative Crusade*. New York: Simon and Schuster, 2000.

Eisler, Kim Isaac. *A Justice for All: William J. Brennan, Jr. and the Decisions that Transformed America*. New York: Simon and Schuster, 1993.

Epstein, Richard. "The Proper Scope of the Commerce Power," *73 Virginia L. Rev. 1387* (1987).

Epstein, Richard. "Rent Control and the Theory of Efficient Regulation," *54 Brooklyn L. Rev.* (1988)

Epstein, Richard. *Takings: Private Property and the Power of Eminent Domain*, Boston: Harvard University Press, 1990.

Freeman, Joanne B., ed. *The Writings of Alexander Hamilton*. New York: Library of America, 2001.

Friedman, Leon. *The Supreme Court Confronts Abortion*. New York: Farrar, Straus and Giroux, 1993.

Friendly, Fred W., and Martha J. H. Elliott. *The Constitution: That Delicate Balance*. New York: Random House, 1984.

Garrow, David J. *Liberty and Sexuality: The Right to Privacy and the Making of Roe v. Wade*. New York: Macmillan, 1994.

Gerhardt, Michael. *The Federal Appointments Process*. Durham, N.C.: Duke University Press, 2000.

Goldman, Sheldon. *Picking Federal Judges*. New Haven: Yale University Press, 1997.

Hall, Kermit L. *The Oxford Guide to United States Supreme Court Decisions*. New York: Oxford University Press, 1999.

Hutchinson, Dennis J., David A. Strauss, and Gregory R. Stone. *The Supreme Court Review 1999*. Chicago: University of Chicago Press, 2000.

Irons, Peter. *Brennan vs. Rehnquist: The Battle for the Constitution*. New York: Alfred A. Knopf, 1994.

Kairys, David. *The Politics of Law: A Progressive Critique*. New York: Pantheon Books, 1982.

Kammen, Michael. *The Machine That Would Go of Itself: The Constitution in American Culture*. New York: Alfred A. Knopf, 1987.

Kennedy, Randall. *Race, Crime and the Law*. New York: Pantheon Books, 1977.

Kesslec-Harris, Alice. *In Pursuit of Equity*. New York: Oxford University Press, 2001.

Kloppenberg, Lisa A. *Playing It Safe*. New York: New York University Press, 2001.

Kluger, Richard. *Simple Justice: The History of Brown v. Board of Education*. New York: Vintage Books, 1975.

Kohut, Green, et al. *The Diminishing Divide*. Washington, D.C.: Brookings Institute, 2000.

Lazarus, Edward. *Closed Chambers: The Rise and Fall and Future of the Modern Supreme Court*. New York: Penguin Books, 1999.

Mayer, Jane, and Jill Abrahamson. *Strange Justice: The Selling of Clarence Thomas*. New York: Houghton Mifflin, 1994.

Michelman, Frank. *Brennan and Democracy*. Princeton: Princeton University Press, 1999.

Murdoch and Price. *Courting Justice*. New York: Basic Books, 2001.

Nagel, Robert F. *The Implosion of American Federalism*. New York: Oxford University Press, 2001.

Orfield, Gary, and Holly J. Lebowitz, eds. *Religion, Race and Justice in a Changing America*. New York: Century Foundation, 1999.

Patterson, James. *Brown v. Board of Education*. New York: Oxford University Press, 2001.

People for the American Way. "Courting Disaster." Washington, D.C. (2000).

Peretti, Terri J. *In Defense of a Political Court*. Princeton: Princeton University Press, 1999.

Phelps, Timothy M., and Helen Winternitz. *Capital Games: Clarence Thomas, Anita Hill and the Story of a Supreme Court Nominee*. New York: Hyperion, 1992.

Pipes, Richard. *Property and Freedom*. New York: Vintage Press, 2000.

Posner, Richard A. *Breaking the Deadlock*. Princeton: Princeton University Press, 2001.

Posner, Richard A. *Economic Analysis of Law*, 3rd ed. Boston: Little, Brown & Company, 1986.

Posner, Richard A. *An Economic Approach*, 2 Journal of Legal Studies (1973).

Posner, Richard A. *Frontiers of Legal Theory*. Cambridge: Harvard University Press, 2001.

Posner, Richard A. "The Jurisprudence of Skepticism." *86 Michigan L. Rev.* 827 (1988).

Powe, Lucas A., Jr. *The Warren Court and American Politics*. Cambridge: Belknap/ Harvard University Press, 2000.

Rakove, Jack N. *Original Meanings: Politics and Ideas in the Making of the Constitution*. New York: Alfred A. Knopf, 1996.

Rosenberg, Gerald N. *The Hollow Hope: Can Courts Bring About Social Change*. Chicago: University of Chicago Press, 1991.

Rosenkranz, Joshua, and Bernard Schwartz. *Reason and Passion*. New York: Norton, 1997.

Rutland, Robert A. *James Madison: The Founding Father*. New York: Macmillan, 1987.

Sargentich, Thomas O. *Uncertain Justice: Politics and American Courts: The Reports of the Task Forces of Citizens for Independent Courts*. Century Foundation Press, 2000.

Savage, David G. *Turning Right: The Making of the Rehnquist Supreme Court*. New York: John Wiley & Sons, Inc. 1993.

Schwartz, Bernard. *The Ascent of Pragmatism: The Burger Court in Action*. Addison-Wesley Publishing, 1990.

Schwartz, Bernard. *Decision: How the Supreme Court Decides Cases*. New York: Oxford University Press, 1996.

Schwartz, Bernard. *Main Currents in American Legal Thought*. Duram, N.C.: Carolina Academic Press, 1993.

Schwartz, Bernard. *The New Right and The Constitution: Turning Back The Legal Clock*. Boston: Northeastern University Press, 1990.

Schwartz, Bernard. *Super Chief: Earl Warren and His Supreme Court, A Judicial Biography*. New York: New York University Press, 1983.

Schwartz, Bernard. *The Unpublished Opinions of the Burger Court*. Oxford University Press, 1988.

Schwartz, Bernard. *The Unpublished Opinions of the Rehnquist Court*. New York: Oxford University Press, 1996.

Schwartz, Herman. *Packing the Courts: The Conservative Campaign to Rewrite the Constitution*. New York: Charles Scribner's & Sons, 1988.

Segal, Jeffrey, and Harold Spaeth. *The Supreme Court and the Attitudinal Model*, Cambridge, 1993.

Simon, James. *The Antagonists*. New York: Simon and Schuster, 1989.

Simon, James F. *The Center Holds: The Power Struggle Inside the Rehnquist Court*. New York: Simon and Schuster, 1995.

Smolla, Rod. *Deliberate Intent: A Lawyer Tells the True Story of Murder by the Book*. New York: Crown Publishers, 1999.

Sunstein, Cass R. *Designing Democracy*. New York: Oxford University Press, 2001.

Sunstein, Cass. R. *One Case at a Time: Judicial Minimalism on the Supreme Court.* Cambridge: Harvard University Press, 1999.

Tribe, Laurence H. *American Constitutional Law.* New York: Foundation Press, 2000.

Tribe, Laurence H. *God Save This Honorable Court: How the Choice of Supreme Court Justices Shapes Our History.* New York: Random House, 1985.

Tushnet, Mark. *Red, White and Blue: A Critical Analysis of Constitutional Law.* Cambridge: Harvard University Press, 1988.

Twentieth Century Fund. *Judicial Roulette.* New York: Priority Press, 1988.

White, Edward G. *The Constitution and the New Deal.* Cambridge: Harvard University Press, 2000.

Wilkinson, J. Harvie, III. *From Brown to Bakke.* New York: Oxford University Press, 1979.

Williams, Joan. *Unbending Gender.* New York: Oxford University Press, 2001.

Yalof, David Alistair. *Pursuit of Justices: Presidential Politics and the Selection of Supreme Court Nominees.* Chicago: University of Chicago Press, 1999.

ACKNOWLEDGMENTS

In preparing this book, I primarily relied on the decisions and transcripts of the Supreme Court, published information, the private decisions of the justices at conferences discussing the cases, the papers of the Supreme Court justices, and the interviews I conducted with participants in those cases. I am indebted to the scholarship and graciousness of Professors Sanford Levinson, Jack Balkin, Marci Hamilton, Jeffrey Rosen, Sheldon Goldman, Tinsley Yarborough, Larry Kramer, Anthony Amsterdam, and Bernard Schwartz, and Norman Redlich, my former professors at New York University Law School, and Marc Stern. I have drawn generously from the materials and analyses contained in their writings. I thank Nan Aron and her colleagues at the Alliance for Justice in Washington, D.C., and Ralph Neas, Elliot Mincberg, and Larry Ottinger of People for the American Way, who for years have fought to stop the conservative court packing and whose annual report, entitled *Courting Disaster*, has played a very important role in keeping the public advised of the path of the law.

Secondary sources on events I was not at included David Savage's *Turning Right: The Making of the Supreme Court* (John Wiley, 1993), Sheldon Goldman's writings in *Judicature* and *Picking Federal Judges* (Yale University Press, 1997), and the books of Bernard Schwartz, including those containing unpublished opinions of the Warren, Burger, and Rehnquist Courts. *The Supreme Court in Conference (1940–1985)*, and *Private Discussions Behind Nearly 300 Supreme Court Decisions* (Oxford, 2001), edited by Del Dickson, supplements the justices' papers and the work of Bernard Schwartz.

I express my appreciation to Susan Leon and David Sobel, two caring editors; to my good friend and agent, Joni Evans; to Lynie T. Fass, my wonderful researcher;

to the Holt staff, including Heather Rodino; and to Pat Gross and Fredda Tourin, who helped transform my scrawls into this book. Comments that I appreciated came from conversations with Marci Hamilton, Michael Gottesman, David Cole, Barry Castro, Dan Troy, Donna Lieberman, Leslie Neuman, Nancy Chang, Helen Hershkoff, Paul Chevigny, Neil Lewis, Ronald Tabak, Julie Goldscheid, Kim Hawkins, Barbara Shack, Marc Stern, Alfred Ross, Dennis Parker, Barry Lynn, Neil Glaser, Art Eisenberg, Jonathan Kandell, Dan Cogan, Steve Rolston, Raymond Steckel, Barry Castro, George Kendall, Will Hellerstein, Theodore Shaw, Leon Polsky, Joan Biskupic, and Joshua Rosenkranz. And to Ali, Cassandra, and Elizabeth Garbus, and Philip and Christopher Enock. And, last but first, of course, to my wife, Sarina.

INDEX

ABOUT THE AUTHOR

Martin Garbus is one of the country's leading trial lawyers, appearing before the Supreme Court and representing high-profile clients from Lenny Bruce to Václav Havel. An NBC, CBS, and CNN legal commentator, his articles have appeared in the *Washington Post,* the *New York Times*, the *Los Angeles Times*, and other publications. He is the author of three previous books and lives in New York City.